SYSTEMS
ANALYSIS
AND DESIGN

SYSTEMS ANALYSIS AND DESIGN

GERALD A. SILVER

Los Angeles City College

MYRNA L. SILVER

ADDISON-WESLEY PUBLISHING COMPANY

Reading, Massachusetts ▲ Menlo Park, California ▲ New York
Don Mills, Ontario ▲ Wokingham, England ▲ Amsterdam ▲ Bonn
Sydney ▲ Singapore ▲ Tokyo ▲ Madrid ▲ San Juan

James T. DeWolf, Sponsoring Editor
Bette J. Aaronson, Production Supervisor
Wendy Calmenson, The Book Company, Production and Art Editor
Juan Vargas and Wendy Calmenson, Text Designers
Marshall Henrichs, Cover Designer
Hugh Crawford, Manufacturing Supervisor
Katherine Harutunian and John Thompson, Photo Researchers

Library of Congress Cataloging-in-Publication Data

Silver, Gerald A.
   Systems analysis and design / by Gerald A. Silver and Myrna L. Silver
   p. cm.
   Includes index.
   ISBN 0-201-06615-7
   1. Systems design. 2. Systems analysis. 3. Management information
   systems. I. Silver, Myrna. II. Title.
   QA76.9.S88S565 1989
   004.2'1—cc19   88-11686
                                               CIP

Photo on p. 141 and p. 161 courtesy of St. John's Military Academy, Delafield, Wisconsin.

Many of the designations used by manufacturers and sellers to distinguish their products are claimed as trademarks. Where those designations appear in this book, and Addison-Wesley was aware of a trademark claim, the designations have been printed in initial caps or all caps.

ABCDEFGHIJ-DO-898

P R E F A C E

Today, systems analysts must solve a wide range of complex and sophisticated information system problems. They may recommend or assist with the expenditure of large sums of money; supervise the selection and installation of expensive, sophisticated computers and communications equipment; alter the physical environment of the business organization; train or retrain hundreds of employees; and deal with customers, employees, vendors, and management.

The costs involved in operating modern information systems have surged upward in the last several years. Therefore, systems must be implemented as nearly perfectly as possible the first time around—there is little room for second chances, trial and error, or experimentation. This underscores the need for careful analysis of each information system problem.

The computer has made significant changes in the way organizations are structured, how they carry out their activities, and how they manage and manipulate their information. The microcomputer, in particular, has had great impact upon both large and small organizations. This directly affects the work of the systems analyst. Not only must analysts deal with a wide range of computer problems, but they must also learn to use computers in their work and fully utilize a computer's problem-solving potential.

This text introduces undergraduate students to the world of systems analysis, information management, and database usage. It defines the role of systems analysts and describes their duties, methods, techniques, and tools. It provides a comprehensive survey of the major aspects, concepts, and theories of information systems.

Systems Analysis and Design strikes a balance between the theoretical and applied aspects of systems analysis, presenting state-of-the-art systems procedures, methodology, and software.

End of Chapter Projects

At the end of each chapter are exercises and a group of projects, which will enable students to explore systems concepts on their own.

Analyst at Work

After the introductory chapters, modules describing an analyst at work provide students with more detailed, hands-on projects. Each module contains data flow diagrams or other visual and descriptive material laying out the system problem. Students then develop one or more work products that may be turned in to the instructor for grading. Each chapter thus contains a range of projects, some unstructured and others more guided.

A running case, UniTrans Company, is integrated in the text. The distinctive UT symbol is printed in the margin throughout the text whenever we refer to UniTrans. This case provides another functional laboratory in which students can apply the theories covered in the chapters. The UniTrans Company is patterned after the very successful overnight air package delivery services widely used by business and industry. Many students may have had contact with these carriers and can relate the case to their personal experiences. The UniTrans case offers a hands-on opportunity to learn how systems are analyzed, screens and forms designed, and systems actually implemented.

Systems analysis concepts are presented in a logical, orderly manner. Planning, analysis, design, development, and implementation concepts form the basis for major parts of this book and coincide with the approach followed in most courses. This text covers fundamental concepts and vocabulary clearly and concisely. It includes an explanation and discussion of the principles of the scientific method and encourages students to rely on these principles as a sound basis for all problem-solving activities.

Modern hardware and software concepts are described, including database design, optical character scanning, and personal computers. Current methods of data input, output, storage, and retrieval are also presented, along with a thorough discussion of microfilm, microfiche, and computer output microfilm.

Computer-Aided Software Engineering

Computer-aided software engineering (CASE) and automated systems analysis tools have been developed within the last several years, and Chapter 14 is devoted to this topic. Automated systems design tools are integrated throughout the text. Data dictionaries, prototyping, and structured programming concepts are thoroughly discussed. In addition, a chapter on project management is included. Both traditional and computerized network scheduling are fully described, with numerous figures and examples.

Cases

The text concludes with a comprehensive group of case histories. Drawn from real-world organizations, these diverse cases explore the wide variety of business systems found in industry today. They expose students to situations and problems that will be encountered on the job, enabling them to integrate the knowledge gained from the text into their careers.

Supplements Package

A complete package of supplemental material for the instructor is available with the text. This package includes the following:

Instructor's Guide

Computerized Test Bank

Transparency Masters

Blank Forms Package

Index Technology's Educational Grant Program

Contained within the Instructor's Guide is an application for participation in Index Technology's Educational Grant Program. Qualifying institutions will be entitled to a free copy of Excelerator, a state-of-the-art integrated workbench designed for the professional systems analyst. For more information about the Educational Grant Program contact your Addison-Wesley sales representative, or Index Technology at One Main St., Cambridge, Ma. 02142, (617) 494-8200.

Acknowledgments

The authors wish to acknowledge the contribution of the many reviewers who commented on several drafts of the manuscript. Their efforts are sincerely appreciated, and the book has certainly improved as a result of their suggestions.

Marilyn Bohl, Digital Research, Inc.

John Tomei, Diablo Valley College

Donald L. Harris, Lincoln Land Community College

C. T. Cadenhead, Richmond College (Dallas County Community College District)

Gary Klotz, Milwaukee Area Technical College

R. H. Howell, Lansing Community College

William Davis, Miami University

Kenneth W. Veatch, San Antonio College

Frank White, Catonsville Community College

R. K. Fanselau, American River College

Encino, California   *G.A.S. and M.L.S.*

C O N T E N T S

INTRODUCTION

INTRODUCTION TO SYSTEMS ANALYSIS

LEARNING OBJECTIVES

After studying this chapter, you should be able to:

1. Describe key system concepts.

2. Contrast business and information systems.

3. Explain, with examples, the concepts of system environment, boundaries, and limits.

4. Contrast open systems and closed systems.

5. List the advantages of systems analysis.

6. Summarize the limitations of systems analysis.

To some, this is the atomic age; to others, the computer age. But perhaps it might better be called the information age. Information and paperwork are the most abundant products generated by modern business. Processing this mountain of information occupies the working hours of hundreds of thousands of office workers, computer operators, clerks, and managers.

Why this overwhelming volume of information and paperwork? Basically, for two reasons: people and government.

Each person throughout his or her lifetime is the subject of an enormous amount of information—medical files, insurance policies, financial records, mortgage loans, employment and school records, to name a few. A growing population generates a tremendous amount of data that needs to be entered, manipulated, processed, and output.

The second reason for the deluge of information and paperwork is the increase in governmental regulations and control. More and more, the transactions of daily business life must be preserved in the form of reports and records for governmental processing.

Private industry spends billions of dollars each year to generate the data required by the government alone. The government spends billions more to process its way through the mass of paperwork created both by citizens and by business. This represents only a small part of the data produced throughout the nation by large and small businesses, schools, hospitals, factories, and others.

Computers, particularly microcomputers, are widely used to cope with this burgeoning volume of paperwork. In this decade there will be a 50-fold increase in the sales of personal computers. By the end of 1990 sales of microcomputer hardware will exceed $50 billion. These machines not only process data, but generate it as well. Thus, the computer provides fuel for the information base upon which large and small business decisions are made. It is used to help management set policy and make better decisions about employment, purchasing, and distribution patterns.

The flow and availability of data has become an indispensable, vital element of almost every human enterprise. Molding this data into coherent, usable form does not occur by chance. It requires planning, people, machines, and money.

WHAT IS A SYSTEM?

System is an overworked word in the English language. It is used to describe many things, conditions, and methods. We refer to an accounting system, a communications system, an air-conditioning system, or a transportation system.

A **system** is a regularly interacting or interdependent group of elements forming a unified whole. Thus, a system is a collection of related parts treated as a unit where its components interact.

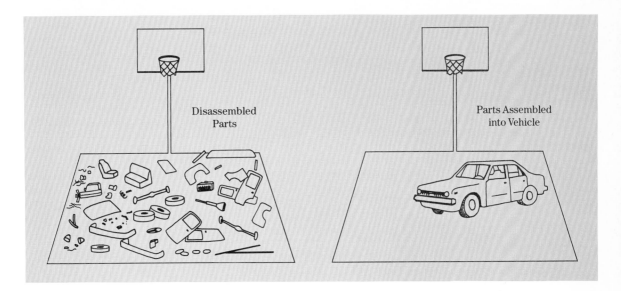

Each day we come into contact with many different types of systems. A city's water system, for example, is made up of pipes, valves, pumping equipment, and reservoirs, as well as operating personnel and management. Plants and animals are elements in our ecological system. The human body is a system composed of many parts that function as a whole. The government operates a tax collection system, and the courts are part of the legal system. Business, too, has its systems for manufacturing goods, preparing payrolls, transferring funds, and keeping track of goods sold, returned, or exchanged.

A major attribute of systems is that they possess qualities and capabilities not found in the individual elements. This attribute—the whole producing results that are greater than the sum of the parts—is the key to understanding systems.

To illustrate, imagine a collection of mechanical and electrical items—bearings, gears, wires, nuts, bolts, stamped parts, etc.—all laid out before you on a gymnasium floor (see Fig. 1.1). Each part has a limited function and is of relatively little use by itself. But assemble all the parts into an automobile, and the collection that had comparatively little utility is now an integrated, functioning system with practical and monetary value. The relative worth of the resulting system is far greater than the sum of its parts.

The same is true of a business system. Computers, personnel, procedures, invoices, and reports functioning as an integrated system may have a far greater value than they have by themselves.

FIGURE 1.1

What Is a System? An assembled automobile is a system possessing qualities and characteristics not present in the collection of disassembled parts.

Business Systems

It is helpful to view a business enterprise as a system (see Fig. 1.2). A **business system** is a collection of policies, procedures, methods, people, machines, and other elements that interact and enable the organization to reach

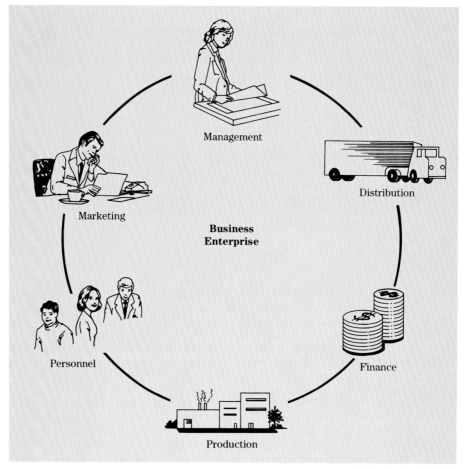

its goals. Business systems often include marketing, personnel, production, finance, and distribution elements. An important task of the business system is the managing and coordinating function.

A goal for some organizations is to maximize profit and return on investment to shareholders. For others, such as mutual benefit associations, the goal is to provide services or facilities to members, rather than profit to shareholders. Still others, such as nonprofit organizations, serve the public by providing health care, housing, or food programs to those in need. In order to accomplish their mission, organizations must use systems. Business systems record deposits and withdrawals, transfer funds, collect and manage data about customers, or guide the production or marketing aspects of an organization.

Information Systems

Information processing and handling is one of the most important components of many businesses. **Information systems** are collections of procedures, programs, equipment, and methods that process data and make it available to management for decision making.

Many analysts draw a distinction between data and information. **Data** is the raw material that is processed and refined to generate information. **Information** is the product that results from processing or manipulating raw data (see Fig. 1.3). It is information, not data, that is ultimately used to make decisions. A store manager, for example, might have difficulty deciding whether to remain open on Saturdays if only raw data were available for inspection. A check of receipts or a printout listing all sales for Saturdays might not be as helpful as a summary figure that reduces the raw data to meaningful information. This important information might show sales by product line and total sales and profit for the current day.

The increase in the amount of information that must be processed has led to a greater reliance upon computerized information systems. Computers are able to process vast amounts of information quickly and inexpensively. They have become indispensable in modern information-processing systems.

FIGURE 1.3

Data and Information Data is the raw material that is processed to generate information.

SYSTEM FUNDAMENTALS

Since we will be working with systems throughout our study, it is essential that we view them from a sound conceptual base. Systems are constructs that operate within an environment (see Fig. 1.4). Systems are separated from the environment by a boundary. Further, all systems have inputs, a processing element, and outputs. Let's look at these terms in greater detail.

A business system is usually composed of many parts or elements called **subsystems** (see Fig. 1.5). A subsystem performs a specified task that is compatible with the goals of the larger system of which it is a part. For example, a

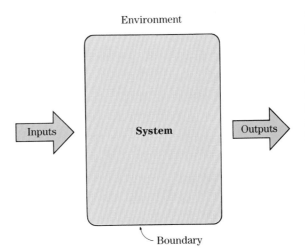

Environment

Inputs

System

Outputs

Boundary

FIGURE 1.4

System Boundaries Systems operate within an environment and are separated from the environment by a boundary.

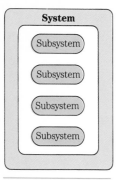

FIGURE 1.5

Subsystems A business system may be composed of many smaller elements known as subsystems.

firm's information system might be composed of a communications network, telephones, computers, and the personnel to operate them.

The Environment

The **environment** is the people, facilities, rules, policies, and regulations that surround a system. Systems do not function in a vacuum. Instead, they exist in relation to other systems and the outside world. Like people, animals, and plants, they exist in an environment. A banking system that processes customers' accounts not only must interact with customers, but also must deal with many other people and systems as well. Its environment may include federal and state banking regulations, national, state, and local economic trends, and a changing demand for and supply of money. It would not be wise to analyze systems without considering the broader context in which they function.

Boundaries

A **boundary** is the perimeter, or line of demarcation, between a system and the environment. It distinguishes between the elements that make up the system and the outside world with which it interacts. Sometimes boundaries are clearly defined. A city, for example, may have clearly drawn lines to denote the area within the incorporated city system. Other systems may have fuzzier boundaries. For example, the members of a social club may constitute a system. However, some individuals may pay dues and be formally listed on the register; others may be in arrears; and still others may drift in and out of social events without ever formally joining the organization.

Inputs

All systems gather or receive some kind of information or data that is subsequently processed, generating results or output (see Fig. 1.6). **Inputs** are those items that enter the boundaries of the system from the environment and are manipulated by the system. For example, students registering for a college class may provide their names to the registrar for further processing by the college's registration system. An automobile assembly plant receives a variety of inputs. These consist of labor, materials, money, marketing information, and goods and services. Without input, a system cannot function or generate output.

Processing

Systems exist to process data, raw material, money, or other inputs. **Processing** is the conversion of inputs, or raw materials, to outputs, or finished results. It is processing that enables an organization to move toward its goals. The processing function in a bakery, for example, involves processing its inputs

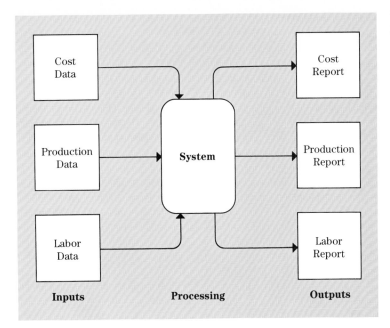

FIGURE 1.6

System Inputs
Systems receive
information, process
it, and generate
results or output.

(labor, foodstuffs) and generating output (cakes and pies). The processing function involves mixing, baking, packaging, and so on. A banking system processes
debits and credits, while an information system processes names, numbers, words,
sentences, and the like. Data processing activities include sorting, searching,
merging, summarizing, calculating, and similar operations.

Outputs

Outputs are the product of processing. They are the end result of receiving data or other input and processing it. Outputs in a small business may consist
of profit to its owner or shareholders. Outputs in an information system might
consist of reports, lists of accounts, printouts of inventories, and so forth.

TYPES OF SYSTEMS

Systems are either open or closed, depending upon whether or not their
outcomes and behavior can be predicted with certainty.

Open Systems

Open systems, also called probabilistic systems, are those in which the
output, or results, cannot be determined precisely, but can only be guessed at.
These systems involve elements of chance or probability (see Fig. 1.7).

FIGURE 1.7

Open System In an airline reservation system, the number of individuals who will purchase a ticket for a given flight cannot be predicted with certainty.

AIRLINE SEAT INVENTORY VS. DEMAND

	Available seats	Demand						
		Mon	**Tue**	**Wed**	**Thur**	**Fri**	**Sat**	**Sun**
Flight 100	360	306	206	296	320	319	410	405
Flight 101	320	212	208	196	260	307	302	308
Flight 102	320	196	230	210	290	240	310	326
Flight 103	215	180	161	112	96	185	203	207
Flight 104	320	172	231	236	183	301	304	298

An airline ticket reservation system is an example of an open system. The airline operator cannot predict with certainty how many individuals will purchase tickets for a given flight. An estimate must be made based upon probability and past experience. The actual number of seats that will be sold for a flight remains unknown until the event occurs.

Closed Systems

In **closed systems**, the result or output can be predicted with certainty (see Fig. 1.8). For example, a videocassette recorder manufacturer knows with certainty how many integrated circuits, motors, switches, and transistors will be needed to assemble a given number of VCRs. The number of required components does not change. It always remains proportional to the number of VCRs being assembled.

The output of closed systems can be predicted with relative ease and accuracy by measuring the input or demands placed upon the system. For this reason, closed systems are easier to manage than open systems.

Most business systems have some attributes of each type. Some elements are known for certain; others behave according to the laws of probability, and must be estimated. The number of customers to be served on a given day is probabilistic—the number cannot be predicted with certainty. The amount of information that can be stored on a magnetic disk, however, is fixed. The same number of characters can always be stored on the disk, since there are a finite number of areas that can be magnetized.

If a major portion of a system is probabilistic, the entire system must be treated according to the laws of chance. For example, suppose an airfreight carrier agrees to ship a fixed number of packages for the same customer each day. The number, weight, and destination of the shipments never change. In addition, the airfreight carrier offers service to other customers whose shipments vary on a day-to-day basis. The result is a transportation system that deals with both open and closed elements. In allocating resources (number of planes,

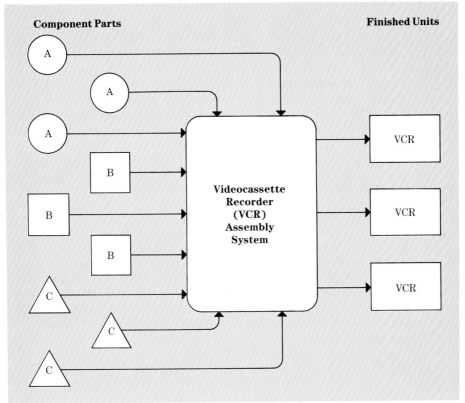

Component Parts   **Finished Units**

FIGURE 1.8

Closed System In a closed system, the results can be predicted with certainty.

pilots, flight schedules, package handlers, etc.), the air carrier must assume that the entire system behaves as though it were open and the amount of resources needed for each day must be estimated.

GROWTH OF THE INFORMATION INDUSTRY

An industry has evolved to process the vast amount of data and information handled by government, industry, and business. The evolution of the information industry has been described as moving through three phases (Arthur D. Little, *Time*, November 23, 1981). In the preindustrial age, information was processed using typewriters, adding machines, and handwritten materials. Thus, information handling was slow, inefficient, and often inaccurate. With the advent of computers, word processing, and copy machines, information processing moved into the industrial age. While mechanized, records were still sent through the mails, handed from one person to another, and physically filed in cabinets.

FIGURE 1.9

Growth of Available Knowledge
The amount of information available for processing has grown geometrically in the past several decades.

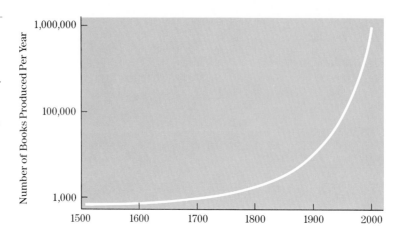

Modern office automation, the personal computer, and breakthroughs in data communications created the information age. In this era, information is routed from terminal to terminal and office to office over communications lines, and can be sorted, stored, and retrieved at many different locations. The basic way we look at, revise, and transmit information is different, both in the speed and in the technology with which it is handled.

The amount of information that organizations process has grown geometrically in the past several decades. Alvin Toffler, in his book *Future Shock,* correctly noted the exponential growth of knowledge and information, which he referred to as the fuel that drives our business, government, and social systems.

Toffler observed that the amount of available knowledge or information has spiraled upward in the last 10,000 years (see Fig. 1.9).* Prior to the invention of movable type in the 1500s, less than 1,000 books were produced in one year in all of Europe. By the 1950s, the number of titles produced exceeded 120,000 per year; by 1960, 360,000 per year. And as anyone who has visited a bookstore, library, or newsstand can attest, today the number of new books is almost uncountable. In addition, business, government, and educational institutions generate millions of articles, reports, technical bulletins, magazines, and pamphlets each year.

THE CHANGING LABOR FORCE

The growth in the volume of data that systems process is reflected in the makeup and size of the labor force. In the early 1950s significantly more people were employed in manufacturing and traditionally blue-collar jobs than in white-collar jobs in finance, banking, communications, and services. Essentially, our

* Alvin Toffler, *Future Shock,* Bantam Books, 1971, p. 30.

Reprinted by permission of Control Data Corporation.

FIGURE 1.10

Knowledge Workers Today many individuals are employed in white-collar, clerical, and knowledge industry–related occupations.

country had a blue-collar, manufacturing-oriented, craftsperson-based economy. But by 1956, the number of white-collar workers exceeded blue-collar workers for the first time. This trend has continued, with many more people today included in white-collar, clerical, knowledge industry–related employment (see Fig. 1.10).

In 1970 there were approximately 19.6 million individuals employed in manufacturing; it is expected that by 1995, this number will reach approximately 21.1 million (see Fig. 1.11). This represents an increase of only 8 percent over 25 years. In the service industries, which include advertising, education, accounting, and so on, the number of employees in 1970 was 14.0 million, but by 1995 it will reach 31.1 million, an increase of 122 percent (Statistical Abstract of the United States, 1987, p. 389).

Similar increases are observed in the banking, insurance, real estate, and finance industries, also heavily information oriented. From these figures it should be clear that our economy is shifting away from manufacturing to a technical-professional-service–oriented workforce. Workers in these categories concentrate on processing data rather than raw materials such as metal, plastic, wood, or paper.

THE STUDY OF SYSTEMS ANALYSIS

This course will concentrate upon the work of **systems analysts**, who are engaged in the broadly expanding field of systems analysis. **Systems analysis** is the investigation of business or information systems. It is the scientific study of the systems process, including investigation of inputs and outputs, in order to find better, more economical, and more efficient means of processing.

As we will see in the chapters ahead, the systems analyst relies upon the scientific method and logical and quantitative tools to develop and improve systems. Systems analysis has developed into an important tool that organiza-

FIGURE 1.11

Makeup of Labor Force

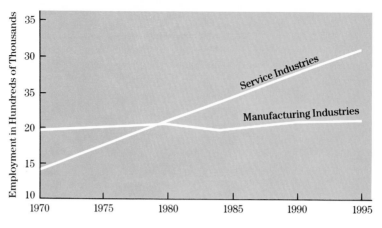

(Source: Statistical Abstract of the U.S., 1987, p. 389)

tions use to improve their productivity. There are many reasons why an organization spends time and money and dedicates resources to the analysis of its systems.

ADVANTAGES OF SYSTEMS ANALYSIS

The application of systems analysis techniques to information processing has many benefits. These include:

1. Greater efficiency. Systems analysis methods help a firm to develop and maintain an organizational structure and operating procedures for maximum efficiency.

2. Maximizing profits. A business firm that operates efficiently and systematically is likely to generate greater profits.

3. Resources used to the best advantage. Systems analysis aids a firm in achieving high-quality output with the least investment of time, material, and other resources.

4. Reduction of human effort. Systems analysis encourages the best utilization and allocation of human effort and labor. Systems analysts attempt to uncover duplication, redundancy, and wasted effort, and to automate procedures whenever practical.

5. Faster turnaround. Efficiently organized procedures and operations make it possible to reach goals faster. This is true whether the output of the firm is the production of goods or services, or the movement of information, data, money, or the like.

6. Reducing or eliminating errors in data and information. An important goal of the systems analyst is to increase the accuracy of data generated and processed by a firm.

7. Consistent operations and procedures. Clearly written policy statements, diagrams, flowcharts, and such make it more likely that a firm's procedures and practices will be followed and maintained in a consistent manner. They also serve as guides for modifications or alterations.

LIMITATIONS OF SYSTEMS ANALYSIS

Systems analysis is not a panacea for all information-handling problems. It has limitations that must be considered. The following list summarizes some of these constraints:

1. Some business problems are beyond the scope of systems analysis techniques. The most skillfully designed data flow system cannot help an organization that is failing because of serious financial problems or because it is marketing a product people no longer want. Problems created by pressures from outside the enterprise, such as from stockholders or the public, are also often beyond the reach of the systems analyst.

2. Systems analysis efforts cost time and money. Finding a long-term, permanent solution to a problem can be an expensive investment, compared to a short-term temporary answer.

3. The human element can cause complications. A systems analyst must take this into consideration. Much of the analyst's activities involve making changes in routines, systems, organizational structures, working patterns and conditions, and in other areas. People tend to oppose change. They resist adjusting to unfamiliar situations, even those that are in their best interests in the long run. The systems analyst has the responsibility of preparing employees, customers, management, vendors, and others to accept the modifications and alterations introduced by a new system.

4. Effort is required to sell a system. No matter how promising a systems analysis project may seem, it cannot sell itself. The people involved must be encouraged to cooperate in the development and implementation of the venture to ensure its success.

UNITRANS CASE

Now that we have laid a foundation for our study of systems analysis, let us look at the UniTrans Company. UniTrans is a fictional composite of several real-life companies. Study the annual report shown in Fig. 1.12. It describes UniTrans's financial condition, physical facilities, and services. Familiarize yourself with UniTrans's organization chart and management and the views of its president, Robert K. Dawson. Throughout our study of systems we will refer to the UniTrans case in order to apply the theories, concepts, and procedures discussed in this book.

UT

FIGURE 1.12

Annual Report of UniTrans Company

UT UNITRANS COMPANY

ROBERT K. DAWSON, President

A MESSAGE FROM THE PRESIDENT

These have been years of rapid growth for UniTrans. We have expanded our air shipping operations by more than 100 percent in the last three years. Our company continues to grow and remain profitable. The key to our success is our excellent service and attention to details. UniTrans continues to add cities to its delivery list. We are automating our operations and bringing in the computer to virtually every aspect of the shipping business.

All of this growth has not been without its problems. Our staff is continually working on creative new solutions to our information-handling and package-shipping problems. As president of UniTrans, I promise our customers even better service in the coming year. Shareholders should continue to receive an above-average return on their investment. And finally, I wish to thank our many employees for their loyalty and fine work. Together, we will help build UniTrans into one of the most successful and specialized package shipping companies in the industry.

UNITRANS COMPANY PICTURE ALBUM

ACCOUNTING DEPARTMENT
Modern computer equipment is used to prepare
payrolls, asset reports, payables, and receivables.

DELIVERY TRUCK FLEET
One of our modern radio-equipped trucks, which
routes packages from our centers to customers.

RETAIL PACKAGE DEPOT
Our staff of courteous employees assist customers
at one of our many retail package centers.

PACKAGE-HANDLING DEPARTMENT
Packages are processed in our modern routing and
sorting facilities.

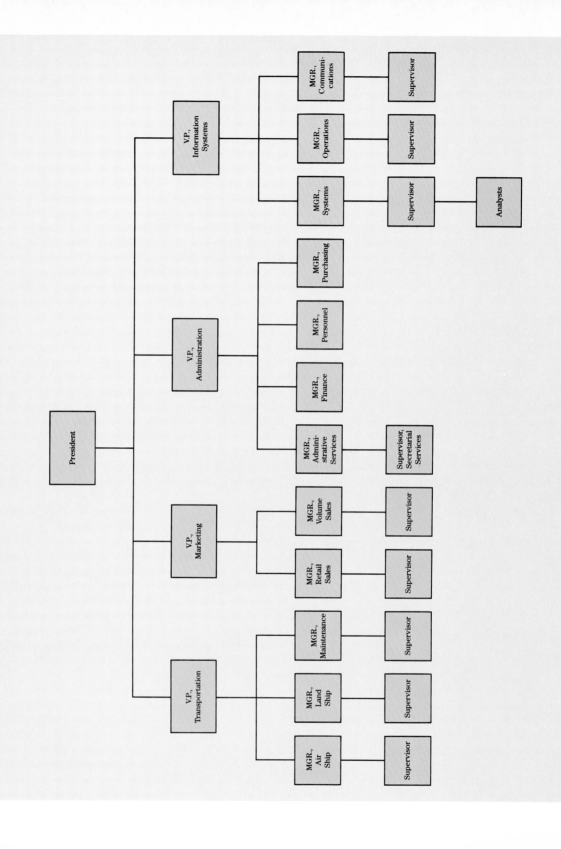

UNITRANS AT A GLANCE

Year	Curr.	Last
Sales (in millions)	$57.6	$51
Net Profit (in millions)	$12.7	$11.3

Employees 2,600
Assets.. $42.6 million
Shares Outstanding .... 1.1 million
52 Week Price Range ....$15 3/4 –$21 1/8
Headquarters .... Central Valley

BALANCE SHEET
(in thousands)

ASSETS

Cash		$ 3,200
Securities		1,600
Accounts receivable		10,800
Total current assets		15,600
Plant and equipment	$31,000	
Less depreciation	4,000	
Net plant and equipment	27,000	
Total assets		**42,600**

LIABILITIES

Accounts payable	$ 3,100
Notes payable	4,200
Accruals	150
Provisions for taxes	4,700
Total current liabilities	12,150
First mortgages	1,000
Bonds	10,500
Common stock	18,950
Total net worth	12,150
Total liabilities	**42,600**

AN INSIDE LOOK AT UNITRANS

TRANSPORTATION DIVISION

The heart of UniTrans is its transportation division. This division operates a fleet of delivery trucks and airplanes. It is responsible for the movement of thousands of packages and parcels each week between the hundreds of locations operated by UniTrans. This division also maintains extensive garage and repair facilities to ensure that all transportation vehicles are maintained at optimum performance.

MARKETING DIVISION

All sales at UniTrans are handled through the marketing division. The retail sales department maintains and operates customer package depots throughout the country. The volume sales department serves large customers who ship a heavy volume of packages and freight each year.

ADMINISTRATION DIVISION

The administration division is an overall service arm of the entire company. The division is responsible for the acquisition of land, the selection of retail sales depots, and the acquisition of property at the Central Valley headquarters. The finance department handles all accounts receivables, accounts payables, and financial transactions for UniTrans. The personnel department is responsible for personnel resources, including training, vacations, and employee benefits. The purchasing department serves as the central facility for the acquisition of all buyout goods and services acquired by UniTrans.

INFORMATION SYSTEMS DIVISION

This division is responsible for the computer facilities, databases, and information flow throughout the organization. The operations department maintains the computer facilities, including its extensive network of communications lines. It also monitors the movement of all shipments throughout the system.

All of UniTrans's divisions are coordinated by the president and his staff. The president holds regular meetings with division vice-presidents, who are involved in long-range planning and the improvement and development of UniTrans's extensive parcel-handling facilities.

Summary

Business organizations are faced with an expanding volume of paperwork, increasing the need for systems. A system is a regularly interacting group of elements that functions as a whole. There are many different types of business systems, including information systems. A business system is a collection of elements that interact to enable an organization to reach its goals. Information systems are collections of elements that process data, making it available for decision making. Data is the raw material to be processed, while information is the product resulting from the manipulation of raw data.

Systems are composed of elements known as subsystems. A system is separated from the environment by a boundary. Systems receive input, process information, and generate output. In open systems, the output cannot be determined precisely, while in closed systems, results can be predicted with certainty.

There has been a great increase in the volume of information generated and manipulated by organizations. This has led to reliance upon office automation, data communications, and computers. The labor force is shifting from blue-collar to white-collar jobs. Systems analysts investigate information systems in order to improve their operation. While systems analysis brings many benefits to an organization, it is not without its limitations or costs.

Key Terms

Boundary	**Open system**
Business system	**Outputs**
Closed system	**Processing**
Data	**Subsystems**
Environment	**System**
Information	**Systems analysis**
Information system	**Systems analyst**
Inputs	

Exercises

1. Define the term *system*.
2. What is meant by system boundaries and the environment?
3. List four common examples of systems.
4. Describe what is meant by an open system.
5. Describe what is meant by a closed system.
6. Summarize the evolution of the information industry.
7. How has the labor force reflected changes in information-processing methods?
8. Contrast system inputs and system outputs.
9. Summarize three advantages of using systems analysis techniques.
10. Describe three limitations of business systems analysis.

Projects

1. Observe the functions of systems in your community. List as many systems as you can, noting whether they are public or private business systems.

2. Interview teachers and staff on your college campus and describe the system used for registering students.

3. Interview five students and ask them to define the term *system*. Contrast their definitions with that given in the text.

4. Discuss the systems used by a small business proprietor. Categorize each system according to its function and purpose.

5. Study a system at your place of employment. Determine whether it is an open or closed system. Make a list of its characteristics.

THE
SYSTEMS
ANALYST

LEARNING OBJECTIVES

After studying this chapter, you should be able to:

1. Discuss the duties and responsibilities of a systems analyst.

2. Describe a systems analyst's career path, working conditions, and salary.

3. Discuss line organization structure.

4. Discuss committee organization structure.

5. Discuss the organization of information departments.

6. List critical success factors of a systems analyst.

Systems analysts provide a key human resource in the planning, improvement, and operation of business organizations. Organizations are made up of more than simply machines, offices, money, and materials. The most essential ingredient in any company is its personnel. Those who wish to succeed must have certain skills, knowledge, and attitudes.

In this chapter we will look at the function and role of the systems analyst and trace the emergence of the business systems department. The chapter describes the structure of business organizations and information-processing departments.

THE EMERGENCE OF THE SYSTEMS ANALYST

Before the advent of computers, orbiting satellites, and industrial robots, life, even in the fast lane of the business world, was slower and more leisurely. The attitudes and atmosphere of business organizations half a century or more ago reflected a pre-information age way of life. Businesses were small, local, individualized, and often family-owned. Information gathering and processing activities were limited to what the proprietor might need in the short term—for example, hours worked by employees or amounts owed by credit customers. Most information management had to be done by hand or simple machines, and it was relatively time consuming and expensive.

The quality of business decisions reflected a lack of precision. Since the influence of a single decision, made by one person, was limited—usually involving only a few people and a small amount of money—guesses and personal experience were often sufficient to solve problems. Errors or mistakes in judgment were also limited in their effects, and most of the time changes and corrections could be made easily.

When business people wanted to improve the information-processing activities in the office, they waited until a salesperson dropped in to show off the latest in manual typewriters or mechanical calculators. If they had the money and the machine seemed practical, the purchase was made on the spur of the moment. This method of solving problems was adequate for the times.

But the population was expanding and technology advancing. Businesses were on the verge of outgrowing many of their traditional, leisurely ways. World War II thrust the nation into a new era. Industry was suddenly faced with the monumental task of supplying the country with the tools of war. These new tools were more complicated than any that had yet been manufactured, and they were needed faster than ever before and in larger quantities.

With the nation's survival at stake, industry could not rely on guesswork, intuition, or hunches for decision making. These methods had high error factors, no cost controls, and too much reliance on isolated individuals rather than on systems. Managers, now under pressure, looked for ways to improve efficiency and output. Scheduling, timing, and planning became critical so that defense plants could meet the demands placed upon them.

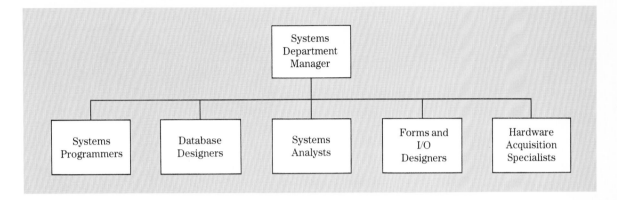

FIGURE 2.1

Systems Department Organization
This chart shows the relationship of systems analysts, engineers, programmers, and others.

The scientific method of problem solving, statistical techniques, and computers pointed the way toward the answers. These tools gave managers powerful systematic procedures for analyzing, defining, and evaluating new techniques and solutions to problems. They were used to develop programs that could find the best mixture of employees, machines, and materials to produce the maximum output in the least amount of time. The science of systems analysis was born.

THE EVOLUTION OF SYSTEMS DEPARTMENTS

It did not take managers very long to realize that many of their business and information problems could be solved using techniques developed by government and research analysts during World War II. As a result, many organizations centralized their problem-solving and information-handling activities into specialized units. These became known as business systems, operations research, or information systems departments. The systems department was responsible for developing information systems, measuring work, and finding solutions to business problems.

During the past several decades the importance of information **systems departments** has continued to grow. Today these departments are staffed by systems analysts, systems engineers, database specialists, programmers, and other individuals with skills in computer use, information processing, and operations research (see Fig. 2.1). Systems departments work together with other units, including the data processing department, to assist in the orderly flow of information throughout an organization. Figure 2.2 illustrates this relationship.

THE DUTIES OF THE SYSTEMS ANALYST

The specific duties of the individuals in the systems department depend upon the size and type of organization involved. Analysts are often concerned with the following areas:

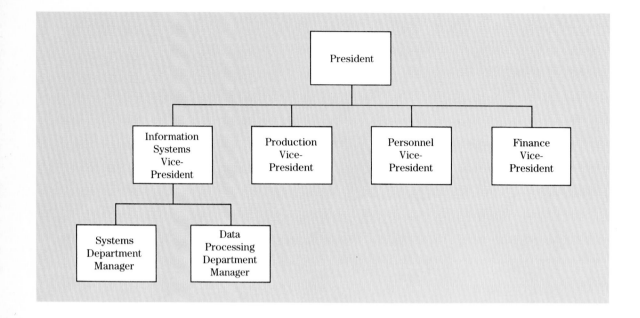

FIGURE 2.2

Typical Organization Structure
The systems department functions as a unit, providing services to the entire organization.

1. Project management. Systems people are sometimes called upon to manage entire projects, coordinating personnel, facilities, and installation procedures.

2. Forecasting and simulation. Systems analysts play an important role in analyzing and planning the goals and growth patterns of a company. They predict financial and economic trends using various computerized mathematical techniques.

3. Sales and marketing of goods and services. Systems analysts supply information and research data for decision makers regarding the sales, marketing, and distribution of a firm's goods.

4. Planning the orderly flow of information throughout an entire business enterprise. Analysts specify what data will be collected, what form it will take, and how it will be processed and reported to management.

5. Modifying or redesigning existing business systems. The systems analyst has the responsibility for proposing changes and improvements in a data flow system to meet new or continuing needs of a business firm.

6. Systems implementation. Once a system has been designed and specified, the systems analyst directs and oversees its orderly implementation. This involves such factors as selecting personnel and equipment and hiring consultants.

7. Computer programming and utilization. Systems analysts indicate the types of computer programs needed for a new system and monitor their development, testing, and final implementation. The actual task of writing programs is often delegated to a programmer.

8. Database design. Systems analysts specify what information will be included in a database and plan the layout of fields, records, and files. They define and develop the procedures necessary to keep the information in the files current and accurate.

9. Forms design and management. Systems analysts plan and design the forms, documents, and records to be used in a system. They select the content, sizes, routing, and storage, and specify forms revision procedures.

10. Establishing system policies and procedures. Systems analysts write the policy manuals that are necessary for a system to work efficiently. They define routines and methods for handling information flow.

11. Employment and training of organization personnel. Systems people are involved in specifying personnel needs for various clerical and office workstations. They describe training programs and procedures.

12. Work measurement. The systems analyst records data on the output of various clerical, management, accounting, and information-processing personnel. This is used to compare, analyze, and report the productivity of personnel involved in the flow of paperwork.

13. Work simplification. Analysts develop easier, faster, more accurate, and improved methods of processing information.

14. Office layout. Systems analysts are involved in planning the office environment. They design and lay out offices and administrative suites, specifying such things as the number and type of desks, cabinets, files, or office copy equipment. The analyst indicates the number of workstations, their locations, and the equipment needed at each.

15. Selection and specification of office and information-processing equipment and supplies. Much time is spent by the analyst in comparing and selecting hardware and machines necessary for the efficient flow of data throughout a firm. This includes computers, copying machines, duplicating equipment, mail handling machines, routing machines, and others.

16. Planning and designing internal and external communications. An important responsibility of the systems analyst involves the firm's data, voice, and video communications facilities. This includes specifying the type and number of telephone lines, data lines, switchboards, dictation equipment, telephones, computer terminals, data transmission equipment, and facsimile machines.

COMMUNICATIONS AND THE ORGANIZATION

Communications, both verbal and written, are vital elements in the daily life of a business enterprise. Identifying and evaluating the activities and communication paths that generate information is one of the basic jobs of the systems

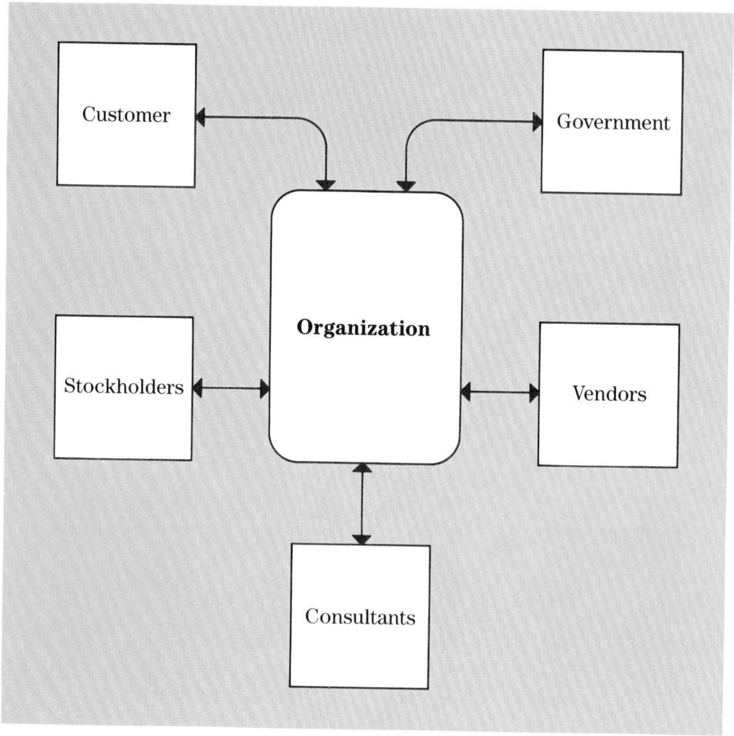

FIGURE 2.3

External Communications
This class of communication takes place between an organization or system and those beyond its boundaries.

analyst. He or she must be able to trace the flow of communications throughout the organizational structure in order to propose and design an information system.

A **communication** is the transmission of a message through a medium, such as the spoken or written word, from a sender to a receiver. Communications are sometimes described as external and internal.

External communications take place between an organization or system and those beyond its boundaries. Examples are communications that flow between a firm and its customers, the government, stockholders, unions, and others (see Fig. 2.3). Documents include purchase orders, bills of lading, sales slips, customer invoices, payments to vendors, tax reports, and more.

Internal communications are letters, memos, and other correspondence that originate and terminate within the same organization (see Fig. 2.4). They include such items as stock records, work reports, expense account records, and check registers.

These internal communications can be further classified by direction—is the movement horizontal or vertical? **Horizontal communications** include the transfer of data and information between individuals at the same level on the organization chart. Examples are one data entry clerk teaching another to prepare an invoice; a report prepared by one office for another on the same level; and the transfer of sales orders from the sales department to accounting.

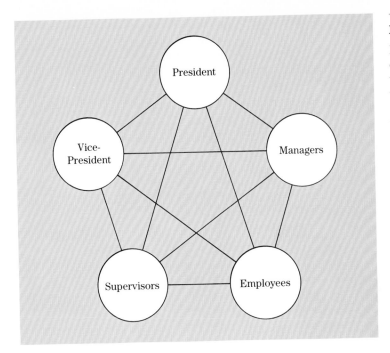

FIGURE 2.4

Internal Communications In this figure, information transfers between individuals within the organization.

Vertical communication is the transfer of information between individuals on different levels of the organization chart. Examples include a request for information from a vice-president of manufacturing to a manager, or a report forwarded by a shipping clerk to his or her supervisor.

JOB DESCRIPTION

Most organizations of any size have drafted formal **job descriptions** that outline the specific duties and responsibilities of systems analysts (see Fig. 2.5). These descriptions usually state the general responsibilities and overall functions of the analyst. Such duties may include working with others, assisting in the development of policies and procedures, designing and developing new systems, and so on.

The specific duties required of the analyst are also defined. The particulars depend upon whether the position is that of a trainee, junior analyst, or senior analyst. As you can see, specific duties include writing reports, interviewing personnel, coordinating functions, and designing files, records, and forms. Some job descriptions also list the individuals with whom the analyst will interact. These descriptions further define the scope of the analyst's work.

It is not uncommon to see salary ranges stated on the job description. The specific training, experience, and knowledge required are stated as well.

FIGURE 2.5

**Systems Analyst
Job Description**

**UNITRANS
COMPANY JOB
DESCRIPTION**

Position: SENIOR SYSTEMS ANALYST

Salary Group: G

Supervisor: SYSTEMS DEPARTMENT MANAGER

Job Description:

Employee will be involved in all phases of systems analysis and design. A large amount of time is spent working with managers from other departments, assisting them with system problems. The job requires the ability to investigate problems, analyze alternatives, and propose solutions. The analyst should exhibit creativity and the ability to work well with others. The applicant should have a knowledge of the transportation industry and be familiar with industry terminology.

Experience and Training:

Previous industry experience necessary, preferably four or more years in the shipping and transportation industry. Bachelor's degree required. Master's strongly recommended. Should have academic training in systems analysis and design, statistics, data processing, and information systems. Familiarity with project management and computerized systems analysis and design software required.

Duties and Responsibilities:

- Define and investigate problems
- Write and prepare feasibility studies
- Write systems software specifications
- Write systems hardware specifications
- Act as liaison between company and vendors
- Conduct benchmark testing
- Perform system evaluation and follow-up
- Perform computer-aided systems analysis and design

SKILLS, KNOWLEDGE, AND TRAINING

Successful systems analysts exhibit certain common skills and traits, sometimes known as critical success factors. These factors include:

Creativity and innovation

Good verbal skills

Good written communication ability

A positive attitude toward others

Technical knowledge of computers and information systems hardware and software

Knowledge of basic business theories and concepts

Willingness to work with others

Ability to solve problems

In addition to the critical success factors, an analyst must master three major domains of skills (see Fig. 2.6). These are described below.

Knowledge of Business

It is essential that an analyst possess a solid foundation in business principles, concepts, and theories. Business systems do not operate in a vacuum.

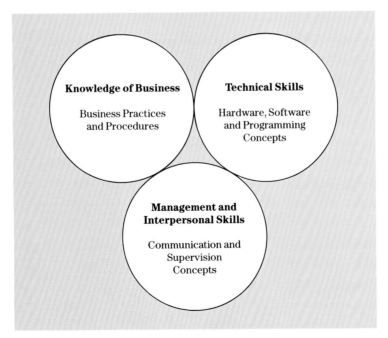

FIGURE 2.6

Domains of Skills The analyst must master three domains of skills to work with systems successfully.

They behave according to common practices, procedures, and principles. Therefore, the analyst must understand basic economics, accounting, marketing concepts, and so forth. Specific business knowledge should relate to the particular organization that employs the analyst.

Without a solid foundation in business, an analyst would be unable to study the system and make the kind of changes and improvements necessary to serve the needs of the firm. The analyst faces a continuing challenge, because conditions change as new technology, products, and methods of manufacturing and distribution come into use.

Technical Skills

The individual should possess a high degree of technical and information-processing skills. Analysts must be aware of modern computer systems, programming and software concepts and the kinds of personnel needed to staff computer and information systems. They should have a grasp of programming, systems design, information-processing methods, advantages and limitations of particular pieces of computer equipment, and communications devices.

One of the key elements in the analyst's bag of technical skills is problem-solving ability. Analysts are called upon to find innovative and creative solutions to the problems faced by businesses.

Management and Interpersonal Skills

Systems analysts work with dozens of individuals throughout the organization. Therefore, they must have good communication skills and be able to articulate concepts clearly. They must also be able to put ideas and concepts in writing in a clear and understandable form.

Analysts must often manage entire projects. This requires an understanding of management theory, motivation, and teamwork. The particular mix of skills varies with the specific assignment. An analyst charged with the responsibility of developing a better personnel management or supervision scheme needs a greater understanding of management skills than one who helps engineer an improved accounting or payroll system.

PREPARING FOR A CAREER
IN SYSTEMS ANALYSIS

The knowledge and skills just described are usually acquired through academic training, on-the-job experience, or a combination of both (see Fig. 2.7). Some analysts complete college coursework and then seek industry experience

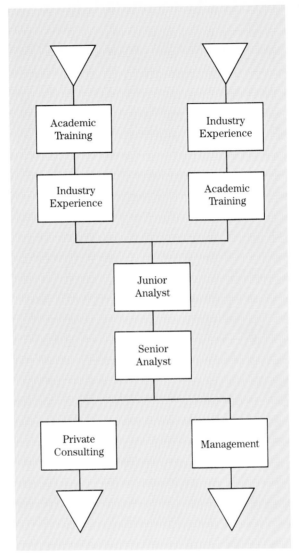

FIGURE 2.7

Systems Analyst's Career Path

after graduation. Others have little academic training in systems analysis; once employed, they may enroll in a formal program of education or alternate between periods of school and work. In any case, this preparation enables an individual to be employed as a **junior analyst**. This position requires less skills and knowledge than that of a **senior analyst**, who may have many years of practical experience and extensive postgraduate training.

     Some analysts may find their career path leading them into management and out of systems analysis. Still others may become private consultants, sharing their skills and knowledge with organizations for a fee.

Academic Preparation

A bachelor's degree in computer science, information systems, systems analysis, or business management is a basic foundation block for work in this field. Coursework should include classes in management, programming languages, computers, programming logic, and similar subjects.

For advanced work in systems, graduate courses are valuable and in some instances required. A master's degree in computers and information systems or in computer science provides some of the required academic skills.

On-the-Job Experience

Many individuals gain on-the-job experience by seeking employment as trainees or entry-level clerks in organizations with systems analysis departments. Some enter as computer operators, junior programmers, librarians, technical writers, or data entry clerks. As they gain skills on the job, they may take on additional responsibilities and be classified as programmers, senior programmers, senior computer operators, and so on. These years of hands-on experience with the hardware and software of information systems prepare these individuals to move ahead in their career path toward senior systems analyst.

Salaries and Benefits

The salaries and benefits paid systems analysts equal or exceed those in similar professional and clerical white-collar occupations. Systems analysts generally work in an air-conditioned environment in well-equipped, modern facilities. They frequently work with managers, executives, and supervisors, as well as with other individuals in key leadership roles in the company.

Salaries vary, depending upon the level of responsibility (see Fig. 2.8). Senior systems analysts and managers are positioned just below data processing directors and vice-presidents on the salary scale. Their annual incomes exceed those of programmers. Even junior systems analysts receive higher than average salaries. This is because of the complex nature of their work and the skills and training required to perform productively.

THE FUTURE OF THE SYSTEMS ANALYST

The career paths of many systems analysts take them into higher levels of organization management. Those analysts possessing strong management, communication, and organizational skills become prime candidates for advancement in upwardly mobile companies.

NATIONAL STATISTICS

Job Description	Number Reported	Lowest Reported Actual Salary	National Average Actual Salary	Median Actual Salary	Mode Actual Salary	Highest Reported Actual Salary
Management						
Top MIS Official	163	384	1131	1078	1153	2403
Manager of Data Processing	435	317	820	800	961	1842
Assistant Manager of Data Processing	105	267	799	865	888	1500
Manager of Database Systems	86	317	725	711	384	1448
Systems Analysis						
Manager/Supervisor of Systems Analysis	233	408	820	826	576	1500
Systems Analyst	706	279	687	686	692	1292
Applications Programming						
Manager/Supervisor of Applications Programming	207	278	796	800	888	1826
Applications Programmer	2610	230	478	423	346	1250
Data/ Telecommunications						
Data/ Telecommunications Manager	50	442	879	902	923	1192
Communications Analyst	126	346	682	692	692	1015
Communications Operator	104	200	323	307	269	673
Computer Operations						
Data Center Manager	179	240	663	634	576	1293
Computer Operator	1226	161	386	384	346	946
Computer Input/Output Control Manager	111	250	440	426	423	823
Tape Librarian	60	223	375	346	269	807
Data Entry Supervisor	108	200	409	384	307	846
Data Entry Operator	786	105	301	291	173	596
Other						
Project/Team Leader	111	484	811	817	817	1184
Information Center Manager	46	326	729	735	769	1332
Information Center Analyst/Trainer	123	274	551	507	500	1011
Manager of Microcomputers	33	140	575	552	576	923
End User Computer Specialist/Office Automation Specialist	84	197	443	428	384	884

FIGURE 2.8

Information Industry Salaries Weekly salary in dollars for all jobs: nationwide.

(Reprinted by permission from Infosystems, Hitchcock Publishing Co., Wheaton, Illinois)

The long-term employment outlook for systems analysts at all levels is very good. As more organizations turn to computers and communications technology to solve their problems, they will rely more heavily upon systems analysts. Rising costs, particularly labor costs, place demands on organizations to find new and better ways to conduct their operations. Systems analysts are basically problem solvers who focus on efficiency.

Analysts who understand new technology and can apply it to solve business problems will always be needed. Robots, artificial intelligence, communications networks, fiber optics, and laser communications are some new technologies waiting for systems analysts to find ways to use them in business.

FORMAL ORGANIZATION STRUCTURE

Since so much of the analyst's time is spent working with others in an organization, it is worthwhile to review some organization structure concepts.

Organizations are composed of individuals who perform specific roles coordinated to enable the company to achieve its goals. Virtually every company has some type of **formal organization** structure. There is usually an official plan that clearly shows the chain of command and the lines of authority and responsibility. Organizations have formal sets of rules that define the various functions and duties at each level of authority and prescribe the relationships among the different roles.

Most business firms are structured according to one of the following three types of formal organizations.

Line Organization

A classical **line organization** resembles a pyramid (see Fig. 2.9). At the top is the manager—chairman of the board, president, chief—with the ultimate decision-making authority. Below the manager are various levels of subordinates.

On the level directly below the manager are the relatively few persons who are next in authority and who have lesser or different responsibilities and decision-making functions. Below them are the other layers of the official hierarchy, each involving a greater number of individuals with lesser responsibility and authority than the one above.

Within this classical line organization exist clear lines of authority, moving from the top down. Each individual is responsible to someone in authority above him or her. Conversely, each individual in authority has persons for whom he or she is directly responsible.

These relationships and lines of authority are often illustrated with a graphic device called an **organization chart**. Figure 2.9 shows the lines of authority and chain of command in a firm organized in the classical line pattern.

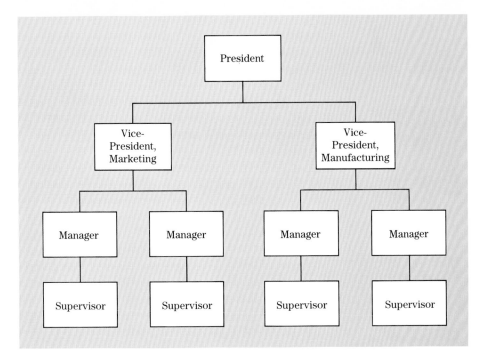

FIGURE 2.9

Line Organization
This structure follows a classical pattern with clear, simple lines of authority.

If individuals are not connected by lines, it is assumed that no authority or responsibility exists between them.

The line organization is a simple, clear structure, but it does contain certain weaknesses. An individual needing advice must follow the lines of authority shown on the organization chart. In theory, he or she cannot approach other organization members not related by a direct line of authority, since no official relationship has been established. However, in practice, these rules are often bent.

Because of this weakness, the line organization is not widely used in modern business or industry. The military is probably one of the few major examples of this type of organization.

Line and Staff Organization

A modified form of business structure is the **line and staff organization**, shown in Fig. 2.10. Line positions are indicated by solid lines; staff positions by dotted lines. This type of structure includes the usual manager and subordinate positions, representing the formal chain of command, with supplemental staff positions.

Staff positions refer to those employees or departments that provide a consulting or advisory service to others in the firm. Usually such departments are not directly involved in producing the goods or services that are the com-

FIGURE 2.10

Line and Staff Organization Staff positions are shown with dotted lines.

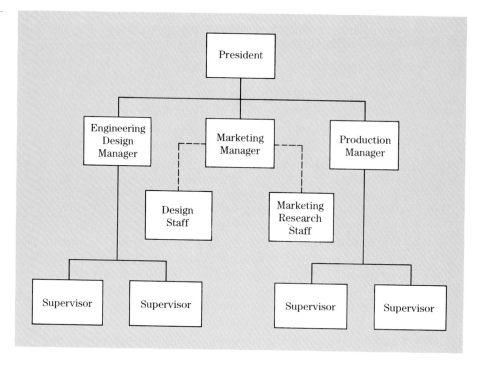

pany's major source of profits. Staff examples are the personnel, accounting, legal, research, and information-processing departments.

The staff member's role is to provide consultation, advice, and support to the line managers in areas outside their expertise. The actual responsibility for the end performance, however, remains with the line manager.

Provisions for consultation and staff support, in addition to the clear lines of authority, give the line and staff organization an important advantage over the line structure. For this reason it has become the most widely used form of business organization.

Committee Organization

Another form of business structure is the **committee organization**, shown in Fig. 2.11. In this arrangement, a position or responsibility is assigned to a group of individuals rather than to a single person. The group shares the responsibilities delegated to that position and makes decisions by consensus. Thus, the talents of several people are involved in solving a single problem or in making a difficult decision.

A major weakness of the committee organization is the difficulty involved in getting several people to act cohesively and to make decisions promptly. Com-

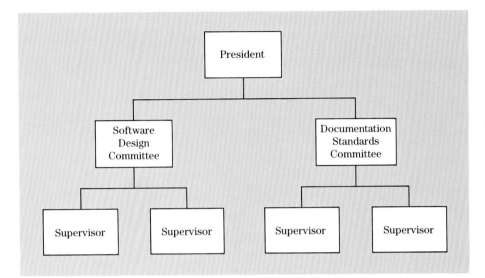

FIGURE 2.11

Committee Organization Responsibility is assigned to a group of individuals rather than a single person.

munications among members of a committee can also pose problems, and it may be hard for an individual to function effectively with a committee rather than a single person as the boss. For these reasons, the committee setup is not a widely used form of business structure in the United States, although it is often found in political and government organizations, and in some other industrialized countries.

Organization of Information Departments

Systems analysts are sometimes employed in information departments, or work under data processing or management information system managers. Figure 2.12 illustrates a typical information department that might be found in a large company. One or more systems analysts may be assigned to the systems group. Programming is handled by various levels of programmers; data entry and computer operators work under the operations supervisor.

As we will see throughout our study of systems, the analyst is engaged in a variety of activities, working with programmers, terminal operators, documentation specialists, and others on the chart. Smaller organizations may have fewer positions than shown in the figure, so one individual may perform several functions.

Now that we have considered the scope of the analyst's activities, we will describe the steps to follow in designing and implementing a new business or information system. The next chapter presents the systems development life cycle, which is the foundation of much of the analyst's work.

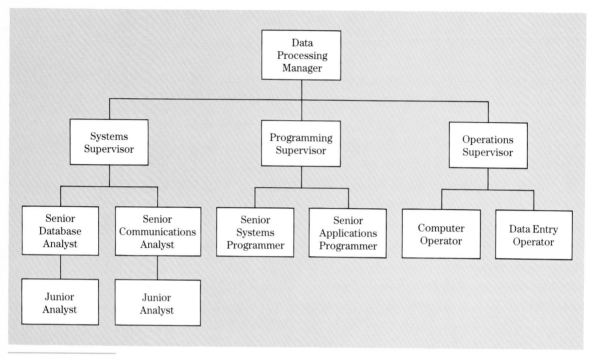

FIGURE 2.12

Organization of Information Department This structure shows the organization
of a typical information department.

Summary   An essential element of an organization is its personnel. The role of the systems
analyst has grown in importance over several decades. Systems departments
have evolved to serve organizations. Analysts are engaged in many tasks, including project management, forecasting, planning, systems implementation, work
measurement, and other activities.

Organizational communications are internal and external, vertical and
horizontal.

A job description defines the skills, knowledge and training required of
the analyst. Analysts gain skills through academic as well as on-the-job experience. The analyst's career path leads toward increasing salaries and benefits.

Common success traits in analysts include creativity, innovation, written
and verbal communication ability, positive attitude, willingness to work with
others, and ability to solve problems.

Organizations are composed of formal structures. They may be based
upon line, line and staff, and committee structures. Information systems departments handle the data processing activities for an organization, and often involve
the work of systems analysts.

Committee organization

Communication

External communications

Formal organization

Horizontal communications

Internal communications

Job description

Junior analyst

Line organization

Line and staff organization

Organization chart

Senior analyst

Systems department

Vertical communications

Exercises

1. List five functions of modern business systems departments.
2. Describe the activities involved in systems analysis.
3. Briefly trace the changing emphasis on business systems analysis.
4. Contrast internal and external communications.
5. Contrast horizontal and vertical communications.
6. What kinds of information are found in a job description?
7. What are some critical success factors exhibited by analysts?
8. Describe at least two formal business organizational structures.
9. Describe the function of organization charts.
10. Describe the organization of information departments.

Projects

1. Draw a formal organization chart showing the relationships of personnel on your college campus.
2. Interview an employee of a business firm and discuss the formal structure of the firm. Draw an organization chart showing these formal relationships.
3. Write a brief essay describing the advantages and limitations of a committee structure in solving problems and making decisions.
4. Interview a systems analyst employed in your community. Discuss wages, salaries, benefits, and working conditions.
5. Interview a systems analyst and discuss his or her duties. List these duties and compare them with those described in the text.

TOOLS OF THE SYSTEMS ANALYST

SYSTEMS DEVELOPMENT LIFE CYCLE

LEARNING OBJECTIVES

After studying this chapter, you should be able to:

1. Discuss cause and effect relationships.

2. Describe the scientific method of problem solving.

3. Contrast structured and classical systems analysis techniques.

4. Describe the cyclic nature of problem solving.

5. Discuss the use of quantitative problem statements.

6. Describe the systems development life cycle (SDLC).

Some problems in life are easily solved. If your car is about to run out of gas, you can drive into a service station and fill up the tank. Other problems take a little more time and effort. If a loud knock develops in the car's engine, you might need to shop around for a mechanic, pay for diagnostic checks, and ultimately pay a large repair bill.

Business problems are similar to personal ones. They too range from simple to complex, from those easily dealt with to those that are insoluble. Each day systems analysts and business managers aggressively apply their intellect and skills and the organization's time and resources to a diversity of problems.

In this chapter we will study problem-solving techniques and look at the systematic approaches that analysts use in dealing with problems. The chapter discusses traditional and structured systems analysis techniques and how to apply the scientific method to solving business problems. It also provides an overview of procedures that will be covered in depth in later chapters.

CAUSE AND EFFECT RELATIONSHIPS

For centuries doctors have known how to operate on patients, but until this century, even when their operations appeared to be successful many patients died. Surgeons in the seventeenth and eighteenth centuries didn't connect the lack of sterilization and cleanliness—the cause—with the infections and high mortality rate that resulted—the effect. It wasn't until 1865, when Joseph Lister associated the lack of antiseptic methods with infections leading to the death of patients, that medicine took a giant step forward.

Today, scientists recognize the **cause and effect relationship.** If a cause and effect relationship exists, the cause will always generate the effect. This certainty allows social scientists, business managers, systems analysts, and others to bring order and structure out of chaos. Cause and effect is the foundation of systems work.

For many years business managers relied upon hunches, guesses, intuition, or tradition to guide them in **problem solving.** It was philosopher John Dewey who outlined the steps of a logical approach for developing sound solutions to problems. His statement of the scientific method is based upon cause and effect relationships. The **scientific method** is a procedure for solving problems that systematically deals with causes and effects, evaluating the results. It is useful for solving a problem with the least expenditure of time and effort.

THE SCIENTIFIC METHOD

The scientific method of problem solving, an important part of the systems analyst's repertoire, is used to develop solutions for a wide range of information flow problems. Its major characteristics are:

1. Reproducibility of results. There is a good deal of assurance that procedures, operations, or tests carried out according to the scientific method will produce the same results each time they are performed.

2. Accuracy of results. Conclusions based on the application of factual knowledge, reproducible experiences, and intellectual proficiency, rather than on guesswork or chance, are more accurate.

3. Efficient expenditure of time and effort. Since procedures are executed logically, there is more assurance that the activities of the systems analyst will achieve specified goals with the least effort.

4. Plan of action. The scientific method gives the systems analyst a reliable and tangible plan to follow when handling a complicated problem with many diverse factors. It ensures that all relevant procedures, elements, and data are considered and that none is omitted accidentally.

5. Transferability of results. Because results obtained from the scientific method are reproducible, the systems analyst can expect similar results to occur in like situations without having to repeat the steps in the process, or to retest data.

The following is a list of the key aspects of the scientific method:

- Precise statement of problem
- Careful attention to detail
- Objectivity in making observations
- Precision in analyzing data and reporting results
- Use of mathematics and statistical techniques
- Systematic, logical plan for solving problems
- Evaluation of results
- Readjustment of system to bring it more in line with objectives

We will review the major elements in the scientific problem-solving process (see Fig. 3.1). This will provide us with a general framework for approaching and solving business problems. Later in the chapter we will see how this set of steps is refined into a process that is routinely followed in systems analysis.

FIGURE 3.1

Scientific Problem-Solving Process

[Flowchart boxes:]
Recognize Problem and Identify Causes

Express Problem in Quantitative Terms

Analyze Choices and Select Plan

Implement the Solution

Evaluate Results and Optimize

Recognize the Problem

Before we can solve a problem, if there is one, we must identify its causes. In this step, the systems analyst describes and isolates the factors pertinent to a particular problem and tries to determine the causes. The analyst investigates the nature of the problem to decide if it is a unique situation, whether it is indicative of other problems, or whether it masks a deeper problem.

Let us use the UniTrans Company, introduced in Chapter 1, as a vehicle to apply some of the concepts in this chapter. Suppose the routing clerks in

UT

FIGURE 3.2

Problem Recognition Delays in entering data at UniTrans could be caused by many different reasons.

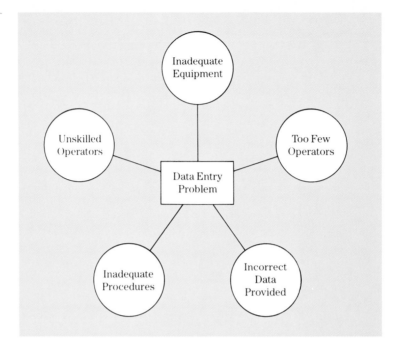

UniTrans Company's transportation division are hampered in their work because the data entry department takes too long to prepare and enter data (see Fig. 3.2). The first step is to identify the factors involved and determine where the problem lies. Is it the fault of the data entry department? How does its output compare to that of similar departments? Are the agents at fault? Are they giving the data entry department sufficient information to prepare documents? Are the forms used to record data adequate and efficient? Is the problem a combination of two or more elements?

In this case the systems analyst decides that the level of output from the data entry department is below what can reasonably be expected. The next question is why? Is the low productivity due to inadequate equipment or malfunctioning computer terminals? Are office arrangements inefficient? Are there problems in the physical environment, such as high noise levels or poor air conditioning? Do the keyboard operators have inadequate skills or insufficient training? Does the company employ too few operators to handle the load?

The problem cannot be solved if the wrong causes are attacked or the wrong solution is implemented. If the problem is caused by inadequate keyboarding skills, rearranging the office furniture will not increase output. The real elements of the problem must be identified before a solution can be found.

Express Problem in Quantitative Terms

The next step in the scientific method involves reducing the problem to **quantitative terms.** A quantitative statement expresses variables in terms of

VARIABLE	QUALITATIVE EXPRESSION	QUANTITATIVE EXPRESSION	FIGURE 3.3
Sales volume	Slow period	$11,500 per day	
Packages handled	Heavy volume	1000 parcels per station	
Delayed shipment	Late delivery	Over four hours late	
Weight limit	Too heavy	Over two pounds	
Size limit	Too long	Over 60 inches	
Hazardous package	Unsafe	On EPA toxic list	
Parts in stock	Almost out	Fewer than three units	

FIGURE 3.3

Quantitative and Qualitative Expressions

numbers, rather than in general qualities or characteristics (see Fig. 3.3). The systems analyst cannot be sure that a problem has been solved unless there is some objective way to measure results or the effects of change on a system. In many cases it is impossible to determine the best way to solve a problem or to see if it has been solved until it has been expressed quantitatively—that is, in numeric terms.

For example, the next step in solving UniTrans Company's data entry problem is to express both the present and expected levels of output in quantitative terms. The systems analyst must know exactly how far below expectations the department falls. If the cause of the low output is identified as poor typing skills, then the next step is to determine exactly which operators are below the norm and by how much. To do this, tools that precisely measure keyboard performance must be obtained or developed. Specially designed sample pages, policies, and forms can be used to test each operator's ability to perform specific tasks required by the company.

Analyze Choices and Select an Alternative

In this phase, the systems analyst develops alternative solutions to the problem after studying various methods of improving the situation. In selecting a plan of action, the analyst uses **if-then logic**—*if* a given solution is implemented, *then* this will happen (see Fig. 3.4).

Risks, costs, and benefits are assessed. One solution may greatly increase accuracy at a slight increase in cost. Another may increase output but not accuracy, at a substantial increase in cost. Still another may increase output slightly and reduce cost at the same time. After identifying the possible alternative actions and their expected outcomes, the systems analyst selects the one that best promises to solve the problem within the constraints of the system.

In our UniTrans Company example, the analyst decides that lack of skills

FIGURE 3.4

If-Then Logic Each path results in a different set of conditions.

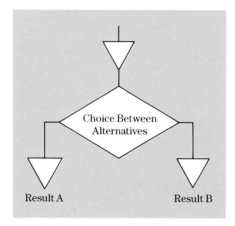

is the problem and that an in-service training program is the best way to upgrade the keyboarding abilities of the present staff. The analyst may also recommend that in the future the company hire only individuals with a high level of keyboarding skills.

Implement the Solution

After a solution has been selected, the next step is to implement it. This phase may involve a considerable expenditure of time and money. Sometimes equipment vendors are called in, employees hired, training courses developed, new forms printed, computers installed, and so on. Patterns of information flow may be changed and new procedures instituted or old ones altered.

Implementing the solution for UniTrans Company involves developing an in-service program to improve keyboard skills. New standards are drawn up for the personnel department so they can select individuals with a high level of keyboarding skills.

Evaluate Results and Optimize

Probably the most important phase of the scientific method is evaluating the results. In this step, the systems analyst determines whether the implemented solution actually solved the problem and whether desired goals were reached.

Few solutions produce perfect results the first time they are implemented. If the original expectations were not met, the analyst must return to earlier steps in the problem-solving procedure. He or she must repeat the activities of the steps, usually with some modifications, in an attempt to adjust the outcomes. This process of reentering the problem-solving loop at the point indicated by the evaluation is called **optimization.**

STRUCTURED SYSTEMS ANALYSIS METHODOLOGY

For many years systems analysts applied the scientific method to problem solving in a traditional way, defining the inputs and outputs of a system and describing how the information would be processed. This could be a difficult and time-consuming effort because it required spending many hours preparing flowcharts and writing lengthy textual descriptions of the information-handling process. Flowcharts (discussed in the next chapter and described in more detail in the appendix) were a major tool of the systems analyst for many years.

This was an unstructured way of describing steps in a solution. Virtually all problems were perceived as being sequential and linear in nature. The traditional systems analysis methodology became inadequate, however, as businesses and organizations undertook solving more complex and interrelated problems. The task of describing all inputs, outputs, processing steps, and contacts with vendors, customers, programmers, managers, and others, using only flowcharts and textual narratives, was too difficult.

To understand what was involved, picture the task a systems analyst might face in documenting all the civil service positions and relationships for a major city, such as New York, Chicago, or Los Angeles. Then suppose that a proposed new plan required a complete restructuring of several major city departments. Using traditional narrative methods, this project would be an overwhelming undertaking.

A new method for solving system problems and describing their solutions was developed by Larry Constantine, Edward Yourdon, Chris Gane, Trish Sarson, and others. This methodology, known as **structured systems analysis,** replaced lengthy textual descriptions with diagrams that substituted words for figures and flowlines for written narratives. Structured analysis enabled analysts to visualize a system graphically, as an interrelated group of elements, rather than merely as a sequence of steps. Thus it became possible to visualize an overall system and its structure in a clearer form (see Fig. 3.5). Structured systems analysis has become the preferred method of analyzing and describing systems. Chapter 4 discusses some of these structured tools in greater detail.

SYSTEMS DEVELOPMENT LIFE CYCLE (SDLC)

Systems analysts have refined the scientific method into a logical strategy that can be applied to many kinds of problems. Figure 3.6 illustrates a five-phase approach known as the **systems development life cycle (SDLC)** that has come into widespread use. The five phases are somewhat arbitrary and often overlap. Some analysts prefer to view the process as having six or more phases.

In many ways the SDLC is like the life cycle of a human being—there is a

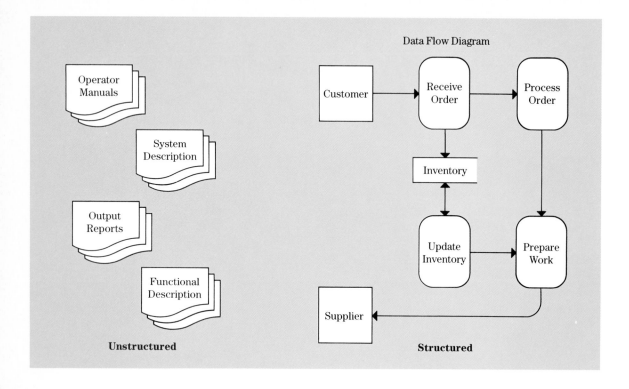

FIGURE 3.5

Structured Systems Analysis This method visualizes the overall system in diagram form.

beginning, a middle, and an end. Just as life does not always run smoothly, so it is with organizations. Most business problems are not solved in a single pass. They may require a series of efforts to bring about the desired results. The process described below reflects a series of repeated attempts at problem solving (see Fig. 3.7).

The SDLC forms the foundation and structure for most systems work. Each phase in the SDLC produces one or more deliverable elements. These elements, or deliverables, are called work products. A **work product** is a finite, measurable amount of work that results from the expenditure of effort during a phase of the SDLC. For example, a particular phase may generate a preliminary report, final report, set of forms, or series of input screens. These are the deliverables for that phase. In some lengthy system studies, payment to consultants may be based upon deliverable work products. Also known as milestones, the work products mark the completion of major phases in the system study.

The Planning Phase

In the **planning phase,** analysts recognize, diagnose, and define the problem. During this phase, they may conduct a study to assess the overall scope of the problem and determine whether more money and time should be expended in solving it. They prepare a plan of attack and select the individuals who will direct a project or serve on a committee. This phase lays the groundwork for further study and the stages that will follow. Chapter 5 will discuss this phase in greater detail.

Let us again turn to UniTrans Company's transportation division for some insight into how a system problem is recognized, diagnosed, and defined. We will listen to a conversation between Mark Stevens, a manager in the transportation division, and Jim Morton, a colleague. You decide if one or more problems exist.

MARK STEVENS: I can't figure out what's wrong with the people in the truck maintenance department. I talked to Ben, the maintenance supervisor, last week, and he told me all of our vans are now on a computerized maintenance schedule. I trust Ben; he has been with us a long time. But when I talk to George in the parts department, he gives me a different story. He says that the vans are having a lot of overheating problems, especially in stop-and-go traffic. They are replacing radiators and water pumps like crazy, and he is blaming the maintenance people.

JIM MORTON: We used to be able to work with Ben until we put in the computer. Now his people spend so much time filling out forms and playing with the computer, they can't keep up with the maintenance schedule. I think they ought to go back to the old manual method where the van drivers kept their own logs. There would be less confusion and everybody would be happier.

MARK STEVENS: Well, something must be done. Ben has to realize that we're in the package delivery business, not the computer business!

Do you think that UniTrans Company's transportation division has problems? If so, which ones can you identify? Look over the list below and decide which apply.

_____ There is no problem

_____ There is a personnel problem

_____ There is a computer hardware problem

_____ There is a computer software problem

_____ There is an economic problem

_____ There is a communication problem

_____ There is a complex problem requiring the services of a systems analyst

Most students will recognize that some kind of problem exists. Chapter 5 will discuss preliminary planning and investigation and give a more detailed look at problem recognition and planning.

The Analysis Phase

During the **analysis phase,** the analyst reviews data and information on the in-place system. He or she takes measurements, conducts audits, gathers information, interviews individuals, samples work, and documents the kinds and

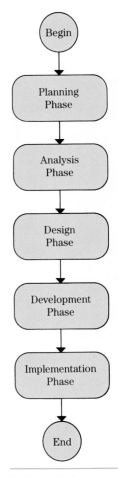

FIGURE 3.6

Systems Development Life Cycle (SDLC) This strategy involves a five-phase approach to problem solving.

Begin → Planning Phase → Analysis Phase → Design Phase → Development Phase → Implementation Phase → End

FIGURE 3.7

SDLC Spiral
A series of attempts
are made to solve a
problem.

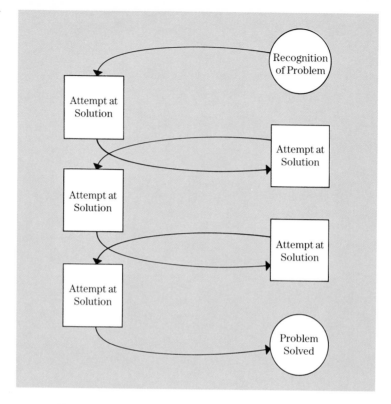

types of information to be processed by the system (see Fig. 3.8). The objective
is to clearly understand the present system, learn what is needed, and discover
the shortcomings or faults that must be corrected or modified.

Mark Stevens has sent a request for systems work to the systems department. A systems analyst has done a preliminary study and is now gathering
information on the in-place system. If you were the analyst, which of the following
documents would you like to review:

_____ Moving vehicle violations by driver

_____ Operator log

_____ Van maintenance log

_____ Replacement parts inventory

_____ Driver routing schedule

_____ Replacement parts price list

_____ Computer program listing

_____ Computer maintenance schedule

Obviously, you will need to gather as much information on the in-place system
as possible. A careful assessment of the problem will help you better determine
the information you need to gather to describe the present system. Chapter 7
discusses systems analysis principles in detail.

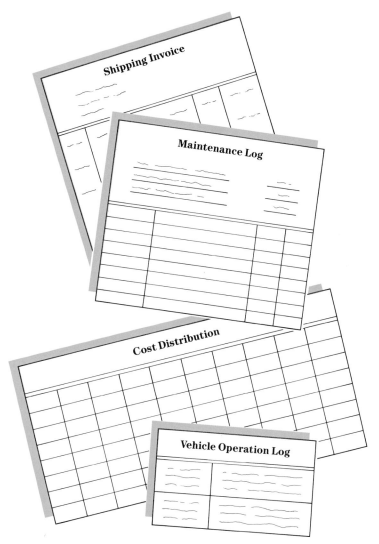

FIGURE 3.8

Analysis Phase
The analyst reviews
the information and
documentation that
describe the existing
system.

The Design Phase

The information gathered in the preceding phases allows the analyst to put down on paper the elements of a new or improved system. In the **design phase,** the analyst identifies and considers alternatives. At some point, he or she will select an alternative and conceive a design. During the design phase, input and output records are prepared, forms laid out, and file specifications written. Figure 3.9 illustrates an input screen designed by an analyst to enter maintenance data into UniTrans's computer.

A major aspect of system design is the structure, organization, and format of the information that will be contained in its database. Time and effort are

FIGURE 3.9

**Input Screen
Design** Analysts
design screens to
facilitate data entry
and reduce errors.

> ### MAINTENANCE SCHEDULING INPUT SCREEN
> ### UniTrans Company
>
> VEHICLE NO. **1321**
>
> | | | | |
> |--------------|---------------------|----------------------|----------------|
> | TYPE: | **Delivery van** | DATE REGISTERED: | **1988** |
> | MILEAGE: | **36,279** | PURCHASE COST $: | **14,360** |
> | VENDOR: | **Wadsworth Leasing** | OWNERSHIP: | **Purchase** |
>
> | DATE | SERVICE | MECHANIC | COMMENTS |
> |------|---------|----------|----------|
> | **02/21/88** | **Lube & O.C.** | **MS** | **5000 mile** |
> | **04/27/88** | **Replace 4 tires** | **RM** | **Warranty** |

spent designing the database, specifying the content of records and files that will be included in it, and describing procedures for entering data and searching, updating, or querying the files.

Assume that you have worked out a careful plan and have analyzed UniTrans's existing system. You are about to design a better system. Which of the following might you recommend:

_____ Recommend employees be fired

_____ Request new input forms

_____ Rework computer software

_____ Repair or replace computer

_____ Report the problem in company newsletter

_____ Install more telephones to improve communications

_____ Ignore problem and hope that Ben can solve it without your help

You will no doubt want to consider the above options and many others. Chapters 8 through 12 will help you better understand system design principles.

The Development Phase

In the **development phase,** the new system is actually built. The analyst concentrates on identifying vendors and suppliers who will be able to provide the necessary equipment or facilities at a reasonable price. Equipment and machines are ordered and set up, computer programs written or purchased, and communications lines leased and installed.

If you were the systems analyst at UniTrans, which of the following might you utilize in this phase:

_____ Schedule appointment to install new telephones

_____ Terminate unsatisfactory employees

_____ Purchase new computer

_____ Assign programmer to test and modify software

_____ Other actions as specified in the design phase

In the development phase we begin the actual process of implementation that will be concluded in the last step. Chapter 13 will help you explore systems development in greater detail.

The Implementation Phase

The last step of the cycle, the **implementation phase,** deals with the changeover to a new or improved system. After the facilities have been installed, programs, software, and hardware must be tested to ensure that they meet design specifications. Final changes and modifications are incorporated in the new system at this stage. The objective is to optimize and fine-tune the system. During this final step, systems documentation, which was begun early on, is completed and reports, paperwork, and diagrams are prepared describing the system now in place.

Now that you have dealt with the problem, as an analyst you should:

_____ Assume problem has been correctly solved

_____ Assume problem was not solved

_____ Invite consultant to second-guess your solution

_____ Fine-tune the system

_____ File a report with management describing how problem was solved

Depending on the circumstances, you may take one or more of the above actions. Your specific course of action will depend upon the results of the previous steps in the problem-solving process. Chapters 15 through 17 describe this phase in more detail.

In practice, the analyst may repeat one or more of the previous steps. Through a repeated series of problem-solving efforts, he or she will reach the goal of designing and engineering a better system. For UniTrans, this may mean fewer overheated vans, better inventory control, cost control of replacement parts, more efficiently scheduled maintenance work, and so on. All of this translates into better service for UniTrans's customers, and more profit for the organization.

There are many facets to problem solving and systems work. Before we proceed further with our discussion of the SDLC, we must learn about certain tools that systems analysts need. The next chapter describes data flow diagrams, decision tables, structured English, and a variety of traditional and structured techniques to help you document and design systems.

Summary

Cause and effect relationships underlie much of the work of the systems analyst. Analysts use the scientific method of problem solving. This approach ensures reproducibility of results, accuracy, and efficiency.

Before a problem can be solved it must be identified, then expressed in quantitative terms and alternatives for solving it must be described. Quantitative terms deal with numeric attributes rather than general characteristics. This facilitates the process of analyzing problems and finding solutions. If-then logic is applied to select the best solution. All reasonable alternatives are considered. After implementation, results are evaluated and optimized.

Traditional approaches to problem solving were unstructured, dealing with problems in a sequential and linear fashion. Structured systems analysis relies upon diagrams rather than written narratives. The systems development life cycle moves through five phases: planning, analysis, design, development, and implementation.

Key Terms

Analysis phase	**Problem solving**
Cause and effect relationship	**Quantitative terms**
Design phase	**Scientific method**
Development phase	**Structured systems analysis**
If-then logic	**Systems development life cycle**
Implementation phase	**(SDLC)**
Optimization	**Work product**
Planning phase	

Exercises

1. Describe what is meant by a cause and effect relationship.
2. Describe the scientific method.
3. Summarize the major characteristics of the scientific method.
4. What is meant by problem recognition?
5. Contrast quantitative and qualitative terms.
6. Explain what is meant by if-then logic.
7. Why is it necessary to evaluate results?
8. Describe traditional systems analysis methodology.
9. Describe structured systems analysis.
10. List the major steps in the systems development life cycle.

1. Discuss cause and effect relationships with a business manager. List specific relationships related to his or her organization.

2. Visit a business establishment and discuss systems documentation. What kinds of forms are used in the in-place system?

3. Visit a business establishment and identify problems that might be solved through a systems analysis effort.

4. Discuss the SDLC with a systems analyst. Determine the work products that are generated as a result of a system study.

5. Visit your library and read about the scientific method and problem solving. Prepare a short essay on problem-solving techniques.

THE TOOLS OF THE ANALYST

LEARNING OBJECTIVES

After studying this chapter, you should be able to:

1. Discuss the value of system modeling techniques.

2. Describe the advantages of design diagrams.

3. Contrast traditional and structured systems analysis tools and give examples of each.

4. Read and understand various traditional design diagrams.

5. Read and understand various structured design diagrams.

6. Read and understand structured English and pseudocode.

Analysts use a variety of system design diagrams to plan, describe, troubleshoot, or document a system. These design tools include Gantt charts, decision trees, decision tables, flowcharts, data dictionaries, data flow diagrams, HIPO charts and Warnier-Orr diagrams, and others that follow the data flow through a system. As systems expand in size and complexity, analysts find a growing need for these tools.

This chapter covers the fundamentals of data flow diagrams, illustrates and describes the symbols used in their preparation, and presents several examples of various diagrams. It also discusses structured English and pseudocode, important tools used by the analyst. Flowcharts are touched upon and described more fully in the appendix.

SYSTEM MODELING

A **system model** is a representation of an in-place or proposed system that describes the data flow throughout the structure. The model describes the points where data or information enters a system and the places where it will be processed, as well as the actions taken and the points where data will be output.

By reducing a system to a model on paper or in a computer, the analyst can visualize, modify, or experiment with changes before they are actually put in place. If these changes were implemented in real life and they were unsuccessful or inefficient, the organization could waste thousands or perhaps millions of dollars.

FIGURE 4.1

System Model
System models are similar to building blueprints.

System models are like blueprints of a building (see Fig. 4.1). It is much easier for architects, engineers, and craftspeople to design and install partitions, plumbing, electrical systems, communications, and other equipment if they have a model on paper. In business, analysts use models to describe billing and accounting systems, inventory and payroll-processing systems, manufacturing systems, and the like.

A system model is documented through a variety of design diagrams. A **design diagram** is a graphic or visual representation of a structure. Design diagrams include data flow diagrams, structured charts, decision trees, and other items.

ADVANTAGES OF DESIGN DIAGRAMS

Analysts use system modeling tools and design diagrams for many reasons. The major advantages of design diagrams are that they:

1. Serve as a communications tool. The design diagram is a convenient method of communicating ideas and concepts among engineers, designers, management, programmers, and other interested personnel. It provides a concrete, visual medium for describing complex plans or problem solutions.

2. Serve as a planning tool. Data flow and other diagrams are flexible tools for planning and designing a new system. They enable designers to diagram concisely the essence of a system and its flowlines. They help analysts visualize the relationships and movements that will exist within a system while it is still in the planning stages. This makes it easy to experiment with different data flow paths and alternative methods.

3. Provide an overview of a system. Design diagrams make it possible to see the important elements and relationships in a system, free of extraneous details. They give a bird's-eye view of major steps and processes.

4. Define roles. The design diagram spells out in pictorial form the roles played by personnel, workstations, and processes in a system. It shows where data, forms, and reports are generated and the end results produced.

5. Demonstrate relationships. Design diagrams point out relationships that may not be readily obvious from verbal or written descriptions. They show how data elements relate to each other, as well as the relationship between parts of a system.

6. Promote logical procedures. Design diagrams require analysts to clarify and refine their thinking and to describe explicitly all paths, branches, and flows in a system. Errors in logic are more easily seen in visual representations than in verbal descriptions. The analyst can identify incorrect branches and missing elements and may discover a more efficient way to implement a part of the system.

DESIGN TOOL	STRUCTURED TOOL	SHOWS DATA FLOW	SHOWS DECISIONS	SHOWS SEQUENCES	VISUAL CHART	TEXTUAL CHART	SHOWS DETAIL
Gantt chart				X	X		
Decision table			X				X
Flowcharts		X	X	X	X		X
Data dictionary	X					X	
Data flow diagram	X	X	X		X		X
HIPO chart	X			X	X		X
Structured English	X			X		X	
Warnier-Orr diagram	X				X		
Nassi-Shneiderman chart	X		X		X		
Presentation graph		X			X		

FIGURE 4.2

Structured and Traditional Design Tools Design tool comparison chart.

7. Facilitate troubleshooting. System problems, breakdowns in communications, or unforeseen developments are usually more readily diagnosed if a design diagram is available. It serves as a blueprint of the inner workings of a system, to which the troubleshooter can refer when diagnosing a system failure.

8. Document a system. Design diagrams record graphically, clearly, and permanently the important elements of a system. This facilitates making changes, revisions, and modifications at a later date. It enables those unfamiliar with a system to grasp its elements easily and quickly.

TRADITIONAL DESIGN TOOLS

For many decades, systems designers have relied upon various traditional tools to illustrate the flow of information throughout a system. These include Gantt charts, system flowcharts, and decision tables. You should be aware of these tools because they are often used by analysts.

It may appear strange that tools only 20 or 30 years old are considered "traditional." But since the world of computers and information systems is so dynamic, even one year can see a generation's worth of change. Figure 4.2 lists both structured and traditional design tools and contrasts some of their features.

THE GANTT CHART

In the early years of the century systems analysts were often called efficiency experts. They sought to document and diagram systems so they could improve operations. In 1914 one of these efficiency experts, Henry L. Gantt,

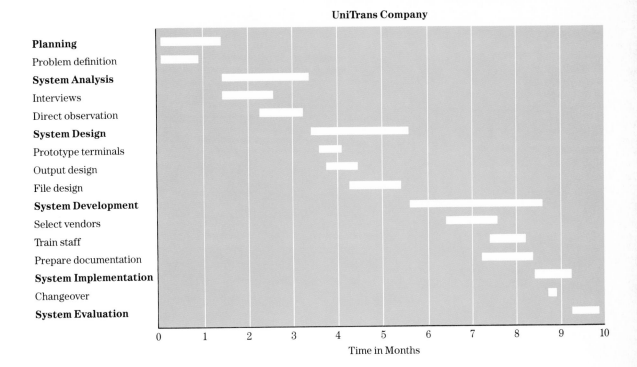

UniTrans Company

Planning
Problem definition
System Analysis
Interviews
Direct observation
System Design
Prototype terminals
Output design
File design
System Development
Select vendors
Train staff
Prepare documentation
System Implementation
Changeover
System Evaluation

Time in Months

introduced a scheduling chart that later became known as a **Gantt chart.** The Gantt chart, shown in Fig. 4.3, is a fundamental planning tool of the analyst. Down the left-hand column are listed the tasks or activities to be performed. The right-hand portion of the chart has horizontal bars that show the duration of each activity. If a complex task is broken down into several subtasks, these are also shown.

The chart marks off time periods in days, weeks, or months. Thus, we can see at a glance what activities are to be performed, when each begins, and when each terminates. But, much like a calendar, the Gantt chart is based upon time intervals and does not show the logical flow of information throughout a system. However, it remains a useful tool for documenting systems work. We will come back to Gantt charts in a later chapter on project management.

FIGURE 4.3

Gantt Chart The chart shows when activities begin and end.

DECISION TREES

Systems analysts are often faced with documenting complex systems that involve making many decisions. The **decision tree** is a tool that is particularly well suited for illustrating such systems. Figure 4.4 depicts a decision tree. It is read from left to right, showing decisions to be made. Tasks such as granting credit, approving a purchase, or handling a customer complaint, which involve making decisions, can be illustrated on this type of chart.

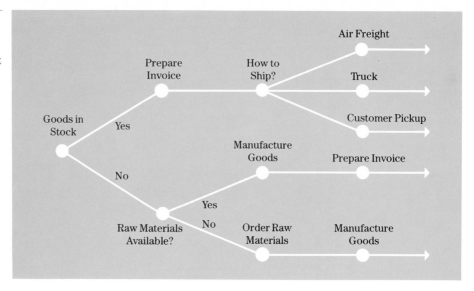

Decision trees sometimes include numbers that express the probability
of an event at each decision. One course of action may have a 30 percent probability of occurring and another 70 percent. By placing values at each juncture,
an analyst can better assess the overall probability of certain events taking place.

DECISION TABLES

Systems analysts often use a design diagram known as a **decision table.**
Decision tables are charts in the form of matrices that graphically display conditions, options, and alternatives to be dealt with when making business decisions.
A decision table is composed of several parts (see Fig. 4.5). The **condition stub** lists all possible conditions that could arise in making a decision. The
action stub lists all possible actions that may be taken. The **condition entry**

Condition Stub	Condition Entry
Action Stub	Action Entry

lists all possible combinations of conditions that may occur, and the **action entry** describes what actions will be followed for each set of conditions. The entry sections are lined off in vertical columns called **rules.** Each rule specifies what actions are to be taken for each set of conditions.

Figure 4.6 illustrates a decision table used in an order-processing system. It defines the various ways to handle orders for items that are low in stock. The analyst begins by completing the upper left quadrant, the condition stub, listing a variety of conditions such as supply out of stock, supply adequate, and item discontinued. Next, the analyst completes the lower left quadrant, the action stub, listing the possible actions that may be taken. For instance, a stock pick order, a purchase requisition, or an invoice may be prepared.

Then the analyst prepares a group of rules. In our example there are 17 rules, indicating that 17 combinations of conditions can occur. The rules are constructed with Yes and No marked in the upper right quadrant of the decision table. Y means that the condition is present, N that the condition is absent, and a blank that the condition is not applicable. Each rule has a unique set of Ys and Ns.

The lower right section, the action entry, is completed last. Action entries define which actions will be taken in light of each rule. The analyst enters an X, meaning that those actions are to be taken in every instance where a given set of conditions occur. To illustrate, in rule 1, a pick order is to be written and an invoice prepared whenever there is an adequate supply of goods and the item is not discontinued.

Decision tables enable the analyst to lay out a complex variety of conditions and to specify how each set of conditions should be handled. The rules developed in a decision table can be used as the basis of a procedures manual for employees, to teach them how to handle various situations and to ensure consistent treatment. Decision tables are also used when designing computer programs. They describe all the possible options in a problem and the specific actions that the computer must execute for each set of conditions.

Decision tables have several advantages. They lessen the possibility of omitting essential elements and ensure that a given set of conditions will be handled consistently. They are easier to understand than lengthy verbal descriptions of choices. As do other tools, they require the analyst to refine his or her thinking and to clarify details. The decision table cannot be completed until the analyst has explicitly defined all the conditions and actions involved.

FLOWCHARTS

As punched cards and unit record equipment came into use in the 1940s, systems designers found it necessary to describe and define systems in new ways. This led to the development of the flowchart as a major means of documenting information flow (see Fig. 4.7). The flowchart was widely used as a design tool until the 1970s, when it lost popularity to some of the newer struc-

RULES

	1	2	3	4	5	6	7	8	9	10	11	12	13	14	15	16	17
Supply—adequate	Y	N	N	N	N	N	N	N	N	N	N	N	N	N	N	N	N
Supply—below minimum	N	Y	Y	Y	Y	Y	Y	Y	Y	Y	Y	Y	Y	Y	Y	Y	Y
Supply—out of stock	N	N	N	N	N	N	N	N	N	N	N	N	N	Y	Y	Y	N
Item discontinued	N	N	N	N	N	N	N	N	N	N	N	N	N	N	N	Y	
Purchase requisition made		Y	N	Y	N	Y	N	Y	N	Y	N	Y	N	Y	N		
Old account		Y	Y	Y	Y	Y	Y	N	N	N	N	N	N				
Large order		Y	Y	Y	Y	N	N	Y	Y	N	N	Y	N				
Sale item		N	N	Y	Y	Y	Y	N			Y	Y					
Write pick order	X			X	X	X	X					X	X				X
Make purchase requisition			X		X	X	X		X		X		X		X		
Cancel order															X	X	
Write order confirmation	X	X	X					X	X	X	X			X	X		
Prepare invoice	X		X	X	X	X	X					X	X				X

FIGURE 4.6

Decision Table Example A decision table that might be used in an order-processing system.

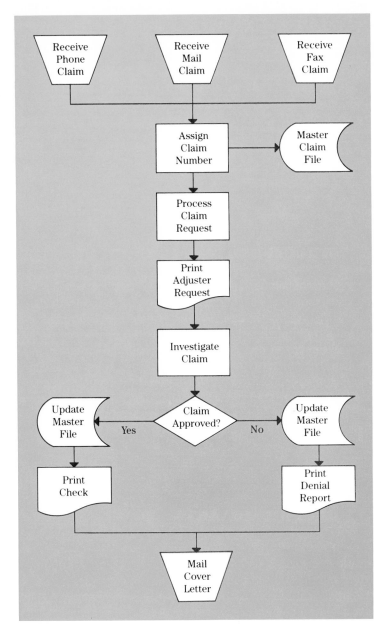

FIGURE 4.7

Flowchart A graphic representation of the information flow in a system.

tured tools discussed later in this chapter. The system flowchart emphasizes processing steps, workstations, and the physical manipulation of data, rather than its logical flow. Nevertheless, it is still used by many analysts.

A **flowchart** is a graphic representation of the steps in the solution of a problem, in which symbols represent operations, data flow, hardware, and the system plan. Flowcharts can document either business systems or computer programs. **System flowchart** diagrams illustrate the movement of data in an organization. They show the sequence of steps through which information moves, including related personnel, workstations, forms, records, processing, and associated activities.

The systems analyst uses program flowcharts when working with computer programs. **Program flowcharts** show the sequence of steps performed in a computer program. System flowcharts document the overall system, while program flowcharts deal with the information flow through the computer. A standard set of symbols for drawing these flowcharts has been approved by the American National Standards Institute (ANSI). Flowcharts are discussed in greater detail in the appendix.

STRUCTURED DESIGN TOOLS

Much experimentation and research has gone into developing new graphic and visual tools for designing and documenting systems. During the past decade these structured tools have become widely used by analysts and are rapidly replacing traditional design tools, such as flowcharts and decision tables.

Structured design tools emphasize the visual or graphic nature of a problem. They break systems down into elements known as modules. A **module** is one component of a system. Structured tools emphasize the logical flow of information rather than physical manipulation. Unstructured or traditional design tools describe systems in terms of written narratives or sequential diagrams that emphasize sequence and physical handling rather than the logical flow throughout a system.

DATA DICTIONARY

In the early 1970s systems analysts realized that they needed more systematic and logical methods of describing systems. The proliferation of computers and the collection of large amounts of information in databases often led to a great deal of confusion and inconsistency. For example, the same type of data might be collected by several different departments in a company. When these databases were merged, inconsistencies in style and content of data fields became obvious. One department might put last names first on employee or customer records, while another department entered first names first. This made sorting and merging files very difficult. The problem was further complicated by the number of reports generated by a system and the number of online terminals that retrieved or displayed information. Clearly, what was needed was a more logical way of structuring data. This led to the development of the data dictionary. A **data dictionary** (see Fig. 4.8) is a composite collection of speci-

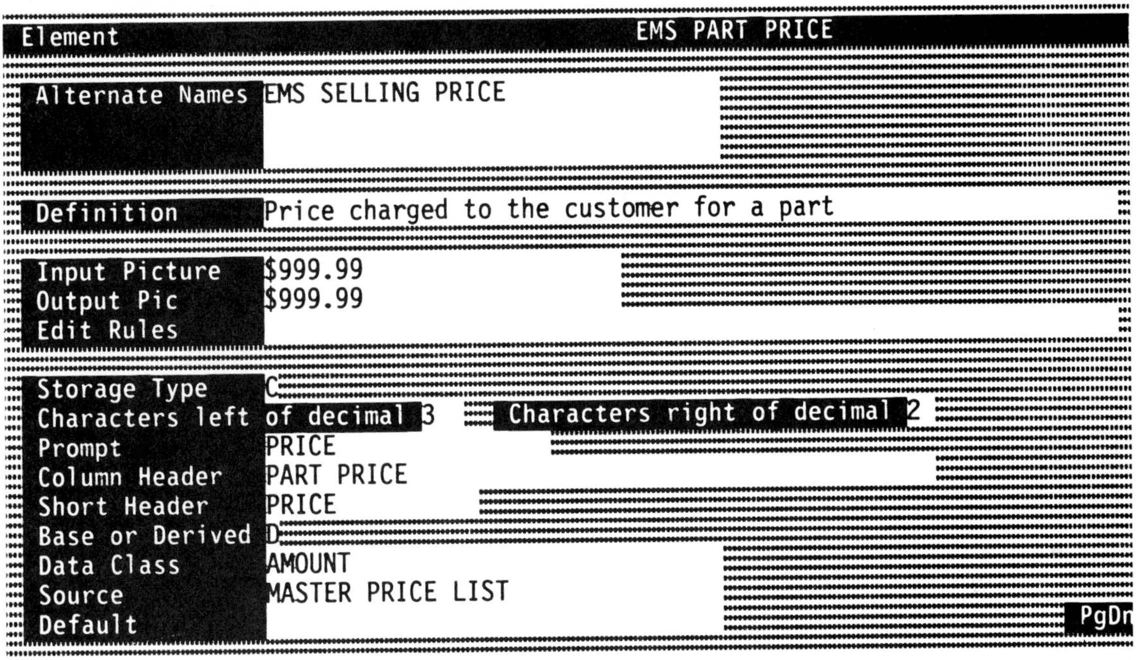

(Source: Index Technology Corp.)

fications about the nature of data and information. It is a repository of descriptions of the form, style, and content of data, as well as of the methods that will be used to process and report it.

The data dictionary is the foundation of structured systems analysis. It provides the standards and uniform format by which all elements or parts of a system are designed and coordinated (see Fig. 4.9). A data dictionary places all information in a structure or hierarchy (see Fig. 4.10). At the top of the hierarchy is the data element. The **data element** is the smallest unit of data that will be processed or become part of a record.

Examples of data elements include dates, employee names, and gross pay. Rules for editing information or length of a field, for example, are characteristics maintained on the data elements within a data dictionary. These data elements are used as a universal guide throughout the system when information is referenced or processed. The data dictionary is much like a printed dictionary, which provides standards for spelling, hyphenation, and so forth.

Below data elements on the hierarchy are data records. A **data record** is a collection of elements, such as names, addresses, or sequences of records, treated as a unit. This means that records will be treated consistently throughout the system.

Next on the hierarchy are the data stores, data model entities, and data flows. **Data stores** describe the files that hold data, **data model entities** define what records and elements will be treated as a unit, and **data flows** specify pathways for moving information.

FIGURE 4.8

Data Dictionary Entry This figure illustrates an order entry system data dictionary entry.

FIGURE 4.9

Data Dictionary Overview The dictionary is the central repository for all system data.

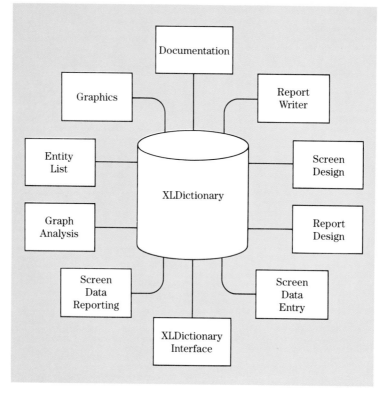

(Source: Index Technology Corp.)

FIGURE 4.10

Data Hierarchy A data dictionary places all information in a hierarchical structure.

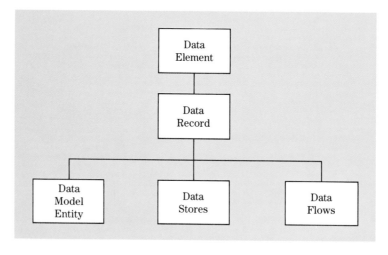

The dictionary may also include standard tables of codes or words and their meanings, as well as alternate names or definitions. For example, EMPLOYEE NUMBER and SERIAL NUMBER might be equated, and both might reference an employee's identification number.

The existence of a data dictionary unifies a system and develops consistency. The dictionary can contain uniform screen displays or standard output reports. It provides a common denominator wherein all reports, data gathering, processing, output functions, input screens, and storage files can be integrated.

DATA FLOW DIAGRAMS

The data flow diagram is used as a system modeling tool because of its great utility. A **data flow diagram** is a graphic illustration that shows the flow of data and logic within a system. Figure 4.11 is a data flow diagram containing a group of symbols that are linked together with lines. The shape of the symbol indicates to the analyst that a specific operation is performed. The arrows that connect the symbols show the direction in which data flows. Descriptive labels are usually placed within each symbol or next to the connecting lines to further describe the flow and transformation of data.

The detail and complexity of a data flow diagram varies with the system being described. As you work with systems, you will find yourself continually relying upon diagrams such as these to show points where data originates, is processed or transformed, and is output.

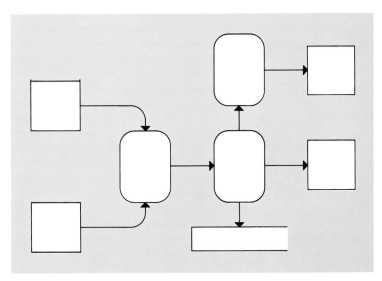

FIGURE 4.11

Data Flow Diagram Symbols are connected to show the flow of data through a system.

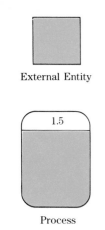

External Entity

Process

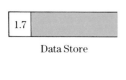

Data Store

Flowline

FIGURE 4.12

Data Flow Diagram Symbols Four symbols are used in Gane and Sarson notation.

Data flow diagrams are composed of four basic symbols (see Fig. 4.12). There are no ANSI standards for data flow diagram symbols. One widely used convention adheres to symbols developed by Edward Yourdon; a similar notation has been developed by Chris Gane and Trish Sarson. Yourdon uses a circle for a process, while Gane and Sarson use a rectangle with rounded corners. Yourdon's data store symbol is a rectangle open at each end. Gane and Sarson show a data store as a rectangle closed at one end. We shall use the Gane and Sarson notation in our examples.

External Entity

An **external entity** is a square box that specifies either the source or the destination of data. It shows where data originates outside a system or where it will be transmitted after processing, always outside the system. External entities are sometimes called sources and sinks. A **source** is a point outside the system that generates data. A **sink** is a point outside the system that receives data. Both are external entities, drawn as square boxes.

Think for a moment about the data in a small retail establishment. Checks are received from customers and orders come in the mail. These are sources. Bills are sent to customers, goods are shipped with invoices, and reports are sent to government agencies. These are sinks. These sources and sinks are common examples of external entities, because they represent movement of data and information into and out of a system.

Process

The **process symbol** is drawn as a rectangle with rounded corners. It represents the transformation or processing of information within a system. The process symbol shows those places in a system where calculations are made or where information is changed in character. Examples of processing in our small retail example include computing payroll, calculating profit, and computing sums, such as in the preparation of a customer invoice or bank deposit. The top of the process box is usually ruled off, leaving space to enter a reference number. The reference number is used to key more detailed data flow diagrams to the box.

Data Store

A **data store** is a point in a system where information is permanently or temporarily stored or held. It is shown as a rectangle with one end open. The left side of the box may be ruled off to enter a reference number, which keys the box to other diagrams. Data may be stored on filing cards, ledger sheets, floppy disks, or even on the check stubs in a checkbook. While stored, the information remains intact and is not changed or modified in any way.

Information Flow

Information **flowlines,** sometimes called **pipes** or vectors, connect external entities, process, and data store elements. These lines, always drawn with an arrowhead, trace the flow of information throughout the system. Information flow may be one-way or two-way. One or two arrows are drawn between boxes to show which way the information flows.

HOW TO DRAW DATA FLOW DIAGRAMS

Data flow diagrams are composed of the common symbols just described. With these symbols the analyst shows where data originates, how it is transformed, and where it is output. While there are no universal standards for drawing data flow diagrams, some guidelines should be followed when preparing them.

1. Do not mix levels of detail on one chart. Instead, draw several data flow diagrams, each with a different level of detail.

2. Select either the Gane and Sarson or Yourdon notations and use them consistently.

3. Use a template to draw uniformly sized and shaped symbols for permanent system documentation. Symbols may be drawn freehand for rough or temporary diagrams.

4. Connect symbols with flowlines. Draw connections using pipes or lines with arrowheads to show the flow of data between symbols. Place an arrowhead at each end of the pipe to show a two-way flow of data. Place an arrowhead at one end of the pipe to show a one-way flow of data.

5. Name and label all symbols and connectors. Select names that are descriptive and reflect what is being done. Place text within each symbol describing the function or transformation taking place. Place textual labels next to flowlines or pipes to describe the movement or transformation of data taking place.

6. Correlate symbols to other data flow diagrams, using reference numbers to show relationships.

7. Desk check all data flow diagrams to make sure each symbol is logically connected to another and that all symbols properly describe the flow within the system.

8. Label the top of each data flow diagram with the system name, date prepared, name of preparer, and other pertinent information. This will be helpful when you or others refer to the diagrams later.

FIGURE 4.13

Context Diagram This diagram shows an order system in its most generalized form.

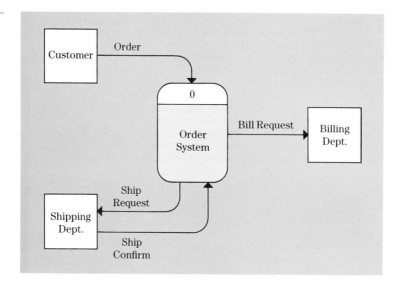

Context Diagrams

It is often helpful to illustrate systems using a broad-brush, undifferentiated data flow figure known as a **context diagram** (see Fig. 4.13). The context diagram shows the entire system as one general element. It is the most overall view we can obtain of a system. All sources and sinks of data are linked to this one entity, using flowlines or pipes.

Figure 4.13 shows a system used to process orders in a manufacturing company. One process symbol, labeled "order system," includes all steps in the process. External entities such as customers, billing department, and shipping department are connected to the system. Note that the process symbol is drawn using an approved shape, a rectangle with rounded corners, and the external entities are drawn using square-shaped symbols. Flowlines or pipes connect each element in the diagram and each is labeled accordingly. Context diagrams are valuable because they show only major items with a minimum of detail that might confuse or cloud the bird's-eye view of the system.

Decomposing Data Flow Diagrams

Since context diagrams do not show detail, it is necessary to draw additional diagrams to refine or expand individual elements. This process is known as **exploding** or **decomposing** elements. Explosion is a method by which a group of related charts explain an operation in increasingly more detailed levels. Figure 4.14 illustrates the process of exploding a diagram. The first level of explosion is an entity taken from the context diagram. Each level 1 symbol is exploded into a level 2 diagram. In turn, each level 2 diagram is further exploded into level 3 diagrams.

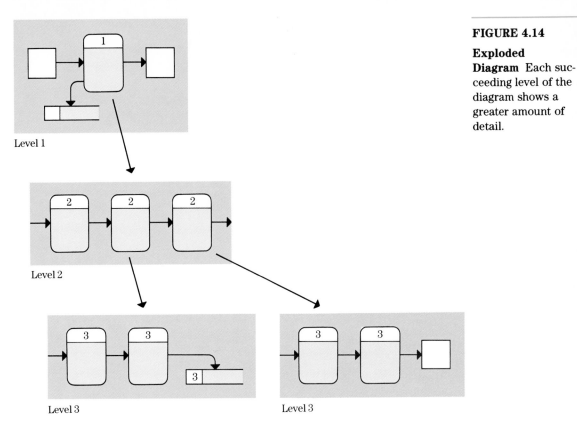

Level 1

Level 2

Level 3

Level 3

FIGURE 4.14

Exploded Diagram Each succeeding level of the diagram shows a greater amount of detail.

Thus we are able to view a system starting at its most generalized level and refining each element step by step. Explosion of a context diagram can be likened to breaking down a road map of the United States into a group of state maps, with each state map further broken down into a group of city maps. The city maps can be reduced to neighborhood maps showing individual streets. This concept is basic to the preparation of data flow diagrams. Explosion allows the designer to build structure into the system, since each symbol can be a self-contained module that in itself can be exploded to detail other modules.

Data Flow Diagram Example

Let's put the concepts and symbols we have discussed to use and see how a set of data flow diagrams are prepared. Suppose we are designing a payroll system that will generate paychecks and tax reports. We begin by drawing a context diagram of the system, illustrated in Fig. 4.15. The entire system is shown in one symbol labeled "Payroll System." Connected to this process are the external entities "Employees" and "Government."

FIGURE 4.15

Payroll System Context Diagram "Employees" and "Government" are external entities.

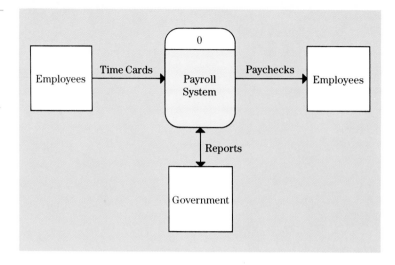

Let us now refine the level of detail. Figure 4.16 illustrates a level 1 diagram of the system. The employees' time cards are drawn as a source (external entity). Hours worked are verified against information in the time card file. Computations of employees' salaries require accessing a tax table file. Tax reports will be prepared from the information provided by these computations. The permanent record of the transaction is saved on the check stub, shown as a data store. Preparing the paychecks is a process step. Since the check leaves the

FIGURE 4.16

Payroll System A level 1 diagram.

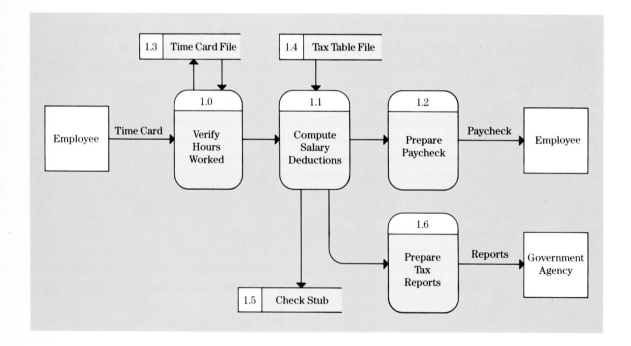

system and is delivered to the employee, it is shown as a sink (external entity). Flowlines are drawn to connect the elements and show the flow of data.

Each process symbol can be broken down into lower levels of detail. For example, the computation step might involve computing deductions, state and federal income tax withholding, and payments to credit unions. This would result in one or more second-level diagrams, which could be further exploded to a third level of detail. In the next example, we will see how this is done.

ORDER SYSTEM DATA FLOW DIAGRAM

Figure 4.13 illustrated an order-processing system context diagram. Figure 4.17 shows a level 1 explosion of the process order system. External entities show points where data originates outside the system and where it is sent. Customers are shown as external entities. The actual processing of the order takes place in a level 1 symbol labeled "Process Order."

When the customer's order is received, the stock is verified. This is done by checking against the stock file of goods in inventory. The order then moves to the process order step. A pick order, shipping order, billing, and other processes are then initiated. The entire process order phase has been shown in one transformation labeled "Process Order."

In Fig. 4.18 we see how this single symbol, "Process Order," is exploded

FIGURE 4.17

Order System This diagram shows level 1 detail.

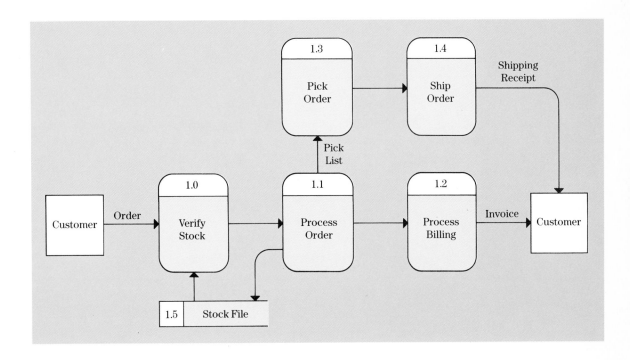

FIGURE 4.18

Order System A
level 2 diagram.

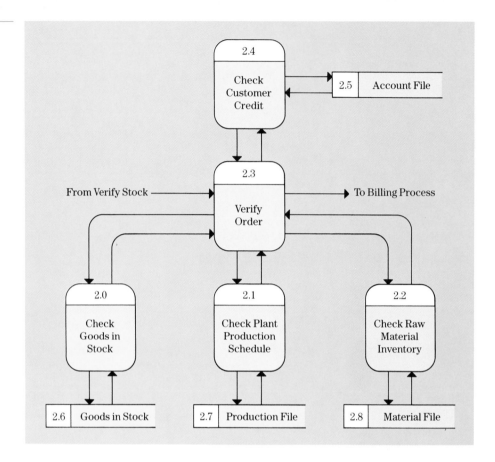

to show the next level of detail. The level 2 diagram includes data stores, additional process steps, and other points where data is transformed. After an order is received it is verified and the customer's credit standing checked. This step involves accessing an account file. In addition, the order is checked against goods in stock. If not enough goods are available to fill the order, a plant production schedule and raw material file are consulted. Then goods are manufactured to fill the order. After the various steps are completed, the order moves on to the billing process.

In Fig. 4.19 we see a third-level diagram. This figure is an explosion of a single process, the credit check, from the level 2 chart. Steps include checking for previous payments, cash sent with order, and so on. This figure shows more detail than the level 2 diagram.

In all three levels of detail a common set of symbols is used. The symbols are connected with flowlines or pipes that show the direction of flow and all symbols and pipes are labeled. Thus the analyst can look at successively more detailed views of a complex system. As many levels of detail may be drawn as are required to adequately document and describe the system under study.

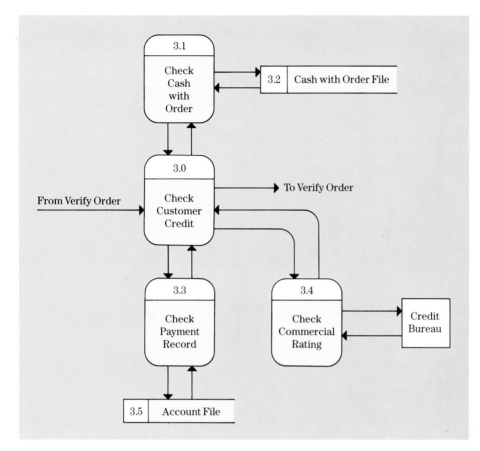

FIGURE 4.19

Order System A level 3 diagram.

HIERARCHY PLUS INPUT-PROCESS-OUTPUT (HIPO)

Hierarchy plus input-process-output (HIPO) diagrams were developed by IBM Corp. in an attempt to provide programmers with better structured tools for dealing with systems. HIPO (pronounced hi-poe) diagrams consist of three distinct types:

- Visual table of contents (VTOC)
- IPO overview diagram
- IPO detail diagram

These diagrams enable analysts to define procedures and operations in a hierarchical manner, correlating input, processing, and output steps with the integrated whole expressed in the visual table of contents.

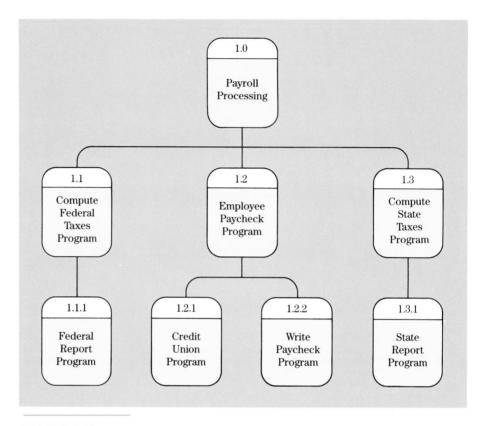

FIGURE 4.20

Visual Table of Contents (VTOC) The level of detail increases from the top to the bottom of the figure.

Figure 4.20 illustrates a **visual table of contents** (VTOC). The chart shows a hierarchy in which the level of detail increases from the top of the chart to the bottom, moving from the general to the specific. This is called top-down development. In our figure, the levels are coded with reference numbers. At the top of the chart is the general level 1.0 module. Think of this as the parent. Below the parent are the children, noted as levels 1.1, 1.2, etc., which further explode the detail of the preceding level. Still lower levels of detail are marked 1.1.1, 1.1,2, etc.

The chart provides a hierarchical view of the problem, which is then supported by two additional charts known as **input-process-output** (IPO) (pronounced eye-poe) charts. The IPO chart may be either general or specific in nature. A general sequence of steps is known as an IPO overview diagram, while a detailed chart is called an IPO detailed diagram. These charts are especially useful for programmers who must code a program (see Fig. 4.21).

The IPO chart is read from left to right. It describes the input, processing activities, and output for any given module on the VTOC.

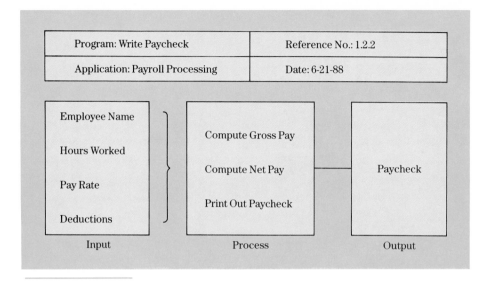

FIGURE 4.21

Input-Process-Output (IPO) Chart This chart describes the processing activities for any given module on the VTOC.

STRUCTURED ENGLISH

Up to this point we have been dealing with diagrams that are visual or pictorial in nature. To actually write a program for the steps illustrated in an IPO chart or a data flow diagram, we must prepare a detailed sequence of instructions in a programming language. Figure 4.22 illustrates a block of programming code. There is obviously a major jump between a VTOC or data flow diagram and the detailed commands required in a program.

Many systems analysts and programmers rely upon a form of **structured English,** also known as **pseudocode** (see Fig. 4.23). Pseudocode expresses language commands in an English-like form that greatly facilitates programming. The structured English in Fig. 4.23 has levels of indentation similar to the levels of detail found on the VTOC. Pseudocode includes key words in capital letters that reflect the major programming commands to be used when actually coding the program.

Structured English is written in a terse sentence form resembling an outline. Steps in the program are listed in sequence. Items are indented to show subordination. Once completed, a set of pseudocode instructions provides an easy bridge to programming. It becomes a communications tool used by both the programmer and the systems analyst.

FIGURE 4.22

COBOL Language Code This code is typical of high-level languages.

```
IDENTIFICATION DIVISION.
PROGRAM ID. LISTING1.
ENVIRONMENT DIVISION.
CONFIGURATION SECTION.
SOURCE COMPUTER. CYBER-170-720.
OBJECT COMPUTER. CYBER-170-720.
SPECIAL-NAMES.
INPUT-OUTPUT SECTION.
FILE CONTROL.
     SELECT IN-FILE ASSIGN TO INPUT.
     SELECT OUT-FILE ASSIGN TO OUTPUT.
DATA DIVISION.
FILE SECTION.
*    DEFINE INPUT OF THE PROGRAM.
FD   IN-FILE
     LABEL RECORDS ARE OMITTED.
01   RECORD-IN              PIC X(80).
*    DEFINE OUTPUT OF THE PROGRAM.
FD   OUT-FILE
     LABEL RECORDS ARE OMITTED.
01   RECORD-OUT.
     02 FILLER             PIC X(01).
     02 DATA-OUT           PIC X(80).
PROCEDURE DIVISION.
LETS-GO.
     OPEN INPUT IN-FILE.
     OPEN OUTPUT OUT-FILE.
     MOVE SPACES TO RECORD-OUT.
     WRITE RECORD-OUT AFTER PAGE.
READ-AND-WRITE.
     READ IN-FILE AT END GO TO CLOSE-UP.
     MOVE RECORD-IN TO DATA-OUT.
     WRITE RECORD-OUT AFTER 1.
     GO TO READ-AND-WRITE.
CLOSE UP.
     CLOSE IN-FILE, OUT-FILE.
     STOP RUN.
```

(Source: Silver and Silver, Computers and Information Systems, *Harper and Row, 1986)*

WARNIER-ORR DIAGRAMS

Programmers and systems analysts sometimes use another form of design diagram known as a **Warnier-Orr diagram** (see Fig. 4.24). Named for its creator, Jean-Dominique Warnier, and Ken Orr, who further developed it, the diagram

```
Prepare invoice record
READ name, account number, cost, balance
    IF balance = 0
        THEN
                skip to next invoice
        ELSE
                compute selling price
                price = cost × .25
        ENDIF
    IF balance = 10.00
        THEN
                print out invoice
        ELSE
                go to next record
        ENDIF
Increment invoice counter
End
```

FIGURE 4.23

Pseudocode
Pseudocode expresses language commands in a structured English-like form.

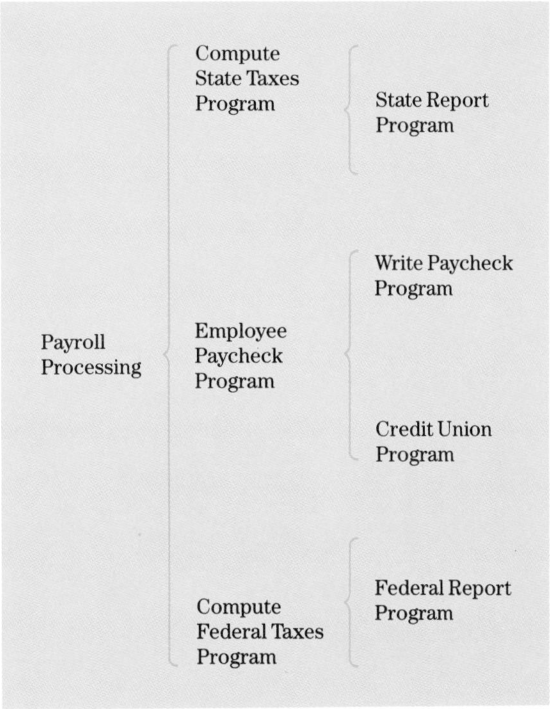

FIGURE 4.24

Warnier-Orr Diagram Brackets define where each subroutine relates to the next higher level.

FIGURE 4.25

**Nassi-Shneiderman
Chart** This type of
chart clearly illus-
trates program logic.

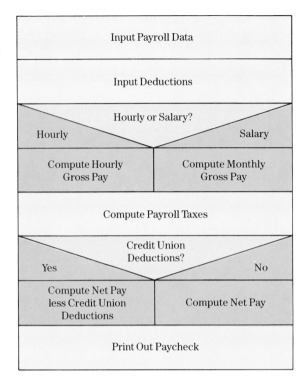

resembles a visual table of contents placed on its side. The major or general
modules are listed at the left of the page, while the right shows the detailed
modules. Brackets define where each subroutine or module relates to the next
higher level.

Many analysts prefer the Warnier-Orr diagram over the VTOC because the
Warnier-Orr chart can be drawn without templates or artists' instruments and
shows at a glance each level in the hierarchy.

NASSI-SHNEIDERMAN CHARTS

In the early 1970s, Isaac Nassi and Ben Shneiderman developed a form
of programming chart that closely resembles the control structures used by
programmers. The **Nassi-Shneiderman chart** shown in Fig. 4.25 describes the
data flow through a computer program. These charts, sometimes known as structured flowcharts, are used by analysts and programmers because they clearly
show the logic in a program.

PRESENTATION GRAPHS

The design diagrams we have described are technical in nature and are used to communicate ideas and concepts between skilled programmers and systems analysts. However, systems analysts must often discuss system concepts with end users and managers. Data flow diagrams, decision tables, and HIPO charts are sometimes too complicated for the untrained person to understand. As a result, analysts use presentation graphs when communicating with non-technical people.

Presentation graphs are visual charts that show the flow of information through a system in a pictorial manner. These charts rely upon pictograms or icons that show people, printouts, terminals, paper files, and so on (see Fig. 4.26). Presentation graphs are used in sales brochures and in manuals that explain to nontechnical operators how to use a system. Once the analyst has discussed end-user needs and communicated concepts with presentation graphs, he or she can then use the more technical design diagrams discussed in this chapter to engineer the system.

This chapter has discussed a variety of design tools. As an analyst, you will be expected to understand and use many of these tools. Learn to rely upon visuals, charts, and graphs to help refine your thinking and to communicate with others. Don't be concerned if you lack artistic or drawing skills, because today's generation of systems analysts can use computers to generate graphics.

With a basic understanding of the tools used in systems analysis, we can now go on to study the steps involved in designing and implementing a system. In the next chapter we come back to UniTrans Company and begin to analyze and solve the company's system problems, following the five major steps in the systems development life cycle (SDLC).

Summary

Analysts reduce systems to models on paper or in the computer to help visualize a new or modified system before it is put in place. System models are like blueprints in that they document a system with design diagrams. Design diagrams serve as communications and planning tools, demonstrate logical relationships, facilitate troubleshooting, and document a system.

The traditional design tools include the Gantt chart, decision trees, decision tables, and flowcharts. System flowcharts diagram the flow of information throughout a system, while program flowcharts trace the flow throughout a computer program. These tools were devised before structured programming concepts came into use.

Structured design tools are more recent developments. They are based upon top-down program logic and modular structures. The data dictionary is a collection of specifications about the nature of data and information. It provides standards and uniform formats for elements in a system. A data dictionary may

(Source: Index Technology Corp.)

FIGURE 4.26

Presentation Graph This type of chart is best suited for communicating with nontechnical people.

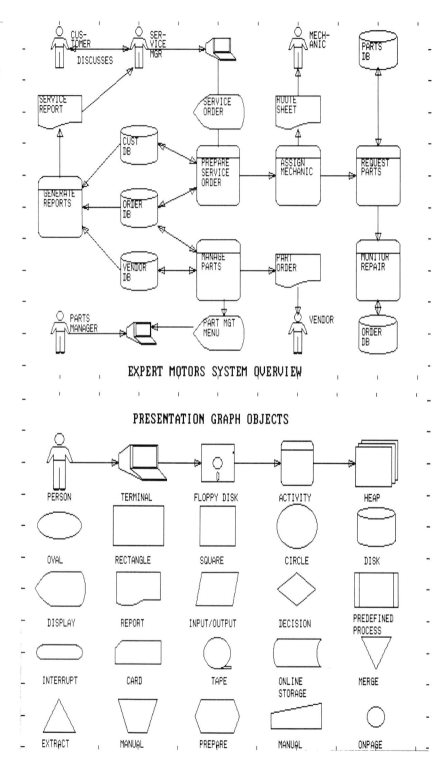

EXPERT MOTORS SYSTEM OVERVIEW

PRESENTATION GRAPH OBJECTS

include data elements, data records, data stores, data model entities, and data flows.

Other structured tools include data flow diagrams, hierarchy plus input-process-output (HIPO) charts, Warnier-Orr diagrams, and Nassi-Shneiderman charts. Structured English, also known as pseudocode, describes logic flow. Presentation graphs show the flow of information in a pictorial manner.

Key Terms

Action entry
Action stub
Condition entry
Condition stub
Context diagram
Data dictionary
Data element
Data flow
Data flow diagram
Data model entity
Data record
Data store
Decision table
Decision tree
Decompose
Design diagram
Explode
External entity
Flowchart
Flowlines

Gantt chart
Hierarchy plus input-process-output (HIPO)
Input-process-output (IPO)
Module
Nassi-Shneiderman chart
Pipes
Presentation graph
Process symbol
Program flowchart
Pseudocode
Rules (decision table)
Sink
Source
Structured design tools
Structured English
System flowchart
System model
Visual table of contents (VTOC)
Warnier-Orr diagram

Exercises

1. List the advantages of design diagrams.
2. List traditional design tools.
3. List structured design tools.
4. Describe a Gantt chart and how it is used.
5. What are the four major parts of a decision table?
6. Define the term *data dictionary*.
7. What is an external entity?
8. What is the function of a data store in a system design?
9. Explain how structured English is used.
10. Describe the function of presentation graphs.

Projects

1. Select a business firm in your area that uses a billing system and prepares invoices. Construct one or more data flow diagrams to illustrate the information flow within the system. Identify sources, sinks, and data files.

2. Visit a systems analyst and discuss the kinds of design diagrams used in his or her work. What types of diagrams are preferred and why?

3. Choose a business firm in your area that operates a payroll-processing system. Prepare a context data flow diagram of the system and several other data flow diagrams showing greater levels of detail.

4. Prepare a context data flow diagram illustrating an inventory system used by a firm in your area. Prepare several other data flow diagrams, each with a greater level of detail.

5. Suppose that you are designing a system involving the shipment of goods using different package delivery services. Each service has its own package weight and size limits. Prepare a decision table that lays out various conditions and actions.

ANALYST AT WORK

AMATEUR ARTIST'S MAGAZINE

DESCRIPTION OF FIRM

Amateur Artist's Magazine (AAM) is an established monthly publication catering to arts and crafts enthusiasts. *AAM* is mailed to subscribers and also sold at magazine stands and bookstores. A limited number of copies are mailed free of charge to an influential group of artists, designers, and crafts supplies retailers. Here is a breakdown of *AAM*'s circulation list:

39,000 copies mailed directly to subscribers

5,000 copies sold through newsstands and bookstores

2,000 copies distributed free
_____

46,000 total copies

Mailing labels are prepared in the subscription office, using a computer and a laser printer. The labels are then given to a mailing service which affixes them to the publications and sends them out.

SYSTEM OVERVIEW

All subscription processing is handled by the subscription department. The department maintains an updated mailing list and prepares the billing sent to subscribers. The data flow diagram in Fig. 4.27 shows the major elements in the subscription-processing system.

The subscription department receives numerous renewals and new subscriptions each week. Some subscribers send in renewal forms and ask to be billed later. Others send in money orders or checks with their renewal applications, so invoices are not necessary. Occasionally, subscribers mail in requests to cancel their subscriptions. Among other requests received are address changes and queries from subscribers who have not received their magazines.

Sometimes renewal requests are received that include checks but make no reference to a specific subscriber's name and address. Occasionally, a subscription renewal request does not specify the length of additional time desired. Such cases require follow-up correspondence.

(continues)

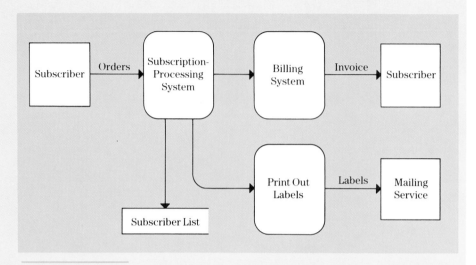

FIGURE 4.27

Amateur Artist's Magazine Data flow diagram.

HANDS-ON APPLICATION

Study the data flow diagram in Fig. 4.27 and prepare a diagram at the next level of detail. In addition, prepare a decision table that lays out the alternative conditions and actions to be taken, depending upon the information provided with the renewal application. Complete the three work products described below.

Work Product No. 1   Analyze *AAM*'s subscription system and prepare a decision table. Label this WP1, Chapter 4. Prepare a task list indicating the steps to be followed in preparing the decision table.

   TASK LIST

_____

_____

_____

_____

_____

_____

The following subscription request conditions may exist:

- Statement sent without payment
- Check received without renewal application
- Length of renewal time not indicated
- Address change requested but old mailing label not included

A few of the possible actions that may be taken are:

- Mail customer a subscription application
- Send request to subscriber for additional information
- Bill customer for subscription charges

Study the conditions described above and prepare a list of the possible conditions that may be encountered in the subscription-processing system. Enter the information below.

POSSIBLE CONDITIONS

_____

_____

_____

_____

_____

Analyze all actions that may be taken in light of these conditions. Enter them in the space below.

POSSIBLE ACTIONS

_____

_____

_____

_____

Your decision table should describe actions to be taken if various conditions occur. Enter the appropriate Y, N, or X to complete the rules.

(continues)

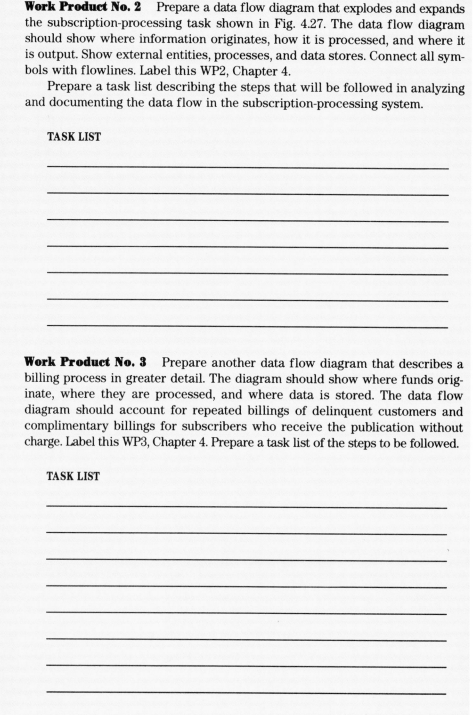

Work Product No. 2   Prepare a data flow diagram that explodes and expands the subscription-processing task shown in Fig. 4.27. The data flow diagram should show where information originates, how it is processed, and where it is output. Show external entities, processes, and data stores. Connect all symbols with flowlines. Label this WP2, Chapter 4.

Prepare a task list describing the steps that will be followed in analyzing and documenting the data flow in the subscription-processing system.

TASK LIST

_____

_____

_____

_____

_____

_____

Work Product No. 3   Prepare another data flow diagram that describes a billing process in greater detail. The diagram should show where funds originate, where they are processed, and where data is stored. The data flow diagram should account for repeated billings of delinquent customers and complimentary billings for subscribers who receive the publication without charge. Label this WP3, Chapter 4. Prepare a task list of the steps to be followed.

TASK LIST

_____

_____

_____

_____

_____

_____

_____

THE
PLANNING
PHASE

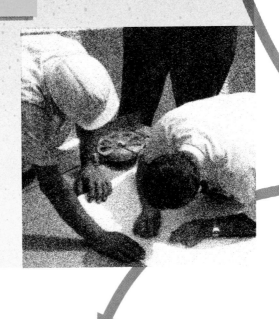

PRELIMINARY PLANNING AND INVESTIGATION

LEARNING OBJECTIVES

After studying this chapter, you should be able to:

1. Describe how problems are brought to the attention of systems analysts.

2. Discuss the function of feasibility studies.

3. Discuss the elements of the feasibility study.

4. Describe how problems are recognized and diagnosed.

5. Describe the steps followed in defining a problem.

6. List various approaches to staffing a study effort.

We are now ready to discuss the planning phase of the systems development life cycle (SDLC). We will use the UniTrans Company and its system problems as a vehicle to analyze the planning process, problem definition, feasibility study, and selection of personnel for conducting an ongoing systems design effort. Throughout this chapter we will mix theory and practice. We will trace the steps that an analyst follows in doing the preliminary planning and investigation necessary to solve a problem.

HOW TO CONDUCT A SYSTEM STUDY

In Chapter 3 we discussed the SDLC. As you recall, the systems analyst methodically moves through phases, applying the scientific method to solve problems and repeating steps when necessary. The objective, of course, is to approach systems design in a logical way, generating a system that will operate with a minimum input of time, money, and effort while producing the desired accuracy and results.

The five major phases in the SDLC are summarized in Fig. 5.1. They may be completed in a matter of a few days or weeks if a relatively simple system is involved. For example, a small retailer might acquire a microcomputer and software for managing a database. The equipment may be delivered in a few days and an operator trained to use the system in a couple of weeks. After a few minor modifications, the system may be fully operational in less than a month at a cost of only a few thousand dollars.

At the other extreme, a large company may spend hundreds of thousands of dollars planning and designing a new system. Many employees may be hired, retrained, or relocated. It may take many months or even years to fully implement the new system. The final project may cost millions of dollars and involve the purchase of hundreds of pieces of equipment, extensive modification of buildings and offices, and the installation of specialized communications facilities.

A system study begins with recognition of a problem, willingness by the organization or the system staff to deal with it, and then delineation of the tasks necessary to solve the problem. Let us see how a problem is assessed and reduced to discrete steps so that it can be resolved.

RECOGNIZING THE PROBLEM

Problems are brought to the analyst's attention in many ways. It is the rare analyst who waits until problems create serious systemic difficulties. Instead, most analysts take an active role in **problem recognition.**

Analysts are continually measuring, examining, studying, and comparing

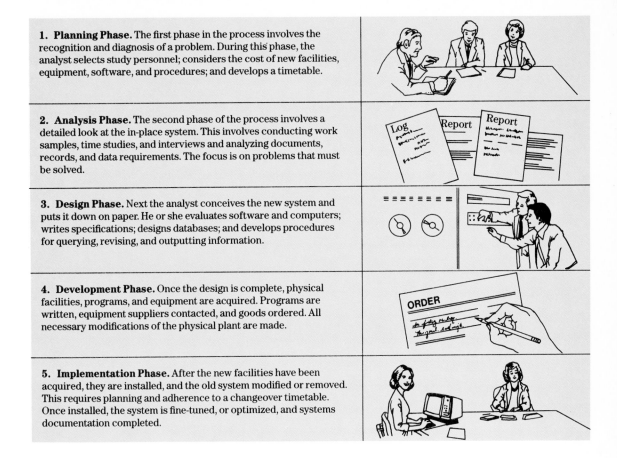

1. **Planning Phase.** The first phase in the process involves the recognition and diagnosis of a problem. During this phase, the analyst selects study personnel; considers the cost of new facilities, equipment, software, and procedures; and develops a timetable.

2. **Analysis Phase.** The second phase of the process involves a detailed look at the in-place system. This involves conducting work samples, time studies, and interviews and analyzing documents, records, and data requirements. The focus is on problems that must be solved.

3. **Design Phase.** Next the analyst conceives the new system and puts it down on paper. He or she evaluates software and computers; writes specifications; designs databases; and develops procedures for querying, revising, and outputting information.

4. **Development Phase.** Once the design is complete, physical facilities, programs, and equipment are acquired. Programs are written, equipment suppliers contacted, and goods ordered. All necessary modifications of the physical plant are made.

5. **Implementation Phase.** After the new facilities have been acquired, they are installed, and the old system modified or removed. This requires planning and adherence to a changeover timetable. Once installed, the system is fine-tuned, or optimized, and systems documentation completed.

elements in a system to pinpoint problem situations before difficulties disrupt the organization. A good analyst looks ahead, incorporating new ideas and techniques to improve efficiency, increase benefits, and prevent obsolescence of a system. Analysts often work with an organization's marketing department to ensure timely design and implementation of the system to cope with new products or enhancements.

Sometimes management approaches the systems analyst about existing problems or with a request to study the feasibility of a specific system or installation. Suggestions or requests for changes or improvements can also come from personnel in other departments or from supervisors or other employees.

Complaints from dissatisfied customers are often indications of serious problems. Accounting records may point to specific problem areas, such as cost analysis reports that show unexplained or unexpected increases in expenses or overhead, ratios that show unreasonably high costs, or excessive overtime or reject rates. Sometimes lost or misrouted data is a sign that problems exist.

FIGURE 5.1

Summary of the Systems Development Life Cycle (SDLC)

REQUEST FOR SYSTEMS SERVICES

Date:	
Submitted by:	
Title:	
Department:	
Phone:	
Supervisor's Signature:	

Request Is For:

_____ New system

_____ Modify existing system

Special Instructions (if any):

Previous Case History

Date	Actions Performed

Status

_____ Immediate Request

_____ As Time Allows

_____ Deferred Pending Budget

_____ Ongoing Project

_____ Other

Reserved for Systems Department

Process form and file with approval

Analyst Assigned:	
Date:	Budget:
Approved by:	
Comments:	

Describe Systems Services Needed:

FIGURE 5.2

Request for Systems Services

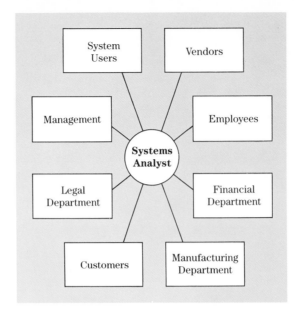

FIGURE 5.3

Sources of Problem Identification
Many different people may bring problems to the analyst's attention.

REQUEST FOR SERVICES

Many organizations have developed a formal procedure for alerting staff to the need for systems services. A **request for services** form, similar to that shown in Fig. 5.2, is frequently used for this purpose. The form provides space to briefly describe a problem and outline the services needed. It is then sent to the systems department, where it will be evaluated. Upon receipt of a form, appropriate staff and resources are assigned to initiate a study. Where merited, a full-blown systems study will be undertaken.

A request for services may come to an analyst in different ways and from different people. Sometimes the analyst, working on one problem, will identify another that requires solution. Or the problem may be brought to the analyst's attention by customers or users of a system (see Fig. 5.3). Less formal procedures may be followed in smaller organizations: a letter or memo sent to the systems department, or simply a phone call or a request for a visit by an analyst.

Letters, memos, and requests for services become part of the systems documentation file. This file is begun early in the SDLC and continues through the completion of the system. Chapter 17 discusses systems documentation in greater detail.

HOW TO INVESTIGATE A SYSTEM

Assume you are an analyst and you have received a request from Mark Stevens, a manager in the transportation division of UniTrans Company, asking

REQUEST FOR SYSTEMS SERVICES

Date: 6/21/89
Submitted by: M. Stevens
Title: Manager
Department:
Phone: x 218
Supervisor's Signature:

Request Is For:
_____ New system
__X__ Modify existing system
Special Instructions (if any):

Previous Case History

Date	Actions Performed
1/3/89	Developed and installed computer-based maintenance schedules.
3/6/89	Software modified to correct bugs in initial data entry program.

Status

__X__ Immediate Request

_____ As Time Allows

_____ Deferred Pending Budget

_____ Ongoing Project

_____ Other

Reserved for Systems Department

Process form and file with approval

Analyst Assigned:	
Date:	Budget:
Approved by:	
Comments:	

Describe Systems Services Needed:
Truck maintenance schedule system not functioning properly. Staff complains paperwork is too time consuming to complete. Discrepancy between maintenance reports and parts availability reports.

FIGURE 5.4

Maintenance Schedule Request for Services

the systems department to delve into a maintenance schedule problem in his department (see Fig. 5.4). You study the request, recognize that it has come from an appropriate manager or supervisor, and want to take action. You will first develop a task list that describes the preliminary steps to be taken. Your task list might look something like this:

TASK LIST, MAINTENANCE REPORTING SYSTEM

1. Study request and review previous documentation and case history.
2. Meet with Mark Stevens and discuss problem.
3. Prepare problem definition statement.
4. Conduct feasibility study.
5. Assign personnel to project.
6. Prepare report for management, including recommendations for dealing with the problem.

You have now studied the case history and met with Mark Stevens. You and he have discussed the maintenance schedule problem, the excessive paperwork in the system, and the discrepancies between maintenance reports and parts department replacement logs. You have already begun preparing a set of notes detailing your observations and further refining the tasks that you expect to perform. It is clear from your observations and discussions with Mark Stevens that a problem exists. But the nature of the problem is still fuzzy.

DEFINING THE PROBLEM

After a problem has been recognized or brought to the analyst's attention, he or she moves on to the next step—**problem definition.** The analyst makes a brief assessment of the ways in which the problem manifests itself. The assessment indicates such conditions as the number of hours a report is delayed, the percentage of rejects, and the number of complaints received (see Fig. 5.5).

Next, the analyst determines what goals, outcomes, or improvements would solve or diminish the problem. These are expressed in such terms as reduction in cost, decrease in turnaround time, increase in fringe benefits, and so forth.

Now the analyst must recommend ways in which the problem can be solved and the goals reached. This may involve modifying, redesigning, or even replacing a system, or in some instances ensuring that an established system is thoroughly documented and is being operated properly.

Once these initial steps have been carried out, the analyst decides whether it is practical to make the recommended changes. Will the benefits gained from modifying an existing system or installing a new one be worth the costs, effort, and disruption involved?

FIGURE 5.5

Complaint Log

Logs such as these record the nature and type of complaint.

	UNITRANS COMPANY	
	PARTS DEPARTMENT COMPLAINT LOG	
Date	**Source**	**Nature of Complaint**
02-16-89	Shipping	Repair parts delivered late
02-23-89	Marketing	Shipment incomplete
02-26-89	Depot 38	Parts charged to wrong account
03-09-89	Marketing	Parts shipped without billing
03-19-89	Depot 73	Maintenance not performed

For extensive, complex changes, this is a critical question that cannot be answered easily or without a thorough analysis of alternatives and outcomes. Firms may have to invest hundreds of personnel hours and thousands of dollars and suffer disruption of office routines or deliveries of goods and services to customers.

You have now completed the first three items on your task list and have generated a precise statement of the problem (see Fig. 5.6). A problem exists and you believe that a feasibility study is in order.

FEASIBILITY STUDY

Systems analysts have developed logical methods of evaluating the practical details involved in implementing a new or modified system. The process begins with a **feasibility study.** Its purpose is to gather, analyze, and document the data needed to make an informed, intelligent decision regarding a system's practicality.

This analysis is done in three stages (see Fig. 5.7). The **preliminary study** is concerned with determining whether or not the direct and indirect benefits gained from the new system will be greater than the costs involved. If the answer is no, the feasibility study ends there and the project is temporarily or permanently abandoned.

If the answer is yes, the analysis enters the second stage—the **investigative study.** There the problem is carefully defined and all details in the solution are specified.

The last stage of the feasibility study is the **final report** (see Fig. 5.8). It fully documents the work done during the first two parts of the study, showing all expected costs, benefits, and outcomes. The final report tells how and when the new system should be implemented. Management will use these recommendations as the basis for decisions regarding the new system.

Project: MAINTENANCE REPORTING SYSTEM

Analyst: S. Vargas

   Date: September 3, 1989

Statement of Problem:

After a careful review of UniTrans Company's maintenance records and discussions with the plant manager,
I have concluded that the following problems exist.
The paperwork requirements for processing inventory
parts are unnecessarily complicated. As a result, many
errors are made in report handling. Items are often
overlooked or charged to the wrong accounts. There is
an inadequate procedure for verifying book inventories
against physical inventories. A communications problem
exists in the department, which results in reports
being transmitted to incorrect destinations or in an
untimely manner.

Suggestions and Recommendations:

An improved system for processing inventory parts
should be developed. This system should be easier to
use than the present arrangement and should make provisions for reconciling physical inventories against
book inventories. A reporting system should be developed to transmit reports to the appropriate departments in a timely manner.

Approximate time needed for development: 50 hours

Redesign and reprint forms

FIGURE 5.6

Statement of Problem

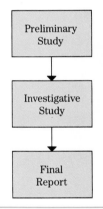

FIGURE 5.7

**Stages of the Fea-
sibility Study**

Who Will Conduct the Study?

After the decision has been made to examine a problem situation or
modify a system, the next question to be addressed is, who will undertake the
task? (see Fig. 5.9). There are at least four methods from which to choose.

1. Consultants and experts. In this arrangement, a firm that specializes in
   performing this type of study is hired. **Consultants** working for such
   firms have skills and training in this area. In some arrangements, the
   consulting firm carries out the feasibility study and implements the new

FIGURE 5.8

Final Report The last step in the feasibility study is to issue a final report.

**FINAL REPORT
PLANNING STUDY ON NEW COMMUNICATIONS SYSTEM**

Prepared by Project Task Force

Outline

I.   Statement of problem
II.   Discussion of communications needs
III. Summary of supervisor's comments
IV.   Description of proposed system
V.   Cost/benefit analysis
VI.   Recommendations

or modified system. In other instances, it only conducts the study and the host firm or other outside experts handle the implementation.

2. Ongoing committee. The **ongoing committee** is a group of individuals who assume continuing responsibility for evaluating new systems. The members usually represent many areas of expertise—management, systems analysts, line employees, supervisors, and so on. New members may be assigned as necessary to maintain a comprehensive and relevant representation on the committee. This approach gives the firm an experienced group that continually monitors the company's information and data flow. This makes it easier to identify and solve problems early and to anticipate situations that should be improved or modified.

3. Task force. A **task force** is a group charged with the one-time responsibility of studying a given system problem. Members of the task force may be

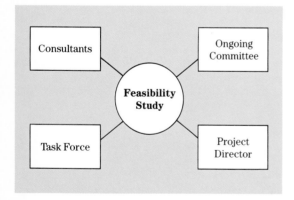

FIGURE 5.9

Staffing the Study Several different approaches can be used to staff the feasibility study.

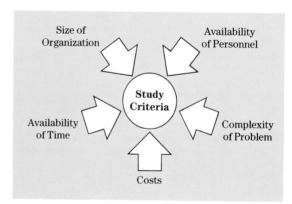

FIGURE 5.10

Study Factors Different factors are considered before launching a feasibility study.

managers, systems analysts, and other employees. After the particular assignment has been completed, the group disbands. If another problem arises later, another task force is formed to address that specific situation.

Project director. Sometimes one person is entrusted with the responsibility of conducting or directing a feasibility study. The **project director** may be an analyst on the systems department staff or may be drawn from management. The director may conduct all the phases of the study alone or supervise one or more assistants who do so.

The arrangement selected to carry out a feasibility study depends on several factors (see Fig. 5.10). These include the size of the organization; how soon the new system is to be installed; the anticipated complexity and cost of the new system; and the availability of personnel with the necessary experience and knowledge.

UNITRANS COMPANY'S FEASIBILITY STUDY

You have discussed the UniTrans problem in detail and have concluded that one individual, a project director, can handle the assignment. You have obtained approval from the systems department manager to move forward with the study and you have been assigned as the project director. Thus you begin the next task on your list, conducting the feasibility study. You will conduct the three parts of the feasibility study consecutively, using the results of one part to guide the development of the next.

Preliminary Study

The first stage of the feasibility study answers the question, "Should further time, money, and resources be spent in studying or developing a new or modified system?" The analyst estimates costs for developing and operating the system compared to the expected direct and indirect benefits. The results of this cost/benefit analysis determine whether or not the next phase should be performed.

In order to assess accurately the costs and benefits of a system, you should document information about the structure of the present system, the projected system, and the organization itself. Study the existing system and calculate time elements involved in performing various actions. Describe the output in quantitative terms, such as minutes, hours, dollars, numbers of replaced parts, and so forth. Gather cost data for operating the system, defining its strengths and weaknesses in quantitative terms.

The improvements expected from a new system should also be stated in quantitative terms. You need to investigate other firms and systems to see how they handle similar situations. Discuss alternative plans and select one or two

FIGURE 5.11

Costs and Benefits Analysis

COSTS	BENEFITS
Temporary disruption of operations	Lower operating costs
New forms	Lower capital investment
Supplies	Lower maintenance costs
New equipment	Reduced salaries
Employee training	Less physical space needed
Facilities alterations	Fewer operators required
Development time	Faster turnaround time
Preparation of computer programs	Greater accuracy
Consultant fees	More comprehensive reports
Conversion costs	Improved morale

for further investigation. Compare equipment capabilities and obtain competitive equipment bids.

Now is the time to evaluate the costs and benefits that will result from the development and operation of the new system in a **cost/benefit analysis** (see Fig. 5.11). This includes the costs incurred in planning, developing, and implementing the system: salaries; preparation of computer programs; materials; commissions to outside consultants or experts; purchase, lease, and installation of new equipment; training personnel to operate the new equipment; and making any necessary modifications to the building. Conversion costs involved in changing from the old system to the new one must also be estimated.

The costs involved in operating the new or modified system include salaries, forms and other materials, equipment maintenance and replacement, updating employee skills, and building maintenance. Figure 5.12 is a preliminary cost assessment of the new system showing the monthly and annual cost savings. Studies such as these quantify increases in profit or reductions in costs. They may be computed on the basis of hourly, daily, weekly, monthly, or even annual time periods. Sometimes cost analysis is based upon units, for example, a specific cost saving per package shipped or check mailed.

Make a study of the benefits that UniTrans expects to derive from implementing the new system. These include direct benefits such as savings in costs and expenses (salaries, physical space, equipment, equipment operation, personnel training), and improved output and service (reduction in errors, faster turnaround time). Direct benefits also include the ability to produce comprehensive reports with more detailed interpretations more frequently.

Benefits that accrue from a system can also be indirect, such as increased morale or greater understanding of the organizational structure of a firm or system. Attitudes may change as well. Increased awareness of the existing situation will sometimes lead to improvements in other departments or systems, even in the organizational structure of the firm itself. A system designed for one particular problem or department may be "exportable," able to be used with little or no modification in other branches or departments, by other firms, or to solve other problems.

	RATE	HOURS REQ.	AMOUNT
Labor costs (includes burden)*			
Systems programmer	$ 17.40	12 hours	$ 208.80
Communications engineer	19.70	31 hours	610.70
Systems analyst	23.50	6.5 hours	152.75
Installation costs			
Install two circuits	260.00	2	520.00
Facilities alterations			2200.00
Material and supplies (per mo.)	73.50	12	882.00
Overhead and operating			
costs (per mo.)	390.00	12	4680.00
FIRST YEAR COSTS			9254.25
SECOND YEAR COSTS			5562.00

FIGURE 5.12

Analysis of System Costs This report shows the costs involved in developing the new system.

*Payroll taxes, FICA, fringe benefits, etc.

  In preparing the cost/benefit analysis you will be concerned with questions such as these:

1. What will be the differences in cost and profit between the old and new systems? Is a new system justified on the basis of cost alone?

2. Will a new system increase UniTrans's output capability? Will the company be able to schedule truck maintenance more efficiently, use less labor, have better control over replacement parts?

3. Will the cost of maintaining the new system be less than the old? What will be the true savings in maintenance costs in both the long and short run?

4. What indirect benefits will result from a new system? Will changing the elements of one system improve the operation of another system?

5. Will the new system be more reliable and dependable? Are there reasonable expectations of less down time and fewer periods of inactivity from equipment breakdowns? How can these changes be quantified?

6. What improvements in personnel attitudes will result? Will the new system produce greater motivation, resulting in less absenteeism and greater productivity? Will it reduce the problems between the maintenance department and the parts department?

  If the cost/benefit analysis suggests that the new or modified system will be feasible, make plans to continue on to the next phase. You may want to call in outside consultants at this point to carry out the remainder of the project.

You will need to recommend a timetable for planning, developing, and implementing the system, or you may suggest that additional time be allowed for more study. You may wish to prepare a progress report detailing the work and recommendations of the study. Based on this report, management decides whether to end the project or begin the investigative study.

Investigative Study

In this stage, you are going to plan the actual specifications, elements, and relationship of the new system in considerable detail. The costs involved in development, implementation, and operation are reviewed and updated to reflect the most recent specifications, estimates, and bids. A detailed time schedule for installing the system is drawn up to serve as a guide during the implementation phase.

Before you begin the design work, it may be necessary to make a more thorough analysis of the situation. You may prepare a more detailed statement of the problem, its causes, and how the new system will meet the objectives set for it.

During this stage, you will use interviews, questionnaires, time studies, direct observations, and other techniques to gather information. You should consider any preexisting limitations that must be built into the new system. New systems or modifications must be compatible with systems already in operation and must cause as little disruption as possible. The new system must be able to accept data generated by other systems and output results in a form suitable for their use.

You must determine how and where the new system and existing systems interact and what changes are necessary to make them compatible. You should indicate which constraints must be designed into the new system and what elements in the old system must be modified.

Existing equipment must be able to perform the type of information processing planned for the new system, or new equipment must be acquired. Personnel retraining must be considered. The availability of employees with the needed skills and experience is often an important factor in systems planning.

The project director designs a system geared to meet the objectives and existing parameters. You may consider alternate designs or methods of solving the problem before selecting the one that best meets the organization's needs.

At this time, you specify all the elements that compose the system. This includes the required equipment and information regarding exact model numbers, price, purchase and leasing details. Spell out the number of workstations, job responsibilities, and locations of equipment, along with salary expectations, training requirements, and availability of suitable personnel. Specify changes that must be made in the physical plant along with the expected costs and anticipated time required to make the changes. Detail the files, records, forms, and reports used or generated by the system.

You must also state information regarding computer programs needed by the system, including costs, who will write the programs, and the configuration of equipment necessary to execute them. Specify the data input and output generated by the programs and estimate the time required for each operation in the system.

Determine and document the movement of information, activities, and personnel in the new system with system design diagrams. Use flowcharts and decision tables wherever necessary to clarify situations with many alternative data flow paths.

A major part of the investigative study is preparing the **implementation schedule.** In this stage, you recommend how the new system should be installed and prepare a timetable to guide the transition from old to new as smoothly as possible.

If necessary, you may describe a temporary **backup system** for use during the changeover. Many times the old system continues to operate while the new system is being implemented. The project director recommends the best way to phase out the old system with the least disruption, and also recommends ways to prepare employees for the new system. These may include training programs, in-service instruction, meetings, or demonstrations. You should state the costs of any programs and give suggested time schedules.

The project director also designates who will carry out the implementation of the new system. You should indicate who will be in charge of specific areas of responsibility. Sometimes the project director does this job; at other times the systems department or other individuals in the firm do it.

Final Report

The last step in the feasibility study is the preparation of the final report. This document summarizes the results of the planning effort and gives your recommendations regarding implementation. Management will use the information in this report as a guide when making decisions.

The final report itemizes the actual costs involved in the new system, describes the objectives that it will accomplish, and gives a statement of the benefits that will accrue to the company. Based upon these recommendations, management may select one of several courses of action. It may:

1. Proceed immediately with the implementation of the new system as outlined in the final report.
2. Forestall implementation until a later date when economic conditions improve or other factors change.
3. Elect not to implement the new system at all, and terminate consideration of the project.

The course of action can be selected intelligently, since all relevant data is at hand. If management decides not to install the new system, they will be aware of the possible direct and indirect benefits that will be lost. If they decide to implement the system, the feasibility study has prepared the guidelines to be followed as the project enters the next phase.

Planning is the foundation upon which a strong structure is built. This chapter has explored the issues that need to be investigated when complex problems are being solved. Before going on to discuss the next steps in the systems development life cycle, we will study project management. The next chapter describes the role of project managers, why projects fail, and how to manage complex projects and keep them on schedule.

Summary

The systems development life cycle (SDLC) begins with the planning and investigative phase. Problems are brought to the analyst's attention from many different sources, including customers, employees, managers, and others. A request for services form is sometimes prepared and sent to the analyst.

Upon recognition of a problem, the analyst usually prepares a task list. This list lays out the steps that will be followed in executing the planning phase. Problem definition is usually initiated early. Then the analyst determines the goals and outcomes that are expected from an improved system.

Sometimes the analyst performs a feasibility study. This effort begins with a preliminary study to decide if it is advisable to proceed with the project. An investigative study and final report follow. Alternatives to staffing the study include using consultants, an ongoing committee, a task force, or a project director.

An assessment of costs and benefits is done in the planning phase. This weighs costs against advantages that will be realized from an improved system. Questions will be asked concerning output capability, maintenance costs, indirect benefits, level of reliability, personnel, attitudes, and motivation.

Key Terms

Backup system	Ongoing committee
Consultant	Preliminary study
Cost/benefit analysis	Problem definition
Feasibility study	Problem recognition
Final report	Project director
Implementation schedule	Request for services
Investigative study	Task force

Exercises

1. What elements are taken into consideration in defining a problem? Give several examples.
2. What is the function of a feasibility study?
3. What are the three major parts of the feasibility study?
4. List at least three different approaches that may be followed in assigning staff to conduct the feasibility study.

5. What is the function of the preliminary study?
6. What is the function of the investigative study?
7. What is the function of the final report?
8. Describe the kind of information found on the request for services form.
9. Suppose you are investigating a problem concerning delays in the flow of paperwork through a system. Prepare a task list showing the preliminary steps that must be taken to solve the problem.
10. Describe the function of an ongoing committee.

Projects

1. Conduct a short feasibility study of an activity such as purchasing a car.
2. Visit a business firm that has conducted or plans to conduct a feasibility study. Discuss the aims of the study and how people were selected to conduct it.
3. Assume you are starting a small retail firm. Conduct a feasibility study of various methods of writing and processing orders.
4. Study your school's registration system. Prepare a feasibility study showing an improved method of registering students.
5. Conduct a feasibility study comparing the installation of electric typewriters versus personal computers in a small office.

ANALYST AT WORK

CARLSON'S DEPARTMENT STORE

DESCRIPTION OF FIRM

Carlson's Department Store was founded by Leonard Carlson over 50 years ago. It is now owned and managed by the Carlson family. The first store was located in a downtown metropolitan area. Subsequently, four additional stores were opened in various suburbs. Carlson's is proud of offering high-fashion styles, a wide selection of merchandise, and reasonably priced goods. Carlson's is a full-line retailer, selling hard and soft goods, furniture, and clothing.

Since Carlson's reputation is based on offering prompt and courteous service, sales clerks are trained in sales and retailing before they are put on the floor. Clerks are taught how to operate the point-of-sale terminals located in each department and how to handle returns, exchanges, and credits on merchandise.

SYSTEM OVERVIEW

Carlson's management cooperated with a computer manufacturer in designing and installing the point-of-sale terminals. Each retail terminal is wired directly to a central computer located in each store. All retail transactions, including returns, exchanges, and credits are processed through the terminals. The system also maintains the inventory. Figure 5.13 is a data flow diagram showing the major elements in Carlson's online terminal and billing system.

Most merchandise sold in the store has tags indicating the price, item number, color, size, and other pertinent information. Items that are either too small or too bulky to carry price tickets are assigned article numbers. Goods sold or returned must bear an article number in order to be properly processed. A log is kept of these articles at each point-of-sale terminal.

The central computer in each store is used to generate several reports each day. These include inventory, cash flow, and merchandise returned reports, as well as sales by station, sales by clerk, and so on. The reports assist management in making decisions.

HANDS-ON APPLICATION

Carlson's has experienced an increased number of customer complaints. These complaints center around transactions related to returns of goods, customers

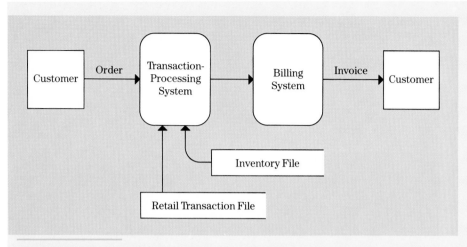

FIGURE 5.13

Carlson's Department Store Data flow diagram for point-of-sale terminal system.

being over- or undercharged, or items with wrong article numbers. Complaints are also received from customers who say that payments made in person were not credited to their accounts.

You have received a request for systems services from the sales manager of Carlson's downtown department store (see Fig. 5.14). She has asked that you study the problem and assist in finding solutions. You are to become involved in a preliminary planning and investigation study to help resolve Carlson's difficulties. The sales manager has also given you a complaint log from several departments. Figure 5.15 is a list of complaints reported by assistant managers in one store.

As a result of your preliminary planning and investigation effort, you will produce the following work products:

1. Written statement of problem
2. List of benefits from an improved system
3. Recommendations for staffing a system study to resolve Carlson's problems
4. Data flow diagram that expands the next level of detail in Fig. 5.13

Work Product No. 1   Analyze the request for systems services and the complaint log shown in Figs. 5.14 and 5.15. Prepare a written statement clearly delineating the problems that must be resolved in Carlson's retail operations. Label this document WP1, Chapter 5.

REQUEST FOR SYSTEMS SERVICES

Date: 9/14/89	**Request Is For:**
Submitted by: Betty Rawlins	_____ New system
Title: Sales manager	__X__ Modify existing system
Department: Downtown store	Special Instructions (if any):
Phone:	Work needs to be completed as soon
Supervisor's Signature:	as possible.

Previous Case History

Date	Actions Performed
3/21/89	Develop transaction-processing system for downtown store
6/5/89	Develop centralized billing system

Status

__X__ Immediate Request

_____ As Time Allows

_____ Deferred Pending Budget

_____ Ongoing Project

_____ Other

Reserved for Systems Department

Process form and file with approval

Analyst Assigned:	
Date:	Budget:
Approved by:	
Comments:	

Describe Systems Services Needed:
Correct problems in billing system involving overcharges, incorrect posting, and errors in charging goods to department and clerk. Improve transaction-processing system problems related to assignment of article numbers (see attached complaint log).

FIGURE 5.14

Request for Systems Services This document was provided by the sales manager of the store.

CUSTOMER COMPLAINTS

Customer overcharged on sale item
Customer credit not posted
Customer credit incorrectly posted
Delay due to lack of assigned article number
Goods charged to wrong customer account
Service charge incorrectly posted
Customer undercharged
Goods rung up with wrong department number
Goods rung up without salesclerk ID number

FIGURE 5.15

Carlson's Complaint Log

Prepare a task list indicating what steps must be carried out in order to properly diagnose and define the problem and to complete Work Product No. 1. Enter your task list below.

TASK LIST

_____

_____

_____

_____

_____

Work Product No. 2   Prepare a benefit and cost analysis list. This list should identify all the costs associated with an improved system and the benefits and improved system performance that will result. Label this document WP2, Chapter 5. To assist in defining the costs and benefits, you should prepare a task list. Enter your task list for Work Product No. 2 below.

TASK LIST

_____

_____

_____

_____

_____

_____

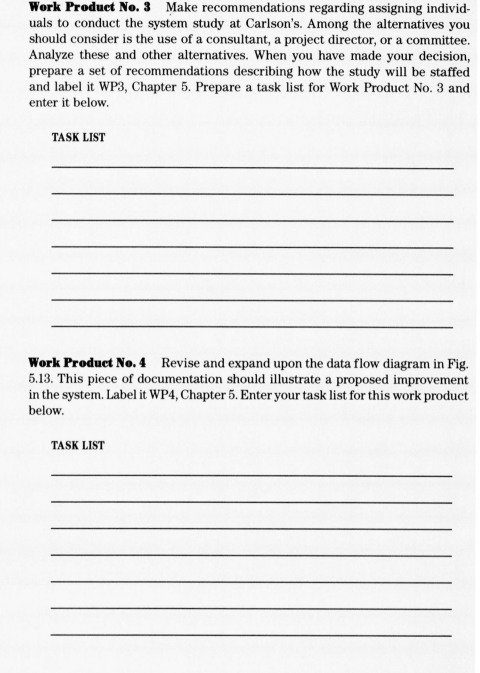

Work Product No. 3   Make recommendations regarding assigning individuals to conduct the system study at Carlson's. Among the alternatives you should consider is the use of a consultant, a project director, or a committee. Analyze these and other alternatives. When you have made your decision, prepare a set of recommendations describing how the study will be staffed and label it WP3, Chapter 5. Prepare a task list for Work Product No. 3 and enter it below.

TASK LIST

_____

_____

_____

_____

_____

_____

Work Product No. 4   Revise and expand upon the data flow diagram in Fig. 5.13. This piece of documentation should illustrate a proposed improvement in the system. Label it WP4, Chapter 5. Enter your task list for this work product below.

TASK LIST

_____

_____

_____

_____

_____

_____

PROJECT MANAGEMENT

LEARNING OBJECTIVES

After studying this chapter, you should be able to:

1. Discuss the need for project management.

2. Describe different ways of staffing a project.

3. Discuss traditional project management.

4. Discuss computerized project management.

5. Describe the role of consultants in project management.

6. Contrast projects and programs.

The Great Wall of China, the pyramids of Egypt, and the Hoover Dam are all examples of major projects. A project is an undertaking, large or small, that involves the coordination of individuals, money, and resources to reach a goal. Some projects produce buildings or roadways, while others generate information systems, computer programs, or databases.

Now that we have described the preliminary planning and investigation phase of the systems development life cycle (SDLC), we will move on to study project management. In this chapter you will learn how projects are created, managed, and kept on schedule and how computers are used in project management. A knowledge of project management provides many concepts to better understand the remaining steps in the SDLC.

PROJECT CONCEPTS

A **project** is a planned undertaking of scheduled activities by an organization and its management to reach a goal. Projects are one-time attempts that draw together human resources, money, and physical facilities to generate a product. Projects are undertaken to solve problems or to create computer programs, billing systems, payroll-processing systems, and the like. The task of developing and managing a project is often assigned to systems analysts.

A project effort should be distinguished from a program effort (see Fig. 6.1). A **program** is an ongoing endeavor by an organization to generate a series of products or reach a sequence of goals. Projects are one-time, nonserial ventures, while programs are continuing efforts to address business system problems. A program may, in fact, be a series of projects. Sometimes a project may turn into a program, while at other times what was conceived as a program turns into a single project.

NEED FOR PROJECT MANAGEMENT

Since a project may involve an extensive financial and personnel commitment on the part of an organization, it must be properly managed. A project should always be planned, the result of an organized, systematic effort.

Project management is the coordination of all aspects of a project so that it is completed on time and within the assigned financial and personnel constraints. The task of project management involves defining the goals of the project, listing the resources assigned to it, scheduling the work, periodic reporting and evaluation, and finally assessing its overall performance.

Applying some of the structured concepts from a previous chapter, let us view the project from a top-down perspective. Figure 6.2 shows a hierarchy with

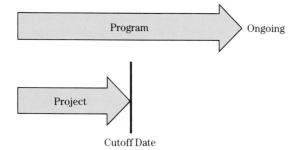

FIGURE 6.1

Programs and Projects Programs are ongoing efforts, while projects have definite ending dates.

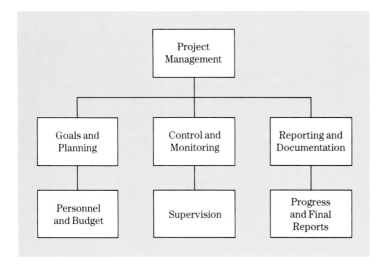

FIGURE 6.2

Elements of a Project A project can be viewed from top-down perspective with different levels of detail.

project management at the top. Lower-level tasks include project planning, control, and documentation. Still lower levels are budgeting, supervising, and generating progress and final reports.

WHY PROJECTS FAIL

A project can fail to reach its designed objectives for a variety of reasons. Sometimes insufficient money or personnel have been assigned to the project. In other instances there may be a lack of commitment on the part of management, or even a conflict of goals. Projects may fail because new technologies are not fully understood before they are implemented. Or there may be cost overruns or personnel difficulties.

A lack of experience on the part of the project manager or analyst may be the cause of some failures. Sometimes a project addresses the wrong goal or involves so many individuals that coordination is lost. The absence of good planning or sound communications also causes projects to fail. Our objective in this chapter is to understand the nature of project management and to learn how to avoid failures.

MANAGING PROJECTS

The essence of project management is coordination and scheduling. Many analysts develop a **task list** that describes the key elements in a project management effort. Suppose UniTrans Company's management wishes to replace 10 of its container tractor-trailer trucks with new vehicles. These trucks haul cargo from UniTrans's airport freight terminal to its regional distribution centers. This is a one-time project to coordinate removing the older vehicles from service and replacing them with a fleet of new tractor-trailers. Here is a task list for this project:

TASK LIST
UNITRANS COMPANY TRACTOR-TRAILER PROJECT

1. Assign individuals to project.
2. Define problem and specify goals.
3. Define budget and allocate resources.
4. Establish timetable, schedule work.
5. Track and monitor project.
6. Generate reports and documentation.

The first step in the project is to assign personnel. There are a variety of approaches to this task.

Project Director

The project director or project manager is the individual assigned to a project to guide it through to completion. He or she assumes responsibility for the overall success of the project. Project directors may have one or more assistants to help them in carrying out their duties. The analyst in the UniTrans case asks to have a mechanical supervisor and someone from the purchasing department assigned to the project. These people will bring supportive skills to the task and work under the project director.

Project Team

A committee or group is sometimes assigned to manage a project. A **project team,** sometimes called a task force, is a collection of people who have diverse knowledge and abilities and who manage the project collectively. The advantage of this approach is that several individuals are responsible for managing the project and are able to pool their skills and knowledge. Individuals in the team may be drawn from many levels of the organization, including managers, supervisors, line employees, and others. Upon completion of the project, the members return to their previous jobs.

Consultants

Particularly complex, technical, or extensive projects are sometimes turned over to a consultant for management. A consultant is an individual or organization who provides project management services to others for a fee. Using consultants has many advantages. It enables organizations to bring in highly skilled individuals for short periods of time. People with these skills may not be readily available on the organization's payroll.

Consultants supplement an organization's workforce and thus do not siphon off key employees, as does the project director or project team. A consultant can also make recommendations or issue project directives that might be politically unpopular if they came from within the organization. Those involved in a project may more willingly accept direction from a consultant rather than a peer, because people often resent following directives given by an equal in the organization.

TRADITIONAL PROJECT MANAGEMENT

For many decades, systems analysts followed a classical approach to project management. Before the advent of computers, all project budgeting, scheduling, monitoring, and reporting was done manually. This usually involved preparing reports computed by hand and drawing charts and graphs with pencil and paper. We will review traditional project management methodology before moving on to a study of computerized project management.

Define Goals

Reference to our task list will show that problem definition and goal specification follows assignment of individuals to the project. Assume that the systems department manager has appointed you the project director to handle

Project: VEHICLE REPLACEMENT PROGRAM

Analyst: A. Wang

   Date: August 24, 1988

Statement of Goals:

I conducted a number of interviews with key individuals regarding the replacement of fleet vehicles. Ten container tractor-trailer trucks must be replaced.

The key goals of this project are to:

1. Increase package-handling capacity per vehicle.

2. Reduce operating and per mile maintenance costs of fleet.

3. Bring tractor-trailer fleet into compliance with state and local air pollution requirements.

4. Increase reliability and dependability of the truck fleet.

I expect that additional capital investment will be required in order to reach these goals. This additional investment should be more than offset by the added reliability and lower operating costs of the new vehicles. The new trucks will also enable UniTrans to meet the stricter vehicle licensing standards now in effect.

the acquisition of the 10 new tractor-trailers. You first interview key individuals and discuss the problems they are having with the present fleet of trucks. Next, you set goals for the replacement vehicles. After discussions with many people in the company, you prepare a goal statement (see Fig. 6.3).

Your discussions lead you to the conclusion that the project goal is to replace the older vehicles with new equipment that meets certain cost and performance criteria.

Define Budget and Allocate Resources

With a set of goals in mind, you are ready to acquire the necessary budget to execute the project. In practice, this involves consulting with the organization's chief financial officer, department managers, and others to assess the price of new vehicles and review bids for salvaging the old trucks.

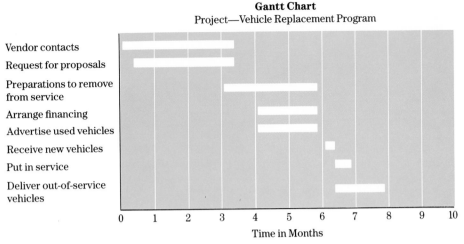

Gantt Chart
Project—Vehicle Replacement Program

Vendor contacts
Request for proposals
Preparations to remove from service
Arrange financing
Advertise used vehicles
Receive new vehicles
Put in service
Deliver out-of-service vehicles

0   1   2   3   4   5   6   7   8   9   10

Time in Months

FIGURE 6.4

Gantt Chart The chart shows the starting and ending dates of each element in a project.

Establish Timetable, Schedule Work

Once budget and resources have been allocated for the project, you must schedule the work to be done and establish a timetable for its completion. On complex projects, this may involve extensive planning and research, defining each beginning and ending segment of the project and examining interdependent relationships. For example, UniTrans will not want to dispose of its existing tractor-trailers until the replacements have been delivered and put into service. You may also want to plan a training schedule to familiarize drivers with the new vehicles. This is a subtask on your task list.

For many years the Gantt chart has been used to document project schedules. Figure 6.4 illustrates the Gantt chart you have prepared for this project. It shows the total time involved from the beginning of the project to its completion. The time that will be spent on each activity is shown in the form of a horizontal bar.

Track and Monitor Projects

Throughout the life of the project you must monitor its progress. Monitoring can be done in several ways. You can show actual time elapsed or consumed in an operation on the Gantt chart, sometimes in different colors. This becomes an easy visual reference of where each part of the project is on the schedule.

You may also issue progress reports. A progress report, shown in Fig. 6.5, conveys to management the status of each stage of the project. It also notes any problems that have occurred and the amount of money spent on the project to

FIGURE 6.5

Progress Report
The report describes
the project's status,
including any prob-
lems that have
occurred.

Project: VEHICLE REPLACEMENT PROGRAM

          PROGRESS REPORT

Analyst: A. Wang

Date: June 1, 1989

Report on Progress For Period Ending 5-31-89:

Vendors were contacted and proposals received by March
15. The proposals were responsive to our bid requests,
though prices appear higher than initially
anticipated.

Plans are under way to remove the 10 tractor-trailer
vehicles from service by 6-30.

Advertisements were placed in trade journals to dispose of the vehicles to be taken out of service. Several written and telephone inquiries were received
from potential buyers.

Contacts were made with our local bank and efforts to
finance the new vehicles are proceeding on schedule.

Anticipated Problems:

Initial indications suggest that the delivered price
of the new vehicles will be about 3 percent higher
than anticipated. This will require a slight increase
in the capital for the project.

The market for used tractor-trailer trucks appears
soft, and additional funds may be necessary to advertise and dispose of the used vehicles at the prices
estimated in the preliminary plans.

---

date. With this type of reporting system, manual tracking is limited. More efficient computer methods, discussed below, provide comprehensive budget and
financial statements.

Reports and Documentation

Upon the completion of the project, it is customary to make a final evaluation and present a report to management. The final report describes the steps
taken throughout the project and the extent to which goals have been achieved,

whether target dates were met, and whether the project fell short of or exceeded the budget. It also discusses problems and recommendations that will assist future planners in avoiding similar difficulties.

COMPUTER PROJECT MANAGEMENT

The computer has had a profound influence on project management, because it allows analysts to plan and manage projects carefully and assess their progress. In the 1950s and '60s, project planning and scheduling programs were developed for large computers. But with the proliferation of microcomputers in the 1980s, planning and scheduling software was developed for many small systems. This enabled sophisticated techniques to be implemented on inexpensive desktop computers. Let us first look at some of the more traditional programs available for large computers and then examine microcomputer software.

Critical Path Method (CPM)

Several computer techniques have been developed to find the most efficient way of **scheduling** the activities involved in a project. These techniques—**critical path method (CPM),** program evaluation and review technique (PERT), and network planning and scheduling—are all ways of showing the time required to complete each task in a project, and indicating the relationship between tasks. They allow the analyst to compare various task schedules to find the one that completes the project in the least amount of time.

The schedule produced by these planning techniques is shown in the form of a network. It represents the total time involved from the beginning of the project to its completion. Time spent on each activity is depicted as an arrow, and the completion point of the activity is indicated by a circle. Figure 6.6 is a time schedule for producing a technical manual. The critical path for this project is shown by the darker lines.

Often several activities that are relatively independent of each other can be done concurrently. They are shown by separate time lines on the schedule. A time delay in one of these independent elements will not usually affect the others.

Other activities are interdependent: activity A must be finished before activity B can be started; activity B must be completed before activity C can begin; and so on. A delay encountered while carrying out one of these dependent activities will retard implementation of all the other activities in that path.

A schedule may contain several paths with dependent activities. The path that represents the greatest time span is called the **critical path.** It represents the shortest possible time in which the project can be completed. A delay at any

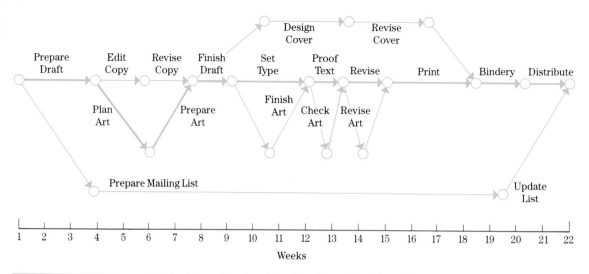

FIGURE 6.6

Critical Path Diagram The critical path is shown by the darker lines.

point in the critical path will adversely affect the entire schedule and delay completion of the project. For this reason, the activities in the critical path must be carefully planned and monitored during implementation to minimize disruptions or problems.

Budgeting Programs

About a decade ago, computer software was developed to facilitate budgeting and make complex economic projections. This software, known as **spreadsheet** analysis, is a form of electronic ledger sheet that enables managers and analysts to make projections. Some popular programs that provide this function include Lotus 1-2-3, MultiPlan, and SuperCalc4. Spreadsheets allow analysts to lay out columns of values in a matrix on the screen of a desktop computer. Each intersection of a column and a row is a **cell** in which data can be entered.

Let's see how you might use a spreadsheet to budget the project for UniTrans. Figure 6.7 illustrates a budget for the acquisition of the new tractor-trailers. It is based upon estimates obtained from research and discussions with truck dealers.

Using spreadsheet software, you enter all the figures as shown and enter formulas in each cell to perform computations. For example, you enter a formula that subtracts the salvage value from the new cost to compute net cost. The computer automatically totals the columns and generates a report. As the project moves forward, you can enter new values in the cells and have other cell values recalculated by the computer. Thus, you can quickly track deviations from the costs originally allocated to the project.

An extremely useful feature of spreadsheets is **what-if analysis.** What-if analysis enables you to change the project's basic assumptions and then have the computer recalculate all other values on the spreadsheet. For example, suppose management has budgeted $80,000 for each new vehicle. However, you find

#1	1	2	3	4	5	6	7
1		UNITRANS TRUCK FLEET BUDGET					
2		(Vehicle Replacement Program)					
3							
4	DESCR.	MILEAGE	COST NEW	SALVAGE	NET COST		
5							
6	Vehicle 1	67000	$80000	$15000	$65000		
7							
8	Vehicle 2	81000	80000	14500	65500		
9							
10	Vehicle 3	93000	80000	12500	67500		
11							
12	Vehicle 4	102000	80000	9500	70500		
13							
14	Vehicle 5	87000	80000	9500	70500		
15							
16	Vehicle 6	109000	80000	9000	71000		
17							
18	Vehicle 7	65000	80000	15500	64500		
19							
20	Vehicle 8	99500	80000	9100	70900		
21							
22	Vehicle 9	105500	80000	10500	69500		
23							
24	Vehicle 10	133000	80000	7900	72100		
25							
26	TOTALS	1076000	$800000	$113000	$687000		

FIGURE 6.7

Spreadsheet Program Columns show amounts budgeted for the acquisition of new equipment.

that because of price increases, each new vehicle will cost $85,000. Using what-if analysis, you enter the new values and direct the computer to recompute all other figures on the spreadsheet. The recalculated spreadsheet shown in Fig. 6.8 displays the new total net cost you must budget for tractor-trailers.

What-if analysis is useful to project directors, since it allows them to experiment with a variety of conditions, changing assumptions throughout the implementation of a project.

MICROCOMPUTER PROJECT MANAGEMENT SOFTWARE

Several programs that run on microcomputers have been developed specifically for project management. PROJECT, from Microsoft Corporation, and Project Scheduler Network (PSN), developed by Scitor Corporation, allow project data to be entered along with planning and control information and other param-

FIGURE 6.8

What-If Analysis
The figures have
been recomputed
based upon new
assumptions.

#1	1	2	3	4	5	6	7
1		UNITRANS TRUCK FLEET BUDGET					
2		(Revised Replacement Program)					
3							
4	DESCR.	MILEAGE	COST NEW	SALVAGE	NET COST		
5							
6	Vehicle 1	67000	$85000	$15000	$70000		
7							
8	Vehicle 2	81000	85000	14500	70500		
9							
10	Vehicle 3	93000	85000	12500	72500		
11							
12	Vehicle 4	102000	85000	9500	75500		
13							
14	Vehicle 5	87000	85000	9500	75500		
15							
16	Vehicle 6	109000	85000	9000	76000		
17							
18	Vehicle 7	65000	85000	15500	69500		
19							
20	Vehicle 8	99500	85000	9100	75900		
21							
22	Vehicle 9	105500	85000	10500	74500		
23							
24	Vehicle 10	133000	85000	7900	77100		
25							
26	TOTALS	1076000	$850000	$113000	$737000		

eters. These packages produce Gantt charts, scheduling calendars, and other management reports. The balance of this chapter describes Scitor's PSN in detail. The Scitor product runs on a desktop computer and can generate Gantt charts, labor cost reports, resource distribution cost reports, and other tables. The discussion will give you an overview of computerized project management techniques.

Scitor Project Scheduler Network (PSN)

The analyst provides information to PSN through a series of screens that it displays. PSN displays schedules and uses the critical path method (CPM) for analysis. It keeps track of the starting date and status of each job in a project and charts the components of a project on a time scale shown in days, weeks, or months. The software can perform what-if analysis, so the analyst can experiment with different data. The program recalculates the critical path and displays a new Gantt chart or network diagram for each modification. It also prints out a variety of reports and plotter graphics.

PROJECT CONSTANTS REPORT—Current Date: 08-30-87

PROJECT INFORMATION

PROJECT NAME:	SALES TERMINALS
MANAGER:	BOB CRANE
PROJECT START DATE:	01/01/88
PROJECT FINISH DATE:	03/25/88

CALENDAR INFORMATION

OVERALL START DATE:	Friday 01/01/88
WORK DAYS:	Monday Tuesday Wednesday Thursday Friday
TIME SCALE:	WEEK
NUMBER OF SHIFTS:	1
HOLIDAYS:	

FIGURE 6.9

Constants Screen
The screen shows constant data and holidays pertaining to the project.

Create the Project

Let's use PSN to manage another UniTrans Company project. UniTrans's management has approved a project called Sales Terminals that will equip one of its sales centers with 50 new computer terminals. The project is to be completed in three months, working a five-day week, single-shift schedule. It involves researching facilities, site design and preparation, installation, and so on. Bob Crane has been assigned as project director, and he has decided to use PSN.

Enter Constants and Holidays

Bob first enters the calendar information shown in Fig. 6.9. The screen shows the starting and finishing dates of the project, defines which days of the week will be work days, and gives the number of shifts.

Enter Resources

The next step involves entering into the computer a list of all resources that will be used throughout the project (see Fig. 6.10). This includes personnel and labor reserves as well as buyout costs and parts and materials. In setting up the project, Bob Crane enters each personnel category with the hourly rate that will be charged to the project. The hourly rate reflects the total cost to the enterprise, including taxes and overhead, for each hour of the resource listed.

FIGURE 6.10

Resources Data
All resources used
in the project are
entered on this
screen.

RESOURCE TABLE REPORT-Current Date: 08-30-87

NO.	RESOURCE NAME	UNIT COST	LABOR/ OTHER	AVAILABILITY
1	SUPERVISOR	55.00	L	0.00
2	SYSTEMS ANALYST	35.00	L	0.00
3	COMMUNICATIONS ANALYST	30.00	L	0.00
4	INSTALLER	25.00	L	0.00
5	DATA ENTRY	15.00	L	0.00
6	SUPPORT	15.00	L	0.00
7	BUYOUTS	70.00	O	0.00
8	PARTS-MATERIALS	40.00	O	0.00

Enter Job Information

In this step, Bob enters each task on the job information screen, followed by the number of hours (duration) it needs. Sometimes tasks are listed under major categories. Date dependencies may be entered. This establishes starting dates based upon predecessor jobs. In other words, it defines which jobs must be completed before succeeding tasks are begun. For example, in a construction project, framing and wall construction cannot begin until after the foundation has been poured.

Set Up the Network

Once all project information has been entered and resources have been assigned to tasks, Bob Crane instructs the computer to generate a visual network. The network, illustrated in Fig. 6.11, shows each step of the project as a network of nodes or points. It displays the starting and ending date of each phase of the project, as well as the relationship of each task or subtask.

The computer automatically calculates the critical path for the project. The critical path is the sequence of tasks that must be completed on schedule in order to finish the entire project on time.

FIGURE 6.11

Network Screen
The screen shows
each node in the
project network.

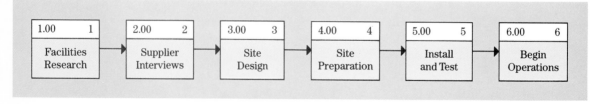

```
GANTT CHART REPORT-Current Date: 08-30-87

SALES TERMINALS          1988
                         JAN                    FEB              MAR
                         1    8    15   22   29  5    12   19   26   4    11   18
                         0    1    2    3    4   5    6    7    8    9    10   11
1.00 FACILITIES RESEARCH >==>.    .    .    .   .    .    .    .    .    .    .
2.00 SUPPLIER INTERVIEWS  .   >======>.   .    .   .    .    .    .    .    .    .
3.00 SITE DESIGN          .    .    .  >==========>.   .    .    .    .    .
4.00 SITE PREPARATION     .    .    .    .    .   .   >==========>.   .    .
5.00 INSTALL AND TEST     .    .    .    .    .   .    .    .    .  >======>.
6.00 BEGIN OPERATIONS     .    .    .    .    .   .    .    .    .    .    .  >==X

>##> Conflict
>::> Completed Duration
   | Milestone
__ Delay
>==> Critical
   X Terminator
>--> Baseline
>..> Noncritical
```

Generate Reports

PSN software is designed to generate a variety of reports. One such report is the Gantt chart, shown in Fig. 6.12. The Gantt chart shows each step of the project laid out across the page, with beginning and ending dates. In addition, the critical path is marked so managers can track important phases carefully.

A variety of other reports can be produced, including histograms, labor reports, and work distribution reports (see Fig. 6.13).

FIGURE 6.12

Project Report
Reports such as this Gantt chart show each step of the project as it progresses.

Modifying a Project

Frequently, projects fall behind schedule or—because of hard work and a measure of luck—are completed ahead of schedule. The PSN program allows the analyst to enter changed information at any point in the project. For example, beginning or ending dates may be changed and resource costs such as labor rates may be altered. Unexpected work stoppages may occur, or additional shifts may be assigned to the project. The analyst enters this information into the entry screens and the software immediately recomputes all other dependent variables. The program reconfigures reports, readjusts the Gantt chart, and revises the network on the screen. The entire project can be easily redesigned. Project scheduling software is a powerful tool for tracking complex projects more quickly and accurately than by manual means.

LABOR REPORT—Current Date: 08-30-87

PROJECT: SALES TERMINALS   DATE RANGE: 01/01/88-03/25/88

NO.	JOB NAME	UNITS	DATES	STATUS	SLACK
LABOR:	1				
1	FACILITIES RESEARCH	4.00	01/01/88-01/08/88	Critical	0
3	SITE DESIGN	9.00	01/22/88-02/12/88	Critical	0
4	SITE PREPARATION	36.00	02/12/88-03/04/88	Critical	0
5	INSTALL AND TEST	8.00	03/04/88-03/18/88	Critical	0
6	BEGIN OPERATIONS	1.00	03/18/88-03/25/88	Critical	0
LABOR:	2				
1	FACILITIES RESEARCH	8.00	01/01/88-01/08/88	Critical	0
2	SUPPLIER INTERVIEWS	4.00	01/08/88-01/22/88	Critical	0
3	SITE DESIGN	36.00	01/22/88-02/12/88	Critical	0
4	SITE PREPARATION	36.00	02/12/88-03/04/88	Critical	0
5	INSTALL AND TEST	8.00	03/04/88-03/18/88	Critical	0
6	BEGIN OPERATIONS	8.00	03/18/88-03/25/88	Critical	0
LABOR:	3				
1	FACILITIES RESEARCH	4.00	01/01/88-01/08/88	Critical	0
2	SUPPLIER INTERVIEWS	4.00	01/08/88-01/22/88	Critical	0
3	SITE DESIGN	36.00	01/22/88-02/12/88	Critical	0
6	BEGIN OPERATIONS	4.00	03/18/88-03/25/88	Critical	0
LABOR:	4				
4	SITE PREPARATION	72.00	02/12/88-03/04/88	Critical	0
5	INSTALL AND TEST	32.00	03/04/88-03/18/88	Critical	0
6	BEGIN OPERATIONS	1.00	03/18/88-03/25/88	Critical	0
LABOR:	5				
5	INSTALL AND TEST	8.00	03/04/88-03/18/88	Critical	0
6	BEGIN OPERATIONS	8.00	03/18/88-03/25/88	Critical	0
LABOR:	6				
3	SITE DESIGN	9.00	01/22/88-02/12/88	Critical	0
4	SITE PREPARATION	36.00	02/12/88-03/04/88	Critical	0
6	BEGIN OPERATIONS	2.00	03/18/88-03/25/88	Critical	0

FIGURE 6.13

Labor Report A
variety of reports
can be produced for
each project.

Now that we have studied how projects are managed, both manually and by computer, we will move on to the next step of the SDLC. In the next chapter we will study systems analysis and see how to analyze in-place systems in order to plan more efficient systems.

Summary

Project management is the coordination of all aspects of a project to ensure that it is completed on time and within assigned constraints. A project is a planned undertaking of scheduled activities to reach a goal or objective. A program is an ongoing endeavor to generate a series of products or reach a sequence of goals. A project may be managed by a director, a task force, or a consultant.

Projects fail because of lack of commitment on the part of management, conflicting goals, technology not being fully understood, or lack of experience on the part of the project manager.

Traditional project management followed a classical approach that did not rely upon the computer. Individuals were assigned to a project, specific goals and budget were defined, a timetable was worked out, and then the project was tracked and reports generated.

The computer has become a valuable tool in project management. It is used for scheduling and finding the critical path. Spreadsheet software is used for budgeting and making complex economic projections. Spreadsheets also perform what-if analysis.

Computerized project management follows a sequence of steps. It involves creating the project and entering constants, holidays, and resources. Then job information is entered and a network set up. Various reports about the project can be produced.

Key Terms

Cell	**Project team**
Critical path	**Scheduling**
Critical path method (CPM)	**Spreadsheet**
Program	**Task list**
Project	**What-if analysis**
Project management	

Exercises

1. Define the term *project*.
2. Define the term *project management*.
3. Give some reasons why projects fail.
4. Prepare a project management task list.
5. Discuss the advantages of hiring a project consultant.
6. Discuss how projects are tracked and monitored.
7. Describe the critical path method of scheduling.
8. Describe how spreadsheets are used in budgeting.
9. Summarize how microcomputer project management software functions.
10. Contrast projects and programs.

Projects

1. Visit a project management site, such as a building under construction or a business system being installed, and discuss project management with the supervisor.

2. Visit a consultant and discuss project management concepts. What services does the consultant provide?

3. Visit a computer store that sells programs and software. Make a list of the major pieces of project management software that are offered for sale.

4. If project management software is available on your campus, obtain a copy and familiarize yourself with it. Execute any tutorial or instructional software provided with the program.

5. Conduct a class project that involves project management software. Obtain the necessary software, set up a project, print out a network schedule, and generate one or more reports.

ANALYST AT WORK

EDELMAN ENGINEERING

DESCRIPTION OF FIRM

Edelman Engineering designs and constructs large commercial and industrial projects. The firm's most recent undertakings include a local area network facility for a finance company, a computer data center for a manufacturing plant, and a communications network and dispatch facility for a city government. Over the years Edelman Engineering has gathered a staff of skilled project engineers, designers, and communications specialists. These employees are experts in office and facilities design and project management.

Many large business and industrial firms call upon Edelman Engineering to do the design and planning for the physical sites of new facilities. This often involves major alterations to physical plants, installation of air conditioning equipment, and provisions for communications and electrical power.

Some of Edelman's contracts have liquidated damages clauses. This means that if a project is not completed on time, Edelman Engineering must pay the client a specific amount for each day of delay. These damages can run into tens of thousands of dollars, so it is necessary to keep projects on a critical timetable. Some contracts provide bonuses for work completed below estimated costs. Therefore, time and money are major considerations in Edelman Engineering's project scheduling.

SYSTEM OVERVIEW

A large insurance company has contracted with Edelman Engineering to do the site planning and installation for a data communications network facility. The network is to link branch offices with their home office. Edelman Engineering must design and schedule the physical plant alterations on the existing premises. A 4000-square-foot room, formerly used for clerical and office purposes, must be converted to house the communications center. Figure 6.14 is a data flow diagram that illustrates some of the functions of the new communications center. The center will handle switching for the terminals located in the insurance company's branch offices. It will also maintain a database of clients and produce reports to be sent to agents in the branch offices.

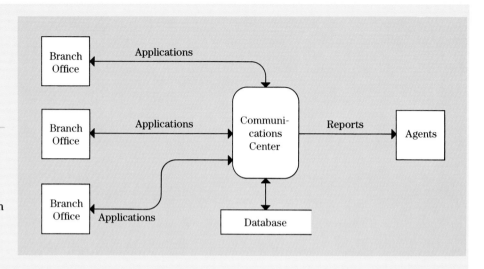

FIGURE 6.14

Communications Center Branch offices are linked to a home office, which maintains a database and generates reports.

HANDS-ON APPLICATION

You have been given the task of managing the design and installation of the new communications facilities for the insurance company. You are responsible for the entire project, including contractual relations with suppliers and the final system checkout. Figure 6.15 illustrates the major steps in the construction and checkout of the new communications center.

Begin by preparing a task list that shows the major steps you will follow in managing the project. Enter your task list below.

TASK LIST

_____

_____

_____

FIGURE 6.15

Steps in Design and Implementation of Communications Center Each task must be completed in time in order to finish the project on schedule.

_____

_____

_____

_____

| Engineering and Design | → | Rough Site Preparation | → | Finish Site Preparation | → | Test Hardware and Facilities | → | Optimize and Fine-Tune Facilities |

Work Product No. 1   Prepare a Gantt chart showing the major steps and timetable in the installation of the new system. Assume you have a total of six months to complete the entire installation. Your Gantt chart should show starting and ending dates of each step shown in Fig. 6.15. Label this document WP1, Chapter 6.

Work Product No. 2   Prepare a resources list for the project. This list should identify the various purchases, buyouts, and other requirements to complete the design and construction of the communications center. Label this document WP2, Chapter 6. You may prepare a task list to organize this effort. Enter your task list below.

TASK LIST

_____

_____

_____

_____

_____

_____

Work Product No. 3   Since this project will involve a variety of skilled and unskilled labor, it will be helpful to prepare a specialized report detailing the major labor costs. Refer to Fig. 6.13 for a sample of this type of report. Complete a labor report and label it WP3, Chapter 6. You can organize this effort by preparing a task list. Enter your task list below.

TASK LIST

_____

_____

_____

_____

_____

_____

THE
ANALYSIS
PHASE

SYSTEMS ANALYSIS PRINCIPLES

LEARNING OBJECTIVES

After studying this chapter, you should be able to:

1. Discuss quantitative systems assessments.

2. List systems study and investigation techniques.

3. Discuss overall systems interrelationships.

4. Describe systems constraints and limitations.

5. Discuss time and motion studies.

6. Describe communications traffic surveys.

Systems analysis is a key step in the analytical process because it establishes reference points by which a new system can be measured or improvements to an old system evaluated. Without the information gathered in this phase, there is no way of knowing whether new hardware, personnel, or communications facilities improve a system.

Once problems have been diagnosed and the decision made to move forward with a project, the systems analyst is faced with choices. Is it better to make improvements in an existing system, or to design a new one from the ground up? If a system already exists, the analyst must study its characteristics and parameters before proceeding.

This chapter describes systems analysis, the second phase of the systems development life cycle (SDLC). Systems analysis is the detailed investigation of an in-place system in order to understand its operation. It consists of work sampling, time studies, interviews, questionnaires, reviewing records and documents, and other fact-finding techniques.

QUANTITATIVE ASSESSMENTS

Systems analysts can solve problems more effectively if they gather information through interviews, observations, audits, and questionnaires and then put this data in quantitative terms. **Quantitative** expressions reduce variables to numbers or discrete terms, while **qualitative** assessments describe conditions in general and subjective terms. By expressing customer complaints, delivery schedules, orders on backlog, orders processed, and the like as amounts, the analyst can measure performance accurately. The direction and magnitude of a change is charted with greater precision and its cost effectiveness more easily assessed when characteristics are reduced to minutes and hours, or dollars and cents.

FACT-FINDING TECHNIQUES

There are numerous methods of gathering the data necessary for analyzing, studying, and redesigning an in-place system. These tools are used to define the elements of a system quantitatively, describe the nature of a problem, and obtain the information necessary for its solution.

Interviews

The interview is a useful tool for gathering data on activities, attitudes, and opinions. Using structured and unstructured interview techniques, the investigator talks to employees, customers, and management, carefully recording responses. Later, the data gathered will be analyzed, categorized, compared, interpreted, and quantified.

The investigator often poses the six classical questions usually asked by journalists to get the facts of a story:

1. *Who?* This question attempts to identify people, roles, and responsibilities. Who does this operation? Who is in charge? Who exhibits the best performance?

2. *What?* This question is used to learn about the elements involved in a procedure or system. What activities are conducted in this department? Through what steps does the paperwork move? What kinds of programs and computers are used? What are the workers' attitudes toward the tasks?

3. *Why?* This question searches for the purpose of an operation and the reasons behind existing attitudes. Why is a job done in a particular way? Why is an operation done at all? Why do employees support or resist a specific change?

4. *When?* This question investigates time elements. How much time does it take to do a given job? When is it finished? When are errors most likely to occur?

5. *Where?* This question is concerned with physical location. Where are computers and workstations located? Where are disks and information stored?

6. *How?* This question uncovers the sequence of steps followed in doing a job. How is a routine done? How are activities performed? How does an employee learn his or her skill?

Types of Interviews

Interviews may be conducted in several ways. One of the most common techniques is the face-to-face interview. In this approach, the analyst sets up an appointment with one or more individuals and obtains information through discussion and questioning.

A second method is the telephone interview. In this arrangement, the systems analyst places telephone calls to employees, managers, customers, vendors, and others. It is usually less expensive to conduct a telephone interview rather than a face-to-face discussion, since travel costs are eliminated.

It may not be possible to interview all the individuals involved in a system study. Therefore, some form of selection and sampling procedure is necessary. Samples may be drawn from particular departments or employee classifications.

How to Conduct an Interview

The systems analyst should first decide whether to use a structured or unstructured technique (see Fig. 7.1). In a **structured interview,** prepared questions are asked in a specific sequence. A given amount of time may be

FIGURE 7.1

Unstructured Versus Structured Interview

UNSTRUCTURED INTERVIEW

Greater flexibility
Wide-ranging questions
Difficult to evaluate results
Possibility of overlooking key questions
Opportunity to redirect interview while questioning
No fixed sequence of questions
Experienced interviewer required

STRUCTURED INTERVIEW

Prepared sequence of questions
Easier to evaluate results
Inflexible format
Questions limited to predefined areas
Simpler and easier to conduct
Time required to prepare structured questions
Less experienced interviewer required

allotted for various blocks of questions. **Unstructured interviews,** while more flexible, make it difficult to draw conclusions, since interviewees may be asked different questions.

Set up appointments to give interviewees time to prepare, and tell them the purpose of the meeting. Be polite, tactful, and objective throughout the discussion. Here are some suggestions to follow when conducting an interview:

- Frame questions so that they are unambiguous and easily understood.
- Allow adequate time for the interviewee to respond.
- Take written notes of responses.
- Work through the interview systematically and unhurriedly.
- Don't lead or bias the interviewee's answers.
- Ask broad questions first and then narrow down to specifics.
- Don't be argumentative. If you are adversarial, the interviewee will provide less information than if you are supportive and unthreatening.
- Provide an opportunity for the interviewee to make additional comments before you conclude the interview.

Advantages and Limitations of the Interview

Interviews are sometimes the only way to obtain information about a system. However, the analyst may spend many days or weeks on interviews. This increases the cost of a system study. Sometimes the analyst's personal bias may color or distort the interview. Interviews based upon a poor sampling may generate inaccurate answers, which in turn lead to systems that malfunction.

Productive interviews require the use of a trained and experienced systems analyst. However, other fact-finding techniques may be less costly and in the long run better than an interview.

UniTrans Interview

Figure 7.2 is an excerpt from an interview conducted by a UniTrans analyst. The analyst is gathering information on the workload and responsibilities of personnel in the secretarial services department in order to design an improved word processing system. You can see how the six key questions are used to draw out the interviewee.

Interviews such as these yield facts as well as insights into the interviewee's attitudes and feelings about the job, fellow workers, and superiors. The investigator uses the facts to build a picture of the interrelated elements of the system. It is difficult to improve a system without thoroughly understanding its nature, strengths, weaknesses, and problems. The insights gathered from interviews enable the systems analyst to assess the behavioral responses of those involved in day-to-day work activities. Attitudes are as important to the success of a system as the physical tasks the employees perform.

Direct Observation

Another important means of gathering data is by **direct observation.** This technique enables the systems analyst to obtain additional knowledge somewhat more objectively than by conducting personal interviews. Both viewpoints are, of course, helpful for a complete understanding of a system.

The analyst attempts to answer the same six questions asked in interviews when making direct observations, keeping careful notes and records. He or she personally observes all aspects of a system, watching as people perform their tasks; noting such details as what they do, where they do it, and how long it takes; examining forms, documents, equipment, and manuals; and observing the physical flow of movement as personnel go from one workstation to another.

The **random clock** observation technique is a common application of this method. At random times throughout the day (determined by a chart such as the one shown in Fig. 7.3) the analyst observes and records work activities. This technique permits sampling the activities of many days or weeks and condensing them into a short, precise form for further study.

Selecting subjects for observation is an important consideration in obtaining accurate results. Analysts frequently use the same sampling techniques for selecting individuals to be observed as those to be interviewed. As with the face-to-face interview, direct observation can be an expensive means of collecting data.

FIGURE 7.2

Excerpt From UniTrans Interview

INTERVIEW NOTES

Project: NEW WORD PROCESSING SYSTEM

Analyst: R. Goldberg   **Interviewee:** Jean Dolan

Date: September 2, 1989   **Department:** Secretarial Services

---

Q: How long have you worked with the present word processing equipment in your department?

A: About three years.

Q: When was the word processing equipment originally installed?

A: About four years ago.

Q: Who has had the responsibility for maintaining the equipment and seeing that it is properly serviced?

A: My immediate supervisor, Ms. Marks.

Q: What kinds of problems are you experiencing with the equipment?

A: The printer is very slow. It requires frequent maintenance and ribbon changes. This slows down our operators and reduces our output.

We often have to call in the maintenance people to repair the keyboards. Keys often malfunction.

Many of our operators complain of eyestrain because of the position of the monitors, which are not located in the line of sight.

Q: If new equipment were to be installed, when would be the best time to do the work? When are your slow months?

A: I would recommend August, since our volume is low during that month.

Advantages and Limitations of Direct Observation

While direct observation can provide a firsthand opportunity to see a system in action, it can be expensive and lead to erroneous conclusions. Direct observation is sometimes the only way to monitor the behavior of individuals in a system. However, people who are the subject of a study may behave differently from those who are not. Therefore, the analyst must be sure that observations are conducted unobtrusively so that the fact finding is not biased.

10:29	8:00	9:11	11:55	4:04	1:19	10:35	8:05
1:10	8:16	4:22	4:29	2:17	8:25	3:53	11:38
2:07	10:40	3:48	10:10	11:46	2:15	3:25	11:49
3:01	10:46	9:08	4:42	2:09	3:45	2:51	11:57
11:36	8:30	9:35	4:20	11:51	4:06	1:40	11:50
9:50	2:47	3:59	2:24	11:31	8:10	11:42	3:36
10:17	10:12	8:15	8:38	9:42	10:19	3:04	1:33
2:03	10:41	10:53	1:38	2:19	9:06	11:34	11:13
4:37	1:28	11:11	2:41	9:38	1:27	4:56	8:47
2:20	2:25	10:52	1:02	9:12	9:46	4:01	1:56
9:56	9:51	10:23	9:23	8:54	3:22	4:23	1:51
4:55	2:38	11:32	2:46	8:45	4:21	1:29	4:19
1:20	1:04	9:39	9:45	10:02	3:14	9:07	11:10
2:02	8:50	10:43	10:18	8:12	9:37	3:30	10:58
1:34	2:27	3:49	10:09	10:34	11:54	1:01	9:17
2:54	10:27	8:20	3:31	9:32	3:44	2:18	3:43
2:10	11:53	11:09	4:28	4:09	4:25	4:24	8:03
9:16	11:16	2:06	4:18	8:33	4:12	2:26	11:39
4:47	11:37	2:08	9:54	3:52	9:31	11:05	10:22
9:10	8:35	8:06	2:28	8:36	2:33	3:24	10:28
4:38	11:58	8:19	11:59	2:21	2:52	8:44	2:55
9:04	9:20	9:58	1:26	4:46	3:17	10:03	2:34
8:41	10:38	2:00	3:57	1:16	10:42	11:26	3:09
3:00	11:06	11:56	10:11	1:37	1:18	2:23	8:49
9:40	9:05	4:16	3:54	8:58	1:46	8:11	1:48
4:13	2:53	3:20	8:22	11:00	4:30	2:16	3:05
8:17	2:40	8:42	4:43	3:40	4:46	1:42	8:31
3:30	10:00	10:47	9:36	11:47	11:52	3:56	3:03
1:39	3:10	8:46	1:58	4:49	9:59	2:29	1:54
9:28	4:36	9:30	10:32	4:40	10:33	11:02	8:40
9:43	2:42	9:53	2:36	3:38	10:31	8:59	3:33
3:12	1:47	2:37	4:51	11:29	9:00	8:14	11:24
8:07	4:27	9:47	2:50	9:15	8:37	10:20	9:26
8:34	1:13	3:27	1:17	3:26	9:13	11:01	3:06
1:00	1:23	2:58	4:00	4:34	1:52	3:32	3:50
10:07	4:52	11:25	3:58	10:36	9:14	10:16	11:19
11:30	10:24	11:45	10:30	1:39	4:30	2:30	1:21
3:19	9:18	4:32	11:44	10:37	1:55	8:23	8:01
11:03	3:08	3:34	8:48	3:16	2:45	3:41	11:41
1:05	10:45	1:57	10:08	4:45	3:55	10:48	2:21
9:19	9:33	10:15	1:11	10:57	10:25	9:03	10:54
11:28	8:51	3:18	1:14	3:23	3:42	9:22	1:41
8:02	11:33	4:58	3:02	11:47	8:53	4:08	9:09
9:01	4:05	10:59	8:32	11:07	2:39	1:32	10:05
9:41	11:21	2:56	2:48	4:50	4:31	4:14	1:22
9:48	8:29	3:21	8:28	3:46	11:14	1:30	9:55
1:53	4:33	1:07	10:56	8:43	8:24	1:50	3:29
2:49	1:24	9:02	3:47	11:35	10:39	9:29	9:57
3:35	1:25	2:32	8:39	3:51	11:43	3:07	3:11
4:27	10:44	4:53	10:13	8:18	4:35	8:08	4:41
1:45	11:18	8:57	2:04	1:36	10:49	4:39	11:48
8:09	4:15	8:56	9:24	1:44	9:44	4:07	11:23
1:03	4:59	1:59	2:22	1:06	1:31	10:55	2:31
10:14	4:57	2:14	2:35	8:27	3:13	10:50	4:26
1:09	4:54	10:01	8:52	10:26	1:15	8:04	11:20
2:57	8:55	1:43	4:10	10:51	9:34	1:49	11:08
2:05	11:12	4:44	8:13	2:01	4:11	10:21	4:17
3:28	1:08	10:06	2:11	2:43	2:44	11:15	2:59

FIGURE 7.3

Random Clock Chart This chart lists random times throughout the business day.

(Source: The Office)

FIGURE 7.4

Task Breakdown

Talking to fellow employees	15%
Using telephone	15%
Typing and keyboarding	30%
Resting	10%
Operating computer	20%
Miscellaneous unaccounted	10%
TOTAL	100%

The Hawthorne Effect

The results of a study done during the 1920s illustrate the complexity of making accurate observations. Psychologist Elton Mayo was studying a group of relay assemblers in the Hawthorne, Chicago plant of Western Electric Company, with the goal of increasing productivity. He performed a series of tests in which he manipulated elements in the working environment—changing lighting levels and work groups, altering rest periods, and so on.

The final evaluation showed quite unexpected results. Mayo had anticipated that productivity would go up as environmental conditions improved and would go down as they declined. What actually happened was that the productivity of the study group went up regardless of what changes were made. Mayo concluded that the knowledge that they are involved in a study and are being monitored affects people's actions and output. This phenomenon is known as the **Hawthorne effect.** You should be aware of the psychological implications of this reaction when considering human elements in systems design.

UniTrans Observation

Figure 7.4 illustrates a breakdown of tasks developed by the analyst at UniTrans who observed an employee in the secretarial services department. The analyst sought to obtain information about a typical work day. Quantitatively breaking down tasks, as shown in the figure, may be helpful in designing a system.

Review of Documentation

Another tool of the systems investigator is the methodical study of the official documents used in a system. The investigator obtains copies of policy and procedure manuals, personnel guides, bulletins, reports, official forms, and similar documents, examines their functions, and follows their movement throughout the organization (see Fig. 7.5). A review of this type gives an indication of whether the operations of a system reflect official goals, and it helps to pinpoint existing omissions, weaknesses, and errors.

Audits

An **audit** of records, ledgers, files, databases, memos, and other pieces of information can uncover a considerable amount of information about the elements of a system and how they interrelate. This is often done by requesting personnel to save or prepare a copy of all working documents, computer disks, notes, or records generated over a given period, say several days or weeks. Special provisions must often be made to gather information from elements such as communications circuits and display terminals.

This information is analyzed and used in several different ways; for example, to study data flow patterns or to rate the efficiency, value, or weaknesses of forms. Data gathered in this way can be used to understand a work distribution pattern. A typical breakdown for a secretarial services worker might look like the one in Fig. 7.6, showing the number and types of documents prepared or handled by an employee in one day. Such information serves as an excellent guide for the systems designer when selecting computers and communications equipment for a particular workstation.

Questionnaires

The use of **questionnaires** is another way to gather information about a system. Employees, customers, managers and others may be asked to complete questionnaires designed to focus on general or specific problems. Short answer, true or false, fill-in, checklist, and multiple choice questions are valuable for eliciting specific data on a particular problem. These types of questionnaires are easiest for respondents to complete. Essay-type questions are often used to gather information of a more general nature or to make an assessment of attitudes and interests.

However, questionnaires may not draw out sufficient information. For example, a question such as "Is Time Card Form 23 adequate for your needs?" may not elicit the kind of information that will help improve the form. It does not allow the user to express dissatisfaction with specific elements on the form. A better approach is to ask the user to modify a form or mark specific changes.

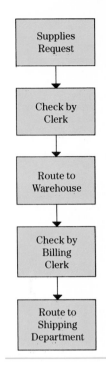

FIGURE 7.5

Record Movement This diagram traces forms as they travel throughout the organization.

Letters typed	6
Reports corrected	2
Memos typed	8
Computer printouts generated	9
Documents proofread	25
Documents filed	11

FIGURE 7.6

Audit Report This report shows a typical breakdown of tasks for one employee.

FIGURE 7.7

Questionnaire Checklist A checklist such as this assists in preparing the final questionnaire.

CHECKLIST

The following items will be incorporated into the paperwork questionnaire:

Name of analyst
Date to return questionnaire
Document name
Document number
Number of pages in document
Color of stock
Is form still needed?
How is form routed in department?
Are additional copies needed?
Open-ended question to solicit comments on form improvements
Name of respondent
Date questionnaire completed

How To Develop Questionnaires

First, decide what kind of information you want to gather. You can prepare a checklist to assist in designing the questionnaire (see Fig. 7.7) so that you will not overlook any items. The checklist also helps you place questions in the proper sequence.

Next, plan the best way to gather the facts. Choose the type of questions—fill-in, multiple choice, etc.—that will provoke answers about your specific problem. Prepare a draft of the questionnaire. State the questions clearly, in the best sequence, and provide adequate space for the answers. Eliminate any unnecessary or confusing questions. Make changes and modify the draft as necessary.

An essential element is the scoring and answer evaluation. Be sure the questionnaire can be easily scored. Avoid check boxes buried in the middle of paragraphs or questions requiring answers that cannot be quantified or categorized into some form of meaningful data. If you distribute a large number of questionnaires, you should have them scored by machine.

Test the questionnaire on a group of subjects. Ask them to complete the questionnaire and to mark questions that are confusing or that cannot be answered precisely. Make any needed modifications in the draft. Proofread the final document carefully before it is printed and distributed.

UniTrans Questionnaire

Figure 7.8 is a paperwork questionnaire used by UniTrans's analysts to gather information on their system. This type of questionnaire would enable an analyst to determine the flow of particular documents throughout a system. It includes fill-in, checklist, and short answer questions.

PAPERWORK QUESTIONNAIRE

Your assistance is requested by the Systems Department in identifying problems in the handling of paperwork in your department. Please complete this questionnaire and return to:

Systems Analyst ___W. Ryan___ Return by ___August 8, 1989___

DOCUMENT DISTRIBUTION

Name of Document _____

Document No. _____ No. of Pages _____ Color _____

The attached document is regularly distributed to you in the chain of distribution. We would like to simplify our paperwork processing and reduce handling and operating costs. Please look over the attached form and determine if you need to receive copies of the report.

_____ This form is no longer needed or used by us. Discontinue distributing to me.

_____ This form is needed. Please keep me on distribution list.

_____ Form is read and not filed.

_____ Form is filed in department.

_____ Additional copies of form should be provided when it is distributed to me.

Please describe ways in which the attached form can be changed or improved to increase its utility. You may mark up the attached document and return it with this form.

Comments:

Submitted by _____ Date _____

FIGURE 7.8

Questionnaire
This form is used to gather information about a system.

Time and Motion Studies

Another method of fact finding, dating back to the early efforts of efficiency experts, is the **time and motion study.** This technique attempts to document and accurately measure the clock times and physical motions involved in performing a given task. Stopwatches and cameras are frequently used. Slow motion and single-frame projections of recorded motions are valuable for analyzing the steps involved in the various operations.

UniTrans Time and Motion Study

The manager of UniTrans's retail sales department wishes to improve the procedures for handling packages at one of the firm's package depots. Customers often bring shipments directly to these depots, where the packages are weighed, forms are completed, and the customer pays the clerk or puts the charges on an open account.

Several techniques could be used to gain information on this operation. An analyst could use a video camera with a telephoto lens focused on a workstation. The camera is located in an unobtrusive spot away from the clerk. Stop-motion cameras are equipped with circuitry that projects the image of a digital stopwatch, shown in Fig. 7.9, on each frame of the tape, recording the actions along with the times required for their performance. The data from these tapes gives clues for changes in procedures and physical arrangements. After the redesigned system is implemented, the same camera equipment can be used to document the new procedures and determine the actual time savings that result.

FIGURE 7.9

Time and Motion Study The camera time-stamps each frame of the film.

Dictation	14 min.	
Keyboarding	13 min.	
Proofing	5 min.	
Computer printout	6 min.	
Preparing envelope	2 min.	
	40 min. @ $12/hr. = $8.00	
Stationery		.46
Postage		.25
Supplies		.20
TOTAL		$8.91

FIGURE 7.10

Cost Analysis This breakdown reports the costs involved in producing a typical letter.

Cost Analysis

Cost analysis is an examination of the elements of a system based on the cost of processing a given unit of work. Discrete tasks such as keyboarding a letter, processing a phone inquiry, or making a database inquiry are analyzed and measured to establish quantitative standards for comparison and study. This technique involves breaking a procedure down into its fundamental operations and determining the costs for each operation. Figure 7.10 shows the cost breakdown of preparing a typical one-page letter. Later, the costs for various procedures are calculated by adding the costs of the individual operations involved. Cost predictions can be made from these figures and then compared to the actual costs incurred.

Statistical Analysis

Other types of information describing a system can be gathered using **statistical analysis** techniques and a computer. This type of quantitative data provides an excellent way to report on the operation and functioning of a system.

Statistical analysis might be applied to measure time delays encountered on the telephone switchboard at various times throughout the day. The analyst might place periodic calls and record the time that elapses before each call is processed. The quality and accuracy of reports produced by the word processing department might be monitored by a careful review of a sample selected at random from the day's output.

Analysts routinely keep records on the speed and quality of the service delivered by a system. They sample such things as peak loads, delivery delays, and service bottlenecks. Comparing these figures with those of other periods enables them to monitor the performance of a system over various intervals of time. They use statistical analysis to keep track of average service call backlogs, customer waiting time at counters, backorder delays, or other problem areas. Other statistical techniques such as correlations, chi-square, and regression analysis help uncover relationships not readily apparent from a cursory examination of the data.

FIGURE 7.11

Population and Sample The sample is a smaller representation of the population.

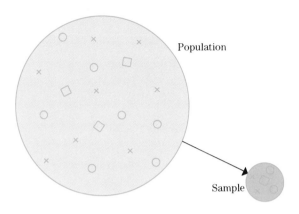

Population

Sample

Sampling Methods

Sampling techniques are widely used in systems analysis to learn the characteristics of a population without examining each individual case. Sampling is used to survey public opinion and employee attitudes, to check the quality of manufactured goods, and to gather information on in-place systems.

Statisticians have developed several reliable ways of selecting samples that are truly representative of a larger group. A **population** comprises all the cases under study, while a **sample** refers to a selected number of units or elements that is representative of the study group (see Fig. 7.11). The size of the sample need not be large to produce accurate results; rather, the sample must be representative of the population being studied. The information gained is assumed to be true of the entire population. Sampling is used where the population under study is very large and it would be too expensive or time consuming to examine each individual case.

Random Sampling   In **random sampling,** all members of a population have an equal chance of being selected for the sample. This method can be used in any situation where all the elements in a group (or numbers representing the elements) are available for selection at the same time. It could be used to sample the kinds of complaints being received by UniTrans's customer service department, without analyzing each individual complaint.

Systematic Sampling   In **systematic sampling,** samples are selected from a group according to an organized pattern; for example, every fifth or tenth complaint. Usually the first element in the sample is selected in a random manner, the rest according to the systematic pattern. If the pattern is every fifth complaint and the first element selected at random was 9, then the second element would be 14, the third, 19, and so on.

Stratified Sampling   **Stratified sampling** is used to obtain a more accurate representation of each subgroup in a population than a random sampling can provide. Suppose a survey was planned of all employees of a firm and it was important that each department be represented in the sample. The elements in the sample could be selected at random, but the analyst could not be absolutely sure that each department was represented. But if all the employees (the population) were first divided into departments (stratified) and a few selected at random from each stratum, the analyst could be sure that each group was represented in the final sample.

In this instance, a smaller number of samples would produce more precise and accurate representation than would random sampling. This method has even more value when the cost for selecting and examining each sample is an important factor.

Cluster Sampling **Cluster sampling,** also called area sampling, is used to cover a large geographic area. The population is first divided into small areas or groups. Then a certain number of these groups are selected by systematic or random sampling methods. The final sample is chosen from the selected groups by systematic or random sampling. Cluster sampling is often used for marketing surveys. It is less accurate than the other methods, but it may be more convenient and economical.

Quota Sampling **Quota sampling** is structured so that a specified number of representatives from each group are included in the final sample. For example, the analyst may be asked to interview five members from the marketing department, two from the communications department, and two from the advertising department.

Communications Traffic Survey

A **traffic survey** is a technique used to analyze the communications links that tie together the parts of a system. UniTrans relies heavily on telephone and data transmission circuits to interconnect offices, branches, and departments of the company. Good communications must be maintained, costs kept low, and disruptions held to a minimum. UniTrans has leased many telephone circuits and uses common carriers to link its facilities. However, communications links frequently create bottlenecks for UniTrans, limiting the flow of information between offices.

UT

The traffic survey is a valuable tool in such situations to pinpoint problems and document throughput. **Throughput** is a measure of the volume of traffic handled by communications circuits. It is usually measured in **transmission rate of information bits (*TRIB*).** The faster the computers, transmission equipment, and facilities, the greater the volume of traffic or number of bits of data that can be handled. The number and types of messages transmitted, their destinations and duration, and line charges for a period of time are carefully recorded. This information is invaluable in producing an overall picture of the communications flow in a given system.

A thorough traffic survey will study and document message response time. The **response time** is the amount of lapsed time between the completion

FIGURE 7.12		EXISTING SYSTEM	NEW SYSTEM
Facilities Inventory This inventory lists in-place and proposed new facilities.	Microcomputers	2	12
	Typewriters	14	3
	Tables, worktops	13	9
	Desks, chairs	12	12
	Telephone stations	21	19
	Microfiche readers	0	3
	Disk storage cabinets	0	1
	File cabinets	14	6

of entering a request for information and the start of receiving an answer. As a rule, the greater the volume of information handled, the slower the system's response time. Analysts must look at slow periods as well as peak periods and then try to determine system averages.

Some errors are bound to occur whenever messages are handled or routed. The **error rate** should be documented for a given system. Manual processing generally exhibits a higher error rate than computerized processing. Further, error rates tend to decline as an operator gains experience at a task.

Facilities Inventory

Organizations sometimes invest hundreds of thousands of dollars in office facilities, computers, terminals, communications equipment, and other hardware. It is helpful for the analyst to have a clear picture of this investment before making changes. **Facilities inventories** are often prepared to describe in-place systems (see Fig. 7.12). After the changeover is made, the new system is inventoried. In this way the analyst can compare capital costs and determine how much of the organization's money is tied up in equipment or made available for other purposes because of the new system, which may be less capital intensive.

EFFECTS ON ENTIRE ORGANIZATION

Another important aspect of systems investigation is the study of the interrelationships of the parts of the system. The analyst must predict the effects that changing one part of a system will have on other parts. How will new equipment affect cost factors? How will morale be affected if the organization is restructured? What other parts of the system will be affected if inventory and credit department data is shifted from large computers to small ones?

The human element is always a major part of a system that must be considered whenever changes or alterations take place. But since people do not always respond predictably, it is often the most difficult one to assess and evaluate.

DETERMINING CONSTRAINTS AND PARAMETERS OF SYSTEMS

Few systems operate without constraints, and a major portion of the analyst's time is spent in defining and evaluating them. Business resources are limited. The analyst must know how much money, time, personnel, equipment, or facilities should be applied to solve a particular problem. The rate of tolerable errors and length of time delays must also be determined.

The demands placed upon a system must be considered before attempting any changes or modifications. For example, UniTrans cannot arbitrarily close down one of its retail package dropoff depots or abandon one of its important package delivery routes for several weeks to change or update its equipment. Other arrangements that take these responsibilities into consideration will have to be made.

Most business systems cannot be closed or put out of service for any length of time without some economic consequences. The systems analyst must predict these consequences and plan for them when altering a system or installing a new one. It is often necessary to develop backup or alternative systems for use while the original system is being modified.

In this chapter, we have looked at the tools and techniques used to develop an accurate picture of an in-place system, its functions, and its problems. With this information in mind, the analyst can go on to design a new or better system. The next chapter describes basic design considerations.

Summary

Systems analysis, the second phase of the SDLC, is the detailed investigation of an in-place system. This includes work sampling, time studies, interviews, reviews of records and documents, and both quantitative and qualitative assessments.

Interviews ask the six classical questions: who, what, why, when, where, and how. Interviews yield facts about workers' attitudes and feelings about a system. Direct observations are also made, and they may be scheduled using a random clock table.

The analyst reviews documents; audits records, files, and databases; circulates questionnaires; and conducts various time and motion studies, cost analysis, and statistical analysis. Common methods include random, systematic, stratified, cluster, and quota sampling.

Communications traffic studies measure throughput, response time, and error rates. The Hawthorne effect should be considered to ensure that individuals under study are being evaluated objectively.

Key Terms

Audit	**Error rate**
Cluster sampling	**Facilities inventory**
Cost analysis	**Hawthorne effect**
Direct observation	**Population**

Qualitative	Structured interview
Quantitative	Systematic sampling
Questionnaire	Throughput
Quota sampling	Time and motion study
Random clock	Traffic survey
Random sampling	Transmission rate of information bits (TRIB)
Response time	
Sample	Unstructured interview
Statistical analysis	
Stratified sampling	

Exercises

1. Contrast quantitative and qualitative data collection.
2. What are the six classical questions used to obtain information about a system?
3. Discuss how questionnaires are used to gather information.
4. Discuss the kinds of data collected using a communications traffic survey.
5. What is throughput?
6. Describe the advantages of a facilities inventory.
7. Describe how the random clock observation technique is used in system study.
8. How are time and motion studies used in analyzing a system?
9. What is the Hawthorne effect and how does it affect system results?
10. List four major sampling methods.

Projects

1. Perform a direct observation analysis on some activity or function in which you are involved. Use the random clock chart and record observations and activities. Summarize your conclusions.
2. Prepare a questionnaire. Collect data on the attitudes of fellow students regarding their degree of satisfaction with their present employers. Administer the questionnaire and prepare conclusions.
3. Conduct a series of interviews to gather the same information discussed in Project 2. Interview a group of students and summarize your conclusions in a written report.
4. Perform a cost analysis on a task with which you are familiar. Classify each component of the activity, assign a cost per hour, and then compute the entire cost for the activity.
5. Perform a facilities inventory. Select a location, such as your place of work or an organization or club office, and prepare a list of equipment and facilities located on the premises.

ANALYST AT WORK
THURSTON ACADEMY

DESCRIPTION OF FIRM

Thurston Academy is a military school operated for profit by Ret. Col. Robert L. Thurston, which enrolls students of junior high and high school age, providing room and board, academic training, and college preparation.

Four hundred and fifty cadets are enrolled at Thurston Academy, many of whom are attending on scholarship or a student loan program. Some students are subsidized by their families, and some are supported by funds from state agencies or endowment programs.

SYSTEM OVERVIEW

Thurston Academy periodically bills parents, state agencies, and other fund providers for resident tuition. Figure 7.13 is a data flow diagram illustrating Thurston Academy's billing system. Prompt collection of tuition fees is important in order to maintain the institution's sound cash flow. Thurston Academy has a substantial payroll to meet each month and this is paid out of student tuition receipts.

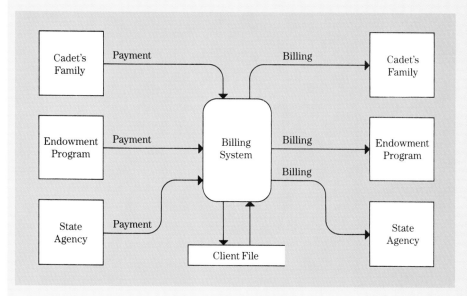

FIGURE 7.13

Thurston Academy Data Flow Diagram.

Continues

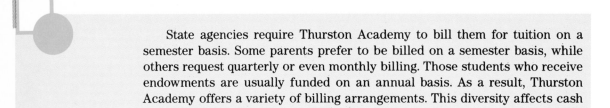

State agencies require Thurston Academy to bill them for tuition on a semester basis. Some parents prefer to be billed on a semester basis, while others request quarterly or even monthly billing. Those students who receive endowments are usually funded on an annual basis. As a result, Thurston Academy offers a variety of billing arrangements. This diversity affects cash flow and makes financial planning difficult.

HANDS-ON APPLICATION

You have been asked by Ret. Col. Thurston to investigate the present billing and tuition accounting system. You are to gather opinions both within the organization and from clients regarding Thurston Academy's billing system.

The objective is to make observations regarding the weaknesses of the present system and to make recommendations for improvement. The observations and recommendations will be used to design and implement a more efficient billing system. The new system should reduce billing costs, smooth out cash flow problems, and facilitate Thurston Academy's long-range financial planning.

Work Product No. 1　Make an analysis of Thurston Academy's clients and prepare a list of individuals or organizations that will either be interviewed or receive a questionnaire. The study should sample clients from all the various billing cycles. Considering the number of students that are enrolled, design a plan that will interview 5 percent of the students and mail questionnaires to 10 percent of Thurston Academy's clients. Label this document WP1, Chapter 7. Prepare a task list to help define the population and sample to be questioned. Enter the task list below.

TASK LIST

_____

_____

_____

_____

_____

_____

_____

Work Product No. 2   Prepare a questionnaire that will be mailed to Thurston Academy's clients. The questionnaire should survey preferences regarding tuition payment. It should assess various billing cycles and the client's willingness to change or to be billed on a monthly, quarterly, semiannual, or annual basis. You may wish to write one or more drafts of your questionnaire before preparing your final draft. Label the questionnaire WP2, Chapter 7. Prepare a task list to assist in this effort. Enter your task list below.

TASK LIST

_____

_____

_____

_____

_____

_____

_____

Work Product No. 3   You are to interview a variety of Thurston Academy's clients and discuss billing procedures. Prepare a set of structured interview questions that will be used to assess the client's billing preferences. Label this structured interview outline WP3, Chapter 7. In the space below prepare a brief outline of the structured interview that you wish to conduct. On a separate sheet of paper prepare your final outline.

INTERVIEW OUTLINE

_____

_____

_____

_____

_____

_____

_____

THE DESIGN PHASE

STRUCTURED SYSTEMS DESIGN

LEARNING OBJECTIVES

After studying this chapter, you should be able to:

1. List and explain the factors evaluated in systems design.

2. Describe the data cycle and give two examples.

3. Discuss the benefits of prototype system design.

4. Discuss software design concepts.

5. Discuss hardware design concepts.

6. Prepare a systems design task list.

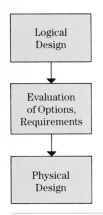

FIGURE 8.1

Logical Design

Some design decisions are easy; others more difficult. Some problems can be solved with a pad of paper and a pencil, while others require sophisticated computer systems. The selection depends upon factors such as volume of information to be processed, accuracy requirements, availability of staff, and cost of equipment and personnel. Before embarking on the design phase, the systems analyst must understand the capabilities and limitations of computer hardware and software.

This chapter introduces systems design fundamentals. It describes logical plans, physical designs, and prototyping. The chapter reviews guidelines for sound design and shows how to prepare a task list outlining the design steps to follow.

SYSTEMS DESIGN

Systems design is the reduction of a plan or concept to a set of specifications that describes a new or modified system. Systems design is the third phase of the systems development life cycle (SDLC). It involves evaluation of software and hardware, preparation of specifications, and design of methods for querying and manipulating databases. Input and output specifications are prepared in this phase.

Throughout the design process the analyst evaluates many hardware, software, and personnel requirements. As each phase of the SDLC moves forward, work products, referred to as **deliverables,** are generated. The deliverables from the systems analysis phase are likely to have been developed from some conceptual ideas about how a system may be improved. These products are often vague and only outline the general parameters for a solution. It is up to the systems analyst to convert these concepts into practical designs that can be physically implemented. In the systems design phase, physical designs are the deliverables, which in turn will be used in the development phase of the SDLC.

LOGICAL AND PHYSICAL DESIGNS

A system design evolves from a logical conception to a physical implementation. For example, if you plan to travel across the country during a holiday break, you make a logical decision before you make a physical one. The logical decision consists of deciding whether the trip is feasible in the time allowed. If so, you select the physical means of implementing that decision. If the trip is short and you have plenty of time, your physical plan may involve bicycling or driving to your destination. If the trip is long and the time short, it may be more practical to fly.

Systems analysts always begin their conceptualization by looking at the **logical design** first (see Fig. 8.1). After evaluating the options and obtaining a

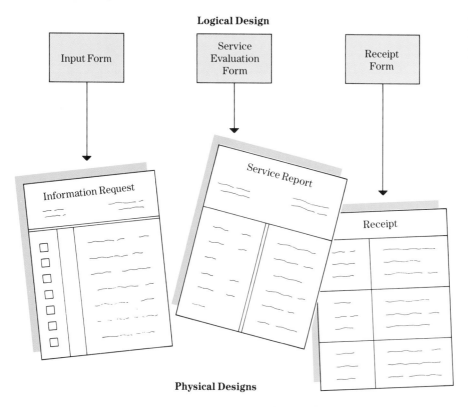

Logical Design

Physical Designs

FIGURE 8.2

Physical Design

clear understanding of the system goals, the analyst can move on to cast the plan into its **physical design.** This involves selecting specific pieces of hardware or programs and designing forms and procedures. In Fig. 8.2, three system forms are reduced to physical designs that can be printed and distributed.

PROTOTYPE DESIGNS

It rarely happens that analysts design perfect solutions to complex problems on their first attempts. More than likely many improvements will be needed. Prior to the advent of the computer, designs could not be easily or inexpensively modified. Early systems analysts were under pressure to design systems as perfectly as possible in the initial attempt. For example, it could cost hundreds of dollars to design and print forms that might later be found unacceptable.

The computer has greatly changed systems work by enabling prototyping and redesign to be done easily. A **prototype** is a mockup or developmental model of a system for test purposes. The prototype is reviewed by the end user and

FIGURE 8.3

Prototyping

repeatedly revised to create a final acceptable model. Through prototyping, designers can revise forms, input screens, databases, and processing methods, submit them to a limited number of system end users for testing, and revise them again if necessary for the final design. Prototyping consists of several steps.

Logical Design

The analyst contacts end users to learn their requirements, develops preliminary logical designs, and writes system specifications. Since the analyst will submit a working model of the system for testing, the design can contain flaws or omissions which will be resolved later (see Fig. 8.3).

Prototype Design

The analyst constructs a system prototype, implementing the logical design in a physical form. Temporary forms are developed and input screens and databases assembled. This is an attempt to actually build a pilot system.

End-User Testing

The prototype system is turned over to a limited number of end users for their testing and evaluation. During this period, end users work with the system, process orders, input data, and so on. In computer program development, end-user testing is known as **Beta testing.** This subjects the computer program to the same real-world conditions it will face in the final release.

Prototype Revision

The prototype is reworked based upon the experiences of end-user tests. If the prototype system design is maintained on the computer, changes in forms, input screens, and procedures can be made easily. Revisions and testing may be repeated several times until an acceptable system is developed.

Final Design

After all end-user comments and suggestions have been evaluated and significant ones implemented into the system, a final design is released. Prototyping has generated a final design that is more functional and has been engineered more quickly than if traditional methods were used.

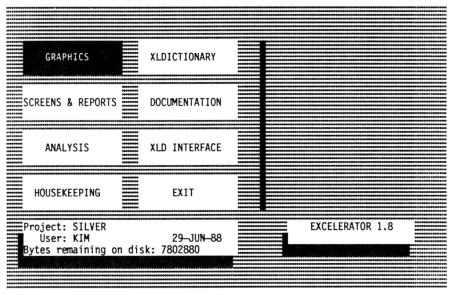

FIGURE 8.4

Excelerator Main Menu

Source: *Index Technology Corporation*

COMPUTERIZED SYSTEM DESIGN

Index Technology Corporation and others have produced computer software to automate systems design and prototyping. Index Technology's Excelerator software is among the most widely used products employed by analysts to develop systems.

Excelerator is menu-driven and designed to operate on a microcomputer (see Fig. 8.4). It contains a data dictionary that stores file, record, and field specifications. Various data flow diagrams, structure charts, and other graphs can be drawn with its graphics capability (see Fig. 8.5). The system uses a series of screens to help designers input information. Prototype forms, input screens, documents, and system specifications are stored in the computer and can be displayed graphically.

Excelerator is well suited for preparing prototype designs because it enables new screens and forms to be generated and tested easily. By using this type of software, designers can maintain consistency in the style and content of new systems.

DESIGN PRINCIPLES

Let us look at some of the basic guidelines that should be followed in systems design work.

FIGURE 8.5

Structured Diagram This diagram was generated with Excelerator software.

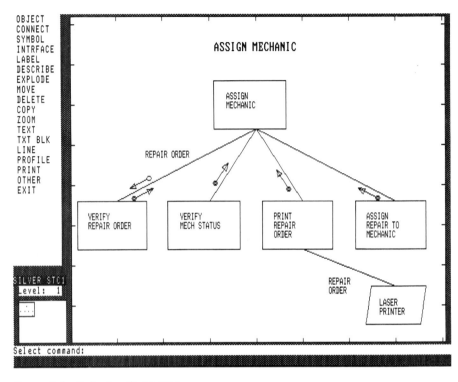

Source: Index Technology Corporation

Top-Down Structure

As a general rule, systems should always be designed as a **top-down structure.** This creates a hierarchy of levels of detail. Figure 8.6 illustrates a system that has been designed using a group of modules. As you can see from the figure, modules at the top level are exploded or decomposed into more modules. Decomposition, also known as explosion, is the process of expanding modules to show more detail.

Complicated systems should always be developed by using groups of modules that explode or decompose procedures. This is fundamental to good systems design. It allows you to reduce complex problems to clearly defined entities that form parts of a logical structure in a hierarchy.

Computer programmers rely heavily upon top-down structure and modules, writing programs in the form of a group of independent modules. Suppose module A performs a payroll accounting calculation and then prints out a report. The programmer could write a separate routine, module B, that prints out a heading for the report. Module B could be called in whenever a heading is needed for any report. Calculations are also performed in modules C, D, and E, which all rely upon module B for their headings. This arrangement, allowing one module to call in another, saves the programmer much time and effort.

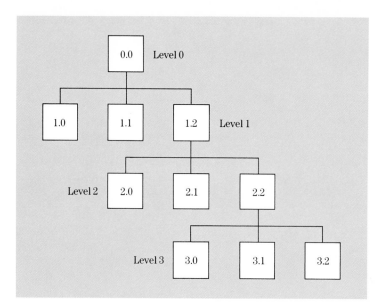

FIGURE 8.6

Top-Down Structure This design is built upon a group of self-contained modules.

The systems analyst applies this concept when routine or repetitive tasks are involved. One module can be called in by others to eliminate the need for preparing duplicate sets of instructions.

Guidelines

Systems analysts follow certain guidelines in order to design and operate a system in the most efficient manner.

Simplicity Designs should be as simple as possible. Select the most precise and direct method of achieving an end result. The simplest system is usually the best.

Modular Structure Develop systems in modules, using exploded or decomposed elements to expand details. These modules should call in others to eliminate redundant effort.

Expandability Design the system so that it can be expanded. It is much easier to add on to a system that has been designed for expansion than to redevelop one that has not.

Audit Trail Well-designed systems include **audit trails.** Audit trails enable analysts to track the information and data flow throughout a system. They make it easier to reconstruct data movement, facilitating problem diagnosis.

FIGURE 8.7

Security and Control Various layers of security should be built into a system.

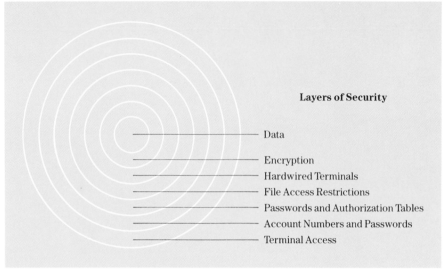

Reprinted by permission from Infosystems, Hitchcock Publishing Co., Wheaton, Illinois.

End-User Orientation Systems should be designed to meet users' needs. Sometimes concentrating on available hardware or resources gives the designer tunnel vision, and he or she overlooks what is really needed. Systems that do not address end users' needs are bound to fail.

User Friendly The system should be comfortable and not intimidating to the user. It should adapt to the user's needs, not the other way around. **User-friendly systems** address human, physical, and psychological aspects of a system. (However, the Internal Revenue Service has been struggling with this problem for years and still has not come up with a user-friendly tax form.)

Consistency All elements of a system should be consistent in their structure and logic. Unless there is a good reason, a given computation should always be performed the same way throughout the system. Fields should be consistent from record to record; printout headings and labels should agree as well.

Efficiency Systems should be designed to manipulate information in the most cost-effective manner. Personnel and computer time are resources that must be used efficiently in any system.

Security and Control Designs should provide the appropriate level of system security and control. The design should include protection against misrouted or lost records, and limit access to qualified users. Figure 8.7 shows various security provisions built into some systems.

THE DATA CYCLE

Before applying some of these guidelines in systems design, we will review the data cycle. In most organizations, data processing moves through three basic steps:

INPUT → PROCESSING → OUTPUT

The sequence of input, processing, and output, known as the **data cycle,** is inherent in virtually all systems. Well-designed systems conform to the logical flow of this cycle.

In some systems the data cycle is performed over a period of several days or weeks. In others, the cycle may be completed in a matter of seconds and repeated hundreds of time throughout the business day. This is typical of online real-time systems.

The first step in the cycle is **input,** consisting of capturing or entering information into the system. Information recorded on source documents is converted, if necessary, into a form suitable for processing by the computer and entered into the system. A **source document** is a record made at the time an original transaction takes place. Source documents may be written in longhand, on sales slips, deposit slips, time cards, or order forms. This data may be prepared for input by keyboarding, optical character scanners, bar code readers, or other methods. In some instances, the source documents themselves are suitable as input media.

The second step involves the **processing** or restructuring of data to make it more useful to the organization. Most common data processing activities involve one or more of the following operations:

Sorting, sequencing, and alphabetizing

Classifying

Storing

Collating and merging

Searching and selecting

Manipulating arithmetically

Converting into a form suitable for further processing

Transmitting from one point to another

The last stage in the data cycle is **output,** the delivery of the results of processing. In this step, the processed data is converted into a form useful to people, such as screens on a video display terminal, printed reports, or documents. Examples include paychecks, statements, invoices, and so on. Output may also be processed into a form suitable for storage or later input to the same or a different system. Examples include accounts receivable, accounts payable, or inventory files stored on magnetic disks.

FIGURE 8.8

**Tasks and
Subtasks** Subtask
lists expand the
detail of specific
items on the task
list.

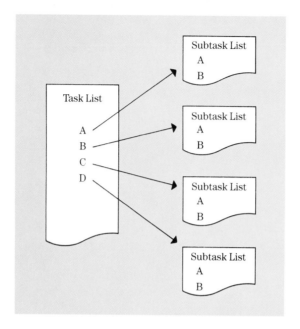

FIGURE 8.8

**Tasks and
Subtasks** Subtask
lists expand the
detail of specific
items on the task
list.

Now that we have discussed some of the general principles of structured
systems design, we will see how analysts reduce these concepts to a sequential
task list that can be executed systematically.

SYSTEMS DESIGN TASK LIST

Almost all systems design problems can be reduced to a series of steps
that begin with an analysis of the technical requirements of the end user and
conclude with the preparation of detailed hardware and program specifications.
The items on a task list, as well as their order, will depend upon many factors,
including the kind and type of system under design, time and economic constraints, availability of vendors, and so on.

There are a number of ways to prepare a task list. Most systems analysts
begin by listing all the activities that must be performed in a given design step,
usually in the form of a checklist. Items are sequenced in the order in which
they are to be carried out. This checklist is reviewed by the analyst, sometimes
with the help of a colleague. They may perform a desk check, mentally walking
through each of the tasks to be done. This sometimes reveals items that were
omitted or that are redundant. After the analyst is satisfied that the tasks are
in the proper sequence, he or she prepares a final task list.

It is helpful to prepare subtask lists for complicated jobs (see Fig. 8.8).
Expanding key tasks into subtask lists further refines the work. You are familiar

with task and subtask lists if you have ever prepared a list of things to do for the day. One of the items on your primary task list may be to take your car to a garage to be serviced. You may also have prepared a separate list including items such as: change oil; lube chassis; adjust brakes; rotate tires. This list is a subtask list expanding on one of the elements on your principal task list.

Let's look at a typical task list developed by an analyst about to undertake a systems design effort.

TASK LIST

1. Determine end-user requirements
2. Investigate hardware, software, and vendor capabilities
3. Write general design specifications
4. Establish benchmark tests
5. Write software design specifications
6. Write hardware design specifications
7. Solicit bids and cost estimates

Determine End-User Requirements

Since systems are designed to serve users, the design phase should always begin by assessing user needs. Specify the physical features, software performance, or communications the user requires.

Much useful information regarding end-user needs has been developed in the previous systems analysis phases. A review of the existing system often gives valuable clues to assist in designing new or improved systems.

Investigate Hardware, Software, Vendor Capabilities

With an understanding of end-user requirements, the analyst can search out available resources to meet these needs, contacting vendors and requesting proposals from suppliers. Sometimes an available hardware or software product may meet the user's requirements, eliminating the need to design a new product.

Write General Specifications

A general design statement defines the specific hardware and software needed in the new system. These specifications also describe the tests and evaluation procedures to be written. This step serves as an overall framework that assists in developing more detailed design specifications in later tasks. Some

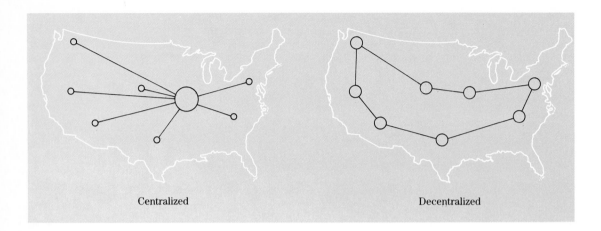

Centralized   Decentralized

FIGURE 8.9

**Centralized and
Decentralized
Systems**

key questions can be asked to narrow the general to the specific. For example, the analyst may ask:

What will be the hardware costs?

What are the programming costs?

Can ready-made software packages be used?

What are the personnel costs?

What security and data integrity considerations apply?

Will databases and information be distributed throughout the system or stored in one place?

What will be the role of data communications in the new system?

Systems analysts are sometimes faced with deciding whether to design a centralized or decentralized data processing system. In a **centralized system** data is processed at one central point. All the data moves back and forth between a central point and users located at some distance from the processing center (see Fig. 8.9). The advantages of a centralized system are uniformity of data processing, more consistent procedures, and better security, since all data is handled at one controlled central point.

A **decentralized system** brings data processing facilities closer to the end user. By eliminating the central processing point, end users are able to process data locally, maintaining better control and often eliminating communications costs associated with a centralized system.

Many organizations further refine their data processing needs into distributed systems. A **distributed data processing** system is one in which data is distributed throughout the network and is available to selected users. By distributing computer resources and databases, the organization is less dependent upon communications facilities and is less subject to total system failure.

Establish Benchmark Tests

In this task, the systems analyst works with vendors and programmers to establish **benchmark testing** requirements. They design specific tests to compare computer processing speeds, software capability, data communications capability, and the like. These tests are used in evaluating the finished hardware and software.

Write Software Design Specifications

In analyzing the software requirements in the design phase for a new business system, the analyst must often decide whether to use a ready-made software package or have one written to solve a problem.

User-Written Programs   Some organizations employ a staff of programmers who work with systems analysts to write computer programs. The programmer begins by studying a problem and defining each step in its solution. Often design diagrams are prepared to assist in developing the sequence of steps to solve the problem. Then the program is coded in a language that the computer can understand. This may require an extensive amount of computer language study.

Applications Packages   A variety of powerful **applications packages** that perform many tasks are available. They do not require users to know a specific programming language. Packages such as WordStar, dBASE III PLUS, Framework, Lotus 1-2-3, Symphony, and others assist in managing databases, performing word processing, and manipulating information in the form of spreadsheets.

Systems analysts often elect to design systems that use off-the-shelf software. This eliminates the necessity for writing and testing detailed code. The tested software is readily available and less expensive than custom-written programs. Finally, there is an increasing pool of skilled software package users. Organizations can employ individuals who already know how to use applications packages.

Write Hardware Design Specifications

With an understanding of the general system specifications and software design requirements, the analyst can prepare hardware design specifications. Some work on this task will already have been completed as a result of contacts with vendors and a careful analysis of the in-place system.

An analyst must often decide whether to design a system using microcomputers or to opt for a larger machine. There is a trend toward the use of microcomputers because of their low cost, availability, and ease of maintenance.

Large **mainframe** computers, however, are capable of serving a greater number of input and output devices than are microcomputers. The heavy data storage demands of some organizations require large mainframe computers with their massive secondary storage capability.

Solicit Bids and Cost Estimates

The last task in the design process is to solicit bids and cost estimates. The system under design must meet the economic constraints placed on it by the organization. If final bid prices are too high or bids from vendors fail to address design requirements, then some redesign may be in order.

Now that we have concluded our overview discussion of the design task, let us turn our attention to the specifics of input design. The next chapter explores input devices, online terminals, and input design criteria.

Summary

The purpose of systems design is to reduce a plan or concept to a set of instructions that describes a new or modified system. A system design evolves from a logical conception to a physical implementation. A prototype or mockup is sometimes constructed for developmental purposes. After end-user testing and revision, a final design is completed. Software packages already on the market enable the systems analyst to computerize the design process.

As a rule, top-down structure should be followed, using modular design. Where necessary, modules are decomposed or exploded into greater detail. Not only should designs be modular in structure, but the analyst should opt for simplicity, expandability, consistency, and efficiency. Designs should also have end-user orientation, be user friendly, and have audit trails, security, and control.

The data cycle begins with a source document and analysis of the input, process, and output steps. Task lists are sometimes used in designing systems. General specifications are written, followed by software and hardware design specifications. Analysts must sometimes choose between centralized and decentralized or distributed systems. The last step in the task is the solicitation of bids and cost estimates.

Key Terms

Applications package	Logical design
Audit trail	Mainframe
Benchmark testing	Output
Beta testing	Physical design
Centralized system	Processing
Data cycle	Prototype
Decentralized system	Source document
Deliverables	Systems design
Distributed data processing	Top-down structure
Input	User-friendly system

1. What are the major steps in the data cycle? Describe the function of each.   ***Exercises***
2. List at least five common data processing activities.
3. Describe what is meant by systems design.
4. Contrast logical and physical designs.
5. Discuss the function of prototype designs.
6. Discuss the concept of top-down structure.
7. Contrast the design of centralized and decentralized systems.
8. Describe the function of benchmark tests.
9. What are the advantages of purchasing software packages?
10. Contrast centralized and decentralized data processing systems.

1. Prepare a typical system design task list.   ***Projects***
2. Interview a business employee and discuss his or her tasks. Determine which method of data processing is used. Is it the best method, in your opinion?
3. Select a business firm that uses microcomputers and describe the system and procedures used.
4. Prepare a system design that is based upon the centralized processing of data at one major location.
5. Prepare a system design that is based upon a decentralized data processing system.

ANALYST AT WORK

BARSTOW PHOTO SUPPLY

DESCRIPTION OF FIRM

Barstow Photo Supply is a well-established distributor of photographic film, cameras, projectors, and other items. The company's sales are concentrated among a group of industrial, commercial, and fashion photographers located within a 25-mile radius of Barstow's retail store and warehouse.

Barstow Photo Supply has built its reputation on good service. The company maintains a large inventory of goods so that orders can be filled promptly. Money is lost if goods cannot be shipped because they are not in stock.

Photographic film and paper make up the bulk of Barstow's inventory. If these items become outdated, they are returned for credit or sold as discount goods. This represents a loss to the company; therefore it is necessary to maintain fresh stock and accurate inventory records.

SYSTEM OVERVIEW

Barstow Photo Supply's inventory system is illustrated in the data flow diagram in Fig. 8.10. Goods and materials are kept in inventory at the company's retail outlet, known as Store 1, or its warehouse, known as Store 2. Retail customers pick up goods at Store 1. All wholesale orders are shipped from Store 2.

Goods and materials are purchased from a variety of wholesale suppliers and distributors. When the goods are received, they are placed in stock in either Store 1 or Store 2. A computerized file of all goods in stock is maintained. When an item is backordered, a record is kept in the backordered goods file. When the item is received, it is placed in inventory and the data transferred from the backordered goods file to the goods in stock file.

The inventory system generates a variety of reports. These include the inventory report, backordered goods report, and inventory turnover report. These reports provide the salespeople with a complete picture of goods in stock or on order.

HANDS-ON APPLICATION

You are designing the inventory system for Barstow Photo Supply. Your task is to design the system that generates the three reports mentioned above.

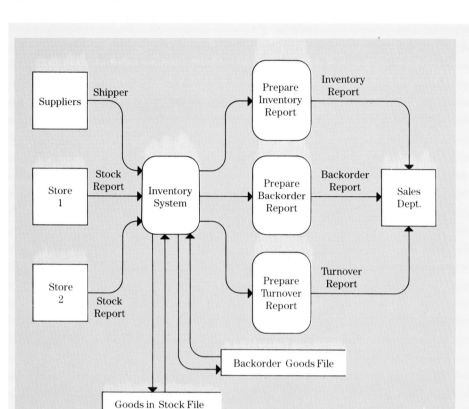

Work Product No. 1   Study the data flow context diagram that describes Barstow Photo Supply's inventory system. Prepare a data flow diagram that describes the company's inventory report system. The inventory report should show goods in stock in both stores. It should reduce stock as goods are sold and increase stock as goods are received. Label this document WP1, Chapter 8. Prepare a task list indicating the steps that must be carried out in preparing WP1. Enter your task list below.

TASK LIST

_____

_____

_____

_____

_____

Work Product No. 2   Refer to the data flow context diagram that describes Barstow Photo Supply's inventory system. Prepare a data flow diagram that describes the company's backorder report system. The report should show goods that are backordered from various suppliers. It should show stock on order and decrease the backorder inventory as goods are received. Label this document WP2, Chapter 8. Make a task list indicating the steps that must be carried out in preparing WP2. Enter your task list below.

TASK LIST

_____

_____

_____

_____

_____

_____

_____

Work Product No. 3   Prepare a data flow diagram that prints out a turnover report for Barstow Photo Supply. The turnover report should show how long goods remain in inventory before they are sold. Reports such as these are particularly helpful where perishable items, such as photo supplies, are kept in stock. Label this document WP3, Chapter 8. Use a task list to assist in carrying out this effort. Enter your task list below.

TASK LIST

_____

_____

_____

_____

_____

_____

INPUT DESIGN AND CONTROL

LEARNING OBJECTIVES

After studying this chapter, you should be able to:

1. Discuss data input concepts.

2. Describe the use of the data dictionary in input systems.

3. Contrast transaction-oriented and batch-processing methods.

4. Discuss data entry modes.

5. Design input screens.

6. Design hard copy input documents.

Each time you use a charge card, write a check, fill out a credit application, or send in your annual automobile registration, you start a chain of events that triggers a system to process, manipulate, store, and output information. The data cycle begins with data input. Data input must be performed efficiently and accurately, because it is the foundation for all subsequent activities.

Data input methods and hardware are undergoing rapid changes. In many systems the greatest expense is data entry because of the high labor costs for keyboarding. These costs are being reduced because much data entry is now done by automated means, such as bar code readers, character recognition devices, and other scanning tools. These devices also increase input speed and accuracy.

This chapter describes input design principles and control concepts. We will see how input forms are laid out and designed, and discuss online terminals, menus, and screen formats.

TRANSACTION-ORIENTED AND BATCH PROCESSING

Data is usually input to a processing system in one of two modes: by the transaction or by the batch. In **transaction-oriented processing,** source data is entered directly into the processing system at the time the transaction occurs without intermediate storage (see Fig. 9.1). Source data is keyboarded directly into a computer. Input is made in **real time**—that is, the data is entered for processing at the time the transaction occurs. This mode is also known as **online data entry.**

No conversion of data from one medium to another takes place. The data entered is usually displayed in a form the operator can see, and at the same time transmitted in machine-readable form to the computer. Examples include bank teller terminals and reservation inquiry systems.

Batch processing involves preparing data to be input to a system at a later time. In this mode, source data is transcribed onto machine-readable storage media, such as floppy disks or magnetic tape. The stored data is held in this form until needed for processing, when it is input to the system. This mode is also known as **offline data entry.**

ELEMENTS OF DATA INPUT

A source document is a record of an original transaction, generated at the time the transaction takes place. Examples include time cards prepared throughout the week by an employee; a list of expense account items gathered by a sales representative; withdrawal slips submitted to a bank teller; or sales slips written by a clerk when items are purchased.

FIGURE 9.1

Transaction-Oriented Processing In this mode, data is entered directly into the processing system.

Source documents contain the data about the procedures or activities initiated during the transaction. Time cards contain data needed to generate paychecks and entries in employment records. Withdrawal slips record data necessary for posting debits to customers' accounts. Sales slips contain the data that initiates activities in the inventory, stock room, delivery, personnel, and accounts receivable departments.

The data on source documents must be made available for processing by the system. Often data is recorded on source documents in longhand. It must be converted into a form acceptable to the processing machines. This involves transferring the data on the source document to another record that is **machine readable.** This may be done by keyboarding, bar coding, or some other method.

Other forms of source documents can be read by both people and machines. Optical character recognition devices, for example, eliminate the need to convert a source document into a machine-readable form in a special step prior to processing.

INPUT MEDIA

Several methods are used to prepare source data for input into a system. The purpose of all input devices is to convert media such as keystrokes, bar codes, or magnetically encoded characters into electronic pulses that can be stored and manipulated by computers or other devices. The most common input media are described below.

Keyboard Terminals

A keyboard terminal connected to a computer is a major means of inputting data. The operator strikes a key, sending electronic pulses representing the character to a computer. At the same time, the data prints out on the terminal or displays on a screen. This method is widely used for data entry in banks, insurance companies, and other offices.

Keyboard terminals are classified as either smart or dumb. **Smart terminals** have an integrated microprocessor. This allows them to check the accuracy of input, proofread entries, display formats on a screen, and prompt operators for data.

Dumb terminals lack this level of sophistication. They cannot perform editing functions since they do not have integrated microprocessors. They simply transmit unformatted data from the terminal to the computer.

Manual Data Entry Devices

The least sophisticated method of input is **manual data entry** done in longhand or on a typewriter. Paychecks are prepared from handwritten time cards. Invoices are prepared from sales slips. Orders are picked and delivered using data written on original order forms. Data gathered manually must be converted into machine-readable form if further processing is required. Manual data entry is slow and prone to error.

Optical Scanning Devices

Optical scanning devices input source data in a form that can be read by both people and machines. Some scanners read only filled-in areas; others can distinguish the letters of the alphabet and numeric digits by their optical characteristics; and still others read bar codes. There are three principal types of optical scanners.

Mark Sense Readers   **Mark sense readers** are optical scanning devices that sense penciled-in areas. The area may be a bubble or a slash in a box. The device converts it to the appropriate electrical pulse for entry to the computer system. This type of document is commonly used for such things as meter readings, inventory control, and test scoring (see Fig. 9.2).

TESTING FORM   **Academic Testing Service**

NAME _____
LAST   FIRST   MIDDLE

COURSE _____ SECTION _____

INSTRUCTOR _____

SOCIAL SECURITY NUMBER

INSTRUCTIONS

• USE NO. 2 PENCIL ONLY
• MAKE DARK MARKS THAT FILL CIRCLE COMPLETELY.
• ERASE CLEANLY ANY ANSWER YOU WISH TO CHANGE.
• MAKE NO STRAY MARKS ON EITHER SIDE OF THIS FORM.

SCORE

FORM NUMBER
① ② ③ ④

NCS Trans-Optic EB01-11380:65

FIGURE 9.2

Mark Sense Form Forms such as these are scanned by a mark sense reader.

FIGURE 9.3

Universal Product Code (UPC) A laser beam sweeps across the bar code pattern, deciphering information.

Laser Beam Scanners A widely used means of optical input is the **laser beam scanner,** which reads parallel lines imprinted on products. The universal product code (UPC), shown in Fig. 9.3, is used for this purpose. A laser scanner sweeps a beam of coherent light across the bar code pattern, deciphering the information. Laser beam scanning is widely used in supermarkets, drugstores, and other retail outlets.

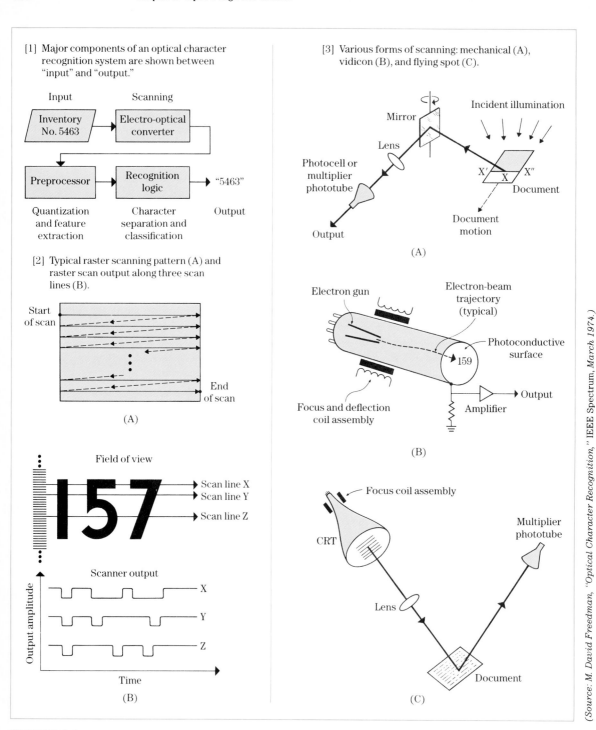

[1] Major components of an optical character recognition system are shown between "input" and "output."

Input   Scanning

Inventory No. 5463 → Electro-optical converter

Preprocessor → Recognition logic → "5463"

Quantization and feature extraction   Character separation and classification   Output

[2] Typical raster scanning pattern (A) and raster scan output along three scan lines (B).

Start of scan   End of scan

(A)

Field of view

157

Scan line X
Scan line Y
Scan line Z

Output amplitude

Scanner output

X
Y
Z

Time

(B)

[3] Various forms of scanning: mechanical (A), vidicon (B), and flying spot (C).

Mirror   Incident illumination

Lens

Photocell or multiplier phototube

X' X X" Document

Output   Document motion

(A)

Electron gun   Electron-beam trajectory (typical)

Photoconductive surface

159

Output

Focus and deflection coil assembly   Amplifier

(B)

Focus coil assembly

Multiplier phototube

CRT

Lens

Document

(C)

(Source: M. David Freedman, "Optical Character Recognition," IEEE Spectrum, March 1974.)

FIGURE 9.4

How Optical Characters Are Scanned

Optical Character Readers (OCR) Optical character readers (OCR) recognize the shape of a letter form (see Fig. 9.4). They can scan neatly printed handwritten numbers and letters as well as typewritten and printed text. The devices convert these images into electrical pulses suitable for computer processing. The chief advantage of OCR input is that the source document can be read by both people and machines. There is no need for data conversion and verification.

Magnetic Ink Character Readers

Magnetic ink character recognition (MICR) is another means of preparing source data for direct entry into a computer system. Characters to be read are printed on a page using a special ink. When these printed letters are passed under a magnetic field the device sends a string of pulses representing a given character to the computer. No conversion of data is necessary, since the source document is used for the data entry to the system.

MICR is widely used in the banking industry to encode account numbers and amounts on checks and deposit slips (see Fig. 9.5). The American Banking Association has approved a standard letter shape and character position for encoding data on checks and forms. The recorded data can be read by both an MICR reader and the human eye.

Voice Recognition Devices

Much research and development is now being done on input devices capable of deciphering the human voice and converting it into electronic pulses sent to a computer for processing. At present, **voice recognition devices** are limited and must be programmed for the individual characteristics of specific human voices in order to interpret a large vocabulary of words. However, they are potentially an important and useful form of data input, since they do not require keyboarding skills on the part of the operator.

FIGURE 9.5

MICR **Form** This form contains letters printed in special magnetic ink.

FOR DEPOSIT TO THE ACCOUNT OF

JAMES C. MORRISON
1765 SHERIDAN DRIVE
YOUR CITY, STATE 01088

DATE_____19____

SIGN HERE FOR LESS CASH IN TELLER'S PRESENCE

CITICORP **+**
SAVINGS
(415) 891-8900
180 Grand Avenue
Oakland, CA 94604

CASH	CURRENCY		
	COIN		
LIST CHECKS SINGLY			
			90-7118/3211
TOTAL FROM OTHER SIDE			
TOTAL			
LESS CASH RECEIVED			
NET DEPOSIT			

90-7118/3211

NOTICE:
A hold for uncollected funds may be placed on funds deposited by check or similar instruments. This could delay your ability to withdraw such funds. The delay, if any, would not exceed the period of time permitted by law.

NOT NEGOTIABLE
SAMPLE - VOID
DO   NOT   CASH!

⑆000067894⑆ 123456 78⑈

HO 40

(Source: Citicorp Savings)

Other Input Devices

A variety of devices such as mice, wands, joysticks, digitizers, and light pens are also suitable for input. They broaden the range of input media available for use on computers. These devices add flexibility to input systems, but are not generally used for entering large volumes of data.

DESIGN OF SOURCE DOCUMENTS

The systems analyst must give careful consideration to the design of source documents. Well-designed source documents make data entry easier and reduce keyboarding costs. A source document should capture data in the sequence in which it will be entered into the system. Figure 9.6 illustrates a source document and a data entry screen for a UniTrans misrouted package form.

Notice that the sequence of fields is the same on the source document and on the input screen. This enables the keyboard operator to key in the data quickly and easily. It eliminates reading fields out of sequence, backtracking, or skipping fields.

The source document should have adequate space for the user to fill in the data. Fields should be labeled, and explanatory notes should be included in the form to make sure that data is entered correctly. Check boxes or checklists may also be used to reduce the amount of material that must be entered. A model showing the style for the entry may be included. For example:

```
MM/DD/YY
06/21/87
```

or:

```
LAST/FIRST/INITIAL
SMITH/ANNA/R.
```

These models ensure that there will be no misunderstanding about how to enter data.

INPUT VERIFICATION AND CONTROL

Everyone has heard stories about a person receiving a refund check from the Internal Revenue Service for $1 million when it should have been for $100, or of the customer who purchased goods for $25 but received a bill for $25,000. The common reaction to these stories is to shrug and say the computer made a

MISROUTED PACKAGE REPORT

UNITRANS COMPANY

Shipper _____   Recipient _____

Address _____   Address _____

City, State, Zip _____   City, State, Zip _____

Shipper No. _____   PACKAGE TRACER INFORMATION:

Date Shipped _____

Retail Depot _____

Charges _____

Tracer No. _____ Code _____

MISROUTED PACKAGE SCREEN

SHIPPER	ADDRESS
CITY, STATE, ZIP	SHIPPER NO.
DATE SHIPPED	RETAIL DEPOT CHARGES
RECIPIENT	ADDRESS
CITY, STATE, ZIP	TRACER NO. CODE
PACKAGE TRACER INFORMATION	

FIGURE 9.6

Source Data and Entry Screen

mistake—but in reality, it was almost certainly a data entry error. These stories illustrate the need for careful control over data entry into a system to ensure that figures are valid and results are accurate.

Well-designed information systems have transaction controls that monitor input data to make sure it is correct, in the proper range, and complete. Systems should prevent a minor keyboard error from converting a $100 refund into a $1 million windfall. In designing input records, the analyst usually programs one or more of the following controls or tests into the entry system.

Range Test

Is the data that has been entered within the range or limit that is expected for the kind of transaction being processed? Computer software controls can flag or reject an out-of-range number to avoid this kind of error. For example, a shoe store might set a credit limit of $200 per returned item, assuming that no pair of shoes with a value exceeding that amount will be returned.

Test For Completeness

Has all data necessary for the processing transaction been entered? This test would, for example, flag a payroll entry for an employee if the name has been entered but the number of hours worked was omitted.

Accuracy Test

Has the data been entered accurately? A common accuracy test is a **check digit** test. A check digit is a number placed at the end of a string of numbers to ensure that no digits have been transposed or omitted. To illustrate, the following number contains a check digit: 364 501 7. The check digit 7 is generated by a mathematical algorithm, which the computer examines each time the number is run. If there is a transposition or other error, the computer detects the error because the check digit is no longer valid. There are several techniques for computing check digits.

Sequence Test

Has the data been entered in the proper sequence? For example, an operator cannot key in a request for confidential information prior to the entry of an approved user ID number or password.

Data Type Check

Is the correct type of data entered in the field? This check ensures that numeric data is not entered in a name field or, conversely, alphabetic data into a numeric field.

Combination Test

Is the information entered into two fields properly related? For example, is a part number compatible with the name of the item being ordered? The system should flag an error if an operator enters part number 1324 for a wrench, for example, when all wrenches have part numbers beginning with 2.

VERIFICATION

Whenever data is transferred from a source document to another medium by a human operator, there is always the possibility of human error. Therefore, the data must be verified. **Verification** involves making comparisons to check the accuracy of the data transferred from one document to another. This step detects errors made during the conversion of the source data.

Verification is accomplished in several ways, depending on the system used. One method is to keyboard information twice. Data keyboarded from source documents is held in storage in the machine while a different operator rekeyboards the data. If the two sets of data agree, the machine completes the transcription and records the converted data in a verified file. If they do not agree, the operators determine where the error occurred, correct it, and move on to the next record.

Another method of verification is the use of **batch totals.** A batch total is a sum of all values in a given field in a batch. After a group of records has been converted from one medium to another, a batch total of the transcribed figures is drawn and compared to a batch total of the original figures from the source documents.

Verified records are assumed to be free of entry errors. Of course, errors in the source documents, such as an incorrect number of hours on a time card, would go undetected.

INPUT DESIGN GUIDELINES

Since data entry can be a large operational cost of an information system, as well as a major source of errors, it is essential to perform this function as efficiently as possible. Review the guidelines discussed below when designing input records. Use a checklist to assess input designs for flaws or omissions, for both physical records and online terminal screens.

- Design input screens for operator convenience. Place related items close together. Avoid shifting between capital letters and lowercase and between figures and numbers unless necessary.
- Use a consistent style. Don't call for a date to be entered one way, for instance 1/29/89, and later ask for it to be entered as January 29, 1989.
- Only variable data should be entered, not constants. Structure records, for example, so that the operator enters "6723," not "EMPLOYEE NUMBER 6723."
- Use common expressions to identify fields: ADDRESS rather than LOCATION or DOMICILE, LAST NAME rather than SURNAME, and so on.
- Enter data in a logical sequence. For instance, name, address, phone number, is more logical than name, phone number, address.
- Use the computer to perform the computations. For example, enter the number of hours worked and the pay rate, and let the computer calculate the gross pay.

FIGURE 9.7

**Style and Format
Specification
Sheet**

INPUT DIALOG SPECIFICATIONS

Input Screen: STANDARD PURCHASE ORDER

Analyst: S. Chang

Date: August 5, 1989

ITEM   COMMENTS

1. The NUMBER field shall not exceed 8 digits and will
   begin sequentially with 1000.

2. The PURCHASE field shall not exceed 25 characters.
   Approved abbreviations: Inc., Co.

3. The ADDRESS field shall not exceed 25 characters of
   alpha data.

4. The CITY field shall not exceed 25 characters of
   alpha data.

5. The ZIP field shall not exceed 10 characters of
   numeric data.

6. The QUANTITY field shall not exceed 6 characters of
   numeric data.

7. The DESCRIPTION field shall not exceed 40 characters
   of alpha data.

8. The UNIT field shall not exceed 10 characters of
   numeric data.

9. The TOTAL field shall not exceed 12 characters of
   numeric data.

FUNCTION: This specification defines the field descriptions for the standard purchase form. Original records
must be maintained for 24 months.

SORT KEY: Purchase Order

- Design forms with the end user in mind. Provide enough space for people
  to write or print required information. For example, leave adequate space
  for names of states or individuals.

- Use codes or abbreviations to simplify data entry. It is obviously easier to
  enter F for female and M for male, rather than having to key in the full
  words.

FIGURE 9.8

Data Dictionary Entry

Data dictionary: Order Processing Function

Name of File: Purchase Order

Designed For: Purchasing Department

Function: Specifies the form of fields in company's standard purchase order

Maintain Records for: 24 months

Storage Medium: Floppy disks

Sort Key: Purchase Order

Name of field	Width	Type	Comments
Number	8	Numeric	Sequential numbers from 1000
Purchased from	25	Alpha	Abbrev. Inc., Co.
Address	25	Alpha	
City	25	Alpha	
Zip	10	Numeric	
Quantity	6	Numeric	
Description	40	Alpha	
Unit	10	Numeric	
Total	12	Numeric	

● Provide entry operators with a guide showing standard abbreviations to be used and explanations of style and format for all fields (see Fig. 9.7).

DATA DICTIONARY

A data dictionary is a tool used to ensure the consistency of all the elements in a system. It specifies such things as a standard field name or data item, whether the field will be alphabetic or numeric, and the field width (see Fig. 9.8). It is particularly helpful in the design of input records.

Minimize the use of aliases in the data dictionary where possible. For instance, design the system to refer to a supplier as VENDOR on all records, rather than VENDOR on some input records and SUPPLIER on others.

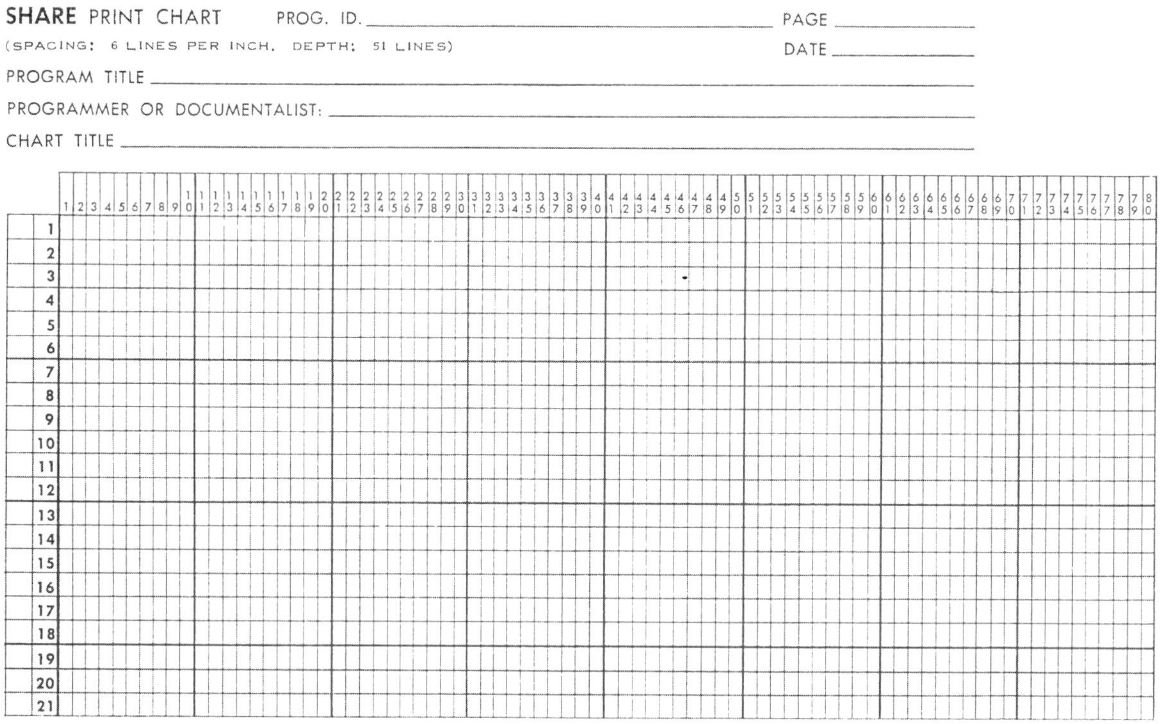

SHARE PRINT CHART   PROG. ID. _____   PAGE _____

(SPACING: 6 LINES PER INCH, DEPTH: 51 LINES)   DATE _____

PROGRAM TITLE _____

PROGRAMMER OR DOCUMENTALIST: _____

CHART TITLE _____

(Source: Courtesy of International Business Machines Corporation)

FIGURE 9.9

Record Layout Form This form is used to design hard copy documents.

HOW TO LAY OUT AN INPUT RECORD

A **hard copy** record is a permanent document, such as a piece of paper or a printed form. A **soft copy** record is displayed on a terminal screen. It cannot be filed as a paper document, although it can be stored electronically in the system. As more interactive systems come into use, systems analysts rely less upon printed forms and more upon computer terminal displays.

Hard Copy Records

Hard copy records, such as printed forms, tab cards, and OCR forms, are best designed using a record layout form like that shown in Fig. 9.9. The form is laid out with horizontal lines and vertical columns. Each line on the record layout form corresponds to a line on the input record. The analyst begins by entering constants, such as words, phrases, lines, or rules, which will be printed on the form and then specifying the variable information.

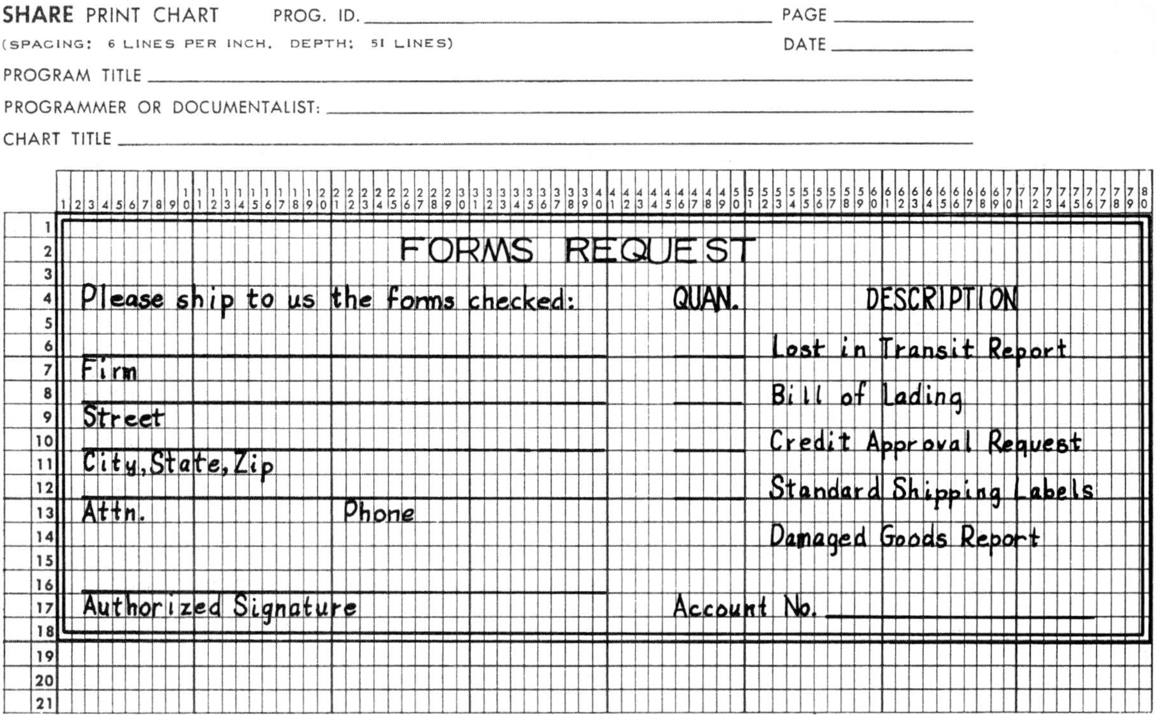

SHARE PRINT CHART PROG. ID. ______ PAGE ______
(SPACING: 6 LINES PER INCH. DEPTH: 51 LINES) DATE ______
PROGRAM TITLE ______
PROGRAMMER OR DOCUMENTALIST: ______
CHART TITLE ______

FORMS REQUEST

Please ship to us the forms checked: QUAN. DESCRIPTION
Lost in Transit Report
Firm
Bill of Lading
Street
Credit Approval Request
City, State, Zip
Standard Shipping Labels
Attn. Phone
Damaged Goods Report
Authorized Signature Account No.

FIGURE 9.10

Completed Form This record was designed using a record layout form.

Figure 9.10 illustrates a form showing all information that will appear on the final record. Adequate space has been provided for entering the necessary information. If the form is to be completed in handwriting, horizontal rules should be included. If data is to be typed into the form, there should be blank spaces conforming to standard typewriter spacing. Most typewriters have 10 to 12 pitch, which means 10 or 12 characters per inch. Standard spacing is usually six lines per inch.

Check boxes should be used to reduce the need for manually typing or writing in data.

The physical size of the form should conform to standard paper sizes. Common business forms usually measure one of the following sizes:

$3\frac{1}{4} \times 7\frac{3}{8}$ inches

$5\frac{1}{2} \times 8\frac{1}{2}$ inches

$8\frac{1}{2} \times 7$ inches

$8\frac{1}{2} \times 11$ inches

$8\frac{1}{2} \times 14$ inches

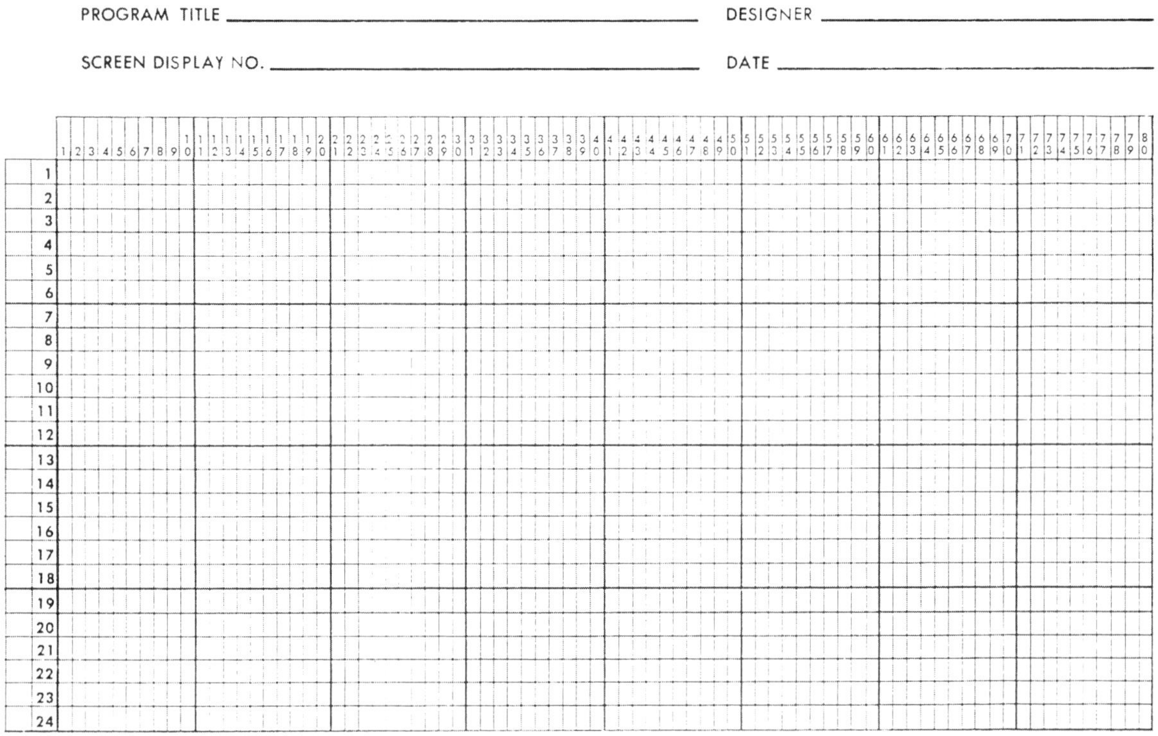

PROGRAM TITLE _____   DESIGNER _____

SCREEN DISPLAY NO. _____   DATE _____

(Source: Courtesy of International Business Machines Corporation)

FIGURE 9.11

Terminal Screen Layout Form

HOW TO LAY OUT TERMINAL SCREENS

The design and layout of input screens is more complex than that of hard copy records. Several screens may be involved, and an operator can carry on a dialog with the computer from a terminal, making queries, entering information, and calling up additional screens.

A terminal screen layout form, shown in Fig. 9.11, is used to design screens. The form is ruled out in horizontal rows and vertical columns, corresponding to common display screens. There are 80 vertical columns and 24 horizontal rows or lines. Each line on the form is equivalent to one line on the screen. Some high-resolution graphics terminals are capable of displaying even more characters. For these screens, use a layout form that corresponds.

Data Entry Modes

There are three common modes of entering data to terminal screens. These include the format, the prompt, and the menu. The selection of mode depends upon the entry requirements of the system.

```
           INSURANCE  LIABILITY  SCREEN

SHIPPER                              CLAIM NO.
ADDRESS                              CONTACT
CITY,  STATE,  ZIP                   DATE
INSURED  VALUE            WEIGHT                  CLERK
DESCRIBE  CONDITION  OF  PACKAGE  WHEN  RECEIVED:    ▮
```

FIGURE 9.12

Formatted Input Mode

```
         CREDIT  AND  COLLECTIONS  SCREEN

ENTER  NAME  OF  ACCOUNT      Forester  Products,  Inc.
ENTER  ADDRESS  OF  ACCOUNT   4934  Millwoods  Dr.
ENTER  CITY,  STATE,  ZIP     Portsville,  ME  02332
ENTER  AMOUNT  OF  PAYMENT    $334.38
ENTER  NO.  DAYS  OVERDUE     ▮
```

FIGURE 9.13

Prompt Input Mode

```
        SPECIAL  ROUTING  SERVICES  MENU

WHICH  OF  THE  FOLLOWING  SPECIAL  SERVICES  ARE  NEEDED?
              1.  INVOICE  TRACKING
              2.  DELIVERY  FOLLOW-UP
              3.  DROP-OFF  LOCATION  SERVICE
              4.  HOLIDAY  DELIVERY  SCHEDULE
              5.  TERMINATE  INPUT
PLEASE  ENTER  YOUR  CHOICE:    ▮
```

FIGURE 9.14

Menu Input Mode

Formatted Input   In the **formatted input** mode, the screen includes blank spaces or leadered lines for input (see Fig. 9.12). To enter data, the operator positions the cursor at the appropriate line and keys in the data. (A **cursor** is a marker on the screen showing where the next character is to be entered.) Fixed data is displayed on the screen and the operator enters the variable data. This form of input is acceptable where relatively fixed data is to be entered.

Prompts   In the **prompt** input mode, the terminal displays one or more queries. The operator enters the data requested, and the terminal then displays the next query. No full-page format is displayed. Figure 9.13 illustrates a series of prompts that are displayed one line at a time. This method of input is easy to design, but may be slow and awkward to use where a large amount of data is to be entered.

Menus   One of the most flexible and easy-to-use methods of data input is the menu mode (see Fig. 9.14). A **menu** is a group of options from which the

FIGURE 9.15

Menu Option

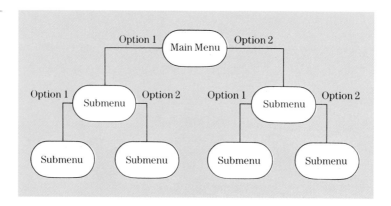

```
                    INVOICE  TRACKING  MENU

WHICH  OF  THE  FOLLOWING  TRACKING  OPTIONS  DO  YOU  NEED?
                1.  TRACE  PACKAGE  BY  DESTINATION
                2.  TRACE  PACKAGE  BY  SHIPPER  NO.
                3.  TRACE  PACKAGE  BY  SHIPPER  LOCATION
                4.  TRACE  PACKAGE  BY  INVOICE  CODE
                5.  TERMINATE  INPUT
    PLEASE  ENTER  YOUR  CHOICE:     ▮
```

FIGURE 9.16

Hierarchy of Menus

operator can choose. After an option is selected, another menu or a formatted screen is displayed, ready for data entry (see Fig. 9.15).

A top-down approach should be employed to design a menu system. Figure 9.16 illustrates a hierarchy of menus. At the top is the main menu, which is displayed at the beginning of the entry program. Submenus may be selected, each displaying another entry screen for inputting different data.

TERMINAL SCREEN DIALOG

Let us go through the steps involved in designing an input screen dialog for UniTrans Company. A systems analyst has studied the input problem and has concluded that an input system needs to be designed to handle telephone requests at the main office. Operators receive requests for standard forms, changes of address, or information about UniTrans's services. Sometimes these requests are received through the mail. Figure 9.17 shows three source documents. A terminal dialog must be written to enter the data on these documents (when completed) into the computer.

FORMS REQUEST

Please ship us the forms checked:

_____
Firm

_____
Street

_____
City, State, Zip

_____
Attn.   Phone

_____
Authorized Signature

Quan.   Description

_____ Lost in Transit Report

_____ Bill of Lading

_____ Credit Approval Request

_____ Standard Shipping Labels

_____ Damaged Goods Report

Account No. _____

CHANGE OF ADDRESS REQUEST FORM

Current Address:

_____
Firm

_____
Present Address

_____
City, State, Zip

_____
Phone

_____
Authorized by

New Address:

_____
Firm

_____
New Address

_____
City, State, Zip

_____
Phone

_____
Account No.

REQUEST FOR INFORMATION

Our firm would like to know more information about your:

_____
Firm

_____
Street

_____
City, State, Zip

_____
Phone

_____
Contact

Please: _____ Phone us

_____ RapidTransit Package Service

_____ OverNighter Rush Service

_____ BudgetPak Service

_____ Personal Courier Delivery

Account No. _____

_____ Mail information

FIGURE 9.17

Source Documents

FIGURE 9.18

Main Menu

UNITRANS COMPANY
INPUT MENU
SELECT AN INPUT OPTION FROM THE LIST BELOW:
  1. FORMS REQUEST
  2. CHANGE OF ADDRESS REQUEST
  3. REQUEST FOR SPECIAL INFORMATION
  4. TERMINATE INPUT
PLEASE ENTER YOUR CHOICE: ▮

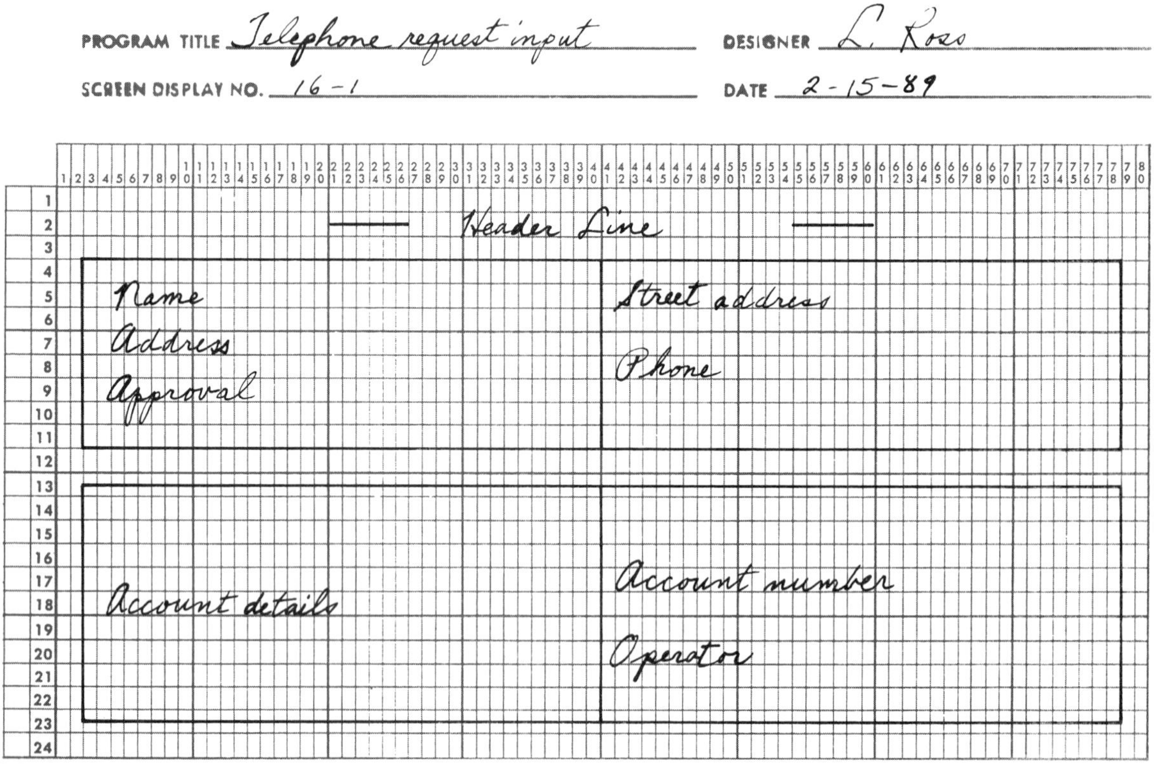

PROGRAM TITLE _Telephone request input_   DESIGNER _L. Ross_

SCREEN DISPLAY NO. _16-1_   DATE _2-15-89_

FIGURE 9.19

Terminal Screen Layout

The analyst develops the following task list:

TASK LIST

1. Review problem and user requirements.

2. Prepare a general layout.

3. Design main menu.

4. Design forms request screen format.

5. Design change of address screen format.

6. Design request for information screen format.

```
                    FORMS  REQUEST  INPUT  SCREEN
FIRM                                  STREET
CITY, STATE, ZIP                      ATTN.
APPROVED SIGNATURE
LOST IN TRANSIT REPORT                BILL OF LADING
CREDIT APPROVAL REPORT                STANDARD SHIPPING LABELS
DAMAGED GOODS REPORT                  ACCOUNT NO.
DATE ENTERED                          OPERATOR NO.
```

FIGURE 9.20

Document Request Screen

```
                  CHANGE  OF  ADDRESS  INPUT  SCREEN

CURRENT FIRM NAME                     ADDRESS
CITY,  STATE,  ZIP                    PHONE
APPROVED SIGNATURE
NEW FIRM NAME                         ADDRESS
CITY, STATE, ZIP                      PHONE
ACCOUNT NO.
DATE ENTERED                          OPERATOR NO.
```

FIGURE 9.21

Change of Address Screen

```
             REQUEST  FOR  INFORMATION  INPUT  SCREEN
FIRM                                  STREET
CITY, STATE, ZIP                      PHONE
CONTACT
RAPIDTRANSIT                          OVERNIGHTER
BUDGETPAK                             COURIER
ACCOUNT NO.
PHONE                                 MAIL
```

FIGURE 9.22

Information Request Screen

The analyst begins the first task by studying the problem and the user requirements. A main menu and three input screens must be designed. Figure 9.18 shows the main menu in the series. The operator will select an option from this screen.

The next step involves designing specific screen formats. This job is done by preparing a general layout, illustrated in Fig. 9.19, which depicts common areas to be implemented in each of the screen formats.

The analyst then designs a set of three input screens, shown in Figs. 9.20, 9.21, and 9.22. Each of these screens is built around the basic layout shown in Fig. 9.19. This completes the design task. The analyst now goes on to write specifications for the program that will be used in UniTrans's computer system to process the input data. The input design for this problem would probably be part of a much broader systems design for UniTrans's operations.

Now that we have studied document and online terminal input design, we need to understand output system design. The next chapter describes computer output systems and the design of records and forms.

Summary

Input designs may be built around transaction-oriented or batch-processing systems. The input process begins with a source document. Some input records are machine readable, while others are not. Common input devices include keyboard terminals, which may be either smart or dumb in nature, manual data entry machines, and optical scanning devices. Magnetic ink character readers, voice recognition devices, and a variety of other machines are used for input.

Pay careful attention to the design of source documents. Make use of input verification and control procedures. Common tests on input media include the range test, test for completeness, accuracy, sequence, combination, and data type check tests. Verification checks the accuracy of data that has been entered.

Systems analysts follow a series of input design guidelines such as designing screens for operator convenience, using logical expressions, and using the computer to perform the computations. A data dictionary ensures consistency of input elements.

Hard copy records are laid out on a form ruled in rows and columns. Terminal screens are laid out using a form that corresponds with the number of characters on the screen. Formatted input, prompt, and menu are common data entry modes.

Key Terms

Batch processing	**Menu**
Batch totals	**Offline data entry**
Check digit	**Online data entry**
Cursor	**Optical character reader (OCR)**
Dumb terminal	**Optical scanning device**
Formatted input	**Prompt**
Hard copy	**Real time**
Laser beam scanner	**Smart terminal**
Machine readable	**Soft copy**
Magnetic ink character recognition (MICR)	**Transaction-oriented processing**
	Verification
Manual data entry	**Voice recognition device**
Mark sense reader	

1. Define *source document* and describe how it differs from other documents used in a business.
2. Define *verification* and explain why it is important.
3. Contrast batch and transaction-oriented processing.
4. List four different input media.
5. How does OCR input differ from MICR input?
6. Contrast smart and dumb terminals.
7. Describe how mark sense readers input data.
8. Discuss how input controls are used.
9. Describe how a data dictionary is used in data entry systems.
10. Describe the menu input mode.

1. Visit the computer center on your campus and describe the input media used. What type of verification, if any, is performed?
2. You have been asked by the proprietor of a small retail establishment to assist in developing a transaction-oriented information-processing system. Lay out and design the necessary input records.
3. Design a group of records for a batch-processing system. The records are to maintain inventory control for a small appliance parts manufacturer.
4. Gather several optical character recognition forms. Select one of them for redesign. Prepare an improved input format and include input verification and control tests.
5. Evaluate and redesign input screens for a computer software package. Obtain a computer program that uses input screens. Modify and change the contents of the screens to improve their input capability.

ANALYST AT WORK

VOLUME TELEMARKETING COMPANY

DESCRIPTION OF FIRM

Volume Telemarketing Company (VTC) is a major distributor of office copiers, supplies, paper, and toner. VTC's customers are scattered over the western United States. Sales are made through direct telephone contacts. The telemarketing department maintains an extensive database of potential customers. The database is broken down geographically by city. It contains customer names, addresses, and phone numbers and information on purchasing agents and their clients' buying patterns.

Sales contacts are made by telemarketing representatives who prospect the list for potential customers. After making an initial phone contact, the representative places follow-up calls to the purchasing agent. Because of VTC's greater purchasing power, it is able to offer lower prices and faster delivery than competitors. As a result, the company can bid successfully on major accounts.

SYSTEM OVERVIEW

VTC's phone prospecting and sales order operation is based upon a computer system with a number of terminals attached. Each telemarketing representative's desk is equipped with a computer terminal and a telephone. The computer contains the database of potential customers and VTC's product mix, including prices, quantity in stock, and other data.

When a customer purchases goods, the representative enters ordering information into the computer terminal. Figure 9.23 is a data flow diagram that describes the system. Periodically, all orders are transferred to VTC's order fulfillment department where they are filled and shipped. Billing, credit, collection, and other services are provided by other departments in the company using data from the telemarketing department's computer system.

A marketing representative will often concentrate on prospects in a given geographic area. This requires displaying appropriate prospect data on the terminal's display screen. During the phone contact, the representative must refer to pricing and inventory information maintained in the computer. After making a sale, the representative calls up an order input screen format and enters the relevant data. Telemarketing representatives must be able to shift quickly between input screens.

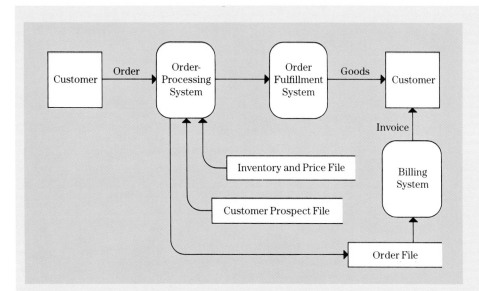

FIGURE 9.23

Volume Telemarketing Company Data Flow Diagram.

HANDS-ON APPLICATION

This project consists of designing the three input screens necessary for this system. Assume that a computer is at your disposal, enabling you to prototype the screens and subject them to end-user testing. The work products in this project consist of three screens and an evaluation report:

1. Customer prospect screen
2. Product price/inventory screen
3. Customer order screen
4. Screen evaluation report

Be sure to include appropriate input verification and controls for each screen you design. The screens should be properly laid out, applying the input design principles discussed in this chapter.

Work Product No. 1.   Design a customer prospect screen. The screen should contain the prospect's name and phone number, the purchasing agent's name and phone number, and other pertinent data. If you have a computer available, prototype the screen and ask other students to critique it before preparing a final design. Label your screen WP1, Chapter 9.

The first step is the preparation of a task list. In the space below list the tasks that must be carried out to design, modify, and fully implement the customer prospect screen layout.

TASK LIST

_____

_____

_____

_____

_____

_____

_____

Work Product No. 2   Design the product/price inventory screen. This screen should include information such as:

STOCK NUMBER	NUMBER	UNIT COST	INVENTORY
6003	Toner, 16 oz.	$29.75	29
6004	Toner, 32 oz.	$52.80	On order

The purpose of this screen is to provide a display of VTC's products, prices, and inventory. Label it WP2, Chapter 9. Use the space below to prepare a task list to assist in designing the screen.

TASK LIST

_____

_____

_____

_____

_____

_____

Work Product No. 3 Design a customer order screen. This screen will be used to enter order data once the customer has agreed to purchase goods. The screen should include such information as customer name, address, purchase order number, and so forth. Consider the needs of an order fulfillment department and decide what information should be entered on the screen to enable clerks to process orders properly. Label this WP3, Chapter 9.

On the lines below prepare the task list you will follow to design, modify, and implement the customer order screen.

TASK LIST

_____

_____

_____

_____

_____

_____

_____

Work Product No. 4 Evaluate your work. You may wish to refer to Chapter 16 for guidance. Prepare a critique of the three layout screens. Describe the contents and use of each screen. Describe improvements that could optimize their use. Label your report WP4, Chapter 9. Use the space below to prepare an outline for the report.

EVALUATION REPORT OUTLINE

_____

_____

_____

_____

OUTPUT
SYSTEM
DESIGN

LEARNING OBJECTIVES

After studying this chapter, you should be able to:

1. Design hard copy and soft copy output forms.

2. Describe printers and various output media.

3. State guidelines for forms design and layout criteria.

4. List techniques for forms control.

5. Explain readability and graphics considerations.

6. Describe commonly used types of forms.

The function of all output systems is to convert electronic pulses stored in a computer system into a form useful to people and organizations. Output systems generate documents, letters, memos, drawings, charts, and graphs and report the results of processing. Without output, the most perfectly designed system would be of little value to an organization.

In this chapter we review the major forms of output, including printers, plotters, display terminals, and other devices. The chapter describes record design and layout and forms control.

OUTPUT DEVICES

A variety of output devices report the results of system processing. Output media vary in cost, permanence, and function. They can be combined in various ways to produce output formats suited to the needs of individual systems. Output devices fall into two categories: hard copy and soft copy (see Fig. 10.1).

FIGURE 10.1

Output Devices

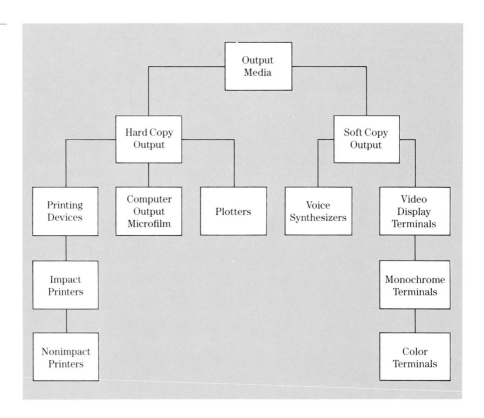

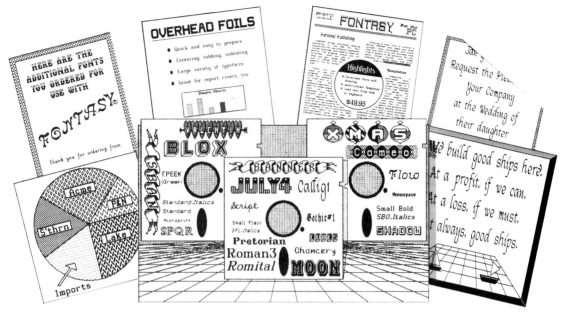

(Source: ® Prosoft)

Hard Copy Output

Hard copy output consists of documents, forms and reports typed or printed on paper (see Fig. 10.2). The hard copy medium is usually selected when the results of processing must be saved permanently, or mailed, handled, and read by people.

There are many hard copy devices available. Printers range from slow speed, impact-type devices to high speed laser and ink jet machines. These devices may cost as little as $200 or as much as $10,000.

Different technologies are used to generate letter forms, including photographic, electrostatic, and thermal imaging techniques. Printers can output from as little as 15 characters per second to over 22,000 lines per minute. The quality ranges from minimally readable to typeset quality. Let us look at some of the devices that produce hard copy.

Impact Printers   **Impact printers** (see Fig. 10.3) strike a letter against a ribbon, which transfers ink to the paper. Fully formed letters may be molded on wheels, type bars, or type elements. **Letter-quality** printers produce fully formed letters. Impact printers are widely used in business systems to generate correspondence, memos, and reports.

FIGURE 10.2

Hard Copy Output
Computers can generate different sizes and styles of type.

FIGURE 10.3

**Daisy Wheel
Printer** This device
outputs letter-
quality characters.

(Source: Darlene Bordwell)

FIGURE 10.4

Laser Printer

(Photo courtesy of Hewlett-Packard Company)

Nonimpact Printers **Nonimpact printers** produce images without
striking a letter form against paper, using instead heat-sensitized paper, ink jets,
and other methods. A **laser printer,** a widely used type of nonimpact printer,
uses a technology closely akin to that of an electrostatic office copier. It produces
letter-quality output at high speed, and can output different sizes and styles of
lettering (see Fig. 10.4). Analysts often select laser printers where a large volume
of output is to be generated and noise levels must be kept to a minimum.

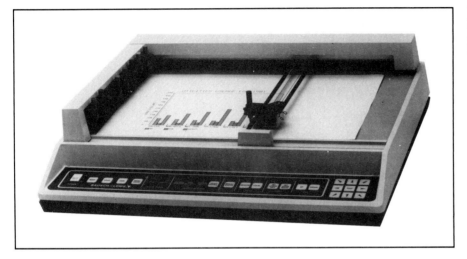

(Source: Houston Instrument Division of AMETEK, Inc.)

FIGURE 10.5

Flatbed Plotter
Plotters draw charts, graphs, lines, and curves.

Plotters **Plotters** are another form of hard copy output device (see Fig. 10.5). Plotters can draw charts, graphs, lines or curves. Some plotters generate single-color images, while others are capable of outputting multicolor plots. These devices are found in businesses and many engineering establishments.

Computer Output Microfilm (COM) **Computer output microfilm (COM)** produces photographic images reduced 50 or more times from their original size. This means great savings in storage space. COM images are exposed on small sheets of film measuring 4 × 6 inches, known as **microfiche** records. Other forms include **microfilm,** where images are stored on strips of film (see Fig. 10.6). Systems designers often select this medium when large volumes of information are to be output and stored. To read COM images, the microfilm or microfiche must be placed in a reader so the image can be enlarged enough to be read by the human eye.

Soft Copy Output

Soft copy output consists of a nonpermanent or temporary display of information. Soft copy encompasses various types of video display terminals and audio output devices. Since these machines do not use paper, ink, or ribbons and are not mechanical, they are selected where the analyst wishes to generate a large volume of nonpermanent output. Soft copy devices require less maintenance than hard copy devices because they have no moving parts.

FIGURE 10.6

Microfilm Reader Strips of microfilm records are wound on reels and can be displayed for easy viewing.

Video Display Terminal (VDT) The **video display terminal (VDT)** is a common means of outputting soft copy (see Fig. 10.7). This type of device may be equipped with a cathode ray tube (CRT) display. VDTs can display both pictures and words on a screen. Some provide only monochrome (one color) output, while others generate full color images. Devices in this category output at high speed and require relatively little maintenance. A display of over 1000 characters can be generated on a screen in a fraction of a second.

Voice Synthesizer The **voice synthesizer** generates spoken words, tones, or audible sounds. It converts pulses from the computer to tones of different frequencies and durations.

The selection of the appropriate output medium depends upon the needs of the system. Hard copy output at high speed from a computer is usually generated by some form of laser or ink jet printer. Images or information needed only temporarily will probably be generated using a VDT. The systems analyst must be knowledgeable about various forms of output media and should be able to specify the devices that will best meet the requirements of the system.

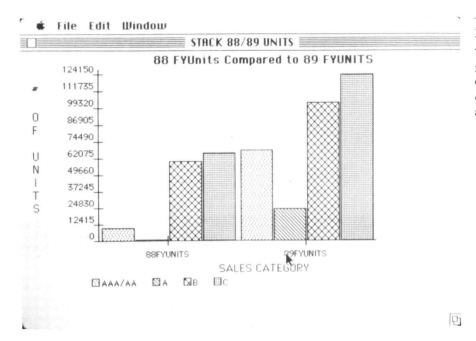

FIGURE 10.7

Video Display Terminal (VDT) Graphics and text can be displayed on a screen.

HOW TO DESIGN DATA OUTPUT

The selection of output media and the design of output forms usually begins with an assessment of system requirements and end-user needs. Output design is frequently conducted concurrently with input design. The systems analyst sometimes uses a data dictionary to ensure consistency between input and output records.

Hard Copy Record Layout Forms

Analysts usually use a layout form when planning and designing hard copy records. The form is laid out in rows and columns consistent with the spacing of the printer. Using a form simplifies the task of record design and helps ensure that columns line up properly and headings are positioned correctly.

Design Example

When preparing an output record, the analyst should first formulate a logical design. This consists of a theoretical layout of records showing only the major elements and specifications for output. Later, these elements will be con-

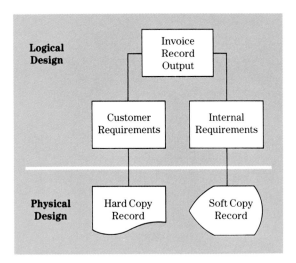

verted into specifics that can be implemented with forms and hardware. For example, an analyst at UniTrans decides that two invoice forms are needed in the volume sales department, one for the customer and the other for internal use (see Fig. 10.8).

Once this logical decision has been made, it is reduced to a physical design. A form is used to lay out the basic elements and their print positions (see Fig. 10.9). In this instance, the form for the customer is generated on a line printer so that a document can be mailed (see Fig. 10.10). The internal document may become a report displayed on a video display screen. The image can be called up as required, so a soft copy is adequate. Thus, the system output requirements are met logically and physically.

Output Considerations

In designing system output, the analyst must assess many factors before preparing specific designs and selecting media. The following are some of the questions that should be asked when executing an output design.

- Is hard or soft copy output needed? The answer to this question will depend upon permanency, speed, cost, and other factors.
- Should the record be textual or graphic? The analyst must decide whether the preferred form of output would be a chart, table, printed text, etc.
- Will the record be stored, transmitted, or mailed? This will determine whether microfilm, printed documents, or screen images are selected.

SHARE PRINT CHART   PROG. ID. _____   PAGE _____

(SPACING: 6 LINES PER INCH, DEPTH: 51 LINES)   DATE _____

PROGRAM TITLE _____

PROGRAMMER OR DOCUMENTALIST: _____

CHART TITLE _____

```
                    CUSTOMER INVOICE

              UNITRANS COMPANY
                      INVOICE NO.

BILL  TO:            DATE:
                     TERMS:
                     SHIPPER NO:

Date     Package No.        Type Service          Charge




              VOLUME DISCOUNTS AVAILABLE

        Shippers who transport over $5000 per month
        are entitled to the following discount:

           8%   (EIGHT PERCENT)


REMIT ALL PAYMENTS TO:
ACCOUNTS RECEIVABLE DEPARTMENT
UNITRANS COMPANY
P.O. BOX 3434,  CENTRAL VALLEY, CA  91605
```

FIGURE 10.9

Layout Example

- Will the document be reproduced? If so, the record must be in a permanent form and an appropriate size must be selected.
- What hardware or viewing aids will be available to the user? Printed documents can be read by virtually everyone. Soft copy output requires a computer terminal and microfilm needs a microfilm reader.
- Is a color image required?

CUSTOMER INVOICE

UNITRANS COMPANY

INVOICE NO. 56542

BILL TO:

DATE: 10—31

CONTINENTAL MANUFACTURING
2382 Riverside Dr.
Los Angeles, CA. 90028

TERMS: Net 10 days

SHIPPER NO. 3458

DATE	PACKAGE NO.	TYPE SERVICE	CHARGE
9—01	1076321	RadidTransit	$ 23.46
9—06	1085483	RapidTransit	45.33
9—14	1099928	BudgetPak Service	8.20
9—14	1099934	OverNighter Rush	67.38
9—22	1100234	OverNighter Rush	87.32
9—23	1102365	RapidTransit	23.46
9—30	1109292	BudgetPak Service	12.10
		AMOUNT DUE	$267.25

VOLUME DISCOUNTS AVAILABLE

Shippers who transport over $5000 per month
are entitled to the following discount:

8% (EIGHT PERCENT)

REMIT ALL PAYMENTS TO:
ACCOUNTS RECEIVABLE DEPARTMENT
UNITRANS COMPANY
P.O. BOX 3434, Central Valley, CA 91605

FIGURE 10.10

Finished Document

FORMS OPTIONS

The systems analyst is often responsible for selecting the type of printed
forms and records used by an organization. Many factors should be considered
when selecting business forms. These include type of data to be recorded, purpose of the form, method of data entry, and physical characteristics of the form
itself. Forms should be easy to understand, convenient to use, and designed to

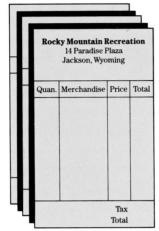
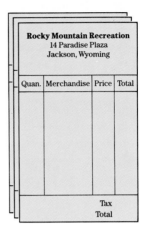

FIGURE 10.11

Types of Forms
Continuous forms
are fan-folded or
printed on a contin-
uous roll.
NCR forms make
multiple copies with-
out using carbon
paper.
The carbon-
interleaved form has
carbons inserted
between each form
in the set.

facilitate business activities and functions. Figure 10.11 shows some commonly used forms.

Cut Forms   **Cut forms** are prepared one form per page. They are usually inserted manually into printers or other output devices. Cut forms are loose
and unbound, and come in a variety of sizes and colors.

Continuous Forms   Forms may be supplied in a **continuous** roll or
fan-folded in boxes. Each form is attached to the forms before and after it,
separated by rows of perforations. Automatic paper-handling machines usually
use continuous forms since they eliminate the need for manual insertion of each
form. Once the first form has been positioned, the machine automatically feeds
subsequent forms. Paychecks prepared on line printers, order confirmation forms,
invoices, and statements are some examples.

The **pin feed form** is a version of the continuous form. Small holes
punched at the sides of the page facilitate proper positioning during automatic
feeding. The pinholes travel over sprockets on each end of the platen roll as the
paper moves through the print unit.

Padded Forms   Forms may be ordered as pads, with or without chip-
board backing. Pads of 50 or 100 forms are bound together with a rubber-based
adhesive at the top of the pages. **Padded forms** keep pages neat and in sequence.
Numbered forms are often padded to facilitate using them in sequential order.
Padded forms are used for such things as interoffice memos, order form books,
or job quotation forms.

NCR Paper Forms   **NCR (no carbon required) forms** eliminate the
need for interleaved carbon sheets or printed carbonized areas on multipart
forms. A special chemical, a substitute for carbon, is applied to the face or back

page. When the forms are written or typed upon, the impression appears on the duplicate copies. NCR forms are clean to use and eliminate the inconvenience of carbon papers. They are often more expensive, however, due to the higher cost of the specially coated paper. They are used for a whole range of business forms for which copies are needed.

Carbon Interleaved Forms   This is a multipart form with a sheet of carbon paper inserted between each page. Duplicate copies are made as the original data is entered. Up to ten copies may be made; however, the quality of each succeeding copy degenerates somewhat.

Carbon interleaved forms are often supplied in a snap-apart format. Pages and carbons are fastened together at the top, creating a stub. When the form has been completed, the stub is pulled off, separating the carbon papers from the pages of the form. This type of form is used for such things as paychecks with carbon copy vouchers or sales order forms with copies for different departments.

DESIGN CONSIDERATIONS

Well-designed forms and records speed entering and processing of data and increase the level of accuracy. The analyst should consider several factors when planning forms.

Paper Selection

Forms can be printed on paper of many different colors, weights, stocks, and sizes.

Colored Paper   Printing on colored paper creates copies that are easily identified and sorted. A common color selection for forms is:

White—First copy

Yellow—Second copy

Pink—Third copy

Blue—Fourth copy

Buff—Fifth copy

Green—Sixth copy

Salmon—Seventh copy

Weight of Stock   Paper is available in different thicknesses, called **weight** or **substance.** The weight of the paper stock should be suitable to the form. Forms that will be used once may be printed on lightweight stock to save storage room and paper costs. Forms that will be handled many times should be printed on durable, heavyweight stock. Most business forms are printed on 16- or 20-lb. bond. Listed below are brief descriptions of the common weights:

9-lb. bond—Very thin, used for multipart forms

11-lb. bond—Thin stock, used for multipart forms

13-lb. bond—Thin stock, used for multipart forms

16-lb. bond—Lightweight stock for general forms

20-lb. bond—Medium-weight stock for general forms

24-lb. bond—Heavyweight paper for durable forms

28-32-lb. ledger—Used for permanent records

90-lb. index bristol—Lightweight card stock for durable records

110-lb. index bristol—Medium-weight card stock for permanent records

140-lb. index bristol—Heavyweight card stock

Type of Stock   Forms may be ordered in a variety of paper types. Newsprint stock is generally not suitable for forms, but is sometimes used when cost is important and large quantities of forms are required. Generally, utility forms are printed on sulphite bond, a paper made entirely of wood pulp. Pen and ink forms and records of a permanent nature are usually printed on rag bond. This paper contains 25 to 100 percent cotton fiber.

Size of Form   Form size depends upon several factors—use, processing, storage. As much as possible, form sizes should be standardized to facilitate handling, storage, and filing. Consult your printer regarding paper sizes before ordering a large quantity of forms. Often a fraction of an inch difference in size can mean a substantial cost saving.

FORMS CONTROL

The systems analyst structures procedures that facilitate **forms control,** which is the orderly, controlled movement of forms through a system. Forms control is concerned with stocking, distributing, revising, printing, and specifying forms, input records, and source documents. Several factors should be considered when planning a forms control system.

FIGURE 10.12

Forms Control A form should contain descriptive data identifying it.

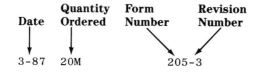

Assignment of Numbers

Number each type of form or record to make reordering or referencing easier. Keep a master list of forms in a forms manual. The form number may include such information as the quantity printed and the date. An example is shown in Fig. 10.12.

Revision Number

If forms or records are revised or updated, a revision number should be assigned to the new form. This aids in keeping track of changes in content. All revisions should be recorded in the master forms book. One person or department should be assigned the responsibility of revising forms. All changes and modifications should be cleared through that person to avoid unnecessary increases in the number of forms and records in use.

Consecutively Numbered Forms

It is sometimes important to keep close control over each copy of a form. Consecutively numbered forms facilitate inventory control and help to maintain accuracy when handling returned merchandise transactions. Keep a record of all numbers in use and check it before ordering new forms, which should follow in the appropriate numbered sequence.

Routing of Forms

If parts of a form are to be sent to different people or workstations, routing information should appear on each part. For example:

Original—Customer copy

Duplicate—Accounting department copy

Triplicate—Marketing department copy

Quadruplicate—Production department copy

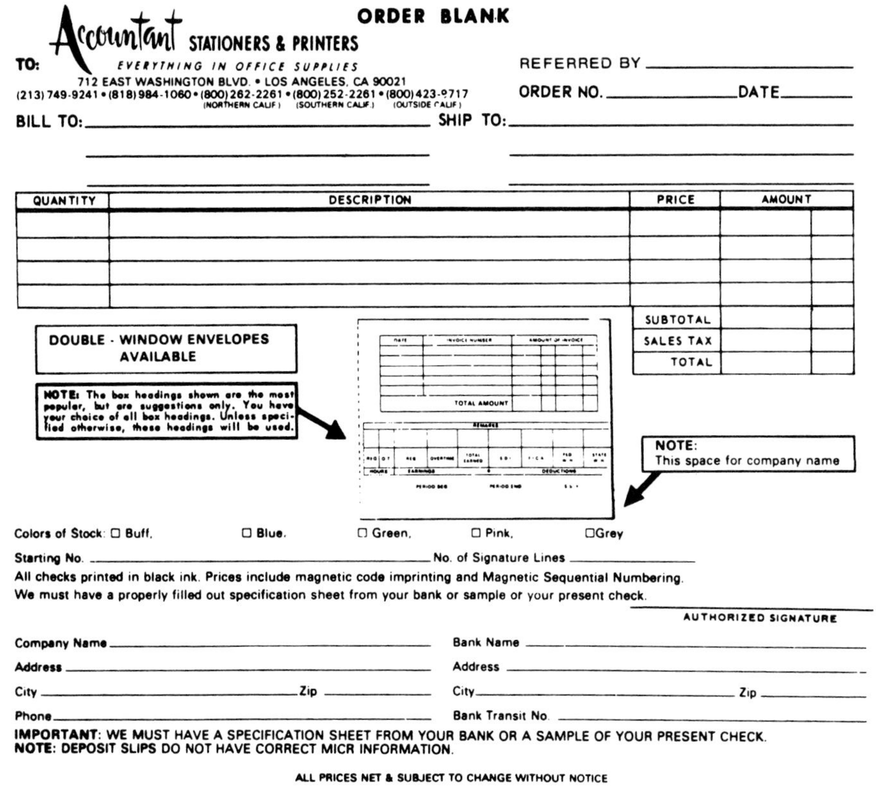

ORDER BLANK

TO: Accountant STATIONERS & PRINTERS
EVERYTHING IN OFFICE SUPPLIES
712 EAST WASHINGTON BLVD. • LOS ANGELES, CA 90021
(213) 749-9241 • (818) 984-1060 • (800) 262-2261 (NORTHERN CALIF.) • (800) 252-2261 (SOUTHERN CALIF.) • (800) 423-9717 (OUTSIDE CALIF.)

REFERRED BY ____________

ORDER NO. ____________ DATE ________

BILL TO: ____________ SHIP TO: ____________

QUANTITY	DESCRIPTION	PRICE	AMOUNT
		SUBTOTAL	
		SALES TAX	
		TOTAL	

DOUBLE - WINDOW ENVELOPES AVAILABLE

NOTE: The box headings shown are the most popular, but are suggestions only. You have your choice of all box headings. Unless specified otherwise, these headings will be used.

NOTE: This space for company name

Colors of Stock: ☐ Buff, ☐ Blue, ☐ Green, ☐ Pink, ☐ Grey

Starting No. ____________ No. of Signature Lines ________

All checks printed in black ink. Prices include magnetic code imprinting and Magnetic Sequential Numbering.

We must have a properly filled out specification sheet from your bank or sample or your present check.

AUTHORIZED SIGNATURE

Company Name ____________ Bank Name ____________

Address ____________ Address ____________

City ________ Zip ________ City ________ Zip ________

Phone ____________ Bank Transit No. ____________

IMPORTANT: WE MUST HAVE A SPECIFICATION SHEET FROM YOUR BANK OR A SAMPLE OF YOUR PRESENT CHECK.
NOTE: DEPOSIT SLIPS DO NOT HAVE CORRECT MICR INFORMATION.

ALL PRICES NET & SUBJECT TO CHANGE WITHOUT NOTICE

(Source: Accountant Stationers & Printers, Los Angeles, Ca.)

FIGURE 10.13

Form With Instructions

Instructions For Use

Any form or record that is not self-explanatory should include descriptive text. Instructions may be printed directly on the form (see Fig. 10.13) or supplied separately with each packet. A copy of the instructions for completing a form should appear in the forms manual.

Inventory Forms

The systems analyst will need to establish an inventory level to make sure that an adequate supply of forms is always available. Reorder promptly to avoid serious system problems. The forms manual should contain a record of the necessary information for reordering forms, such as supplier, cost, and specifications.

Deleting Unnecessary Forms

All forms and records should be reviewed periodically and unnecessary ones should be eliminated. The reviewer should examine the need for a form, its routing locations, revisions, and improvements. Eliminate forms that are no longer needed.

DESIGNING SCREEN OUTPUT

Many of the considerations that apply to designing hard copy documents also apply to the design of screen records. The analyst usually uses a layout form that conforms to the number of columns and lines on the display screen. The following questions should be asked when evaluating screen output:

- Should a color or monochrome display be used?
- Should cursors or flashing images be incorporated into the screen?
- Should some words, phrases, or areas be displayed in reverse or highlighted?
- Should a sequence of screens be used to display the output? If so, what information should be organized into specific displays?
- How should totals, columns, or other special features be aligned and labeled?

READABILITY AND GRAPHICS

Data placement is an important element in output design, whether for a printed form or a display on a screen. The design should be carefully planned for maximum ease of use and legibility. Consider the items below when designing records.

1. Spacing. Factors to be considered include spacing, arrangement of headings, size of type, and margins. If the form is to be used in longhand, adequate space must be provided for fill-ins or completion items. If it is to be used on a typewriter, the spacing should conform to the standard six lines to the inch.

2. Order of items. Important items should be placed at the top of the record. Fields on a record should be grouped so that related items are in adjacent positions. The order of fields should bear a logical relationship to the order in which the data is acquired or entered. Items copied from a source

document or other form should be in the same sequence. The flow of data on a record should be output from left to right and from top to bottom.

3. Identification. Reports, lists, forms, and screens should be titled to identify their purpose. Columns and rows should be clearly labeled whenever necessary.

4. Maximum readability. Reports, forms, and output screens should be designed for maximum readability. This requires attention to column spacing, placement of identifying text, or arrangement of output data. Lines should be properly spaced and the columns well separated.

5. Physical considerations. The graphic details of output reports and forms should be carefully planned. Adequate margins and space around text improve readability. Pages should always be numbered.

6. Permanence. The output medium should be durable enough for its intended use. Forms and documents that are to be handled many times should be prepared on heavy paper. Information of a transitory nature may be output as soft copy on a video display screen.

7. Logical sequence. Information being input should be in the order used in normal business practice. For example, a measurement should be reported as 3'10", not 10"3'.

Now that we have discussed some of the principles of system output design, we will turn to the details of file design. The next chapter describes how to design files and records and evaluate storage systems.

Summary

Output reports the results of processing. Hard copy output consists of documents, forms, or reports printed on paper. Impact and nonimpact printers create readable images. Plotters generate output such as charts, graphs, lines, or curves. Microfiche and microfilm are also output from computers. Soft copy output consists of nonpermanent information, such as displays on a screen. Audio output is generated by voice synthesizers.

Output design begins with an assessment of system and end-user needs. First a logical design is developed, then a physical design is implemented. A variety of options are available, including cut, fan-folded, pin feed, padded, NCR, and carbon interleaved forms. There are a variety of paper weights, colors, stocks, and sizes.

Techniques used in forms control include assignment of numbers, sequential numbering, routing instructions, and methods for eliminating unnecessary forms. Screen output should be designed to promote readability. Considerations include spacing, order of items, and outputting a logical sequence of information. Color or monochrome display can be used.

Key Terms

Carbon interleaved form

Computer output microfilm (COM)

Continuous form

Cut form

Fan-folded form

Forms control

Impact printer

Laser printer

Letter quality

Microfiche

Microfilm

NCR (no carbon required) form

Nonimpact printer

Padded form

Paper substance

Paper weight

Pin feed form

Plotters

Video display terminal (VDT)

Voice synthesizer

Exercises

1. How does soft copy output differ from hard copy output?

2. What questions should be asked when evaluating an output screen?

3. If a microfilm reader is available at your campus, obtain a microfilm record and display it on the reader.

4. List some of the factors that must be considered in designing business forms.

5. List several of the choices involved in selecting the paper for forms.

6. What are the major considerations in planning output records?

7. What factors are normally considered in forms control?

8. Give an example of a typical quadruplicate routing for a set of forms.

9. List a common color scheme for identifying multipart forms.

10. Describe the type of output generated by plotters.

Projects

1. Determine the approximate weight and volume of 10,000 hard copy documents that are 8½″ × 11″. What would be the approximate weight and volume if this data were to be stored on microfilm?

2. Gather several examples of business forms. Write a brief evaluation of each, using the criteria discussed in this chapter.

3. Obtain several samples of paper used to print forms. Determine the type and weight. What recommendations for improvement would you make?

4. Obtain six different samples of computer-generated output. Study them carefully and determine which are letter quality and which are near letter quality. Are there any unique characteristics of the printouts?

5. Visit a local printing firm and discuss the elements of forms design. What suggestions do they have to improve printed forms?

ANALYST AT WORK

KENNEDY GRAPHICS

DESCRIPTION OF FIRM

Kennedy Graphics is a commercial printing company that produces a large volume of catalogs, sales brochures, announcements, and stationery. The company's fully equipped plant includes several one-color and multicolor offset presses, camera equipment, platemaking facilities, and a complete bindery.

When Kennedy Graphics receives an invitation to bid, a printing estimator reviews the job specifications. Using a computer, the estimator records the type of stock, amount required, color of ink, and other data needed for the job, and then prepares an estimate. The computer prints out a price estimate, which is then given to the customer. The same computer system is used for production control and job scheduling.

SYSTEM OVERVIEW

When the bid is accepted by the customer, an order is prepared and the job goes into production. The production department determines whether the necessary amount of paper and other materials are available in stock. This is done by checking the goods inventory file. As orders are accepted, materials are reserved for each job. If not enough goods are in stock, orders are placed with suppliers for the necessary materials.

Figure 10.14 is a data flow diagram that illustrates Kennedy's estimating and production scheduling systems. Job specifications and supplier prices are input to the system. Paper inventory reports, purchase orders, and information on jobs in progress are generated by the system. The goods inventory and jobs in production files are updated as goods come into stock or work is produced. An estimator or production manager can determine the status of a job or the amount of goods in inventory at any time by checking these files.

HANDS-ON APPLICATION

Design several of the output records used in the system: a paper stock inventory report, a jobs in production report, and a purchase order form.

Work Product No. 1   Design a paper stock inventory report that shows the goods in Kennedy's inventory. The hard copy form will be 8½″ × 11″ in size.

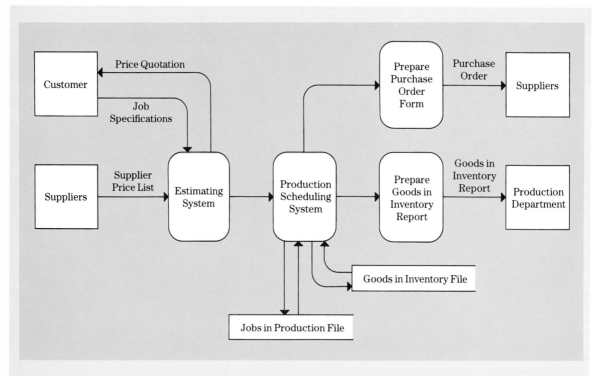

FIGURE 10.14

Kennedy Graphics
Data Flow Diagram

The report should contain headings and other pertinent information. Below is a sample of the data to be contained in the report. The data is listed in a single column and only one item is shown. Your report will include numerous such items, with data laid out in tabular form in vertical columns.

> Date placed in inventory: 02/17/88
> Type of paper: Coated book stock
> Quantity: 2500
> Size: 25" × 38"
> Weight: 65 lb.

Design this document and label it WP1, Chapter 10. Prepare a task list to assist in designing this output record and enter it below.

TASK LIST

_____

_____

_____

_____

_____

_____

_____

Work Product No. 2 Design a jobs in production report showing the jobs in progress. This report should be designed as a display on a video screen and contain headings and other pertinent data. Below is a sample of the data to be incorporated into the report:

> Name of customer: Orion Manufacturing Company
>
> Date ordered: 11/1/88
>
> Date to production: 11/3/88
>
> Delivery date: 11/21/88
>
> Item: 64-page booklets
>
> Stock: Uncoated book stock, 65 lb.

Design your report so that data is displayed in a readable format. Be sure all items are properly labeled with headings. Label this document WP2, Chapter 10. Prepare a task list to assist you in designing the screen and enter it below.

TASK LIST

_____

_____

_____

_____

_____

_____

Work Product No. 3 Design a purchase order form for purchasing goods and supplies. This form will be 8½" wide and 7" deep. It should contain headings and other pertinent data needed on a purchase order. Below is a sample of the data to be contained on the purchase order form:

> Date ordered: 10/20/88
>
> Purchase order no.: 39125

Purchased from: Malcolm Ink Company

Shipped to: Kennedy Graphics

Quantity ordered: 20 lbs.

Item: Offset black ink

Catalog no.: 217

Price per lb.: $8.50

Design the purchase order form in an easy-to-read format. Provide space for several items to be purchased on the same order form. Label the form WP3, Chapter 10. Begin your design effort with a task list and enter it below.

TASK LIST

_____

_____

_____

_____

_____

_____

RECORD, FILE, AND STORAGE DESIGN

LEARNING OBJECTIVES

After studying this chapter, you should be able to:

1. Describe data storage media.

2. Discuss data storage selection criteria.

3. Contrast fixed-length and variable-length records.

4. Explain file design considerations.

5. Contrast master records and detail records.

6. Describe different types of coding systems.

Much of the systems analyst's work involves planning and designing records and files and the storage systems to maintain them. Cost, accessibility, record permanence, file security, and physical space are some of the factors to be dealt with.

For organizations that handle relatively small amounts of data, simple records and storage methods suffice. For larger organizations, however, elaborate and sophisticated methods of storing and retrieving data must be used. This requires a systematic approach to designing records and files.

In this chapter we review the fundamental elements in designing records, files, and storage systems. Records and files serve as the building blocks for a larger structure, the database, to hold and manipulate data. The next chapter describes database structure and design. Thus we move from a discussion of individual records to the broader scope of the database.

DATA STORAGE MEDIA

The analyst must understand storage media before moving on to design files and records. The most commonly used media for storing data are described below. Each has its advantages and limitations; no one medium serves all functions. The media selected by the systems analyst will depend upon cost, permanence, accessibility, and security, as well as other factors.

Magnetic Storage Media

Magnetic storage media are the most widely used means of storing large volumes of data. They store data that has been converted from source documents into electrical pulses. Because the stored data is subject to accidental erasure, measures must be taken to assure file security. The accessibility of the data stored on these media is indirect. The stored data must be converted back into printed characters by a computer or a peripheral device before it can be used by humans. The principal methods of magnetic storage are on floppy disk, hard disk, or magnetic tape.

Floppy Disk Storage   **Floppy disks** are an inexpensive and convenient means of storing relatively limited amounts of data (see Fig. 11.1). They are manufactured in a variety of sizes including 8″, 5¼″ and 3½″. These disks can hold from 160,000 to almost two million characters, depending upon the type, and are easily filed and mailed. Floppy disks must be handled carefully, since data can be lost if the disk is exposed to magnetic fields, damaged, or otherwise mishandled. Disk storage is known as **random access** because data can be retrieved without searching every record in sequence.

(Source: Photo Courtesy of Hewlett-Packard Company)

Hard Disk Storage Rigid **hard disks** can hold millions of characters of data, which are recorded on the disk on tracks. The data can be retrieved almost instantaneously. Figure 11.2 illustrates a hard disk system used on microcomputers. Devices such as these can store 90 million characters or more of data. Even more data can be stored on hard disk systems designed for mainframes. These systems use disks 14 inches in diameter and can store upwards of 200 million characters per drive.

FIGURE 11.3

**Magnetic Tape
Storage** This
medium, by its
nature, permits only
sequential access.

*(Source: Photograph printed with permission from BASF Corporation Information Systems,
Bedford, MA)*

Magnetic Tape Storage   Data may be stored on reels of **magnetic
tape.** The tape measures one-half inch wide and is wound on reels in lengths
of 1200 feet and 2400 feet. The reel of tape is placed on a tape drive, where
read/write heads encode information or read the data already recorded. Because
of its nature, recording tape is a **sequential access** medium. The records on
the tape must be searched in sequence until the desired record is located. Other
tape systems include Phillips-type cassettes and tape cartridges (see Figure
11.3). These media are used for microcomputer storage systems.

Optical Storage Media

A recent innovation in computer storage media is the **laser beam** optical
storage system. Data is recorded on tracks on the surface of plastic or metal
disks. The rotating disk is placed under a laser beam and the information encoded
by deforming or distorting the surface of the disk. Data is read off the disk by a
laser beam that senses the stored information. Laser disks are capable of storing
millions of characters. These disks are not subject to erasure from magnetic
fields.

SELECTION OF DATA STORAGE MEDIA

The hardware selected by the analyst depends on the requirements of the user, the amount of data to be stored, and the type of access needed. The following variables should be considered when designing a storage system.

Cost

Cost is an important criterion when selecting a storage system, but it is particularly important when large volumes of data are to be stored and retrieved. The two major considerations in figuring costs are the space available for storage and the amount of data to be stored.

As a rule, it is very expensive to store large volumes of source documents in their original format. They require bulky file cabinets of some type and often a considerable amount of floor space. Magnetic tape or some form of microfilm is the most inexpensive means of storing a large volume of data. A file recorded on microfilm requires only two percent of the space occupied by the paper source document.

If only a small amount of data is involved, saving original documents in file cabinets may be convenient and adequate. Medium amounts of data, such as an accounts receivable file for a small retailer, are often stored on floppy disks or magnetic tape. Large amounts of data, including graphics or visuals, are best stored on such media as microfilm or microfiche.

Permanence

Another important consideration in storage media selection is **permanence.** Some documents and records must be kept for long periods of time for tax, legal or audit purposes. Often original documents must be saved even though the data they contain has been transferred to another medium. Other data may need to be saved only for short periods, until confirmation has been received or transactions completed.

The degree of permanency and protection varies with the storage medium. Magnetic tape, for example, can be erased. Computer centers are subject to fire and vandalism. Errors in processing can occur, erasing old data or producing new files with erroneous data. If source documents have been saved, it is sometimes possible to regenerate damaged files. If microfilm or magnetic disks are used, backup or duplicate files should be kept to preserve data in case of emergency.

Activity

Another major consideration is the frequency with which a file is accessed. Magnetic tape is less suitable than disk where records must be accessed repeatedly. It is time consuming to retrieve reels of tape, mount them on drives, etc. Files that must be accessed often are usually maintained on magnetic disk.

Legal Considerations

The legality or validity of the form in which data is saved on a storage medium must be considered when designing a system. Copies of signatures, contracts, or other documents are not always acceptable; often only the original document will suffice. In the insurance industry, for example, files of original signatures of policyholders must be maintained, even though all other data has been transferred from source documents to machine-processable records.

Accessibility

Accessibility refers to the degree of difficulty involved in retrieving documents or data from storage. Often the most direct form of data accessibility is simply to keep source documents or records filed in cabinets directly available to the person who needs them. This system, however, is cumbersome.

Data stored magnetically is an indirect means of accessibility. When large amounts of data are involved, however, magnetic storage is the most convenient and fastest method.

Access Time

Access time is the time required to locate a given record in a file. Average access time is determined by the number of records to be searched and the speed of the retrieval system. Access time is also determined by the type of search performed. Random access searches consume far less time than sequential searches, especially if the file is large and the object of the search is not near the beginning.

There is a trade-off between access time and cost—the faster the access time, the greater the storage cost. It costs more money to store large volumes of records on magnetic disk, for example, than on magnetic tape, but the average access time is less for disk than for tape.

Security

Another important consideration when designing a storage system is the possible degree of **security** and document protection. Confidential information such as wholesale prices, client lists, or discount rates is often part of data files and access should be limited. Protecting and preserving this type of data is essential to the survival of an organization.

FIGURE 11.4

**Information
Hierarchy**

Database—The collection of an organization's libraries.
Library—A collection of related files.
File—A group of related records.
Record—A group of related fields.
Field—A group of related characters.
Byte—Bits that represent a character.
Bit—The smallest piece of data that can be processed.

Data storage systems should be designed with this need in mind. Confidential files should be placed in controlled areas where they can be accessed only by authorized personnel. Special code numbers, passwords, and security checks are techniques used to maintain the security of data in storage systems. Systems can control not only who accesses what data but with what privileges. For example, files may be defined as read only, read and write, copy only, and so forth.

Files must also be protected against physical threats. Fire, earthquakes, or water damage threaten the security of data and documents. Backup or duplicate files are often maintained as security measures. In the event of the loss or destruction of a file, the data can be regenerated from the backup file.

RECORD DESIGN AND LAYOUT

All data in an organization may be viewed in a hierarchical structure (see Fig. 11.4). The smallest unit of data is the **bit.** Bits form characters; 8-bit characters are stored in 8-bit locations known as **bytes.** Bytes make up **fields,** such as names and addresses. The fundamental unit of the information system is the **record.** The record may be a source document containing data related to a transaction, an invoice showing details on a purchase, or an image on a screen displaying the hours worked by an employee. A group of records may be organized into a **file** and a group of related files into a **library.** Libraries make up a **database.**

Systems analysts must select and arrange the contents of a record. Several factors are usually considered:

- Available space on each record
- Data to be included
- Bytes to be allotted to each field
- Order of the items
- Storage media

Fixed-Length and Variable-Length Records

The length of a record determines how much data it can hold. Some records, such as printed forms, have fixed sizes and can hold only a limited number of characters. A **fixed-length record** consumes the same amount of space in a storage device regardless of how much data is recorded on it.

Other records have variable lengths and consume only as much space as needed to hold the required data. Some records may be short and others long, depending on the amount of data. Records on magnetic tape or disk can be either fixed or variable in length. **Variable-length records** are more efficient in terms of storage space, but they are often more complicated to use, since a means of determining the length of each record must be developed.

Design of Data Fields

The data to be included in a record is determined by the purpose of the record, the data that will be needed for processing, and how the data is to be obtained and accessed. An invoice record will contain data that is different from a request for a quotation (see Fig. 11.5).

The analyst must decide what size field should be allotted for each item. For example, a field 20 characters wide may be reserved for a name. If a name requires only 12 characters, then eight spaces will be left unused on that record while a name with more than 20 characters will be truncated. A field to record the year may be only two or four characters wide.

Field size is an important element when working with fixed-length records or data that will be processed by some computer programs. It directly affects the selection of what and how much data can be included in a record.

Variable-length records, of course, will be able to hold fields of differing lengths. A name with 12 characters will only require a field 12 characters wide. However, since most records are stored on magnetic disks, a standard field width of 20 or more characters will probably be used.

Another specification is the type of data that will be entered in a field. Some fields are restricted to **numeric** data, others to **alphabetic** data, and some to a combination—**alphanumeric** data (see Fig. 11.6). This depends on the format of the source data, the purpose of the record, and the way it will be processed and stored.

After defining the number and type of fields on a record, the analyst must

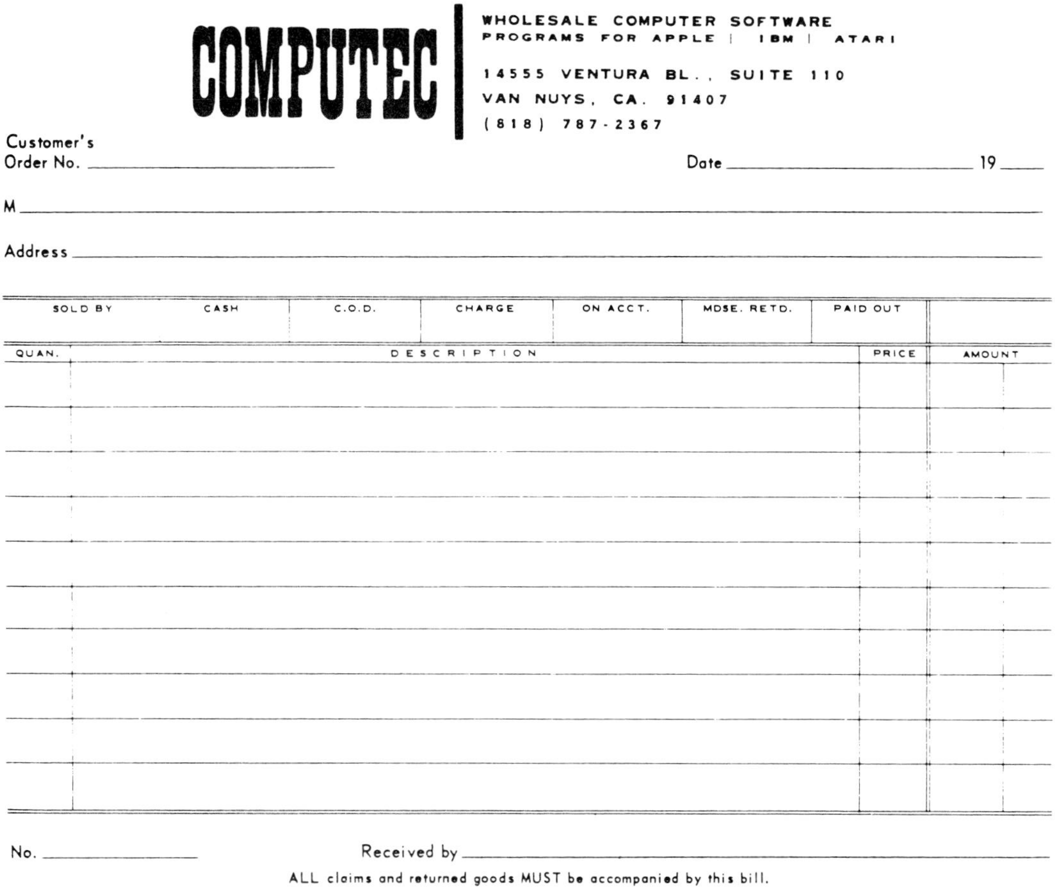

COMPUTEC

WHOLESALE COMPUTER SOFTWARE
PROGRAMS FOR APPLE | IBM | ATARI

14555 VENTURA BL., SUITE 110
VAN NUYS, CA. 91407
(818) 787-2367

Customer's
Order No. _____   Date _____ 19 _____

M _____

Address _____

SOLD BY	CASH	C.O.D.	CHARGE	ON ACCT.	MDSE. RETD.	PAID OUT	

QUAN.	DESCRIPTION	PRICE	AMOUNT

No. _____   Received by _____

ALL claims and returned goods MUST be accompanied by this bill.

select the basic sequence, or order, in which these fields will appear. This is largely influenced by how the record will be prepared, the order and availability of source data, and the order in which the fields will be accessed during processing. Fields on a record should be ordered to increase efficiency and accuracy as much as possible. Fields that will be accessed frequently should be placed first on the records.

FIGURE 11.5

Forms Records contain fields designed for specific kinds of information.

Master Records and Detail Records

Records are often categorized into one of two groups, depending on the nature of the data they contain. Records with data of a permanent nature are called **master records.** Those with data relating to a specific transaction or activity are called **transaction** or **detail records** (see Fig. 11.7).

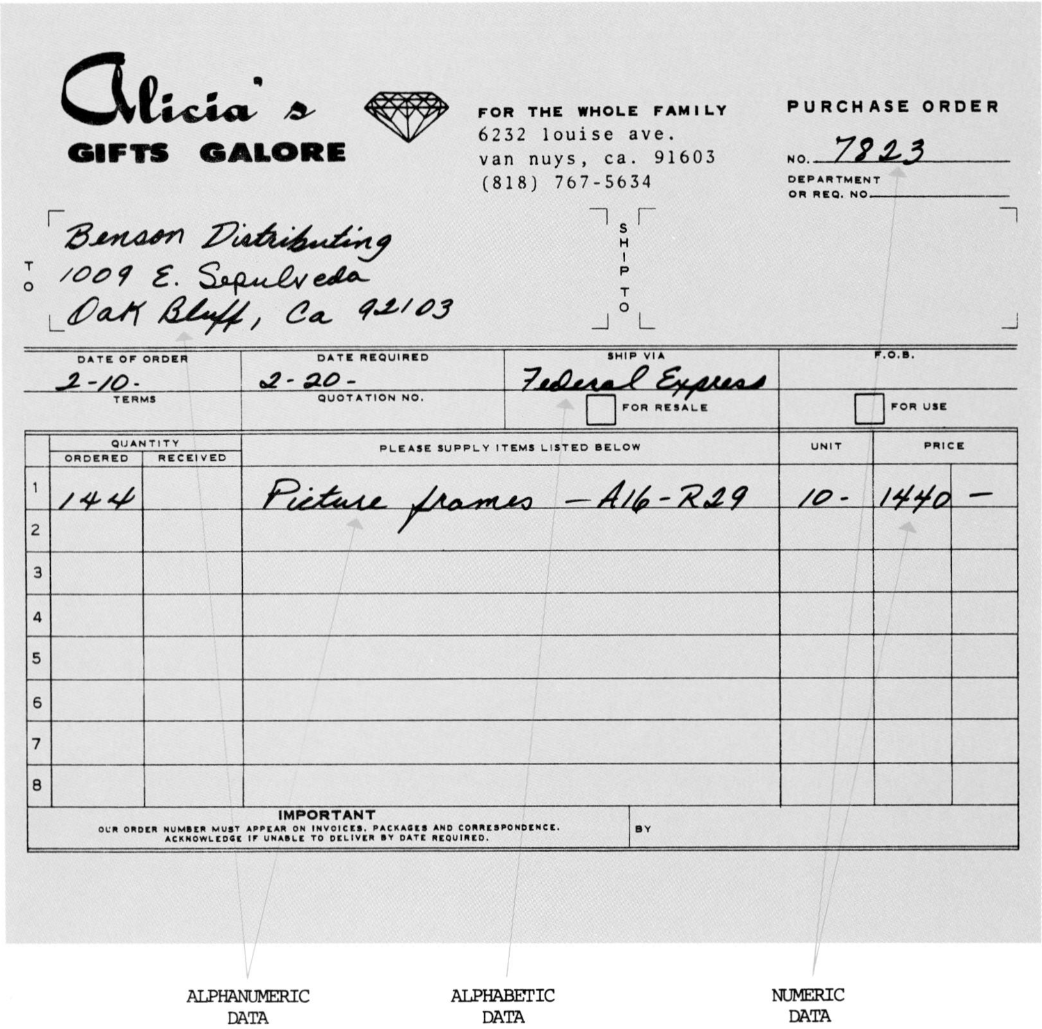

Alicia's
GIFTS GALORE

FOR THE WHOLE FAMILY
6232 louise ave.
van nuys, ca. 91603
(818) 767-5634

PURCHASE ORDER
NO. *7823*

DEPARTMENT
OR REQ. NO.

TO: *Benson Distributing*
1009 E. Sepulveda
Oak Bluff, Ca 92103

SHIP TO

DATE OF ORDER	DATE REQUIRED	SHIP VIA	F.O.B.
2-10-	*2-20-*	*Federal Express*	
TERMS	QUOTATION NO.	☐ FOR RESALE	☐ FOR USE

QUANTITY		PLEASE SUPPLY ITEMS LISTED BELOW	UNIT	PRICE
ORDERED	RECEIVED			
1 *144*		*Picture frames — A16-R29*	*10-*	*1440 —*
2				
3				
4				
5				
6				
7				
8				

IMPORTANT
OUR ORDER NUMBER MUST APPEAR ON INVOICES, PACKAGES AND CORRESPONDENCE.
ACKNOWLEDGE IF UNABLE TO DELIVER BY DATE REQUIRED.

BY

ALPHANUMERIC
DATA

ALPHABETIC
DATA

NUMERIC
DATA

FIGURE 11.6

Fields Fields may
contain numeric,
alphabetic, or
alphanumeric data.

A master record might include an employee's name, address, phone number, social security number, exemptions, deductions, and pay rate, as well as other data of a relatively permanent nature. The detail record might contain the number of hours worked, overtime, commission sales, business expenses incurred, or any other data related to a particular work week. The distinction between detail and master records is blurred in computerized database file management.

Records can also be defined by certain characteristics. A **physical record** can be a specific, tangible document, such as an optical scanning form or a particular portion of a magnetic tape or disk. It may also be all the data available in one read or write operation. A **logical record** refers to a collection of related items that contain data on the same subject.

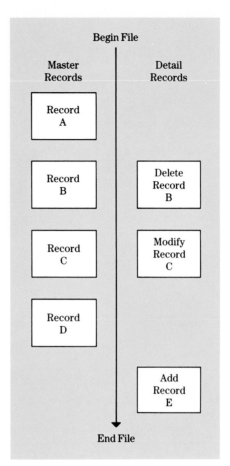

FIGURE 11.7

Master and Detail Records The master record contains permanent data, while transaction data is on the detail record.

FILE DESIGN

Records are grouped together in various relationships and orders to form files. The contents of a particular file depend on its function, the storage medium utilized, and the processing it will undergo. Some files may be composed of master records and others of detail records.

For example, a **master file** contains all the master records of customers with balances due. It holds data such as name, address, charge number, and current balance. A **detail file** includes all detail records, showing charges made during the current month. Detail files are also known as **transaction files.** The information from the detail file is used to update the master file.

Scratch files are temporary files used to hold data during processing. The temporary data can be erased when the task is finished.

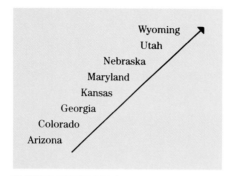

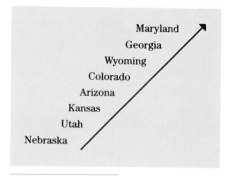

FIGURE 11.8

Sequential Records
Records are arranged in alphabetic order.

FIGURE 11.9

Random Order
Records in the file are in no specific order.

Sequential and Random Order

The way in which records in a file are ordered depends on its purpose and the medium involved. Files can be in sequential or random order, or a combination of both. **Sequential order** means that the records follow each other successively in a particular arrangement (see Fig. 11.8). This might be alphabetic, chronologic, or numeric. Records being added to the file must be placed in the appropriate position to maintain the sequential order.

Random order files contain records placed one after the other with no regard to succession (see Fig. 11.9). Additional records are added to the file at the end or in the position vacated by a deleted record. A combination of both sequential and random order can be used. This type of file is known as **indexed file access.** In this arrangement, records are stored in sequential blocks and within each block in random order. The computer first searches for a block; specific records are found by searching the block sequentially.

Depending on the medium used, records in a file can be accessed either sequentially or randomly, regardless of how they are ordered. Any file can be searched sequentially until the appropriate data is found in the identification or key field on the record.

Media with random access locate a record by going directly to the **address** of the location where it is stored. The address will be indicated by a key or identification code, or determined from a reference table.

Files that are being merged or processed simultaneously will have to be in the same or corresponding order. For example, suppose monthly statements are being prepared from a master file and two detail files. The records in all three files must be in the same order. Usually, sequence and matching tests are performed to make sure that the appropriate records are merged.

DATABASES

The highest unit in the hierarchy of data organization is the database. A database is a collection of files and records maintained at one or more sites that allows many users to share the data within it. A database may contain all the files related to personnel, or all those used by the sales or inventory departments. Databases may be so comprehensive as to contain all of the essential data for an entire business or organization.

The particular structure of a database will depend on the kind of data to be stored and retrieved, the way the data is to be retrieved, the storage medium used, the type of processing to be performed, and the type of output needed. Databases are described in detail in the next chapter.

CODING SYSTEMS

Coding systems save space and allow more information to be entered on a record. A code that represents data is entered on the record instead of the actual data. For example, two-digit numbers may be assigned to represent sales-people rather than spelling out their names. This requires only two characters on a record rather than 10 or 20.

Codes such as these should be sufficiently generalized to allow for expansion as new items are added, but specific enough to allow reference to each individual data item. The code should also bear a meaningful relationship to the item it represents. For example, a code to represent the months of the year should range from 1 to 12 rather than from 10 to 21. The coding system should be compatible with the type of processing—manual, machine, computer—that will be employed.

Significant Digit Code

In the **significant digit code,** each element in the code represents a different characteristic of the data item. This arrangement allows considerable descriptive information to be recorded with a few characters. For example:

Code	Type of Media	Length in Minutes	Year Copyrighted
TA 15 87	Tape recording	15	1987
DI 08 86	Disk recording	08	1986
CD 18 87	Compact disk	18	1987

Sequence Code

Another method of encoding data on a record is the **sequence code.** A group of items is assigned numbers in sequence. Then the assigned number is used instead of the longer piece of data, as in the following example:

Code	Item
01	Carpets
02	Kitchen goods
03	Lighting fixtures
04	Hardware
05	Cosmetics

Mnemonic Code

This system uses a shortened or contracted code symbol to stand for a longer term. The **mnemonic code** should bear a close relationship to the item it represents. For example:

PAYPRO—Payroll procedures

STINOP—Standard inventory ordering procedures

EMTRED—Employee training and educational department

Last Digit Code

In the **last digit code** a final or trailing character is placed after a number or name to indicate the class to which it belongs. Either alphabetic letters or numeric characters may be used. For example:

Code	Meaning
103R	Retail item
104W	Wholesale item
105E	Export item

Identifiers

Social security numbers are often used as **identifiers** on records along with or instead of names. This makes it easier to sequence and search records, and to avoid complications that arise from similar or duplicate names.

Since duplicate social security numbers have sometimes been assigned, using this type of identifier is not without some risk. In addition, the use of social security numbers is legally restricted to specific applications. To avoid these problems, multidigit numbers may be assigned in sequence. Careful records must be maintained to avoid duplication or omission of numbers in the series.

Check Digit Codes

Check digit codes are used to detect clerical errors made when identifiers or other number codes were recorded. A check digit is a number added to the end of the code number, representing the result of a mathematical formula that has been performed on the code number. The computer processing the data performs the operations on the code number and compares the answer to the check digit. A disparity indicates that a transposition or other error has been made. Several formulas have been developed to calculate the check digit.

Now that we have reviewed the key concepts of data storage and record and file design, we will want to integrate this information into a broader system context. The next chapter discusses database design, incorporating the record and file design features discussed in this chapter.

Summary

Many of the analyst's activities involve records, files, and storage design. Magnetic media, including both floppy and hard disks, are widely used. Optical storage devices record data on plastic or metal disks, using laser beams. When selecting data storage media, the analyst considers cost, permanence, activity, and legal considerations. Accessibility, access time, and security are also considerations.

Bits make up bytes, bytes make up fields, fields make up records, which in turn make up files. Fixed and variable-length records, as well as master and detail records, are used. Records may be stored in sequential or random order. A group of files may be organized into a library, and a group of libraries make up a database.

Coding systems save space on a record. Common systems include the significant digit, sequence, mnemonic, identifier, and check digit codes. Data may be organized into physical records. Records may be stored either sequentially or in random order. A master file contains permanent data, while a detail file includes records of transactions. Scratch files are temporary files used in processing.

Key Terms

Access time	**Byte**
Accessibility	**Check digit code**
Address	**Coding system**
Alphabetic data	**Database**
Alphanumeric data	**Detail file**
Bit	**Detail record**

	Mnemonic code
Field	Numeric data
File	Permanence
Fixed-length record	Physical record
Floppy disk	Random access
Hard disk	Random order
Identifier	Record
Indexed file access	Scratch file
Laser beam	Security
Last digit code	Sequence code
Library	Sequential access
Logical record	Sequential order
Magnetic storage media	Significant digit code
Magnetic tape	Transaction file
Master file	Transaction record
Master record	Variable-length record

Exercises

1. What are the major factors to consider in record layout and design?
2. Describe how data is stored on optical media.
3. Define what is meant by the term *access time*.
4. Discuss the topic of security as it relates to storage systems.
5. Contrast master and detail records.
6. Discuss how check digit codes are used.
7. Contrast physical and logical records.
8. Discuss the design of data fields.
9. Discuss cost with respect to selection of data storage media.
10. What factors are usually considered when arranging the contents of a record?

Projects

1. Visit a local computer store and discuss secondary storage devices with a salesperson. Determine which devices have the maximum capacity and speed and which devices are the least expensive.
2. Design three records that would be needed by the credit department of a firm that sells musical instruments and albums.
3. Specify the files that will be needed by the firm in project 2.
4. Make a list of six kinds of businesses. Describe the types of files that you think would be used in each. Would they be direct, sequential, or indexed files? Why?
5. Visit a local business firm. Determine what types of files, records, and storage devices are used in the organization.

ANALYST AT WORK
FIRESIDE BAKERY

DESCRIPTION OF FIRM

Fireside Bakery is a large wholesale bakery that sells to supermarkets, restaurants, and retail outlets throughout the city and neighboring communities. Fireside's product line consists of a variety of packaged cookies, breads, pies, doughnuts, cakes, and other baked goods.

Goods are delivered to Fireside's outlets by their fleet of 32 trucks that service customers daily. Drivers maintain the financial records for their own accounts. Customers place orders on a standard form which they give to drivers. When drivers return to the garage, they turn in their order forms for processing in the company computer. The resulting information generates driver route reports, bakers' production schedules, and customer delivery invoices and statements.

SYSTEM OVERVIEW

The data flow diagram in Fig. 11.10 illustrates Fireside Bakery's order-processing system. One of three input documents is used, depending upon the type of account. Retail outlets, restaurants, and institutional accounts each use a specially designed form to record their requirements. These sales forms indicate the number and type of baked goods required.

The order-processing system generates a driver route report for each driver. This report indicates the goods that have been ordered and sequences deliveries according to a predefined routing schedule. These reports are given to the driver at the start of each day's delivery run.

The bakers' production schedule describes what baked goods will be needed for the following day. The report categorizes the amount of baked goods as well as the ingredients needed for standard commercial recipes.

The system generates a group of delivery invoices that are given to each driver. These are signed by the customer when the goods are delivered. The system also generates periodic statements that are mailed to accounts.

HANDS-ON APPLICATION

Design the various records and files needed in Fireside Bakery's order-processing operations. Study the data flow diagram and decide what kinds of data are

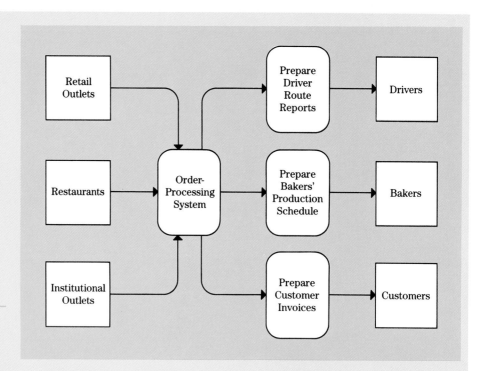

FIGURE 11.10

Fireside Bakery
Data Flow Diagram

needed on the various reports. Complete the three work products described below.

Work Product No. 1 Determine the type of data that would be needed for the driver route report and design the necessary files and records. Use whatever type of file access and storage media you think is appropriate. Label these documents WP1, Chapter 11. Prepare a task list indicating what steps must be carried out to complete this work product. Enter your task list below.

TASK LIST

_____

_____

_____

_____

_____

_____

_____

Work Product No. 2 Prepare the bakers' production schedule. This work product consists of designing appropriate records and files that summarize the baked goods required for the next day. This schedule will be used by the bakers in planning the next day's output. Label this document WP2, Chapter 11. Prepare a task list to assist in this effort and enter it below.

TASK LIST

_____

_____

_____

_____

_____

_____

_____

Work Product No. 3 Weekly invoices should be sent to Fireside Bakery's customers. Design the appropriate files and records for this purpose. Label these documents WP3, Chapter 11. Enter your task list below.

TASK LIST

_____

_____

_____

_____

_____

DATABASE DESIGN

LEARNING OBJECTIVES

After studying this chapter, you should be able to:

1. Discuss the evolution of database usage.

2. Describe management information systems (MIS).

3. Describe decision support systems (DSS).

4. Contrast different database schemas.

5. Describe database configurations and state the advantages of each.

6. Discuss database software packages.

Database management software has become an essential tool of business organizations. As a result, an understanding of database design is crucial for the systems analyst. In this chapter we discuss the evolution of databases, file processing, management information systems (MIS), and decision support systems (DSS). We describe the data dictionary, the heart of the database management system, and cover single-user, multiuser, and distributed information networks, including off-the-shelf software packages.

THE EVOLUTION OF THE DATABASE

Business, educational, and governmental organizations are continually growing in size and complexity. Information systems, too, are becoming more sophisticated. Early data processing methods were designed around files. When the computer was developed, electronic file processing took over. Essentially, the computer performed electronically those tasks previously done manually or by mechanical devices. Computers were viewed as superfast, giant electronic sorters.

The computer's potential was not fully realized, however, until adequate software was written to manage large databases. This introduced the era of database management, a new way of manipulating and managing data.

A database is a collection of files and records, maintained at one or more sites, in an environment that allows an integrated use of its data. Databases enable one or more users to share common data, thereby eliminating redundancy and maximizing the efficiency of the data processing system. Information management has evolved through three major methodologies.

File Processing Systems

A **file** is a collection of records that can be manipulated by people or machines to perform such tasks as sorting, alphabetizing, and sequencing (see Fig. 12.1). Early **file processing** systems relied upon the human hand and eye, and usually involved relatively small numbers of records. With the advent of punched card processing equipment, file processing could be done by machines but was still based upon the manipulation of records in some linear or sequential order. Management reports were generated by summarizing the data stored on the records.

Management Information Systems (MIS)

When computers came into widespread use in the 1950s and '60s, organizations started using them to manipulate records and files. The modern high-speed computer made possible the **management information system (MIS).**

Employee	Shift	Hours Worked
Dodson, Glenn	1	42
Plantin, Suzanne	2	40
Diaz, William	1	38
Paulis, Jim	3	39
Lancer, Robert	1	40

FIGURE 12.1

File This collection of records can be sorted, alphabetized, or resequenced.

A management information system is a user-oriented means of manipulating data to generate reports. The MIS takes advantage of the high speed of the computer to sort, sequence, alphabetize, and organize data.

The evolution from file processing to the MIS was more one of speed than of changes in design or concept. The computer was simply applied to the task of sorting or manipulating records that formerly had been managed by the human hand or machine. Management reports were prepared by categorizing or summarizing data stored on computer files and printing out descriptive data upon which decisions could be made. Conceptually, the MIS is based upon files as a means of accessing, sequencing, and managing data.

Decision Support System (DSS)

The **decision support system (DSS)** is a more sophisticated way of looking at data processing and information. It focuses upon the needs of the end user, who will most likely be a decision maker, rather than upon the needs or requirements of the data processing manager. The trend today is toward the DSS and away from the MIS. This is because organizations maintain files and records ultimately for the purpose of making decisions. Frequently key decision makers are not computer and data processing experts.

The DSS allows data to be gathered, processed, and manipulated using little or no formal structure. It is often only after the data is collected that management has a clear idea of the specific data processing tasks that must be done. The DSS emphasizes the needs of the decision makers, allowing them to display data, prepare reports, and summarize information.

A DSS focuses on relationships rather than on the physical structure of the database. It utilizes interactive processing techniques that enable the user to respond to questions or prompts and to select alternatives. Thus, a manager can go to a computer terminal, access a database, and, without having to know a specific programming language, be able to print out reports or display information on a screen. For example, with only a few keystrokes a manager can direct a database in a DSS to print out a list of all clients who have purchased more than $10,000 worth of merchandise in the last 60 days, and whose billing addresses are within three specific zip codes.

DATABASE ADMINISTRATOR

The task of coordinating database usage sometimes fell to the systems analyst. But it soon became clear that this was a specialized task. The **database administrator** has the responsibility of coordinating software, records, file design, and data management activities. The goal is to achieve consistency in the way data is processed throughout the organization. Consolidation eliminates redundancy and wasted effort.

Before database administrators came on the scene, organizations assigned the responsibility of forms, record, and file design to a systems analyst or other individual, who saw to it that forms were properly prepared, revised, printed, and distributed within the organization. But the problem of data management became overwhelming when computers came into widespread use. Individuals, departments, and divisions began using computers to collect and manage data. There was little consistency or control over who put what on which computer. Chaos was imminent, with files being duplicated in different forms by many people within an organization. A database administrator's job is to bring order out of this chaos. He or she addresses the broader task of designing and implementing databases to support the total organizational needs.

DATABASE DESIGN

The basic design of a database is defined by its schema. The **schema** is the model, plan, or structure around which fields, records, and files are organized. The particular schema selected depends upon many factors, including the kind and type of data to be processed, the number and types of users, and the physical hardware available.

Data Dictionary

The syntax and rules of the schema or structure are usually stored in a data dictionary. The data dictionary specifies the basic elements of the schema. It defines the data model, the form of all records, the design of the data fields, which data can be accessed globally by all users of the system, and which data is restricted and can be accessed only by selected users or workstations.

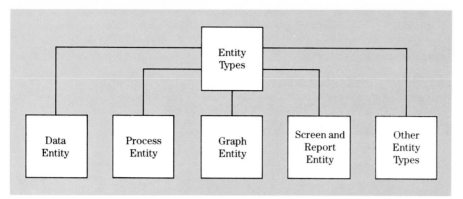

FIGURE 12.2

Excelerator Entity Categories

It is unfortunate that even though the data dictionary is the heart of the database system, no standards that define its content, structure, and style have yet been developed. Therefore, its design is left to the designer of the system or software. To help you understand data dictionaries, we will discuss Excelerator's project dictionary, developed by Index Technology Corp., which provides a good model. Excelerator is a computerized systems design tool that allows analysts to develop systems, prototype forms, and document systems.

The basic unit of the Excelerator dictionary is the **entity.** The entity describes relationships or properties that can be attributed to a unit of information. For example, in a printed dictionary the basic entity is the word. Properties and meanings are attributed to words. These fundamental units are alphabetized and contained in one document—the dictionary—that is read by many people to understand the meaning of the entities (words) and use them consistently. In the same way, Excelerator's electronic dictionary uses many different entity types grouped into five major categories (see Fig. 12.2).

Data Entities   Data entities describe the properties and relationships of items of data. They relate to records, files, or flows of information. In Excelerator's dictionary there are seven different types of data entities:

Data elements

Data records

Data stores

Data model entities

Data flows

Tables of codes

Data relationships

These entities have specific meanings, which are defined in Excelerator's dictionary.

Process Entities   **Process entities** describe processes, destinations, and sources of data, and the properties of various modules. For instance, they define the symbols that will be drawn in a graph. There are five process entities in this category:

Processes

Functions

External entities

Modules

Presentation graph objects

Graph Entities   Since analysts use an extensive amount of graphics and design models, it is essential that these be standardized and integrated into the data dictionary. **Graph entities** describe where diagrams are stored and the type and names of entities within diagrams. There are seven entities in this category:

Data flow diagrams

Structure charts

Structure diagrams

Data model diagrams

Entity relationship diagrams

Presentation graphs

Document graphs

Screen and Report Entities   Analysts frequently prepare reports and design terminal screen displays. This creates a need for a group of **screen and report entities.** For example, these entities show the date a report or screen was created and when it was modified, and names all the elements that are used. There are four entities in this category:

Report designs

Screen designs

Screen data entries

Screen data reports

Other Entity Types   A miscellaneous group of entities are included in Excelerator's dictionary. For instance, individuals need to be associated with documents they create or modify. Sometimes groups of entities are treated as a list, and the list needs to be described. There are five entities in this category:

Document groups

Document fragments

Reports

Entity lists

Users

At first glance, the names of the entities may seem confusing. But they are quickly learned by the Excelerator user as he or she becomes familiar with the software.

Data Dictionary Example

UniTrans Company maintains a computerized file of data on three computers in several departments. One supervisor directs data entry operators to input all employee names, surname first, followed by a comma, and then the first name and any initial. The second supervisor wants the names to be entered first name followed by last. Still another supervisor requires names to be entered with the surname followed by the first name, without any punctuation separating the last and first names. Further, the supervisors have specified field widths of 20, 22, and 30 characters, respectively.

The system serves each department well. However, problems arise when the supervisors seek to merge their data files into a single sorted list of names. The inconsistencies among the three files makes it difficult, if not impossible, to generate a single logical file. Had the supervisors relied upon a data dictionary, which would have set up a standard format (see Fig. 12.3), merging their lists would have been a simple task.

Data Dictionary—Marketing Division

Name of File: Employee Roster

Name of Field	Width	Type	Comments
Name	25	Alpha	Last name, first, sep. comma
Address	25	Alpha numeric	Sep. comma, abbrev, N. E. S. W.
City	25	Alpha	Include city, state, no zip
Zip	10	Numeric	xxxxx-xxxx

FIGURE 12.3

Sample UniTrans Data Dictionary Entry

SCHEMAS

A variety of different database schemas have been developed by information systems managers. These allow data to be quickly and easily collected, restructured, and queried. The following three schemas are widely used in database design.

Linked-List Schema

One of the most common tasks performed in a database is that of sorting or resequencing data. Suppose a list of 1000 names has been stored on magnetic disk in the computer. The records are in no specific order. The manager wishes to obtain a printout of all of the names in alphabetical order. It would be very time consuming to shuffle the records individually, as one might sort out a pack of index cards.

Sorting can be done easily, however, using a **linked-list schema.** The linked list depends upon pointers that are part of each record. The **pointer** directs the computer to the next record in the logical sequence (see Fig. 12.4), which may not necessarily be the next physical record in the sequence. Using pointers, records can be easily deleted by simply changing a pointer to bypass one or more records; or records may be conveniently added to the end of a file. Pointers in appropriate records direct the computer to the newly added records, which in turn point to the next logical record in the sequence. The advantage

FIGURE 12.4

Linked-List Schema

	Record Number	Customer Name	Account Number	Pointer
Begin ●●●	10	Benson Mfg.	2302	20
	20	Emerson Mfg.	3412	70
	30	Gabe Industries	3234	50
	40	Lampson Mfg.	1200	60
	50	Keystone Service	4320	40
	60	Union Mfg.	3203	80
	70	Forrester Co.	3200	30
	80	End-of-file		

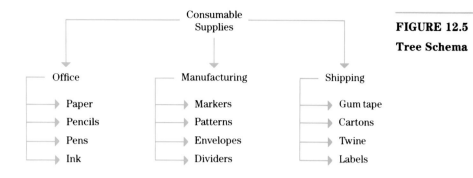

FIGURE 12.5

Tree Schema

of this schema is that records may be easily added or deleted without being physically rearranged on the storage medium.

The Tree Schema

The **tree schema** is another means of structuring data. The tree structure shown in Fig. 12.5 resembles an inverted tree with a trunk and branches. Genealogists who study the lineage of families use the tree structure. The same concept can be applied to a database.

In Fig. 12.5 we see that each **parent record** has several children (subordinate records). Each **subordinate record,** in turn, has its own subordinate records. If information is sought from one of the subordinate records, the computer first accesses the master or parent record. This directs the machine to a subordinate record. The subordinate, in turn, directs the machine to its subordinates. Thus, all records in the file are related and easily accessed by placing them in a tree structure.

Relational Database

The **relational database** is a schema predicated upon relationships, which are defined by means of values in named columns in **tables** (see Fig. 12.6). Rather than relying upon pointers or a parent-child fixed relationship, the relational schema associates records (rows) via column values in the tables. A row in one table can be associated with rows in several other tables by means of matching column values. Since values can change, relationships can change. In the example in Fig. 12.6 data can be sorted or displayed based upon any of the attributes in the composite record. This creates a flexible means of organizing data.

Relational databases have become very popular because they allow access to records without the necessity of sequencing, sorting, or organizing files prior to querying them or generating reports.

DATABASE

Account Number	Account Name	Distributor	Representative
1230	Benson Pharmacy	Drugs	Bill Welch
1240	Save More Drugs	Drugs	Tony Wisner
1250	Ralph's Pharmacy	Toys, drugs	Marcy Greene
1260	Ben's Discount	Notions, drugs	Benjamin Farnham

DISTRIBUTOR TABLE

Drugs	Benson Pharmacy
Drugs	Save More Drugs
Toys, drugs	Ralph's Pharmacy
Notions, drugs	Ben's Discount

REPRESENTATIVE TABLE

Benson Pharmacy	Bill Welch
Save More Drugs	Tony Wisner
Ralph's Pharmacy	Marcy Greene
Ben's Discount	Benjamin Farnham

DATABASE LANGUAGES

In the early years of database usage, they were accessed by writing programs in a high-level **procedural language** such as COBOL or PL/I. This required the skills of an experienced programmer who had a thorough knowledge of database design as well as familiarity with a language. As a result, access to databases was limited to those with procedural language skills.

Modern databases can be accessed through easy-to-use **query languages.** Query languages are similar to English and require little programming knowledge. Commands entered through a computer terminal direct the machine to search files, make comparisons, and generate reports. The utility of databases has greatly expanded because of query languages. Even the most novice user can easily access complex databases, searching out specific pieces of data and generating reports quickly and easily.

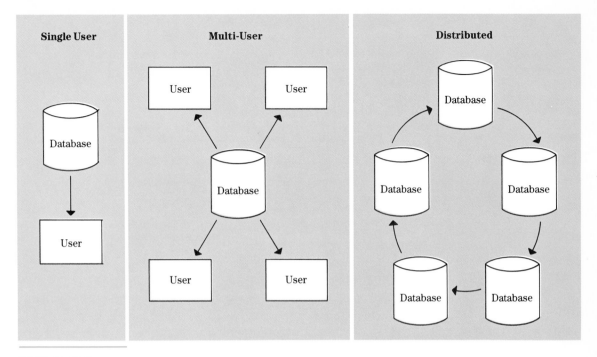

FIGURE 12.7

Data Base Configurations In the single-user database, only one user can access the data. With a multiuser database, several users can access the single database simultaneously. The distributed database permits any user on the system to access information in any of the database files.

DATABASE HARDWARE CONFIGURATIONS

A variety of **hardware** configurations are implemented to enable one or more users to access a database. The most common configurations are single-user, multiuser, and distributed databases (see Fig. 12.7).

Single-User Database

In a **single-user database,** data is stored on disk or other storage device and can be accessed only by one user. Databases such as these, containing millions of characters, are easily stored on hard disk drives within microcomputer systems. To access the database, the user merely turns on the computer. Using a simple query language, he or she can directly access the data.

Single-user systems are inexpensive. Since the system is entirely under the control of one individual, access problems and security are easy to deal with. No communications circuits or software sharing are required.

Multiuser Database

In the **multiuser** configuration, two or more users simultaneously access a single database. Multiuser systems are efficient, since they enable multiple access to one database. Depending upon the communications facilities available, users can be located in the same building or at locations hundreds of miles apart.

Multiuser systems require mechanisms to deal with access. The database software and hardware must provide **record lock** capability. This prevents two users from simultaneously accessing the same data. In the absence of a record lock, several users could access the same record, make changes in its content, create confusion, and generate errors.

Distributed Database

In a **distributed database,** the contents of the database are physically stored at several geographic locations. Users can access any part of the database located at any geographic point in the system. Distributed databases are sometimes known as network databases.

Distributed databases require communications facilities as well as data security and file protection measures. In addition, record locks and other controls must be put in place. These controls, for example, might permit only certain terminals or locations to update records, while the records may be accessed from any terminal in the network. A major advantage of the distributed database over the multiuser system is that no single central computer is required to maintain the database. Centralized systems are more prone to total system failures than distributed databases.

DATABASE SOFTWARE PACKAGES

The proliferation of microcomputers has brought about increased usage of database **software packages.** Packages such as dBASE III PLUS, R:BASE 5000, Cornerstone, and others run on microcomputers yet can manage databases containing thousands of records. These packages were patterned after database management systems used on large mainframe computers.

Database management system (DBMS) software packages are designed to help users with few programming skills to manipulate data. Before entering data into a database, the user must create a **structure** to hold the data. The structure defines the format of the data. Once the structure has been set up, the data is loaded into it. The operator can then enter queries and generate a variety of special or general-purpose reports.

Creating a File Structure

Let us use dBASE III PLUS, a popular database package marketed by Ashton-Tate, to illustrate how a structure is created. A buyer in the purchasing department at UniTrans needs a file containing an account number, name, buyer's name, previous order, and a description of the last goods purchased. The analyst has listed the fields that must be contained in each record (see Fig. 12.8).

The analyst starts dBASE III PLUS and enters the CREATE command. Prompts on the screen assist in setting up the fields. In our example there are nine fields (see Fig. 12.9). Each field is assigned a name. Either characters (C) or numeric values (N) will be entered. The width of each field is also specified. A provision is made for decimal places, if needed.

| Number |
| Vendor |
| Agent |
| Address |
| City |
| Phone |
| Date |
| Previous |
| Item |

FIGURE 12.8

Listing of Fields The analyst has listed the fields required in each record.

```
Structure for file: VENDORS
Number of records: 00000
Date of last update: 01/15/88
Primary use database
Fld      Name        Type Width   Dec
001      NUMBER       N     010
002      VENDOR       C     020
003      AGENT        C     020
004      ADDRESS      C     020
005      CITY         C     020
006      PHONE        C     020
007      DATE         C     020
008      PREVIOUS     N     010
009      ITEM         C     020
** Total **                00161
```

FIGURE 12.9

Creating the File Structure

Loading Data

Once the structure has been set up, the data is loaded. This is accomplished by keyboarding data into the structure as displayed on the screen. Figure 12.10 illustrates a record containing data on one of UniTrans's vendors.

Following this procedure, the operator may load hundreds of records, thus building a vendor database. The database contains vendor names, agents, addresses, and other pertinent data.

FIGURE 12.10

**Loading the
Data** This record
contains data on one
account.

```
RECORD #  00001
NUMBER     :         6245:
VENDOR     : Thompson Carton Co.  :
AGENT      : Ellen Cranston        :
ADDRESS    : 234 S. Flower St.     :
CITY       : Glendale, CA 91405    :
PHONE      : (818) 555-3623        :
DATE       : 2/6/88                :
PREVIOUS   :       24563:
ITEM       : Corrugated cartons    :
```

Querying the Database

DBMS software allows a user to enter a query, causing the computer to display information. If a manager wishes to find out who has ordered goods costing $1500, he or she simply directs the computer to display the list, using a one-line command. There are dozens of options available to obtain displays of subsets of related information.

Generating Reports

A DBMS package has the ability to generate a variety of printouts and reports. The information in these reports can be the result of requests to search, sort, resequence, or rearrange data in a multitude of different ways. Using relatively simple commands, the user can direct the computer to print out all goods ordered from a specific supplier for a given period of time, or list the names and telephone numbers of all vendors so they can be contacted. A marketing manager can print out a report listing customers who have not used UniTrans's services within the last six months or past year. The same database that is used to generate these reports can also generate labels for mailing customer notices or promotional materials.

The most perfectly conceived system cannot be productive unless it is converted into physical equipment and resources, and placed at the disposal of the organization. In the next chapter we will discuss the purchase and actual acquisition of equipment, programs, and facilities.

Summary

Databases have evolved through file processing, management information systems (MIS), and decision support systems (DSS). A database is a collection of files and records maintained at one or more sites. File processing systems manipulate records in a file context. Management information systems process records at high speed and are able to generate reports. Decision support systems are based upon end-user needs and are less structured than other database systems.

A database administrator is often given the responsibility of coordinating an organization's data management activities. Databases are built upon a plan or schema. The syntax and rules of the schema are stored in the data dictionary. The entity is the most basic element of the data dictionary.

In the linked-list schema, a pointer directs the computer to the next record in a logical sequence. In the tree schema, subordinate records are related to parent records. In the relational database, data is viewed as though it were stored in simple tables, and tables are related by means of matching column values.

Procedural or query languages may be used to access a database. Single-user, multiuser, and distributed are common database configurations. A variety of software packages is available to manage databases.

Key Terms

Database administrator

Data entity

Decision support system (DSS)

Distributed database

Entity

File

File processing

Graph entity

Hardware

Linked-list schema

Management information system (MIS)

Multiuser database

Parent record

Pointer

Procedural language

Process entity

Query language

Record lock

Relational database

Schema

Screen and report entities

Single-user database

Software packages

Structure

Subordinate record

Table

Tree schema

Exercises

1. Describe how management information systems operate.
2. Describe the functions of decision support systems.
3. Define *database schema.*
4. Describe the functions of the data dictionary.
5. Describe the linked-list schema.
6. Describe the tree schema.
7. Describe relational databases.
8. Describe query languages.

9. Describe the distributed database.
10. Describe the single-user database.

Projects

1. Describe a file structure for a database that will catalog and index all the books in your personal library.
2. Design a file structure for a database that will store data for a small clothing retailer.
3. Design a file structure for a database that will store data for a small pharmacy.
4. Visit a local computer store or software retailer and discuss off-the-shelf database software available for microcomputers. Describe the products for sale and their capabilities.
5. Visit a business establishment and discuss the kinds of databases and files used in the organization. List the types of files and the kinds of data stored in each.

ANALYST AT WORK

MIDTOWN AUTO SALES

DESCRIPTION OF FIRM

Midtown Auto Sales is a large suburban automobile dealership that specializes in foreign and domestic new car sales. Because of Midtown Auto's large volume, the company also maintains several used car lots to dispose of trade-ins. Most of Midtown Auto's new car inventory is maintained on their main sales lot. A second inventory of new cars is kept at their storage lot. Their inventory of used cars is sold from two other locations. Used vehicles that are not sold within a reasonable length of time are disposed of through wholesalers.

SYSTEM OVERVIEW

It is essential that Midtown Auto's personnel be aware of both the new and used car inventory. Salespeople regularly check inventory using a group of terminals located in the sales offices and storage lots. Management frequently checks inventory using similar terminals available at the main office. Hard copy inventory reports that summarize the number and type of vehicles in stock as well as their location are distributed only to managers.

Figure 12.11 is a data flow diagram that shows Midtown Auto's inventory system. A database of information on both new and used cars is maintained in an inventory file. The database also stores information on vehicles that are on order but have not yet been received by the dealership. A complete inventory of new and used vehicles is maintained, showing their location, wholesale cost, and available features.

HANDS-ON APPLICATION

You are the systems analyst who has been asked to design the database inventory system for Midtown Auto Sales. You are to design a file structure, display screens, and printed reports for the system. You will prepare the three work products described below.

Work Product No. 1   Study Midtown Auto's inventory system. Design a file structure for the database that will store such data as vehicle make, model, extras, wholesale cost, sticker price, and lot location. Show the structure with sample data. Label this document WP1, Chapter 12. Use a task list to assist in this effort and enter it below.

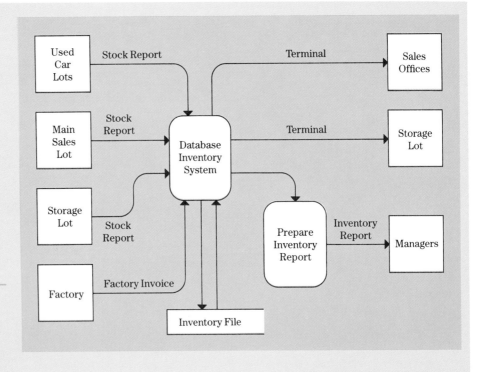

FIGURE 12.11

**Midtown Auto
Sales** Data Flow
Diagram

TASK LIST

_____

_____

_____

_____

_____

_____

_____

Work Product No. 2   Design a display screen that will output information
from the database to be used at the sales offices and storage lots. The screen
should display such pertinent data as automobiles in stock by make, model,
color, and other features. Label this screen design WP2, Chapter 12. Prepare
a task list to assist in this effort and enter it below.

TASK LIST

_____

_____

_____

_____

_____

_____

Work Product No. 3   Design an inventory report that will summarize information from the database for the managers. This should be a printed report that will be used by management for decision making. It should include the total number of vehicles in stock, total investment in inventory, value of inventory at retail, stock turnover, and so on. Label this document WP3, Chapter 12. You should prepare a task list to assist in writing this report. Enter your task list below.

TASK LIST

_____

_____

_____

_____

_____

_____

THE DEVELOPMENT PHASE

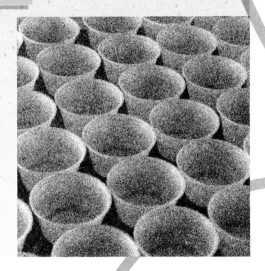

SYSTEMS DEVELOPMENT

LEARNING OBJECTIVES

After studying this chapter, you should be able to:

1. List major criteria in vendor selection.

2. Explain how lead time considerations affect vendor and product selection.

3. List major terms in a purchase contract.

4. Discuss benchmark testing.

5. Contrast lease versus purchase of equipment.

6. Explain why an analyst may recommend use of an employment agency at this point in the SDLC.

Once a system has been designed, the analyst must begin the fourth phase of the systems development life cycle (SDLC). During systems development, equipment is assembled, personnel hired, physical facilities acquired, and orders placed for the necessary software, hardware, and communications devices. This phase may take many months.

In this chapter we will discuss the hardware and personnel aspects of systems development. This includes vendor relationships, lead time schedules, contractual requirements, and warranties. We also discuss whether to purchase or lease equipment and software. The next chapter describes the software aspects of systems development, including computer-aided software engineering (CASE).

THE TASK OF SYSTEMS DEVELOPMENT

Systems development is the stage during which the system is actually built, based upon the designs conceived in earlier phases. Now the analyst must identify vendors and suppliers and begin the purchasing cycle. The necessary computers, software, equipment, and machines are received and installed at this time.

Throughout the systems development process, the analyst negotiates with vendors, prepares contracts, and enters into buying agreements. The major documents used in this stage are the request for proposal (RFP), proposal, purchase order, and contract. Many systems are developed in steps, necessitating a prototype installation. We first discuss vendor selection and the purchasing process, and then move on to describe prototype installations and benchmark testing procedures.

Vendor Selection

The individual or organization that provides equipment or services is known as a vendor. A **vendor** is a provider of resources. The selection of the appropriate vendor is extremely important so that system facilities will be acquired at the best possible price. The systems analyst often makes recommendations with regard to vendor selection.

The decision to buy a piece of equipment from a particular company often hinges on price. However, price may not be a good indicator of the vendor's ability to deliver the quality of goods specified. Let us look at key criteria that are evaluated when selecting a vendor.

Proposal Preparation　Some vendors help their customers select and order specific pieces of equipment. The process begins with a **request for proposal (RFP).** A company sends the RFP to vendors, stating their intent to acquire certain pieces of hardware and software. In turn, the vendor, working with the organization, provides a detailed written **proposal** addressing these needs.

REQUEST FOR PROPOSAL

UNITRANS COMPANY P.O. Box 3434 Central Valley, CA 91605	**RFP #:** 87—432 Date: 02—01—89

V E N D O R	Mason Business Machines Co. 1290 E. Plymouth St. San Francisco, CA 91415	We ask that you provide us with a proposal for the delivery and installation of the goods and merchandise described below. In preparing your proposal, please adhere strictly to the specifications. Please note any deviations in your proposal.

Requested By: George Seagrave	Dept: Purchasing	Required Date: 03-01-89

Item No.	Qty	Description
1	16	Word processing systems, complete with all necessary hardware, cables, and software. The units are to be supplied stand-alone, but with built-in network capability. Installation shall include one letter-quality printer with each system. In addition, three laser printers shall be provided. The proposal shall also include necessary supplies and toner for the laser printers. Price out each component of the system separately, including supplies.

Special Instructions All equipment on this order is to be delivered between 07—05—89 and 07—18—89.	Approval: _____ Date:

Comments:

Analysts generally prefer vendors who provide ordering assistance and a written proposal as part of the purchase process. The proposal assists in defining the organization's needs and puts in writing specifics that might otherwise go unconsidered.

Suppose the systems analyst and management of UniTrans have agreed that a new word processing system is to be installed in the secretarial services department. The analyst prepares an RFP, shown in Fig. 13.1, which is sent to a

FIGURE 13.1

Request for Proposal (RFP) This document invites vendors to submit proposals.

FIGURE 13.2

Proposal This proposal specifies facilities to be acquired.

PROPOSAL

Presented to:

UNITRANS COMPANY

By

MASON BUSINESS MACHINES CO.

1290 E. Plymouth St.
San Francisco, CA 91415

For the Acquisition of a
16-Station Word Processing System with
Laser and Letter-Quality Printers

number of vendors asking for their assistance in preparing a proposal. The vendors will respond with a written proposal similar to that shown in Fig. 13.2.

Vendor Reputation   Some equipment vendors have been in business for many years, while others are new to the industry. The analyst should assess the vendor's reputation and performance. Vendors with established reputations may be in a better position to provide services than those who are less well known.

Vendor Experience and Training   Much of the equipment used in modern business systems is highly technical. It is preferable to order from vendors who are experienced and whose staff has taken training courses in the operation and installation of the equipment they sell and service.

Vendor Maintenance and Services   When purchasing a piece of equipment or software, the analyst should determine whether the vendor will provide adequate maintenance, which is essential for complex software and equipment. An organization may have no place to turn if it acquires, for example,

FIGURE 13.3

Vendor-Sponsored Training Course Training courses allow personnel to become productive more quickly.

a computer program that cannot be changed or modified to reflect changes in tax laws or business usage. Vendors who scrimp on maintenance services may be able to offer lower prices, but in the long run this may be very expensive for the purchaser.

Training and Orientation   The analyst should determine whether the vendor is able to provide training on the goods or software delivered. Qualified vendors will be able to offer training courses at their facility or at the user's site (see Fig. 13.3). Training courses are important because they allow personnel to become more productive faster than if they are forced to learn by trial and error.

Manuals and Documentation   Will the vendor provide documentation for all equipment and software purchased? Some vendors offer installation, operation, service, maintenance, and repair manuals for all equipment and software they sell or distribute (see Fig. 13.4). The absence of adequate documentation can be costly, because it is more expensive to repair, maintain, or update equipment without it.

Convenient Service Depots   Many vendors operate local service depots. These repair stations are equipped to service or maintain equipment promptly. Some vendors use a single central service depot and require that all equipment be returned to the central location for repair. Doing so may cause costly delays

FIGURE 13.4

**Manuals and
Documentation**
Vendors provide a
variety of
documentation.

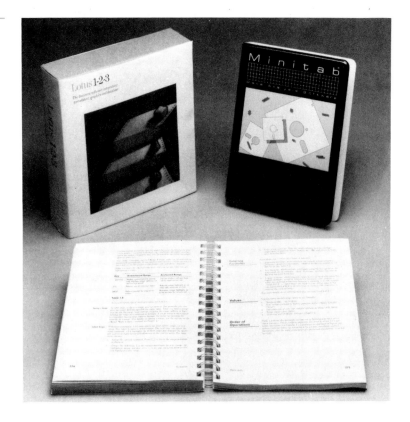

and interruptions in service. Still others offer no service depots and instead require customers to look to other sources for service and maintenance.

LEAD TIME SCHEDULES

The period between ordering a piece of equipment and its actual delivery is known as **lead time.** Lead time can vary from several days to many weeks or months. The systems analyst must consider lead time when acquiring and ordering equipment.

If only a small number of units are to be purchased and they are readily available from a local vendor, then lead times are usually short. If the systems design calls for hundreds or thousands of units, adequate time must be allowed for the manufacture and delivery of the goods. The systems analyst often prepares a lead time schedule that projects the delivery dates for various pieces of equipment. This will ensure that goods are ordered in a timely manner. Figure

ITEM PURCHASED	DATE ORDERED	DELIVERY	DAYS LEAD TIME	
PC/AT	2/1/88	2/15/88	15	FIGURE 13.5 **Lead Time Schedule**
Office copier	2/1/88	2/20/88	20	
Toner, supplies	2/1/88	2/5/88	5	
Fan-fold paper	2/1/88	2/18/88	18	
Floppy disks	2/1/88	2/5/88	5	

13.5 shows a lead time schedule prepared by an analyst at UniTrans for some supplies and equipment routinely used in one of the company's divisions.

CONTRACT TERMS

Systems analysts reduce systems design details to specific contractual terms when ordering equipment. The **contract** between the purchaser and the vendor should clearly spell out the responsibilities of both parties (see Fig. 13.6). The more details that are defined in the contract, the less chance for misunderstanding or confusion regarding the vendor's responsibilities. The following key elements are generally included in a purchase or lease contract:

- Purchase price
- Terms of payment
- Delivery date
- Warranty terms
- Quantity discounts
- Incidental charges
- Overtime charges
- Termination of agreement
- Hours when equipment will be available for service
- Exchange or return privileges

A detailed statement regarding **warranties** on goods is particularly important (see Fig. 13.7). Warranties state the terms and conditions for handling defective goods. The warranty should describe the period of coverage and who shall pay shipping charges when goods must be returned to the factory. Warranties usually exclude damage from abuse or misuse of equipment or goods operated contrary to the manufacturer's instructions.

International Business Machines Corporation

Armonk, New York 10504

Amendment for IBM Service/Exchange Center Services

Name and Address of Customer:

Customer No.:

IBM Branch Office Address:

IBM Branch Office No.:

International Business Machines Corporation (IBM) and the Customer agree that this Amendment applies to the following Agreements which have been or will be signed by the Customer and IBM only with respect to machines for which IBM offers Service/Exchange Center services. Such machines and the Customer's selections of available services will be confirmed by IBM as provided under the following Agreements. These Agreements are 1) Agreements for purchase of IBM machines, 2) IBM Maintenance Agreement, 3) IBM Maintenance Agreement II, and 4) Agreements for lease or rental of IBM machines. As used in this Amendment, the term "machines" refers to machines and/or machine elements.

WARRANTY, WARRANTY OPTION AND MAINTENANCE SERVICE

Warranty, warranty option and maintenance service will be provided by exchanging or repairing the machines under one or more of the service offerings described on the reverse side. The specific offerings available for any machine will be determined by IBM. For machines which have more than one service offering available, the Customer will select one offering per machine and notify IBM. The Customer may change such a selection for any machine upon 15 days' notice to IBM.

Warranty options, available for a charge, provide alternative types of services, as described below, in place of that provided under the warranty provisions of the applicable IBM purchase agreements. A selected warranty option for a machine commences on its Date of Installation, or any later date selected by the Customer within the warranty period, and expires at the end of the warranty period or one year from the machine's Date of Installation, whichever is later. The type of service selected by the Customer under a warranty option will continue under the applicable IBM Maintenance Agreement for the then current charge.

A failing machine is a machine requiring warranty, warranty option or maintenance service (failing machine). A failing machine owned by other than IBM, when presented by the Customer under an exchange offering, and accepted by IBM, becomes the property of IBM at the time of exchange. A machine provided by IBM under an exchange offering (exchange machine) may not be new, but will be in good working order, and becomes the property of the Customer at the time of exchange.

When a failing machine is exchanged, all programs, programming, data and removable storage media, and all non-IBM parts, options, alterations and attachments must be removed by the Customer before such exchange. When a failing machine is to be repaired, all programs, programming, data and removable storage media must be removed by the Customer before such repair. The Customer agrees that all items not removed will be deemed to have been discarded by the Customer.

Problem Determination

It is the Customer's responsibility to determine that warranty, warranty option or maintenance service for a machine is required by following problem determination procedures provided by IBM. It is also the Customer's responsibility to follow service request procedures provided by IBM. IBM reserves the right to verify that the requested service is required prior to providing an exchange machine.

THE ADDITIONAL TERMS AND CONDITIONS ON THE REVERSE SIDE ARE PART OF THIS AMENDMENT. THE CUSTOMER ACKNOWLEDGES THAT THE CUSTOMER HAS READ THE APPLICABLE LISTED AGREEMENTS AND THIS AMENDMENT, UNDERSTANDS THEM, AND AGREES TO BE BOUND BY THEIR TERMS AND CONDITIONS. FURTHER, THE CUSTOMER AGREES THAT THE APPLICABLE LISTED AGREEMENTS AND THIS AMENDMENT ARE THE COMPLETE AND EXCLUSIVE STATEMENT OF THE AGREEMENT BETWEEN THE PARTIES, SUPERSEDING ALL PROPOSALS OR PRIOR AGREEMENTS, ORAL OR WRITTEN, AND ALL OTHER COMMUNICATIONS BETWEEN THE PARTIES RELATING TO THE SUBJECT MATTER HEREIN.

Accepted by:
International Business Machines Corporation

By _____
Authorized Signature

Name (Type or Print) _____ Date _____

Customer

By _____
Authorized Signature

Name (Type or Print) _____ Date _____

Z125-3385-01(U/M001)6/84   Please send all communications to IBM at its Branch Office unless advised to the contrary.

FIGURE 13.6

Contract A contract specifies the terms and conditions of the agreement.

FIGURE 13.7

Product Warranty

HARDWARE PERFORMANCE

A **purchase order** specifies the detailed characteristics desired in the equipment being bought (see Fig. 13.8). The analyst often faces a trade-off between cost and performance: maximum performance at a higher cost or lesser performance for less money. The final determination is made by weighing cost against the organization's requirements.

Computers are among the most frequently acquired devices in a system. The following key equipment capabilities should be evaluated when purchasing a computer:

- CPU performance
- Input/output performance
- Primary storage capability
- Secondary storage capability
- Maintenance costs
- System expandability
- Multiprocessing capability
- Communications capability
- Air conditioning requirements
- Electrical requirements
- Physical dimensions

When purchasing large mainframe computers, the systems analyst must pay particular attention to central processing unit (CPU) performance to be sure

PURCHASE ORDER

UNITRANS COMPANY **P.O. Box 3434** **Central Valley, CA 91605**	**PO #:** 87–143 Order Date: 4–15–89

V E N D O R	Mason Business Machines Co. 1290 E. Plymouth St. San Francisco, CA 91415	S H I P T O	UniTrans Company Secretarial Services Dept. 314 E. Industrial Parkway Central Valley, CA 91605

Requested By: George Seagrave | Dept: Purchasing | Required Date: 07–05–89

Ship Via: Best way

Item No.	Qty	Part Number	Description	Price	Extension
1	16	780–341	Word processing systems, complete with monitors, printers, cables	$5100	$81,600
2	16	780–346	Word processing software packages, with manuals	$325	$5200
3	16	343–211	Desk consoles with chairs	$519	$8304
4	3	780–566	Laser printers with software	$3650	$10,950
5	10	780–569	Laser printer toner cartridges	$69	$690

Special Instructions
All equipment on this order is to be
delivered between 07–05–89 and 07–18–89.

Approval:

Charles Landes
_____
Date: 04–20–89

PLEASE DO NOT MAKE ANY CHANGES OR SUBSTITUTIONS IN THIS ORDER WITHOUT A
WRITTEN CONFIRMATION FROM THE PURCHASING DEPT.

BILL SHIPPING AND FREIGHT CHARGES AS SEPARATE ITEMS.

FIGURE 13.8

Purchase Order This form specifies the detailed characteristics of the equipment
being purchased.

that it can provide the necessary processing capability. Consider the following elements when rating CPU performance:

- Number of processors
- Processor speed (millions of instructions per second—MIPS)
- Instruction cycle time
- Number of programmable registers
- Word size
- Number of input/output channels
- Primary memory capacity
- Operating system characteristics
- Memory cycle time
- Clock speed

The capabilities of the input/output (I/O) devices are another key factor when purchasing computer equipment. Slow or inadequate I/O devices can limit the processing capabilities of an otherwise fast system. Some of the elements considered when evaluating I/O devices are:

- Speed of printers—lines per minute (LPM) or characters per second (CPS)
- Dot matrix vs. letter quality (LQ)
- Number of characters displayed on a video screen
- Data transfer speed between CPU and I/O devices
- Optical character scanning (OCR) capability
- Magnetic ink character recognition (MICR) capability
- Color capability
- Graphics capability
- Kind and type of plotters
- Voice recognition or voice synthesizer capability

The capacity of secondary storage devices is an important factor to be evaluated. If a large amount of data must be accessible to the CPU, adequate secondary storage facilities must be provided. The following list summarizes some of the elements to consider when acquiring secondary storage devices:

- Number of disk drives on the system
- Number of tape drives on the system
- Density of storage media
- Capacity in bytes per device
- Cost to store each kilobyte
- Fixed versus flexible (floppy) disks

The overall computer system performance should be evaluated. A well-functioning system is one that is integrated and produces a high volume of output per unit of input. In assessing the overall system, the analyst should determine whether all the elements function properly and interact with one another correctly. Devices manufactured by different vendors may function well by themselves but, when integrated to form a complex computer system, may exhibit degraded performance or may not function at all.

SOFTWARE PERFORMANCE

On most systems software performance plays a role equally as important as that of hardware. When ordering or specifying computer software, the analyst must be assured that it will function properly. Many hours may be spent testing and debugging software before it is finally integrated into the system.

It is often the systems analyst's task to recommend whether to purchase software from an outside vendor or to write it in-house. In either instance program documentation, flowcharts, and input/output requirements must be clearly specified. If software is acquired from an outside vendor, the analyst should consider the following items:

- Outright purchase vs. license agreement
- Program documentation
- Tutorial and instructional software
- Responsibility for debugging
- Software revisions and updates
- Site license arrangements
- Copy protection schemes
- Ability to meet user requirements
- Ease of modification or facilities that allow tailoring to satisfy user requirements
- Availability of vendor support

COMMUNICATIONS EQUIPMENT PERFORMANCE

Communications equipment plays a key role in many information systems. Business systems may include a variety of connective arrangements including microcomputer to mainframe links, local area networks (LANs), wide area networks (WANs), and value-added networks (VANs). Originally most business systems relied principally upon voice communications—the telephone. Later, data communications, using TELEX and TWX to send digital information, was added. Today video is becoming increasingly important in communications.

It is sometimes possible to gain operating economy and efficiency by integrating the three major domains of communications—voice, data, and video—into a single system. Systems analysts are turning to integrated systems when acquiring new hardware because of the reduced cost. It is more economical to use one system that handles all three domains than three parallel systems.

When preparing specifications for communications equipment, the analyst should consider the following elements:

- Conformance to American National Standards Institute (ANSI), Electronic Industries Association (EIA), or other standards
- Data transmission speed in bits per second (BPS)
- Number and types of communications circuits
- Transmission codes and protocols
- Modulator/demodulator (modem) speed and features
- Multiplexer capability
- Voice, data, and video integration
- Mileage between points of the system
- Connective arrangements such as LANs
- Installation costs
- Maintenance costs
- Public versus private lines
- Traffic volume that can be accommodated
- How facilities integrate with existing communications facilities

PROTOTYPE INSTALLATION

Sometimes a fullblown systems development effort is premature. Instead, a prototype installation may be called for. A **prototype installation** is a pilot project in which hardware and software are acquired and put in place in a limited environment, primarily for testing and evaluation. The prototype installation is monitored carefully to see that end-user needs have been properly met.

Changes and alterations in the system are made as necessary. Once the prototype installation has proven successful, a complete systems development effort is undertaken. Prototype installations are becoming more prevalent because computers allow analysts to develop sample forms, terminal screen input designs, and data flow procedures. These can be easily modified as often as necessary to improve system performance.

Reprinted by permission of Control Data Corporation

BENCHMARK TESTING

During the systems development phase the analyst often specifies benchmark tests that will be used later during the implementation phase to ensure
that the new system is installed and working properly. Benchmark tests may
measure and time computer hardware and software performance or the efficiency of communications equipment (see Fig. 13.9).

Benchmark testing specifications are sometimes written into purchase
orders and proposals. These tests establish performance criteria that must be
met by the vendor before final sign-off and payment for equipment. The design
of the benchmark test should measure the important characteristics that the
system is expected to deliver. Failure to meet established benchmark tests may
require that the vendor modify the equipment or software during the implementation phase. Without benchmark tests and performance criteria, the analyst
would have no way of knowing for certain whether the equipment delivered
actually performs as required.

LEASE VS. PURCHASE

A major decision to be made during the systems development phase is
whether to lease or purchase equipment outright. The decision depends upon

		FIGURE 13.10
Job title:	Computer operator	**Job Description**
Salary range:	$1600–$2300 per month	This document spec-
Responsibilities:	The computer operator is the advanced level in the computer operator group and operates a computer console or machine control panel, tape units, printers, OCR, MICR, and other related I/O units. Other work may be done as required, including some equipment maintenance. The operator will also prepare payroll records for staff in the department.	ifies the education, training, and experi- ence required for a computer operator position.
Requirements:	Must have completed at least two years in a community college program leading to a degree in operations. Should also have experience in employee training. Must be familiar with existing computer equipment in plant facility. Must work cooperatively with others. Some evening and weekend assignments.	
Employee contacts:	Employed under Data Processing Dept. Manager. Supervise staff of five employees. Coordinate work with Systems Dept. Work with programmers.	

many factors. Organizations tend to purchase equipment where capital costs are low and the technology is slow to change. Conversely, high capital costs in a rapidly changing technology argue for equipment leasing. Economics and tax considerations also play an important role in the decision to lease or buy.

A variety of leasing arrangements may be made when acquiring equipment. The **lessor** is the one who provides the equipment, and the **lessee** is the one who uses it. Some contracts require the lessor to cover all installation and maintenance costs. Others shift this burden onto the lessee. Some contracts specify a minimum lease period; others provide for an open-ended lease. When technology is changing rapidly, it is usually advantageous to lease equipment. Technologically obsolete equipment that has been leased can be turned in and replaced by new state-of-the-art devices when they become available.

On the other hand, outright purchase means owning the equipment. A company can modify its own equipment without having to ask permission. Owners can sell equipment that no longer meets their needs; sometimes they even make a profit on it. The systems development phase is when the lease versus purchase issue must be resolved.

PERSONNEL

Finding personnel who will operate the new or modified system is another part of the systems development phase. The job description, shown in Fig. 13.10, specifies the education, training, and experience required of new personnel.

Sometimes people can be moved about within an organization to meet staffing requirements. At other times, employment agencies are called upon to provide personnel.

Employment agencies, sometimes known as head hunters, specialize in interviewing prospective employees and finding the right person for each job. The cost for this service may be borne by either the employer or the employee, or the costs may be shared. The use of an employment agency enables employers to hire skilled individuals who have already been screened, thus eliminating advertising, testing, and interviewing costs.

Preparation of software for a system is as important as hardware acquisition. The next chapter will round out our discussion of systems development with a look at computer-aided software engineering (CASE).

Summary

In the systems development phase, equipment is assembled, personnel hired, physical facilities acquired, and orders placed for the necessary software and facilities. This involves working with and selecting vendors as required. The process begins with a request for proposal (RFP). The vendor responds with a proposal, and after consideration a purchase order is issued for the acquisition of the software and facilities.

Vendors are assessed on the basis of their reputation, experience, and services, among other elements. The period between placing an order with a vendor and delivery of goods is known as lead time. Contracts spell out such things as purchase price, payment terms, delivery date, warranty terms, and other items.

Hardware should be assessed in terms of CPU performance characteristics, I/O facilities, and secondary storage capacity. Software criteria include program documentation, copy protection schemes, site license arrangements, and so forth.

Sometimes prototype installations are called for. These are monitored to see that end-user needs are being met by a proposed system. Benchmark tests are conducted to evaluate hardware and software performance. The question of lease versus purchase must also be resolved.

Key Terms

Contract	**Purchase order**
Lead time	**Request for proposal (RFP)**
Lessee	**Systems development**
Lessor	**Vendor**
Proposal	**Warranty**
Prototype installation	

1. Describe the function of the systems development phase.
2. List the major elements in vendor selection.
3. Discuss lead time schedules.
4. List some key items that are usually included in a purchase contract.
5. List some major equipment capabilities evaluated when purchasing computers.
6. List some elements usually considered when rating CPU performance.
7. List the elements considered when acquiring secondary storage devices.
8. List some items considered when specifying communications equipment.
9. Why are benchmark testing specifications written into purchase orders or proposals?
10. What is a major advantage of leasing equipment?

1. Visit a computer store and discuss delivery times. Prepare a lead time schedule for selected pieces of equipment.
2. Obtain a sample purchase contract from a computer vendor. Study it and determine what contract clauses it includes.
3. Visit a computer store and discuss the performance of a specific piece of computer equipment. Prepare a list describing its characteristics.
4. Obtain a piece of computer software, including the operating manual and other documentation. Study the documentation and make a list of performance criteria.
5. Select a brand of computer equipment and determine what factory service facilities are available in your community. Use your local Yellow Pages to assist you.

ANALYST AT WORK
HOFFMAN PLASTICS

DESCRIPTION OF FIRM

Hoffman Plastics maintains a large production plant that produces extruded and molded plastic products. The firm manufactures a variety of commercial and domestic plastic goods, such as storage containers, trays, jars, and bottles, using modern high-speed injection and molding equipment. New plastic products require many hours of design time, including the manufacture of molding dies. Once dies have been made, they are mounted on the production machines that turn out the goods in volume. Costing out design, die making, and production runs are important aspects of Hoffman Plastics' work.

A key factor in the success of the operation is the company's ability to bid competitively on production runs. This requires using a computerized cost accounting system and inputting valid cost data from suppliers, as well as accurate production standards. Production standards are output norms obtained from the plant's engineers. They provide figures on the capacity and speed of various molding machines.

SYSTEM OVERVIEW

Whenever Hoffman Plastics bids on the manufacture of a product, they use their cost accounting system to price out the job. A designer inputs specifications such as the length of the production run, type of raw material, dimensions, and shape. A computer program generates a production estimate that shows the per unit cost based upon various lengths of run. A price quotation is prepared and presented to the customer. After the job has been produced, an invoice is sent. Figure 13.11 is a data flow diagram illustrating the company's cost accounting system.

HANDS-ON APPLICATION

You have been asked to assist Hoffman Plastics in acquiring a new computer system on which to run their cost accounting program. You must define the criteria for evaluating the new system and prepare a request for proposal (RFP) and purchase contract. These work products are described below.

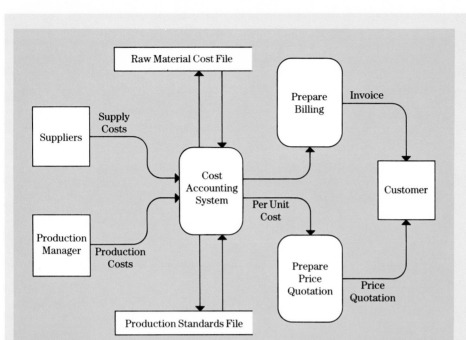

FIGURE 13.11

Hoffman Plastics
Data Flow Diagram

Work Product No. 1   Review Hoffman Plastics' data flow diagram and prepare a list of criteria for a small computer system that will handle the company's cost accounting needs. Label this document WP1, Chapter 13. Use a task list to assist you in this effort and enter it below.

TASK LIST

_____

_____

_____

_____

_____

_____

_____

(continues)

Work Product No. 2 Once you have completed the hardware evaluation criteria, prepare a request for proposal. Study the sample RFP in Fig. 13.1 and draft one that is appropriate for the company's needs. Label this document WP2, Chapter 13. Develop an outline of the important items that must be included in your RFP. Enter your outline below.

OUTLINE

_____

_____

_____

_____

_____

_____

_____

Work Product No. 3 You have successfully identified a vendor and intend to purchase the computer for the cost accounting system. Draft a list of terms and conditions to be included in a contract. Label this document WP3, Chapter 13. Organize your effort by preparing an outline of the key contract terms and enter it below.

TASK LIST

_____

_____

_____

_____

_____

_____

_____

COMPUTER-AIDED SOFTWARE ENGINEERING

LEARNING OBJECTIVES

After studying this chapter, you should be able to:

1. Define computer-aided software engineering (CASE).

2. Discuss traditional software development techniques.

3. Summarize the evolution of programming languages.

4. Discuss language selection criteria.

5. List the steps in the software development life cycle.

6. List some CASE packages currently available and describe their capabilities.

For many decades the computer was used to automate business systems and manufacturing and industrial processes. It became an indispensable tool in almost every office. But until very recently an important application was overlooked—using the computer to automate developing and writing programs and software. With the advent of computer-aided software engineering (CASE), a sophisticated group of tools has been devised to facilitate program development.

In some systems development efforts, computer software and programming account for as much as 80 percent of the costs. The preparation of this software may involve dozens of programmers working for many months on writing, developing, and testing programs.

CASE is the process of automating the design and development of computer software. CASE not only assists in developing data flow diagrams and structured charts, but also actually writes the programming code. This represents a revolutionary step in software development.

In the previous chapter we reviewed the hardware and personnel aspects of systems development, and we now turn our attention to software development. In this chapter we will study traditional software development techniques, review the evolution of languages, and learn how software specifications are prepared. The chapter discusses the software development life cycle and concludes with a discussion of computer-aided software engineering.

WHAT IS CASE?

Computer-aided software engineering (CASE) is the application of the computer to the software development process. CASE automates program design and coordinates design specifications. It also facilitates screen and report design and writes code. CASE is a rapidly emerging methodology wherein the computer takes over tasks that traditionally were performed manually.

CASE consists of a group of software tools and techniques that may be run on a desktop computer or large mainframe to handle the development task in an environment of maximum programmer productivity. It uses data dictionaries, data models, and other elements. With CASE, software developers can produce software more quickly and at a lower cost.

TRADITIONAL SOFTWARE DEVELOPMENT

Before going on to discuss CASE concepts, let us look at the traditional software development process and how computer languages have evolved to meet programmer needs. When programming efforts were first begun in the early 1950s, programmers generally worked alone to analyze the problem, write the code in a language the computer could understand, and then test and debug the program. These pioneers were not only conversant with the software, but were more than likely able to make repairs and refinements in the computer hardware as well. Programs were generally short and uncomplicated, and team efforts were not involved. Program logic was relatively uncomplicated, so little documentation was required.

The actual coding of programs was usually done by the programmer or an assistant who was conversant with a programming language and the particular computer's idiosyncrasies. Since programs were short and usually uncomplicated, manual coding was satisfactory. An exceptionally long program in the early days might involve 300 or 400 lines of code, so the process of finding errors was relatively easy.

Today, however, complex computer programs may have thousands of lines of code and may occupy millions of bytes of memory. They are written in joint efforts that may involve dozens of programmers. This requires the coordination of a team, the scheduling of their activities, and the assurance that each element or module will act consistently and will function with all other elements in the program.

Flowcharting was the traditional tool of the programmer. But as we have seen, structured programming has changed the demands on design diagramming. Today programmers use a variety of tools to document their programs.

EVOLUTION OF PROGRAMMING LANGUAGES

Programming languages are continually evolving (see Fig. 14.1). The earliest language developed for computers was **machine language.** This consisted of code written as strings of ones and zeros that directed the machine to perform specific functions. These instructions were executed directly by the computer. Even today, computers still operate as directed by machine-language instructions. However, most programmers prefer not to use machine languages when writing programs.

Shortly after machine language was introduced, **assembler languages** came on the scene. An assembler language consisted of a group of abbreviations, or mnemonics, known as operation codes or simply op codes. Each op code was converted by the computer into a machine language that the computer could execute. In a sense, this represented the first step toward automation, since the computer did the conversion.

The 1950s and '60s saw the introduction of a third generation of languages, including FORTRAN, COBOL, PL/I, BASIC, and others. These languages were developed to reflect the way programmers thought and worked. For instance, FORTRAN was patterned after mathematical equations and COBOL after ordinary business English (see Fig. 14.2). Since computers do not understand English, or mathematics for that matter, special conversion programs known as **compilers**

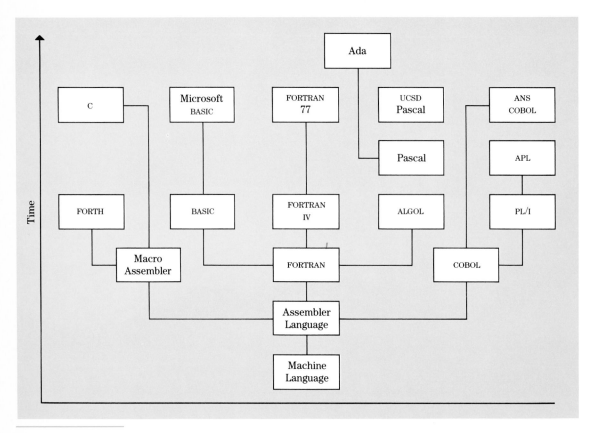

FIGURE 14.1

Evolution of Programming Languages

were needed. These compilers converted English or mathematic instructions into machine language. This represented another step toward automation.

In the 1970s and early '80s, other third-generation languages were developed, refinements and extensions of earlier languages. Ada, Pascal, C, and some advanced dialects of BASIC came into use (see Fig. 14.3). These further separated the programmer from the details of the machine. Yet the programmer still had to write the code that would be converted by the computer into machine language.

Today, development is going forward on **fourth-generation languages** which do not require the programmer to adhere strictly to rules of language syntax and structure. These new high-level languages are an attempt to further remove programmers from language details and allow them to focus on the problems being solved. Obviously, an ideal language would be one that lets a programmer state a problem in ordinary business English or common mathematical notation. It would then translate the statement of the problem into a set of instructions the computer could execute. No such language yet exists, but developmental efforts are moving in that direction.

```
IDENTIFICATION DIVISION.
PROGRAM ID. LISTING1.
ENVIRONMENT DIVISION.
CONFIGURATION SECTION.
SOURCE COMPUTER.  CYBER-170-720.
OBJECT COMPUTER.  CYBER-170-720.
SPECIAL-NAMES.
INPUT-OUTPUT SECTION.
FILE CONTROL.
      SELECT IN-FILE ASSIGN TO INPUT.
      SELECT OUT-FILE ASSIGN TO OUTPUT.
DATA DIVISION.
FILE SECTION.
*     DEFINE INPUT OF THE PROGRAM.
FD    IN-FILE
      LABEL RECORDS ARE OMITTED.
01    RECORD-IN             PIC x(80).
*     DEFINE OUTPUT OF THE PROGRAM.
FD    OUT-FILE
      LABEL RECORDS ARE OMITTED.
01    RECORD-OUT.
      02 FILLER            PIC X(01).
      02 DATA-OUT          PIC X(80).
PROCEDURE DIVISION.
LETS-GO.
      OPEN INPUT IN-FILE.
      OPEN OUTPUT OUT-FILE.
      MOVE SPACES TO RECORD-OUT.
      WRITE RECORD-OUT AFTER PAGE.
READ-AND-WRITE.
      READ IN-FILE AT END GO TO CLOSE-UP.
      MOVE RECORD-IN TO DATA-OUT.
      WRITE RECORD-OUT AFTER 1.
      GO TO READ-AND-WRITE.
CLOSE UP.
      CLOSE IN-FILE, OUT-FILE.
      STOP RUN.
```

FIGURE 14.2

COBOL Example
COBOL closely resembles ordinary business English.

Source: Silver and Silver, Computers and Information Processing, *Harper and Row, 1986*

LANGUAGE SELECTION CRITERIA

In selecting a language, the analyst must consider the application, the program's complexity, the end user's needs, the languages known by suitable programmers, the compilers available, and whether the program will be exported to other systems (see Fig. 14.4). Computer languages have been developed for

```
PROGRAM AVERAGE  (INPUT,  OUTPUT);
   VAR
      NUMBER,  TOTAL,  AVERAGE  :  REAL;
      COUNT  :  INTEGER;
   BEGIN
      TOTAL  : =  0;
      COUNT  : =  0;
      READ(NUMBER);
      WHILE  NOT  EOF  DO
         BEGIN
            TOTAL  : =  TOTAL  +  NUMBER;
            COUNT  : =  COUNT  +  1;
            READ(NUMBER);
         END;
      IF  COUNT  >  0
         THEN
            BEGIN
               AVERAGE  : =  TOTAL  /  COUNT;
               WRITELN(COUNT,  'NUMBERS  WERE  READ,  AVERAGE  IS  ',AVERAGE);
            END;
         ELSE  WRITELN('NO  NUMBERS  WERE  READ');
   END.
```

Source: Silver and Silver, Computers and Information Processing, Harper and Row, 1986

FIGURE 14.3

Pascal Example Pascal is a structured language in which logic levels are shown by indentation.

	ASSEMBLER	ADA	BASIC	C	COBOL	FORTRAN	PASCAL	PL/I
Wide availability	X		X		X			
Standardized		X	X		X	X	X	X
Structured		X		X			X	
Oriented to professional programmer	X	X		X	X		X	X
Suited to novices			X			X		
Business applications			X		X			X
Educational applications			X			X	X	
Operating systems programming	X	X		X				
Scientific and mathematical applications			X			X		X
Interactive applications		X	X	X			X	X
Resembles English					X		X	X

FIGURE 14.4

Language Selection Criteria

Program: PACKAGE TRACER MODULE

Analyst: W. Kline

Date: 9-18-89

General Comments:

This module is part of the shipment control master program. The purpose of this module is to trace misrouted package requests. It will scan input from a variety of sources, tracking an entity by shipping date, shipper, shipper number, point of origin, and destination.

Specific Requirements:

Language: Advanced BASIC

System Requirements: Desktop computer, 640K memory
                      20M hard disk
                      Monochrome monitor

Operating System: MS/DOS

Maximum Program Size: 256K

Documentation: Full set to conform to shipment control
                master program

Data Prototype Completed: 07-15-89

Date Module Completed: 08-15-89

FIGURE 14.5

Software Specifications

various applications. Some languages are best suited for education, mathematics, or business applications, others for scientific or process control uses.

COBOL, for example, generates large, relatively unwieldy programs, but resembles ordinary business English. C is more compact and best suited for developing microcomputer operating systems, while Pascal lends itself to the educational environment.

PREPARING SOFTWARE SPECIFICATIONS

Systems analysts often must prepare software specifications before programs are written. A set of specifications is drawn up, defining the language, memory limits, language standards, and other requirements (see Fig. 14.5). The

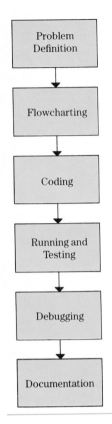

FIGURE 14.6

Traditional Software Development Life Cycle

software specifications should define program length, input and output parameters, computations to be performed, and documentation requirements. Once a set of specifications has been written, it can be turned over to programmers for software development and coding.

SOFTWARE DEVELOPMENT LIFE CYCLE

Most traditional program development efforts follow the **software development life cycle** (see Fig. 14.6). The process begins with a definition of the problem, followed by diagramming. The problem is then coded in a specific language, creating a program. The program is tested and debugged, and then documentation is completed. The steps involved in flowcharting, coding, running, and debugging may be repeated many times until a functional program is developed.

To facilitate the process, a design walkthrough is often undertaken. A **design walkthrough** is a procedure in which a programmer or analyst manually checks through each module or block of program code to check its accuracy and completeness. Design walkthroughs detect errors in logic and coding early in the programming cycle so that they can be corrected easily.

The difficulty with the traditional life cycle is that the process is not computer based or automated, even though computer programs are being written. Errors and inconsistencies in programming style and logic may occur. Further, the entire process is based upon the assumption that a clearly defined set of end-user needs has been developed. There is no provision for prototyping or involvement with the end user. Since the process is manual, diagrams must be drawn over and over to reflect changes, and the debugging stage can become a lengthy and time-consuming effort.

Further complicating the programmer's task are the many changes that may be made to a program as it goes through the development life cycle. It is not uncommon for an input screen or output record to be changed many times until a satisfactory screen image or report is generated. This may require repeated recoding, which again introduces the chances of errors or bugs in the program.

CASE CONCEPTS

CASE is based upon a shared computer environment for software development (see Fig. 14.7). Instead of programmers manually preparing flowcharts and code, they use CASE to automate the process, usually from a desktop computer or a terminal on a larger system; thus CASE software is sometimes called a programmer's workbench. Since several programmers may be involved in the effort, the process is designed to be modular in nature. CASE is provided by

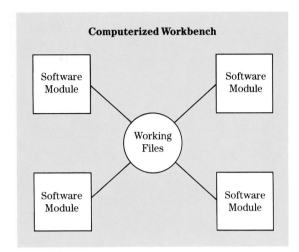

FIGURE 14.7

**CASE
Environment**

installing a software package, such as Knowledgeware's Information Engineering Workbench/Workstation or Index Technology's Excelerator. Some of these packages are described in Fig. 14.8.

To illustrate CASE concepts, we shall use Excelerator. Excelerator requires each user who wants to gain access to the system to enter a unique name and password (see Fig. 14.9). In a large system, access to various projects is controlled so that individuals working on specific modules can access only the part of the system they are concerned with.

Once the project has been accessed, a group of options is presented to the user. The programmer can elect to generate data flow diagrams, input/output screens, and so forth. Main programming modules are developed first, describing the major components of the system. These are then decomposed or exploded into smaller modules. Individual programmers may be assigned to specific modules.

Each programmer accesses files that are common to other programmers working on the project. A consistent programming effort is possible because of the use of a data dictionary. The data dictionary is the repository of the entities or elements that compose a system. Each programmer working on a module develops a component based upon standards entered in the data dictionary. This assures consistency and proper interaction when all the elements are brought together. The data dictionary is the heart of Excelerator. We have already discussed the data dictionary and how it is used in systems development. It performs the same function in Excelerator.

The major steps in the CASE process are:

- Problem definition
- Construction of data dictionary
- Construction of screens and reports

FIGURE 14.8

CASE Software

Computer-Aided Software Engineering (CASE)
A Review of Software Engineering Packages

Using a variety of software engineering packages helps programmers increase their productivity. Packages vary in scope and capability; prices range from under $200 to over $6000. At present, there are no national standards for this type of software, and a diversity of approaches are used. Some of the major CASE products are described below.

EasyFlow   HavenTree Software Ltd.
                                           Thousand Island Park, NY 13692

An onscreen processor for preparing flowcharts and organization charts. Prepares multiple-page charts using either standard or custom flowchart symbols. Runs on IBM PCs and compatibles.

ANATOOL   Abvent
                                           Beverly Hills, CA 90212

A structured systems analysis tool for the Macintosh computer, which automates the software engineering process. Implements the Yourdon Structured Systems Analysis methodology. Incorporates a data dictionary and generates data flow diagrams as well as program and system documentation. Uses the Macintosh Tool Box and icons to create and revise diagrams.

Excelerator   Index Technology Corp.
                                           Cambridge, MA 02142

A comprehensive, fully integrated workbench, used widely by professional systems analysts and programmers. Has a broad range of capabilities and runs on an IBM PC. Prepares data flow diagrams, structure charts, and presentation graphics. Maintains a project dictionary and will prototype screens and reports. Can generate data maps in BASIC, C, COBOL, and PL/I.

- Analysis
- Code generation
- Integrated documentation

Traditional programming takes a linear, noninteractive approach. A sequence of steps, beginning with problem definition and followed by flowcharting, ends

The Visible Analyst   Visible Systems Corp.
Workbench   Newton, MA 02165

A software engineering workbench composed of a diagramming tool, an analyzing tool, and an organizing tool. Runs on an IBM PC and prepares Gane and Sarson as well as Yourdon diagrams. Maintains a data dictionary and can decompose modules at an unlimited number of levels. Uses both standard and custom symbols.

ProMod   ProMod Company
                    Lake Forest, CA

A software engineering tool that includes an automatic structure charting option. Runs on an IBM PC and creates highly detailed structure charts and other diagrams used throughout the development cycle. Charts can be displayed on the screen, edited, and output on either a plotter or laser printer. Creates network charts that connect major system structures.

Information Engineering   KnowledgeWare
Workbench   Atlanta, GA 30026

An extensive menu-driven software development workbench that runs on an IBM PC. Produces data flow, decomposition, and entity diagrams. Prepares reports and analyses and uses an encyclopedia to store entities. Generates action and context diagrams. Designed for engineering information systems and to automate program development. Generates program code based upon detailed designs. Can run as a stand-alone workbench or as a workstation on a larger mainframe system.

---

with a debugged, documented program. CASE uses an interactive, online methodology. Throughout the development life cycle, changes and modifications are made in software parameters, with systematic interaction between elements. For example, a tentative screen design may be developed, followed by a prototype report.

    As the software is prepared, changes are made in the screen design and

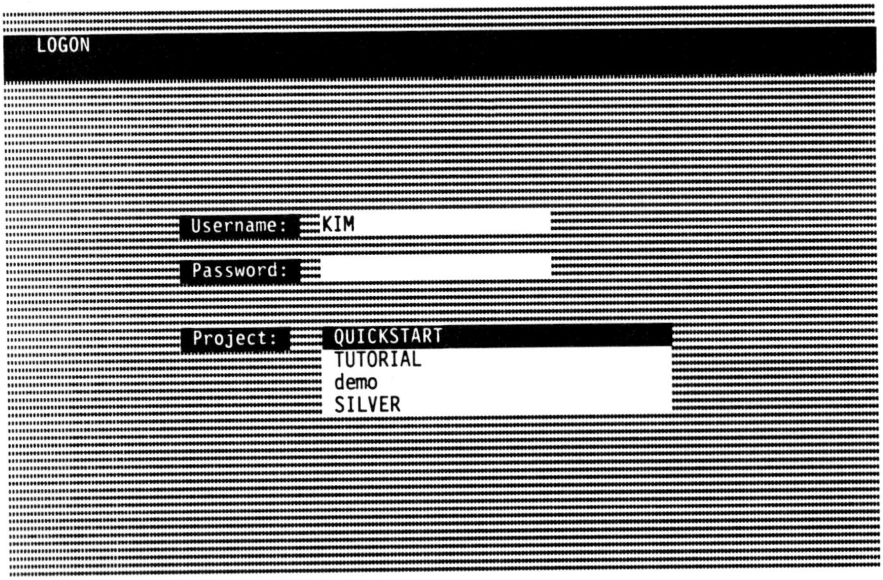

FIGURE 14.9

Excelerator Log-On Screen The user must enter name and password before proceeding.

```
LOGON



                    Username:  KIM

                    Password:


            Project:    QUICKSTART
                        TUTORIAL
                        demo
                        SILVER
```

Source: Index Technology

FIGURE 14.10

CASE Elements

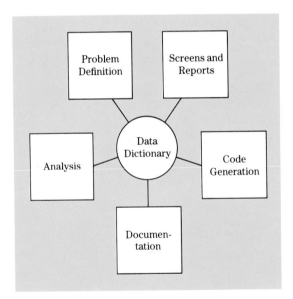

the output report, which in turn affect the program. The data dictionary is used to coordinate the effort, assuring consistency in the development process. Let us look at the major elements in CASE (see Fig. 14.10). Although we describe them in a sequential order, they are not undertaken in a linear fashion, but are performed interactively throughout the development of the software on an online computer system.

Problem Definition

As in traditional programming, the first step is the preparation of a clear problem statement. Before a program can be written, user needs must be assessed and input and output requirements defined.

Data Dictionary

Throughout the process a data dictionary is used to provide consistency of variables, entities, and screens (see Fig. 14.11). This is an important distinction between traditional programming and CASE. In traditional programming, a programmer may select inconsistent variable names or establish illogical relationships that cannot be detected without a great deal of debugging time and effort. By using a central repository, consistency in variable names, elements within a record, and record design is assured.

Screens and Reports

In this phase prototype screen designs and reports are generated with the help of routines available within the CASE software (see Fig. 14.12). The screens are built from entities stored in the data dictionary. This ensures consistent usage of terms, variables, fields, and records.

An entire system of reports and screens can be prototyped. These designs are then tested by the end user to make sure that the software is performing properly. If changes are required, CASE facilitates the process. As in the other steps, changes made on screens and reports are always tracked by the data dictionary.

Analysis

A variety of analytical tools are available in Excelerator. For example, a program's logic can be analyzed for inconsistencies, omissions, or redundancies, using available graphics techniques. Excelerator can analyze logic levels and detect programming logic in an exploded module that may properly belong in a lower or higher level module. The analysis and detection of these kinds of inconsistencies are extremely difficult using traditional programming methodology.

Code Generation

One of the most laborious tasks in programming is the actual writing of code. **Code** is the conversion of logical steps or screen and report content into

FIGURE 14.11

Excelerator Data Dictionary

(a)

(b)

Source: Index Technology

instructions that the computer can understand. Not only is the process time consuming, but it is also prone to error.

Some CASE software has provisions for code generation. Figure 14.13 illustrates a display screen that must be coded in order to run in a finished application program. If Excelerator is used, for example, the specific language

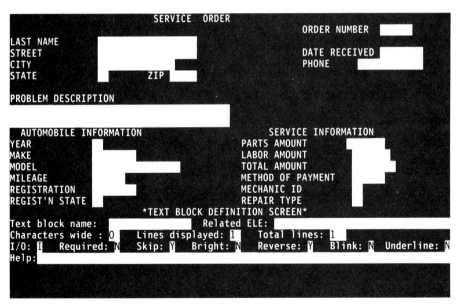

```
1...+...10....+...20....+...30....+...40....+...50....+...60....+...70....+...
1


                        EXPERT MOTORS

                   WEEKLY CAR REPAIRS BY TYPE


      FRONT END ALIGNMENT

10    CUSTOMER NAME           PARTS($)         LABOR($)         MECHANIC ID
      XXXXXXXXXXXXXXXXX       $999.99          $9,999.99            XX
      XXXXXXXXXXXXXXXXX       $999.99          $9,999.99            XX
      XXXXXXXXXXXXXXXXX       $999.99          $9,999.99            XX
      XXXXXXXXXXXXXXXXX       $999.99          $9,999.99            XX
      XXXXXXXXXXXXXXXXX       $999.99          $9,999.99            XX
      XXXXXXXXXXXXXXXXX       $999.99          $9,999.99            XX
      XXXXXXXXXXXXXXXXX       $999.99          $9,999.99            XX
      XXXXXXXXXXXXXXXXX       $999.99          $9,999.99            XX
      XXXXXXXXXXXXXXXXX       $999.99          $9,999.99            XX
20    TOTAL                   $99,999.99       $99,999.99



          3 EXIT      1,8 COLUMN    8 REPEAT    10 FIELD
```

Source: Index Technology

FIGURE 14.12

Report Design Description Screen

```
                    SERVICE   ORDER
                                        ORDER NUMBER    [      ]
LAST NAME        [               ]
STREET                                  DATE RECEIVED   [      ]
CITY                                    PHONE           [         ]
STATE            ZIP    [      ]

PROBLEM DESCRIPTION


  AUTOMOBILE INFORMATION                SERVICE INFORMATION
YEAR                                   PARTS AMOUNT
MAKE                                   LABOR AMOUNT
MODEL                                  TOTAL AMOUNT
MILEAGE                                METHOD OF PAYMENT
REGISTRATION                           MECHANIC ID
REGIST'N STATE                         REPAIR TYPE
                   *TEXT BLOCK DEFINITION SCREEN*
Text block name:                 Related ELE:
Characters wide : 0    Lines displayed: 1    Total lines: 1
I/O: I    Required: N    Skip: Y    Bright: N    Reverse: Y    Blink: N    Underline: N
Help:
```

Source: Index Technology

FIGURE 14.13

Display Screen Fields

selected is entered on the screen (see Fig. 14.14). The programmer can choose BASIC, C, COBOL, or PL/I. Once a selection has been made, the software generates a **data map** (see Fig. 14.15). The data map is consistent with the variable names used, not only on the display screen but throughout the program, and is easily converted to programming code.

FIGURE 14.14

Language Selection

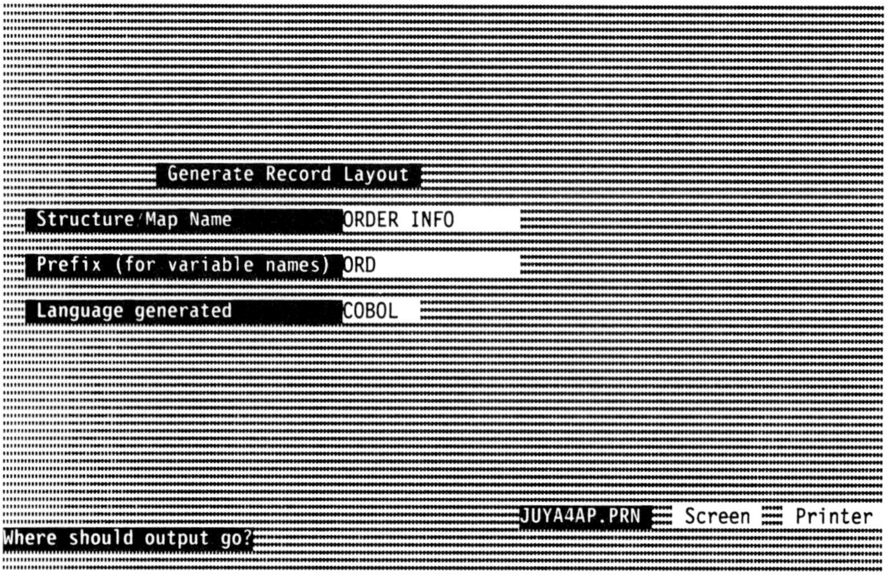

```
                    ┌─ Generate Record Layout ─┐
  Structure/Map Name              ORDER INFO
  Prefix (for variable names)  ORD
  Language generated            COBOL




                                          JUYA4AP.PRN   Screen   Printer
Where should output go?
```

Source: *Index Technology*

Documentation

In traditional programming, documentation is the last step completed in the process, often done after the programmer has forgotten specific details. In CASE, the documentation process automatically begins early in the software development cycle. At any time the programmer can display or print out data flow diagrams and screen or record layouts. Because the documentation is integrated with the data dictionary, it will be complete, consistent, and accurate.

While CASE is new to the programming scene, it promises to play a major role in software development and will almost certainly become important for the systems analyst. Now that we have learned how the systems development effort is conducted, let us turn to systems implementation. The next chapter will discuss the systems implementation process in detail.

Summary

CASE is the process of automating the design and development of computer software. It is an emerging technology that differs from traditional software development, which uses manual flowcharting and coding techniques. CASE has shifted these tasks to the computer, thus increasing programmer productivity.

Programming languages undergo a continual process of evolution and development. First machine languages were introduced, followed by assembler

```
*Record ORDER-INFO. Compiled:   2-Jul-86
 01   ORDER-INFO
      05   ORDOrder-Number   PIC X(11).
      05   ORDDate           PIC X(8).
      05   ORDCustomer       PIC X(29).
      05   ORDAttention      PIC X(32).
      05   ORDProduct-Info. OCCURS 15 TIMES.
           10   ORDProduct-Number
                          PIC X(8).
           10   ORDQuantity  PIC XXXX.
           10   ORDUnit-Price
                          PIC X(7).
           10   ORDTotal-Price
                          PIC X(7).
      05   ORDTax           PIC X(7).
      05   ORDSubtotal      PIC X(8).
      05   ORDTotal         PIC $9999.99.
      05   ORDShipping-Address
                          OCCURS 6 TIMES.
           10   ORDShipping-Address
                          PIC X(25).
      05   ORDAddress        OCCURS 6 TIMES.
           10   ORDShipping-Address
                          PIC X(25).
      05   ORDOrder-Taken-By
                          PIC XXX.
      05   ORDMarketing-Rep.
                          PIC XXX.
      05   ORDInvoice-Number
                          PIC X(8).
```

FIGURE 14.15

COBOL Data Map

Source: *Index Technology*

languages. Later, FORTRAN, COBOL, PL/I, and BASIC became available. Still higher level languages are being developed. Languages are selected using criteria based upon applications to be programmed. Some languages are more suited to specific applications than others.

In traditional software development, a problem is defined, flowcharted, coded, debugged, and documented. Design walkthroughs are sometimes conducted. This process is prone to error and inconsistencies.

CASE implies that a computer environment for software development exists. First the problem is defined, then a data dictionary constructed. Next, screens and reports are developed, followed by an analysis for consistency. Programming code can be automatically generated by the CASE software. Documentation is prepared systematically as part of the CASE process.

Key Terms

Assembler language

Code

Compiler

Computer-aided software
engineering (CASE)

Data map

Design walkthrough

Fourth-generation language

Machine language

Software development life cycle

Exercises

1. Write a definition of CASE.
2. Describe traditional software development methodology.
3. Describe how early programming languages evolved.
4. Discuss language selection criteria.
5. Discuss design walkthrough and its purpose.
6. List the major steps in the CASE methodology.
7. Discuss how screens and reports can be prototyped using CASE.
8. Discuss how analytical tools are used in CASE.
9. Discuss the provisions in CASE for code generation.
10. Contrast traditional documentation techniques with those used by CASE.

Projects

1. Visit a computer store that sells programs and software. Make a list of the language compilers and interpreters that are for sale.
2. Visit a computer programmer and discuss language attributes. What languages are favored? Why? For what kinds of applications?
3. Visit a small business establishment that uses a software package. Discuss reasons why the software package was selected. What are its features and limitations?
4. Obtain a piece of CASE software such as that described in the text. Review the documentation and determine what tasks it performs for the programmer.
5. Visit a systems software developer. Identify the kinds of software used by the organization and discuss software engineering.

ANALYST AT WORK
BRYAN SOFTWARE

DESCRIPTION OF FIRM

Bob Bryan and his brother John became fascinated with programming when they took a course in BASIC at college. Upon graduation, both continued their programming efforts for their respective employers. After several years Bob and John decided to team up and begin writing computer software as a business enterprise.

Today Bryan Software employs several dozen software programmers. The company specializes in writing medical billing programs for doctors, dentists, hospitals, and other medical providers.

Bryan Software frequently contracts to write custom medical billing packages. The packages are put on a developmental timetable. These contracts require that a finished, debugged package be delivered at a specific date. It is therefore essential that Bryan Software develop programs in a systematic and predictable manner.

SYSTEM OVERVIEW

Figure 14.16 illustrates a diagram of the steps followed in developing a new program at Bryan Software. Projects begin with a review of customer requirements and specifications. Then, using data flow diagrams, logical and physical designs are developed.

After the program has been coded, it is run and tested. When Bryan Software is satisfied that bugs have been removed and the software is operating properly, they install it at the customer's site. After additional testing and modifications, a final release is installed for the client. At this time, the customer makes final payment on the program.

Sometimes Bryan Software executes a sales contract with customers that provides for software maintenance. In this instance, the maintenance fee provides for software changes and modifications on an ongoing basis as required by the customer.

HANDS-ON APPLICATION

You have been hired by Bryan Software to assist in the development of software for several new clients. You are to generate the three work products below that involve writing specifications, data flow diagrams, and software evaluation criteria. *(continues)*

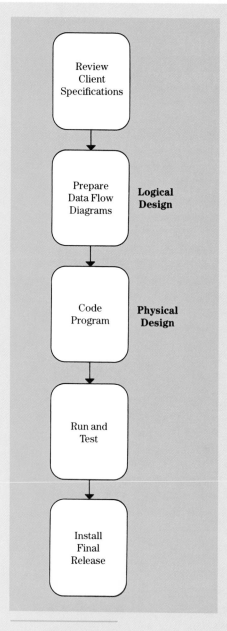

FIGURE 14.16

Bryan Software's Development Cycle

Work Product No. 1   You are to write a set of software specifications for a medical billing program. Refer to Fig. 14.5, which shows a sample software specification sheet. Prepare a similar set of specifications and label it WP1, Chapter 14. Organize your effort by preparing an outline of your specifications before you prepare a final draft. Enter your outline below.

OUTLINE OF SOFTWARE SPECIFICATIONS

_____

_____

_____

_____

_____

_____

_____

Work Product No. 2   Prepare a data flow diagram for a basic medical billing system. The diagram should include steps that process debits and credits, prepare invoices, and generate periodic statements. Label this document WP2, Chapter 14. Use a task list to organize this effort. Enter the task list below.

TASK LIST

_____

_____

_____

_____

_____

_____

_____

(continues)

Work Product No. 3   Prepare a list of performance criteria that you will use to evaluate the medical billing program software. The criteria should specify the characteristics and performance standards that you expect in the final program. Label this document WP3, Chapter 14. Prepare a task list to assist in this effort and enter it below.

TASK LIST

_____

_____

_____

_____

_____

_____

_____

THE IMPLEMEN- TATION PHASE

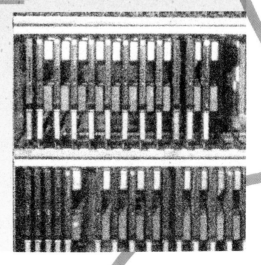

SYSTEMS IMPLEMENTATION

LEARNING OBJECTIVES

After studying this chapter, you should be able to:

1. Describe three common approaches to system changeover.

2. Discuss the human and psychological aspects of systems implementation.

3. Discuss in-service training and education requirements.

4. Identify potential systems implementation trouble spots and suggest how to avoid them.

5. Describe the kinds and types of assistance available during implementation.

6. Discuss the effects of the learning curve.

During systems implementation, the new system is installed, brought online, and made available to users. However, the purchase and installation of facilities with up-to-date hardware, software, and trained personnel does not necessarily mean that a well-functioning information system will result.

Systems implementation is complex and many factors must be considered. Time schedules for implementing the new system must be established. Human reactions must be anticipated and dealt with. Personnel training programs may be necessary. Interruptions in organizational procedures and services must be minimized, and a host of other expected—and unexpected—problems are likely to require attention. Even a small change in a system may have dramatic consequences. More than one system failure has been traced to poor implementation, rather than to inherent weaknesses in the system design. This chapter deals with the last phase of the systems development life cycle, systems implementation.

HOW TO UNDERTAKE SYSTEMS IMPLEMENTATION

Systems implementation is the planned and orderly conversion from an existing system to a new one. It involves fine-tuning system elements in order to maximize efficiency and productivity. Part of the task includes completing documentation and evaluating the final design to make sure that the system meets desired goals and objectives.

A task list may be developed, specifying what must be done. Here is an example of a task list that might be developed to implement a new system.

TASK LIST

1. Prepare changeover timetable.
2. Notify employees.
3. Undertake training and in-service program.
4. Monitor system for trouble spots.
5. Evaluate performance.
6. Optimize performance.
7. Complete system documentation.

The remainder of this chapter will discuss the first four tasks on our list. The next two chapters complete our discussion of the task list.

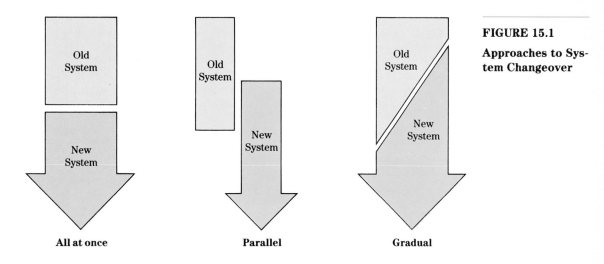

All at once   Parallel   Gradual

FIGURE 15.1

Approaches to System Changeover

THE CHANGEOVER TIMETABLE

A major task in the systems implementation phase is the development of a **changeover timetable.** There are three basic approaches used in converting to a new system: an immediate, all-at-once changeover; a gradual, step-by-step changeover; or a parallel system changeover, when the new and old systems operate at the same time (see Fig. 15.1).

All-at-Once Changeover

In the **all-at-once changeover,** the old system is abandoned and the new system becomes completely operational on a specific date. This approach is sometimes known as a direct, crash, or abrupt changeover. All planning and design, purchasing, training, ordering, and the like are finished before this date, so that the new system is ready to go at the moment the old one ceases to operate.

The major advantage of this approach is cost. Since one system is dropped as the other is started, the organization pays for operating only one system at a time. No backup or temporary systems costs are involved. The all-at-once changeover also eliminates backsliding. Employees are not able to go back to an older, inefficient method, since it no longer exists. The adjustment period to the new system may be difficult and trying, but once made it is complete and the period of disruption is kept to a minimum.

The all-at-once changeover is completed in less time than the other alternatives. The benefits of the new system are realized at once. Having an improved system operational before the competition can institute a similar system is often a major advantage in a crowded marketplace.

A limitation of this approach, however, is that by its very nature it is sudden and abrupt. Employees may have trouble adjusting to it and unexpected problems may develop, causing serious disruptions and confusion. The absence of a backup system during the changeover can result in loss of data, errors in processing, misshipped goods, or interruption of service.

Parallel System Operation

A second approach to the changeover is **parallel system operation.** In this method, both the old and new systems are operated concurrently for a period of time. Data is processed or moved through both systems at the same time. Only when the new system is fully debugged and operational is the old system abandoned.

Advantages of this approach are that the old system is available as a backup in the event of the new system's failure, and the results processed by the new system can be compared to the output of the old. In addition, changes and adjustments can be made in the new system without disturbing customer relations or data flow.

This approach is used in cases where loss of data or system failure cannot be tolerated. In such instances, the parallel system continues until it is certain that the new facilities are functioning properly.

The major limitation of the parallel method is the cost involved in operating both systems during the transition period. The old system must be maintained and operated even after it is no longer productive. Extra shifts, overtime, and leasing duplicate equipment may be required. Another limitation is the confusion that may ensue when two systems are operating simultaneously. Employees may not be sure which system to use or which to rely upon. Orders may be misrouted, errors made, or paperwork incorrectly processed.

Gradual Changeover

A **gradual changeover** is a third commonly used technique of converting to a new system. In this mode, the new system is introduced in steps. As one part of the new system is tested and perfected, that portion of the old system is phased out. This process continues until the new system is fully implemented. For example, accounts payable may be put on the new system first, then accounts receivables, payroll, asset inventory, and so on until the last remaining functions are changed over. This method is sometimes known as the staggered or phased-in approach.

A gradual changeover has many advantages. It gives the employees time to adjust to the new system, allowing them to learn details and ask questions without being rushed or under the pressure of a sudden change. A gradual changeover reduces the chances of an unexpected total system failure. Since only part of the system is being implemented at any one time, a single catastrophic failure is less likely to occur.

There are, however, limitations to this approach. The gradual changeover may take a longer period of time—months, sometimes even years. In the meantime, the organization cannot realize all of the benefits or economic gains resulting from the new system. This may give competitors an advantage. For example, competitors who have already changed to new systems may give better service to customers, ship goods faster, and misprocess fewer orders. While one organization has opted for a gradual changeover, another has made an all-at-once change, gaining immediate benefits in terms of costs and improved customer relations.

The full effects of a new system may not be obvious for months. Thus, a malfunctioning condition may go unrecognized until the problem becomes critical. For example, goods may be misshipped or misbilled for several months before a system error is detected, and then it may be too late to undo the damage. An all-at-once changeover would have shown the error immediately, minimizing losses to the company.

The UniTrans Case

In Chapter 13 we discussed an effort undertaken by an analyst at UniTrans to implement a new and improved word processing system in the secretarial services department. Now the equipment is scheduled for delivery and the analyst must begin the systems implementation phase.

The analyst has learned that August is a very slow month for the secretarial services department and has recommended an all-at-once changeover to take place then. This will minimize organization disruptions and, in the analyst's view, be most cost effective. Figure 15.2 illustrates a changeover timetable developed by the UniTrans analyst. In planning this timetable, the analyst establishes goals and benchmarks to serve as checkpoints during implementation. By setting specific dates for the arrival of equipment, debugging, employee training, and so on, the analyst minimizes the disruption to the organization. Figure 15.3 is a Gantt chart detailing the implementation process.

THE HUMAN ELEMENT

Human and psychological factors are important in systems implementation. People tend to resist change, and employees often need to be convinced

Word Processing Installation	START DATE	END DATE
Notify employees	06/27	07/05
Delivery of equipment	07/05	07/18
Test equipment	07/18	07/25
Install and debug software	07/25	08/01
Operator training	08/01	08/15
System trial startup	08/08	08/15
Changeover date	08/15	08/15
System operational	08/08	08/22
Evaluation and optimization	08/15	08/29
Complete documentation	06/27	09/05

FIGURE 15.3

Gantt Chart The chart shows the timetable of the implementation process.

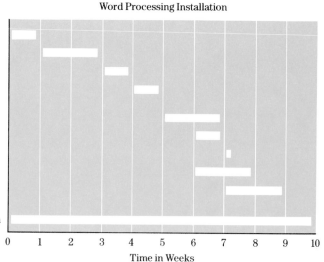

Gantt Chart
Word Processing Installation

that the new system is in everyone's best interests. As soon as word gets around that a new system is contemplated, psychological reactions such as fear, uncertainty, and doubt may become evident. This is sometimes called the FUD factor (see Fig. 15.4).

The systems analyst should understand why people react this way, as well as how feelings of cooperation, interest, and involvement can be generated. Some employees may feel threatened with loss of status, position, or power within the organization. When a change in procedure or structure occurs, some workers fear they will suffer loss of wages or end up with degraded working conditions,

FIGURE 15.4
Word Travels Fast in Organizations
Fear, uncertainty, and doubt may be felt when individuals are exposed to new systems.

increased inconveniences, longer hours, or exposure to criticism. Others resist a new system simply because it is new.

Reactions such as these can lead to serious problems that may delay systems implementation, hinder retraining programs, add considerably to costs and time elements, and even prevent the new system from working properly. One way to avoid such problems is to involve all personnel in planning and assure them that the new system will improve their working situation.

A fundamental rule in this regard is to talk to people. Involve them while the system is still in the design stage and use their input in the systems development and implementation phases. Personnel involved in the genesis of a new system are more apt to support it and to aid in its successful implementation.

The UniTrans analyst has decided to recommend the following suggestions to management in order to encourage positive personnel reactions to the new word processing system.

Announce New System Formally

Officially inform workers of the possibility of system changes. Explain how the changes will affect employees and their working environment. If employees hear the news through the grapevine, they may receive misleading information (see Fig. 15.5).

FIGURE 15.5

Conversations with Employees
System changes should be discussed directly with employees.

Courtesy of International Business Machines Corporation

Involve Personnel Early

Talk to people early in the implementation stage. Discuss their needs and attitudes toward the new system and get them actively participating in the process.

Stress Benefits to be Gained from New System

Describe in tangible terms the advantages and benefits that will result when the new system is operational: ease of use of new equipment, reliability, increased output at lower cost, better looking finished documents, fewer errors.

Report Progress Periodically

Circulate regular bulletins to update employees on the status of the system development and implementation efforts. Such communications are particularly important if many steps or prolonged periods of implementation are involved.

TRAINER	TRAINEE
Project leader	Top management
Analysts	Supervisory personnel
Supervisory management	Clerical personnel
Project leader and analysts	Data processing staff

Encourage Positive Support

Reward individuals who are cooperative and particularly helpful during the implementation of the new system. Acknowledge those who help by recognizing their service, perhaps providing bonuses or vacation time after the implementation is completed.

TRAINING AND IN-SERVICE EDUCATION

Some form of education or retraining is usually needed to teach personnel to operate new machines and to handle new procedures and methods. Many weeks or months may be spent in developing and conducting training programs. Training at different levels, especially during conversion, should include many positions in the organization. Programs may be aimed at top management, supervisory management, clerical workers, the data processing staff, and others. Figure 15.6 shows the various relationships of trainers and trainees.

The systems analyst should consider the following elements when planning a training program.

Special Training

Which activities in the new system will require special training? What new machines will be installed, and how many operators will be needed? Will an intensive training course be needed, or just a demonstration? What new forms will be used, and which personnel should be instructed in their routing and use? Which employees will need explanations about new procedures and how to handle exceptions, failures, overloads, or maintenance?

Training Curriculum

The content and scheduling of the training program must be decided (see Fig. 15.7). This may involve considerable research. The knowledge, skills, and attitudes necessary for each task must be defined. Since many activities will

FIGURE 15.7

Training Programs Employees need to be instructed on how to operate new systems.

FIGURE 15.7

Training Programs Employees need to be instructed on how to operate new systems.

not be too different from those already being performed, many jobs in the new system will require only an orientation or demonstration. Other jobs, involving operating new devices or carrying out unfamiliar procedures, may need intensive classroom instruction and a period of practice.

Training may be conducted in many ways. Some vendors and suppliers provide free or low cost training programs for their equipment. Other vendors offer programmed instruction courses by mail. These courses are self-taught and may be used by the trainee at home.

The systems department may design part or all of the training program. Instructors may have to visit equipment installations or vendors, write training manuals, duplicate instructional materials, and prepare teaching aids and visuals.

After the contents of the training program have been designed, practical considerations must be solved. Instructors must be selected and trained, classroom space provided, and class schedules arranged. Should the classes be held during the work day, during lunch, on weekends, or at night? Who should pay for them? If vendor training programs or programmed instruction courses are utilized, should employees be paid while attending classes?

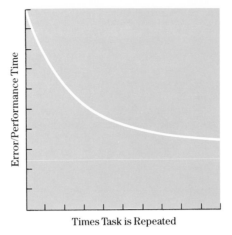

FIGURE 15.8

The Learning Curve Continued practice results in a gain in speed and accuracy.

Y-axis: Error/Performance Time

X-axis: Times Task is Repeated

Personnel for New Positions

The method of selecting individuals for various positions in the new system must be determined. Should existing personnel be sent to classes to learn to use new computer software? Or should new people be hired who already have these skills? How should new positions be filled: appointment by department manager, seniority, competitive examinations, previous training, or requests by employees? Factors that should be considered when making these decisions include the company's personnel policies, psychological effects on employees and morale, and the availability of trained personnel.

Proficiency and the Learning Curve

The analyst should understand the **learning curve** and its effect on training and productivity. The learning curve illustrates the relationship between continued practice at a given task and the resultant gains in proficiency, speed, and accuracy.

Figure 15.8 is a learning curve showing that the performance of an employee beginning a new task is relatively slow, with a high error rate. As the employee practices the task, speed and accuracy increase—up to a certain point, where a plateau is reached. Further practice will probably be of little use beyond this point.

The learning curve reflects the fact that when a new system is first installed, performance is slow, the error rate is high, and output is undependable. As employees learn to use forms, equipment, and procedures, their speed and accuracy go up. After a certain period of time, however, performance stabilizes and further practice yields little change in output.

IMPLEMENTATION TROUBLE SPOTS

It takes time to make a new system function properly. The analyst must expect delays, errors, questions, and problems when a new system is first installed. As personnel gain expertise in the new operations, these problems should subside. If they do not, they may be symptoms of other difficulties elsewhere in the system and the analyst should review the steps involved in the systems design and analysis phase. Certain areas are more likely to be trouble spots. These include the following.

Excessive Costs

Costs may increase much faster than anticipated during periods of change. Because of unfamiliarity with new routines, new sources of supply, and new equipment, or lack of adequate accounting or inventory procedures, costs can sometimes be difficult to predict or control.

The systems analyst must be alert to this potential trouble spot. To avoid or minimize the problem, careful cost control and accounting measures must be instituted early. Costs of goods, services, and supplies must be watched closely during these periods of change.

Inconvenience to Employees

A new system may bring many profitable improvements to an organization and its customers or clients, but the short-term effects often bring inconvenience and disrupted working conditions. Implementation of a new system may require overtime or rescheduling of vacations. If a new system is to be implemented during the period when employees normally take vacations, the expected disruption should be announced well in advance. Employees need time to make changes or to revise their plans.

If employees are expected to put in longer hours or to help in other ways during the implementation phase, their responsibilities should be clearly defined. Last-minute recruitment or hastily drawn work schedules and assignments can create many problems and lead to resentment and lack of cooperation by employees.

Inconvenience to Customers

Sometimes a new system causes temporary interruption of service to customers. Patrons should be forewarned of any possible inconvenience and measures taken to reduce disruption as much as possible during the changeover. If necessary, alternate means of continuing services, such as contracting with outside vendors, should be considered. After the system has been implemented, customers should be thanked for their patience and cooperation.

Time Delays

An important aspect of systems implementation is dealing with the period between when a system is installed and when it is finally up and running. Office machines, computers, communications equipment, and software must be thoroughly tested before they are released for routine use. The testing may take several weeks or even months. Neglecting to account for this time lapse when planning new schedules can lead to serious disruptions of service or other difficulties.

Time must be allotted to install special floors, air conditioning equipment, or wiring for a new mainframe computer system. Hardware that does not meet specifications may have to be redesigned, modified, and reinstalled.

Debugging Software

Time must be allowed to test and install software in a new system. It may take many months of careful effort to fully test and debug a complex computer program. **Debugging,** which is finding and removing errors from a program, can be very time consuming. Test data must be prepared, run through the program, and the results compared to those computed manually from the same data or by the old system.

ASSISTANCE DURING IMPLEMENTATION

The period of systems implementation may be a trying one for customers, employees, and management. The systems analyst should draw upon as many resources as possible to make the systems implementation phase go smoothly.

Assistance from Vendors

Equipment and supply vendors are valuable resources for advice and assistance when implementing a new system. They have an economic stake in the success of the system and are usually willing to provide the necessary customer support.

For example, computer manufacturers may offer their technical expertise and assistance by monitoring a computer's installation, testing its operation, and training operators. Some vendors provide fully tested and debugged programs along with the hardware. These services are sometimes described as **hand holding.**

Some vendors offer training programs to teach operators how to run their equipment. Classes in equipment operation, maintenance, and programming are held either at their site or at the customer's offices. In some instances, vendors make their own equipment, computers, and communications devices available to the customer until the ordered equipment is ready. This allows a firm to develop a new inventory or accounting system, for example, and test and debug it on the vendor's equipment before theirs is delivered. When the new computers finally arrive, little time and effort are lost getting under way.

In addition, some vendors continue to make their own equipment available in case the customer suffers a system failure after installation. If a machine must be taken out of service for repairs or modification, the vendor provides backup facilities.

Use of Consultants

Another approach to systems implementation is to obtain the services of an outside consultant. Systems designers and implementation consultants offer their services to organizations for a fee. They do not sell equipment, only services, and are in a position to be more objective. It may be more economical for an organization to hire a knowledgeable and experienced consultant than to have its own personnel waste valuable time experimenting or using trial and error techniques on a new installation. For many organizations, systems implementation is a one-time experience, and the skills necessary to make the transition are of little value later.

In-House Resources

The pool of personnel already on the payroll is a sometimes overlooked resource in implementing a new system. It is not uncommon for an organization to turn to outside vendors or consultants for assistance without first checking to see if someone on their staff has the needed skills. Employees involved in installing a new system may gain valuable skills and experience useful for running or maintaining the system later.

However, the systems analyst who relies solely on his or her own staff, regardless of their capabilities and range of experience, may be making a serious mistake. It takes time to acquire the necessary information to do an adequate job of systems implementation. Relying on unqualified or inexperienced personnel during a difficult period may delay implementation, add considerably to the cost, and produce an inferior system as the final result. The analyst must weigh the consultant versus in-house staff issue carefully.

Now that we have dealt with the system changeover, we can move on to systems evaluation and optimization. The next chapter describes how systems are fine-tuned and modified for maximum performance.

Summary

Systems implementation is the process in which new equipment is installed, brought online, and fully implemented. It involves the orderly conversion from an existing system to a new one. The objective is to fine-tune elements and maximize efficiency and productivity.

The process usually involves a changeover timetable. The most common conversion procedures are the all-at-once changeover, parallel system operation, and the gradual changeover. These differ in their cost and effect upon the organization. The human element must be considered when making a conversion. Personnel should be involved early, benefits stressed, progress reports issued, and positive support solicited.

New systems involve training and in-service education for employees. A variety of training techniques are available. Employees exhibit a learning curve as they begin a new task. With experience comes speed and efficiency.

Common implementation trouble spots include excessive costs, inconvenience to employees and customers, time delays, and problems debugging software. Conversion assistance can be obtained from vendors, outside consultants, and in-house staff already on the payroll. Sometimes vendors are used only to assist in the conversion process, while the continued operation of the system is turned over to in-house staff.

Key Terms

All-at-once changeover

Changeover timetable

Debugging

Gradual changeover

Hand holding

Learning curve

Parallel system operation

Systems implementation

Exercises

1. Describe the all-at-once changeover.

2. Describe the parallel system changeover.

3. Describe the gradual changeover.

4. What psychological considerations must be evaluated when making a system change?

5. List three training considerations that must be evaluated when implementing a new system.

6. Describe some of the inconveniences that employees may face during a system change.

7. List several sources of help that can be solicited during systems implementation.

8. Describe the efforts involved in installing and testing new hardware.

9. Describe the efforts involved in installing and testing new software.

10. Discuss the effect of the learning curve on employee performance.

Projects

1. Suppose you were going to install a new data processing system in a business organization. Write a one-page statement that will be distributed to employees, soliciting their cooperation and describing the new system.

2. Contact an equipment supplier and ask what training aids, manuals, and instructional materials are available with the equipment.

3. Assume that you are to handle a system conversion and, as a result, the sales desk will be closed for a day and a half. Prepare a one-page letter for customers informing them of this fact and encouraging them to place orders prior to the system shutdown.

4. Carry out an activity that involves following a set of instructions; for example, install a new piece of software on your personal computer. Repeat the operation several times and keep a log of how long it took you each time.

5. Visit an organization that has recently made a system conversion. Discuss the problems encountered with a systems analyst or manager at the organization.

ANALYST AT WORK

THOMPSON COMMUNICATIONS

DESCRIPTION OF FIRM

Thompson Communications began as a private telephone installation company. Initially, the company set up private telephone systems and installed pushbutton telephones and switchboards. During the last several years, Thompson Communications has expanded its operations to include the installation of data transmitting equipment.

Much of the company's work involves the installation of local area networks (LANs). These LANs consist of digital communications networks that tie together computers and terminals. The terminals are generally located within a radius of five miles.

A large brokerage firm has asked Thompson Communications to replace a voice telephone system with a digital network. The new system will involve an extensive conversion and some unavoidable disruption of service to the brokers' clients.

SYSTEM OVERVIEW

Figure 15.9 is a diagram of a local area network that Thompson Communications has contracted to install. In the present system, short messages are routed by telephone. Lengthier reports and documents are physically carried by messengers from office to office. The new system consists of 40 data terminals capable of transmitting reports, files, buy and sell orders, and so forth. The terminals will be used by stockbrokers to route information within their office and between offices.

Figure 15.9 shows only three voice and data terminals. The complete system will include 40 such devices. The system will also have a gateway. A gateway is a circuit that allows the LAN to route messages to other LANs or to other communications systems through common carriers.

HANDS-ON APPLICATION

You are on the staff of Thompson Communications and you have been asked to assist in the conversion to the new system. It will be your task to plan the timetable, evaluate alternatives, and train staff to use the new facilities. Three work products will be generated.

(continues)

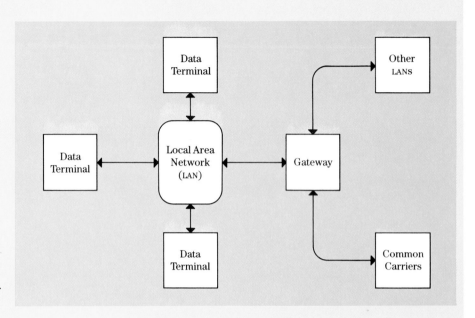

FIGURE 15.9

Thompson Communications Project

Work Product No. 1   Evaluate various approaches to the system changeover. Refer to the discussion in the text of the all-at-once, parallel, and gradual conversions. Assess the effectiveness of each approach. Prepare a report describing the effects of each approach on the brokerage firm's customers. Label this document WP1, Chapter 15. Prepare a task list to assist in this effort and enter it below.

TASK LIST

_____

_____

_____

_____

_____

_____

_____

Work Product No. 2   A decision has been made for an all-at-once conversion as of January 1. Prepare a changeover timetable that specifies the starting and ending dates of various activities. Label this document WP2, Chapter 15. Prepare a task list to help organize the preparation of the changeover timetable and enter it below.

TASK LIST

_____

_____

_____

_____

_____

_____

_____

Work Product No. 3   Analyze the training that will be required to teach personnel how to operate the new system. Prepare a report describing the training needed. Label this document WP3, Chapter 15. Prepare an outline to assist in drafting your report. Enter your outline below.

REPORT OUTLINE

_____

_____

_____

_____

_____

_____

SYSTEMS EVALUATION AND OPTIMIZATION

LEARNING OBJECTIVES

After studying this chapter, you should be able to:

1. Describe quantitative performance criteria.

2. Contrast response time and turnaround time.

3. List major costs evaluated in systems performance.

4. Discuss information security needs.

5. Discuss employee morale assessment.

6. Discuss systems optimization.

At this point in the systems development life cycle, the new system has been installed and is operational. However, analysts should not assume that a new system is operating properly just because it is functioning. It is possible for a system to be malfunctioning, even though employees and others praise it. Without an objective and careful evaluation of performance, the analyst cannot arrive at reliable conclusions.

Some systems analysts expend energy and effort to design and implement an elaborate system, and then assume it will perform as planned. Without measurement tools and benchmarks, the actual performance, improvements, and benefits of a new system can only be guessed at or hypothesized.

Systems evaluation is the systematic assessment of system performance to determine whether goals have been reached. It is a vital and important part of the implementation phase. Its purpose is to measure the performance and output of a system quantitatively and compare it to the goals established in the planning phase. If the goals are met, the system was implemented properly. If not, the analyst must study or redesign the system.

The advent of new hardware or software sometimes makes redesign necessary. This fine-tuning is called systems optimization, because it achieves maximum performance from the resources. **Systems optimization** is the redesign and refinement of system components to improve their performance.

PERFORMANCE CRITERIA

It has been said that if you cannot measure a phenomenon you cannot control it. This is true in many areas of human endeavor, and it is a requirement in systems analysis. Precise **performance criteria** are usually established during the design phase. They should be stated in measurable terms. Statements such as "The new system is operating okay," "We are offering better service to customers," or "There are fewer troubles in the office" are difficult to understand and compare. Instead, the degree of success or failure of a system should be expressed in such terms as percentage increase in productivity, improvement in error rate, or increase in units produced for a given period or work shift.

A system should perform through several complete cycles before being fully evaluated. If a cycle is repeated several times daily, it can be evaluated after a few days. A system that operates on a monthly cycle will not provide reliable results until several months have elapsed. Systems working on an annual basis will require two to three years before an accurate assessment can be made.

Some of the common criteria used to measure the performance of a system include time, costs, performance of hardware and software, productivity, accuracy, security, morale, and user and customer response.

SIZE OF JOB	DESIGN ESTIMATE TIME	INSTALLED SYSTEM TIME
Less than 10 pages or 10 minutes	2 hours	2 hours, 10 minutes
11–30 pages or 11–30 minutes	3 hours, 15 minutes	3 hours, 32 minutes
31–60 pages or 31–60 minutes	6 hours	4 hours, 8 minutes
More than 60 pages or 60 minutes	24 hours	18 hours, 30 minutes

FIGURE 16.1

Design Time Estimate Versus Installed System Time

Time Element

The clock is an important tool of systems evaluation, used to document the time units required for a particular action to be performed. For example, the clock can measure the speed at which information moves through a particular workstation or the time required for a program to be executed. It does not, however, measure the quality of the performance.

Response Time   **Response time** is the time that elapses before a system responds to a demand placed upon it. In some systems, several hours or days may elapse before an order is acknowledged and its processing begun. Other systems may have virtually no delay before processing an order.

Turnaround Time   **Turnaround time** is the period during which a system carries out a demand placed upon it; in other words, the length of time required before results are returned. A slow turnaround means a comparatively long period of time is required for processing, and a fast turnaround means a short period is needed.

UniTrans Word Processing System

In Chapter 15 we described how a UniTrans systems analyst implemented an improved word processing system in the secretarial services department. The system has been installed and is operational. Figure 16.1 contrasts the design time estimate versus the actual time required after the new system was installed and modified. The installed system time was slightly greater than the estimated time on small jobs. Greater than expected time savings were realized on larger jobs.

UT

FIGURE 16.2

Overhead Costs Comparison

DESCRIPTION	IN-PLACE SYSTEM	NEW SYSTEM
Square footage	$1900	$1200
Utilities	118	119
Supplies	360	510
Equipment lease	300	670
TOTAL	$2678	$2499
No. of jobs handled	1400	2675

Response time and turnaround time are not synonymous. A system can have a long response time and a short turnaround time—once the action begins, results are returned promptly. Both time factors must be considered when evaluating system performance. Sometimes an increase in one is made at the expense of the other.

Cost Element

The cost of operating a system is a quantitative measure of performance, sometimes the only measure applied. Dollars are used to measure such things as profit, return on investment, or errors in manufacture and shipping. Certainly a good system requires less money to service a given demand than a poor system. Costs are used to determine whether various parts of the system are performing up to financial expectations.

Labor Costs   The amount of money that must be paid to employees to perform given operations is measured in dollars. Salaries, pay rates, and commissions are convenient quantitative measures of the **labor costs** of a system.

Overhead Costs   System costs that do not change with the volume of output produced are called **overhead,** fixed costs, or burden. These costs include expenses for machines, equipment, physical plant, computers, and lighting. A system using considerable automatic equipment may have a low labor cost, but a high overhead cost. Another system with many manual operations or inadequate hardware may have a high labor cost and a low materials cost. The cost of the facilities must be assessed and evaluated in relation to offsetting factors. Figure 16.2 compares the overhead costs of an existing system and a new system.

Variable Costs   Those costs that change with the volume of output are called **variable costs.** They are incurred as goods are produced or data is processed. Examples are the cost of paper, floppy disks, printer or typewriter ribbons, and other supplies used during systems operation. Variable costs differ

		NEW SYSTEM		FIGURE 16.3
	IN-PLACE SYSTEM	**ESTIMATED COST**	**ACTUAL COST**	**Maintenance Cost Report**
Emergency repairs	$3100	$550	$450	
Regular maintenance	$100/month	$150/month	$150/month	

from system to system. A computerized system might have a higher overhead cost and lower variable and labor costs than a manual system.

Maintenance Costs **Maintenance costs** for the physical plant, office equipment, communications lines, and computer hardware and software must be evaluated after a system has been installed. These costs will exist throughout the life of the system and must be examined during systems evaluation. They sometimes increase disproportionately as a system ages. Figure 16.3 describes a system whose actual emergency maintenance costs were less than estimated and whose regular costs were accurately predicted. A successful system should have a relatively low maintenance cost.

Expansion and Modification Costs **Expansion costs** are incurred when a system is modified, revised, or altered. Some systems are easily expanded at low cost, while others may require extensive changes in design and equipment.

Training Costs The costs of training personnel to operate a system must be assessed during systems evaluation. Generally, the more complex the equipment in a system, the greater the **training costs.** If such costs are considerably above expectations, training programs or even personnel selection techniques should be reevaluated.

Data Entry Costs The costs of **data entry** must be measured in relation to other factors, such as output, processing and equipment costs. Manual systems may involve sizable labor costs but a minimal investment in equipment. Automated data entry systems such as those using OCR, MICR, or bar codes may involve low data entry costs but have higher equipment expenses.

Data Storage Costs **Data storage costs** vary greatly and must be evaluated in relation to other relevant factors: accessibility, type of storage device, and file security. The cost of floppy disks, magnetic tape, or other media differs from system to system. Systems that store large volumes of data with short access times usually require expensive equipment.

Other Costs Miscellaneous costs—communications line charges, duplicating services, consulting fees, lease of backup equipment—must be assessed and considered during systems evaluation.

	ITEM	RATING UNIT
FIGURE 16.4	Central processing unit speed	Millions of instructions per second (MIPS)
Performance Rating Measures	Primary memory speed	Nanoseconds
	Primary memory capacity	Kilobytes, megabytes
	Printer speed	Characters per second (CPS)
		Lines per minute (LPM)
	Data transmission speed	Bits per second (BPS)
	Secondary storage capacity	Kilobytes, megabytes

Hardware Performance

Speed, reliability, service, maintenance, operating costs, and power requirements are factors of **hardware performance** that should be assessed. Figure 16.4 lists some common performance rating measures.

Computer Systems   Since computer systems usually represent a major portion of the costs involved in a business system, their operation is vital to overall performance. Many elements in the computer system must be evaluated and compared against initial expectations. These include processing time, reliability of equipment, maintenance costs, speed of input/output devices, and performance of secondary storage equipment.

A common means of quantifying computer performance is the number of instructions that can be processed in one second. Central processing units are rated by the manufacturer in millions of instructions per second (MIPS). A larger or faster computer may have a higher MIPS rating than a smaller or slower system. This is often the determining factor that causes an analyst to select one system over another.

The system should also be evaluated in terms of the training required by operators and users. Are the training programs adequate and relevant? Do operators have sufficient knowledge to run the machines with little or no difficulty? Do users receive sufficient instructions to enable them to process data or to perform other tasks on the computers?

Total operating costs for the computer system must be evaluated in light of estimated costs and any differences investigated. Figure 16.5 reports the cost differences between the in-place system and the new word processing system after one year's performance.

Other System Hardware   Other devices and equipment used in the system must also be evaluated and compared to expected performance. These include computerized switchboards, word processing machines, copying machines, and microfilm devices.

ITEM	IN-PLACE SYSTEM	NEW SYSTEM
Equipment lease	$ 1,440	$ 3,800
Maintenance	1,200	800
Labor	44,000	22,000
Training	300	4,000
Operating costs	6,000	8,000
TOTAL	$52,940	$38,600

FIGURE 16.5

Cost Comparison Report

Software Performance

Software performance must be evaluated for both user-written and purchased program packages. Key factors to assess are speed of processing, quantity and quality of output, accuracy, reliability, and amount of maintenance and updating necessary to keep the software current.

Productivity

Productivity is a measure of system performance that states the relationship or ratio between input and output. The productivity of an entire system or its parts can be measured to gain insight into system performance.

Productivity is found by dividing output produced by the system by the input costs. Relatively low input costs and a high output volume produce a high productivity factor. When the output volume is low and input costs are high, low productivity results.

Figure 16.6 is a productivity report showing a comparison of costs and output level between UniTrans's old and new systems. In this case, the old system produced 14 acceptable reports and the new system, 57.3.

Accuracy

Accuracy is a measure of the freedom from errors, or conformity to truth, achieved by a system. Obviously a high degree of accuracy is a desirable goal, since a low accuracy rate may diminish the utility of an entire system.

Accuracy is usually related to productivity. The error rate tends to rise along with the output volume—as speed goes up, accuracy goes down.

The accuracy rate can be determined in several ways. The output of processing from one system can be compared to the output from another or to results already known. The number of errors that occur during a given period,

FIGURE 16.6

**Productivity
Report**

CATEGORY	IN-PLACE SYSTEM	NEW SYSTEM
No. employees	30	15
Equipment lease	$600	$300
Output units per person	420	860
Productivity ratio:		
$\dfrac{\text{Units}}{\text{Employee}}$	14	57.3

such as the number of misfiled orders or mistransmitted data, is a measure of system performance. The magnitude of the errors should also be assessed. Many small mistakes may do less harm than one large, gross error.

Information Security

Good **information security** means that records are kept safe, confidential, and under system control at all times. There is no leakage of vital or proprietary data to outsiders or to those who have no need for the information.

High security is sometimes achieved at the expense of increased operating costs. But a system with low operating costs and high output that results in many lost records or little control over the dissemination of confidential information may not be acceptable either. A suitable compromise must be found.

Morale

Morale is reflected in the satisfaction and acceptance that employees feel toward their jobs. The higher the morale, the greater the expected work performance level. Improvements in some areas of a system—output volume, turnaround time, costs—may be achieved, but the changes in procedures and working environment may have a detrimental effect on morale. This may result in many employee grievances, high absenteeism, discourteous treatment of customers, or other signs of dissatisfaction.

Morale is difficult to measure directly. It is a complex matter involving many psychological considerations. However, absentee rate or employee turnover are two factors that can be used to assess morale in an organization.

Figure 16.7 is a report comparing the number of absences and late arrivals that occurred before and after installation of the new word processing system at UniTrans. It shows that absenteeism was definitely lower after the new system was implemented, suggesting an improved level of employee morale. Compari-

REASON	IN-PLACE SYSTEM	NEW SYSTEM	
Absenteeism:			
approved	33	29	
nonapproved	18	6	
Partial days	16	4	
Late arrivals	16	6	

FIGURE 16.7

Monthly Personnel Absentee Report

TYPE OF COMPLAINT	IN-PLACE SYSTEM	NEW SYSTEM	
Late reports	18	6	
Spelling/accuracy	29	12	
Incorrect format	14	8	
Misfiled/misrouted	81	15	
Slow turnaround	16	7	
Incomplete report	3	3	
TOTAL	161	51	

FIGURE 16.8

End-User Evaluation Report

sons such as these are valid only when they take into account the number of employees.

Manifestations of high morale may include, for example, an employee giving extra cooperation during a difficult period or averting a troublesome situation.

User and Customer Reactions

The responses of those who use the system or will be affected by it afford another means of measuring system performance. Large numbers of complaints from customers concerning errors or changes in monthly statements, for example, could indicate poor performance. Fewer complaints might suggest that a new billing procedure is better than the old one. Similarly, requests from other departments for additional information or different kinds of reports could indicate awareness of the ability of the new system to manipulate or process data.

Figure 16.8 compares the number and kinds of complaints from users of the old system with those made after UniTrans's new word processing system was installed.

SYSTEMS OPTIMIZATION

If all the established goals have been reached, systems implementation can be considered a success. More likely, however, there will be some differences between goals and actual achievements. New machines, technology, or software may have come on the market. This is where systems optimization plays a role.

The data accumulated during the systems evaluation process should be studied to pinpoint the reasons why performance did not reach expectations. Fine-tuning is done at this stage. The analyst must balance the costs involved for time spent in further systems analysis, design, and implementation against the possible improvement of benefits gained.

In areas that are not crucial to overall systems performance, or where differences between achievements and expectations are minimal, optimizing may not be worth the additional investment of time and money. If, on the other hand, the deficiencies are in areas of critical importance to the organization or other parts of the system, or the amount of disparity is great, it will most likely be best to return to an earlier point in the systems design process to find an improved solution. Consultants may be hired, new equipment purchased, or newly installed facilities modified.

The evaluation and optimization processes give the analyst an excellent opportunity to observe the system in operation, leading to even more improvements in performance. Often these improvements are not apparent until after the activities of the new system are actually performed. Suggestions for fine-tuning the system may come from employees, users, customers, managers, and members of the information-processing or systems analysis departments.

Summary

Systems evaluation is the assessment of system performance to determine whether goals have been reached. Systems optimization involves the redesign or refinement of a system to improve performance. Common system performance criteria include response time and turnaround time. Cost criteria include labor, overhead, variable, maintenance, and expansion costs. Also considered when assessing a system's performance are training, data entry, and storage costs.

Speed, reliability, service, maintenance, operating costs, and power requirements are factors that are assessed in hardware performance. In addition, software performance is evaluated, including the reliability, maintenance, and updating necessary to keep software current. Freedom from errors, security level, productivity, and employee morale are other factors by which systems are assessed. The responses of those who use the system or will be affected by it are also valid measures of performance.

New equipment, technology, or software may have come on the market since a system was originally designed. This would call for optimization in order to maximize the performance and productivity of the system. Some of the improvements envisioned in this stage may not have been apparent until after the procedures of the new system were actually put in place.

Accuracy

Data entry costs

Data storage costs

Expansion costs

Hardware performance

Information security

Labor costs

Maintenance costs

Morale

Overhead

Performance criteria

Productivity

Response time

Software performance

Systems evaluation

Systems optimization

Training costs

Turnaround time

Variable costs

Exercises

1. Describe the purpose of systems evaluation and why it is important.
2. List some common criteria used to measure systems performance.
3. Define turnaround time.
4. List the major cost elements generally evaluated when reviewing systems performance.
5. Define productivity and discuss how it is measured.
6. Discuss some of the ways in which employee morale may be observed.
7. Describe the turnaround time analysis report and indicate what kinds of information are generally found in it.
8. Describe a productivity report and indicate what kinds of information are found in it.
9. Describe how the customer service evaluation report is useful in measuring systems performance.
10. Discuss system security and why it is important to an organization.

Projects

1. Visit a business and talk to several employees. Discuss their attitudes toward the organization. Prepare a short statement describing their perceptions.
2. Observe a clerical operation, noting the volume of documents handled and the number of personnel involved. Compare productivity during several visits.
3. Visit a business and discuss system operating costs with a manager or supervisor. Prepare a short statement describing these costs.
4. Visit a business operating computers or communications equipment. Discuss system maintenance costs. Prepare a short paper on this topic.
5. Visit a computer store or other supplier of computer hardware. Discuss hardware performance criteria and prepare a short paper on this topic.

ANALYST AT WORK

GRANVILLE FINANCIAL COMPANY

DESCRIPTION OF FIRM

Granville Financial Co. specializes in buying and selling second trust deeds and making loans on commercial and residential properties. Granville's customer base consists of approximately 400 clients who invest money with the company and receive monthly interest payments and annual reports describing the status of their investments. Individuals who borrow money from Granville Financial Co. receive a book of coupons and return one coupon with each payment. Thus, the company serves both lenders and borrowers. The company collects a loan processing fee from the borrower, as well as a service charge for handling the transaction for the lender.

SYSTEM OVERVIEW

Figure 16.9 illustrates a data flow diagram of Granville Financial's loan-processing system. When a request for a loan is received, Granville initiates several actions: appraising the property that serves as collateral for the loan, and checking the borrower's credit rating. Independent appraisers are used and an outside credit bureau is consulted.

After all reports are in and all criteria are met, the loan is approved. Next, a set of loan documents, to be signed by all parties, is drawn up. After the papers are signed, they are sent to the County Recorder. Then a coupon book is prepared and sent to the borrower.

HANDS-ON APPLICATION

As systems analyst for Granville Financial, it is your task to evaluate the loan-processing system periodically and to make improvements and optimizations. Begin your work by preparing a data flow diagram at the next level of detail for the loan-processing system. Then prepare a report evaluating the problems in the system. Finally, make recommendations for improvements.

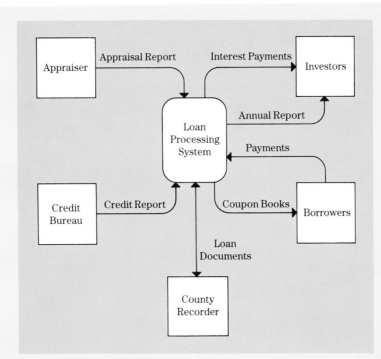

Work Product No. 1   Study the data flow context diagram in Fig. 16.9 and prepare another diagram of the loan-processing system at the next level of detail. This diagram should show where documents originate and how data is processed in the system. Label this document WP1, Chapter 16. Develop a task list to assist in organizing this effort. Enter the task list below.

TASK LIST

_____

_____

_____

_____

_____

_____

_____

(continues)

Work Product No. 2   Study both your data flow diagram and the context diagram presented in Fig. 16.9. Evaluate the system for potential problems. Assess time and cost elements and system security. Prepare a report discussing these concerns. Label this document WP2, Chapter 16. Before you start, prepare an outline to help organize your report. Enter the outline below.

REPORT OUTLINE

_____

_____

_____

_____

_____

_____

_____

Work Product No. 3   Now that you have evaluated Granville Financial's system, recommend improvements. Prepare a report on improvements and optimizations, together with data flow diagrams. Label these documents WP3, Chapter 16. Begin by preparing an outline of the report. Enter your outline in the space below.

REPORT OUTLINE

_____

_____

_____

_____

_____

_____

17

SYSTEMS DOCUMENTATION

LEARNING OBJECTIVES

After studying this chapter, you should be able to:

1. Discuss the need for systems documentation.

2. Describe major pieces of systems documentation.

3. Describe guidelines for preparing clear documentation.

4. Discuss documentation distribution and revision.

5. List major pieces of software documentation.

6. Discuss the use of graphics and illustrations in documentation.

When systems were less complicated and hardware costs lower, details on systems operations could be memorized or recorded on a few sheets of paper. Today, however, the complexity and sophistication of modern information systems require a reliable method of documenting a system.

The last step in systems analysis is the completion of documentation, a process that was begun in the early planning stages. This involves creating, collecting, organizing, storing, citing, and disseminating documents containing information relating to the structure and details of a system. Documentation on an information system or computer program consists of written manuals, system and data flow diagrams, text narratives, layouts of input or output records, photographs, and drawings of how the system functions.

The completion of formal documentation of a system marks its change in status from a project under development to a functioning entity, capable of operation without the guidance and control of its designers. It can now be understood, operated, and modified by others as the need arises.

NEED FOR DOCUMENTATION

The nature, size, and complexity of a system determine the optimum amount and scope of documentation. It is particularly important to document complex computer programs and data processing and communications systems. The intricate details of such systems cannot be left to someone's memory. Documentation has several advantages, discussed below.

Communications Tool

Documents, data flow diagrams, and descriptive material on a system enable analysts and programmers to communicate with each other effectively. System details can be discussed and related to each other on a common ground. Graphically documenting elements of a system reduces the possibility of ambiguous explanations or inaccurate references.

Facilitates Troubleshooting

Adequate documentation aids detection and correction of malfunctions or error conditions in a system, analyzing a system, and tracing its inner workings. It gives the troubleshooter a basis for comparing the present level of performance to the normal level indicated in the documentation. Such documentation is as much a diagnostic tool to the systems analyst as is the X-ray machine to the physician.

Facilitates Systems Revision

Thorough documentation facilitates revising, changing, or modifying an existing system. It gives an analyst a clear picture of how the system operates and how its elements interrelate. Without this information, it would be virtually impossible to change any part of the system without disrupting one or more of the other elements involved.

Operator and Personnel Training

Documentation is a key reference used when designing training programs for operators and personnel who staff the workstations in a system. It contains the specifications that indicate how a job is to be done, by whom, where, and why. The training director will rely on this information to ascertain the knowledge and skills needed by employees to perform their jobs adequately.

Consistency

One advantage of adequate documentation is the increased level of consistency and uniformity throughout a system. This is especially valuable in a decentralized system where operations take place in different offices or locations. Good documentation facilitates maintaining consistent application of procedures throughout a system. It ensures that similar demands will receive the same responses regardless of where requests are processed. It also encourages consistency of action over time, helping to avoid the introduction of minor deviations into established procedures during day-to-day operations.

Management Tool

Documentation provides management with a picture of how a system operates and with much of the background information needed to make intelligent decisions. It is used for planning long-term objectives as well. Without it management would experience difficulty in coordinating the operation of the elements in a large-scale system, especially if they are scattered geographically.

Elimination of Redundancy

The task of documenting a system forces the analyst to take a critical look at the entire system. This scrutiny sometimes uncovers nonessential details and duplication of effort, equipment, or personnel.

Auditing

Most business organizations are subject to auditing and review by many agencies. Complete systems documentation helps auditors to identify personnel, records, facts, and data quickly and accurately.

GUIDELINES FOR PREPARING DOCUMENTATION

The usefulness of documentation is limited if it is not well written and understandable to the user. The following guidelines will help ensure that effective documentation is prepared.

Maintain Clarity and Conciseness

All descriptive and text matter, such as manuals, reports, instructions, and descriptions, should be written in simple, straightforward English. Technical jargon and terms unfamiliar to most people should be avoided. Good technical reports are written from the readers' viewpoint—if they knew or understood the material in the first place, they probably would not be reading the documents.

Any good style manual offers suggestions for a documentation writer. Short words and sentences and direct action words, instead of passive terms and long, complex sentences, increase clarity and interest. Short paragraphs and the liberal use of headings and subheads help to outline written material and facilitate referencing data and subjects. Outline the material before writing it. Organize topics carefully and place them in logical order.

Use Graphics Liberally

Use plenty of diagrams, drawings, and artwork to illustrate concepts that are more easily explained with graphics than with written text. A series of steps described in text form and illustrated with design diagrams will be understood more easily than those without graphics.

A set of photographs showing how to do a given operation is often more effective than written instructions. For example, photographs can illustrate damaged goods in a way that no words could describe.

Relate Pieces of Documentation

The items in the documentation file should be designed to relate to each other in an organized, structured way. Outline or summarize the various documents included in the file. Number paragraphs for easy reference. Cross reference documents to figures and illustrations. Organize items so that each element relates only to a specific area or topic.

Emphasize Data Flow

Organize and design documents to follow the movement of data throughout a system. Show how each piece of documentation relates to a process. Follow a top-down design.

Keep the Reader in Mind

Do not make assumptions regarding the reader's knowledge. Define all terms carefully. Use examples and illustrations liberally. Move from the simple to the complex. Do not begin a detailed technical description unless you are sure your reader is ready to follow it.

Use introductory paragraphs to explain what will be covered in the section, and follow up the presentation of the material with a summary to reinforce important points.

Write Task-Oriented Documentation

Focus your material for a particular audience that is reading for a specific purpose. Tell readers what they need to know to do their job.

MAJOR SYSTEMS DOCUMENTATION

Systems analysts sometimes categorize documentation into four categories: systems, program, operations, and user documentation. Systems documentation describes the overall function and data flow in a system. This provides a macro view of the system elements. Program documentation includes program specifications, program listings, and sample input/output records. Operations documentation relates to the day-to-day running of the system and provides operators with guidelines on how to use the system. It gives a micro view of the system elements. User documentation gives the end user the information needed to properly interface with the system. The amount of documentation required in each class depends upon the kind of system under development and the sophistication of the user. We will review some of the major pieces of documentation related to systems operation. You will be familiar with some of it, since documentation has been described throughout the systems development life cycle (SDLC).

FIGURE 17.1

**Mail Room and
Telephone Policy**

The mail room and switchboard are designed to serve the needs of our customers and our employees in carrying out their duties with the company. All employees are requested to adhere to the following policy regarding use of telephone and mail facilities:

Mail

1. Where possible, use first class mail. Identify the originator and room number in the left-hand corner.

2. Use only approved company stationery.

3. Type recipient's name, address, and zip code.

4. Personal mail cannot be mailed at company expense.

Telephone

1. Answer all phone calls promptly. If necessary, transfer the call by informing the caller and signaling the operator. Remain on line until operator has acknowledged.

2. Local calls may be placed from your extensions. Out-of-area calls will be intercepted by automatic dialing equipment. Place out-of-area calls directly through switchboard.

3. When leaving your name and telephone number, also give extension number.

4. Employees are requested not to make personal calls through the firm's switchboard or extensions. Phone booths are available in the rest areas, locker rooms, and personnel department, for use by employees.

Policy Manuals

Policy manuals are documents that state the goals of the system. These manuals clarify and simplify operational tasks. They indicate priorities and the hierarchy of decisions. Policy manuals state policies and guidelines that direct action, not step-by-step detailed procedures on how to carry out a given task. They enable managers, supervisors, and others to direct subordinates in a manner consistent with company policy. Figure 17.1 illustrates a mail and telephone use policy.

Procedure Manuals

Procedure manuals are documents that spell out in detail the steps involved in carrying out a given routine or action. They establish the daily pro-

AIC

ALLIED

INSURANCE

CORPORATION

System ___Policy Processing___

Procedure ___Agent Claim___

Effective Date ___03/11/89___

Page ___1___ of ___1___

Procedure for processing claims:

Claim Clerk:
1. Review claim form received from agent to be sure it is complete and contains all necessary data.
2. If claim form is incomplete, fill out pink "request for additional information," attach to form, and return to agent. Complete yellow "out for data" card and file in cabinet.
3. Process completed forms as follows: Type green "detail report" using data provided on original claim form. Answer questions accurately and completely. Place the CL number in the box at top of form. Review form to check your accuracy.

Supervisor:
4. Submit form to supervisor. When returned, enter necessary adjustments and changes.

Claim Clerk:
5. Photocopy detail form. Send original to payment department, file duplicate in office, send third copy to agent.
6. Complete blue "claim processed card." Indicate disposition of claim. Include CL number. Forward card to supervisor.

FIGURE 17.2

Page from Procedure Manual

cedures of the company by defining how each task is to be done, always in accordance with stated company policy. The procedure manual defines each specific step in handling such things as payrolls, credits and collections, and returns of merchandise. Figure 17.2 is a page from a procedure manual for an insurance company. It states the steps involved in processing claims.

Procedure manuals are sometimes organized by department. The procedures related to the operation of a given department are gathered together in a single manual and placed in that department for easy reference by personnel.

FIGURE 17.3

Page from Forms Manual

REQUEST FOR CONFIDENTIAL INFORMATION

The employee below has requested that you, as the employer, provide our firm with the following information. It will be used in processing an employment application

Please complete all items below and return the form to us within 10 days.

Name _____

Address _____

_____

Phone _____ Birthdate _____

Presently employed by _____

Address _____

_____

Supervisor _____ Badge No. _____

Date Employed _____

Salary _____ Position _____

Has employee been continuously employed during this period? Yes _____

No _____ . Please explain any interruption in service:

_____

_____

FORM P29

A descriptive annotation should be placed in the forms manual along with the form.

```
Form name: Request for Confidential Information
Stock: No. 4 sulphite bond
Form number: P29
Origination: Personnel Department
Color: Green
Dissemination: Copy to employer
Size: 5½ × 8½
Standard order quantity: 5000
Reorder point: 500
Approved by: J. C. Connors
Date approved: 2/14/89
```

Forms Manuals

Forms manuals are collections of all the business forms used in a system. They specify the layout, size, type of stock, and other relevant details for each form, and list the source of supply, order points, and storage information. They may include details on how to complete or fill out each form, and information for handling and routing. The manual should also specify the procedures to follow if modifications or revisions become necessary.

Assembling all forms into a single manual facilitates the development of a comprehensive forms program. This ensures the consistent appearance, quality, and utility of the forms used within a system, reduces costs, and builds a better corporate image. Figure 17.3 is an example of a page from a forms manual.

Order-Processing Manuals

Order-processing manuals define how orders are to be written and processed. They outline methods for such things as recording sales, prices, and credits. They describe the routing procedures and authorizations necessary to process an order.

Training Manuals

Training manuals describe the programs that prepare personnel to operate the system. They document the level of ability needed to operate each workstation, any prerequisite skills, and the details of instructional programs that train employees for the various jobs.

Assembling this information into a single manual encourages consistency of training programs and reduces time spent on teaching skills previously acquired or attempting to teach skills to personnel who do not have the prerequisite background. By documenting the situations and procedures that employees have been trained to handle, it allows them to upgrade their level of skills more efficiently to achieve higher job classifications.

Organization Manuals

The organizational chart of the firm shows the direct lines of authority and the relationship of managers and subordinates. The **organization manual** describes these responsibilities and relationships in graphic form, indicating how each role in the firm fits into the overall organization scheme.

Systems Manuals

Systems manuals contain documents that trace the flow of information or goods throughout a system. They provide an effective means of detecting

FIGURE 17.4

Sample Customer Documentation

UNITRANS COMPANY

Instructions For Filing a Claim

Packages shipped by our company are insured under our Shipper's Guarantee Program. Unless otherwise noted the maximum claim allowed is $100 per package. We shall not be liable for claims exceeding this amount unless you expressly declared a greater value at the time of shipment. We are not responsible for consequential damages.

Shipper ———————————— Claim No. ——————

Address ———————————— Contact ——————————

City, State, Zip ——————————— Date of Claim ——————

Insured Value ———— Weight ———— Clerk ————————————

Describe condition of package when received:

Instructions for filing a claim:
1.   Complete this form and mail to the claims department:
        UniTrans Company, P.O. Box 3434, Central Valley, CA 91605
2.   Retain damaged package, shipping labels, and routing slips in your file.
3.   Your claim will be processed within 90 days of receipt.

---

errors or malfunctions in systems performance. These manuals show where data originates, where it is processed within the system, and where it is output. They show the workstations, personnel, and paths that data and goods follow as they are processed. System flowcharts, structure charts, and decision tables are the major types of documents used for illustration in this category.

Consumer Documentation

Consumer documentation includes any documents prepared for the consumer of an organization's services or goods. They include informative materials, directions for using services, instructions for filing claims, or any other explanatory text designed to meet customers' needs. Figure 17.4 is a form used by UniTrans to process a customer's claim.

`C:\WS2000>`

```
                WordStar 2000 Tutor Menu

      Lesson 1: Instant Letter
      Lesson 2: Special Effects
      Lesson 3: Moving Text & Inserting Page Breaks
      Lesson 4: Locate and Replace
      Lesson 5: Key Macros
      Lesson 6: Spelling Correction & Thesaurus
      Lesson 7: Tabs and Margins


        Press ↑ ↓ to move the highlighting.
        Press ←┘ to choose a lesson.
                                    Esc to quit
```

Reprinted with the express written permission of MicroPro International Corporation

FIGURE 17.5

Software Tutorial

Collecting these documents into a single file makes them an efficient and coordinated communications link with the customer. It ensures that the documents are adequate, consistent, and comprehensive. The file allows employees to make revisions or deletions in one or more pieces of documentation without invalidating information or specifications contained in another.

Software Documentation

Reliance upon computers has increased the importance of **software documentation.** This documentation serves as a major means of communication between programmer, manager, and computer operator. Software packages purchased from outside vendors generally come with manuals, instructions, and tutorials (see Fig. 17.5). Some have online documentation called **help screens.** Help screens, such as that in Fig. 17.6, can be displayed by a computer operator to assist in using the software. This eliminates the need for user-prepared documentation.

If end users write their own software they must provide their own documentation file. A documentation file is usually prepared for computer programs that are relatively complex. All the data regarding a particular program is collected into a single file available to managers, systems analysts, operators, programmers, and others. This file usually contains the following information.

Abstract   The **abstract** is a short, written description that summarizes the function of the program, the logic it follows, and the general routines available. Figure 17.7 is an abstract for a program that updates UniTrans's personnel mailing list.

Design Diagrams   Data flow diagrams and flowcharts are included to illustrate program flow. These design diagrams are graphic, visual descriptions of the steps followed during program execution.

FIGURE 17.6

Help Screen

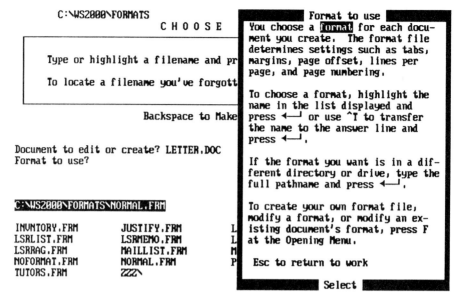

Reprinted with the express written permission of MicroPro International Corporation

Written Narrative   A written narrative describes the logic followed in coding the program. It explains in detail the algorithm, branches, options, and formulas used in manipulating the data in the program.

Program Listing   A program listing that shows the coded instructions in the program, including its branches, is an important item in the file.

Screen Layout   Sketches or printouts that show the **terminal screen layout** are kept in the file. These show the menu options and describe the kind of information entered on various screens.

Record Layout   A sketch or outline illustrates the layout of the input and output records. A detailed description of the data fields, codes, and abbreviations may be included in the **record layout.**

Operating Instructions   **Operating instructions** tell how to run the program and what branches and routines are available. These instructions also indicate any error messages and program reentry routines, if available. They may also describe console operating procedures required by the program.

Data Dictionary   A data dictionary is prepared for database management system software. It specifies the form, style, and content of the records in the database so that all entries will conform to a uniform standard. This greatly expands the utility of the database.

FIGURE 17.7

Computer Program Abstract

Program Number: CA127

Program Name: UniTrans Personnel Mailing List

Department: Personnel

Date Written: 4/14/88

Approved By: J. White

Documentation File Number: 1066

Program Abstract

This program is designed to process the personnel department's mailing list. The program maintains a database of all employees, both hourly and salaried. It merges new employees, deletes terminated employees, and updates all addresses. The program prepares a mailing list based upon zip code for bulk mailing purposes. It also sorts employees by department, division, and other category codes.

Environment

1. Language–Pascal
2. System–IBM AT with 640K
3. I/O devices–CRT and laser printer

DISTRIBUTION OF DOCUMENTATION

Some items of documentation are historical in nature and should be kept in a permanent file not readily accessible to system users. Other items must be constantly available—near computers, workstations, telephones, and so on.

Some documentation is prepared for the exclusive use of the systems analyst and may be looked at only when making major changes in the system. Other items are prepared for the user. These manuals should be given to department managers, supervisors, operators, and other appropriate people.

Some systems analysts organize three-ring binders containing the related documentation for each department in the organization. Each binder, clearly labeled, is placed in the appropriate department to document the established routines and procedures that are performed there. The contents should always be kept current, and any changes should be brought to the attention of the proper person.

REVISION OF DOCUMENTATION

Documentation is of value only if it reflects the present and complete status of a system. An outdated piece of documentation will probably cause more confusion than anything else. An organized, systematic review of all documentation should be undertaken periodically to keep the contents current. Records should be maintained on any changes, indicating which documents were involved and the text of the revision. Revision dates should be printed at the bottom of all forms and on all pages in manuals. Appropriate personnel should be promptly notified of changes. Outdated material should be removed from the documentation or placed in a separate file.

This chapter concludes our discussion of the systems development life cycle. Now that we have studied the key elements in the process, we will analyze some case histories. Before going on to the next chapter, which presents a group of applied case problems, we will conclude the UniTrans case problem that has been woven throughout this book.

CONCLUDING THE UNITRANS CASE

We began to document the UniTrans case problem in Chapter 1. Before going on to solve various UniTrans problems, we reviewed the company's function and structure. The annual report served as an excellent means of documenting many aspects of the organization. We then began a methodical process of identifying system problems and moved through the SDLC to solve them. It became clear that complex organizations such as UniTrans may have a variety of information flow problems to be addressed. As each problem was identified and solved, it was documented.

Our documentation file expanded as we added reports, logs, notes of observations, and work records. As we found solutions to various problems, we developed screen layouts, printer layouts, questionnaires, and systematic procedures. The deliverables from the systems analysis phase involve terminal screen dialogues, printed reports, formats, data flow diagrams, and the like. These were added to our growing documentation file.

Now that we have reached the end of the UniTrans case, we have a comprehensive file describing and documenting not only the system problems but their solutions as well. This file is extremely valuable. It can be used to introduce new analysts or other personnel to the inner workings of the UniTrans Company. It will assist them in making changes or modifications to any of the UniTrans subsystems.

Business and information systems are not static. They are continually changing as organizational goals, structure, and personnel change. Thus we cannot formally conclude the UniTrans case documentation and file it. Instead, we must treat it as a living file that is dynamic and undergoing continual change.

Armed with this file, the analyst is in a position to solve UniTrans's problems quickly and efficiently.

The next chapter presents a group of applied case problems. These cases will give you the opportunity to apply the principles and concepts learned from the UniTrans case and from the rest of the text.

Summary

The completion of documentation is the last step in the systems analysis process. Documentation includes written manuals, data flow diagrams, text narratives, layout of input and output records, and other items. This marks a change in status from a project under development to a fully functioning system.

Documentation is necessary because it serves as a communication tool and facilitates troubleshooting and systems revision. It also helps with personnel training, eliminates redundancy, ensures consistency, and provides an audit record for the system. Documentation should be clear and concise, use graphics liberally, and relate elements to one another.

Major system documentation includes policy, procedure, forms, order processing, and training manuals. Organization and systems manuals, as well as consumer documentation, are often prepared. A computer program documentation file usually includes an abstract, design diagrams, written narrative, program listing, screen layout, record layout, and operating instructions.

Some pieces of documentation are kept in a permanent file, while others may be made available near computers, workstations, or telephones. Documentation should be regularly revised and updated to reflect the current status of the system.

Key Terms

Abstract	**Policy manuals**
Consumer documentation	**Procedure manuals**
Forms manuals	**Record layout**
Help screens	**Software documentation**
Operating instructions	**Systems manuals**
Order-processing manuals	**Terminal screen layout**
Organization manuals	**Training manuals**

Exercises

1. Summarize the need for documenting a system.
2. List six major pieces of systems documentation.
3. Describe the information contained in an organization's policy manual.
4. Describe the information contained in an organization's forms manuals.
5. List the major pieces of information contained in a computer program documentation file.
6. List the major guidelines to follow when preparing systems documentation.

7. Describe the writing style and rules to follow in preparing manuals, reports, or systems documentation.

8. Summarize the guidelines for preparing clear documentation.

9. Discuss how document revisions are handled.

10. Discuss the function of consumer documentation.

Projects

1. Visit a business firm and collect several pieces of systems documentation. Describe the function of each.

2. Rewrite or modify the documentation you obtained to improve its content, style, and comprehensiveness.

3. Write a policy statement on some phase of a school activity.

4. Prepare an organization chart of your campus administration.

5. Visit a computer center and observe the kinds of documentation prepared for their system and programs.

ANALYST AT WORK

JOHNSON BEAUTY SUPPLY

DESCRIPTION OF FIRM

Johnson Beauty Supply is a major wholesaler of cosmetics, beauty aids, and beauty salon equipment. The company has a staff of approximately 60 sales representatives who call upon beauty salons, hair stylists, drug stores, and department stores. These salespeople inform customers of new products, discontinued products, price changes, and so on.

Orders for goods may be placed directly with the sales representative in the field or they may be mailed or phoned in to the sales office. The orders are then filled and shipped within 72 hours. After the receipt of goods, invoices are sent. This system works well for Johnson Beauty Supply but requires the use of a number of forms and documents.

Control must be maintained over all orders, since lost orders mean less profit. Good customer relations are maintained because the system processes orders promptly and goods are shipped within a reasonable length of time.

SYSTEM OVERVIEW

Figure 17.8 is a data flow context diagram that describes Johnson Beauty Supply's order-processing system. Orders are received from three sources: telephone, mail, or field representative. A pick list is then generated and sent to the warehouse so that the order can be filled.

After orders are shipped, invoices are prepared and mailed to customers. At the end of every month statements are mailed summarizing each customer's activity. In addition, a monthly commission report is generated. This report is distributed to each representative and shows the commission earned on all products. The amount of sales commission varies depending upon the type of goods sold, manufacturer's discount, and other factors.

HANDS-ON APPLICATION

Johnson Beauty Supply has hired you to generate the forms and documentation needed for the system. You are to prepare a detailed data flow diagram as well as the necessary documents that will be used in the system. In addition, you are to set up a forms inventory system to keep track of the printing and distribution of forms.

(continues)

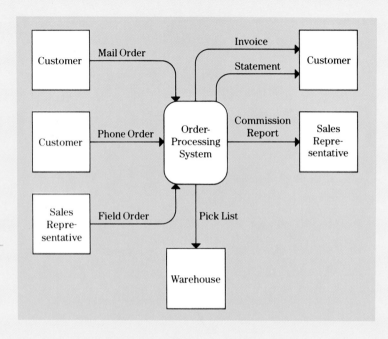

FIGURE 17.8

Johnson's Order-Processing System Data Flow Context Diagram

Work Product No. 1 Refer to Fig. 17.8, which describes Johnson Beauty Supply's order-processing system. Generate a detailed data flow diagram that shows how data flows throughout the system. Label this document WP1, Chapter 17. Organize your effort by preparing a task list and enter it below.

TASK LIST

_____

_____

_____

_____

_____

_____

_____

Work Product No. 2   Generate a set of forms and records that will be used in the system. Include order forms, pick lists, invoices, statements, and commission reports. Label these documents WP2, Chapter 17. Prepare a task list to organize this effort and enter it below.

TASK LIST

_____

_____

_____

_____

_____

_____

Work Product No. 3   Develop a procedure to maintain the inventory and to revise forms. Document this procedure with a record that describes where forms originate, how they are processed, and where they are filed. Label this document WP3, Chapter 17. Prepare a task list to organize this effort and enter it below.

TASK LIST

_____

_____

_____

_____

_____

_____

APPLIED INFORMATION SYSTEMS

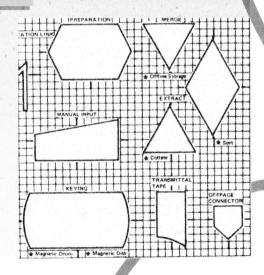

CASE
PROBLEMS

LEARNING OBJECTIVES

After studying this chapter, you should be able to:

1. Discuss typical case history applications.

2. Assess systems functions and recommend changes and improvements.

3. Trace data flow throughout a system.

4. Assess systems advantages and limitations.

This chapter presents a group of case histories that illustrate many of the concepts described in this text. The case histories include word processing systems, management information systems, order processing, reservations, database management, and other applications.

HOW TO USE THESE CASES

Case histories provide an excellent vehicle for applying systems concepts. The cases in this chapter offer you a hands-on opportunity to apply the five phases of the SDLC in detail. You will analyze system requirements, prepare detailed data flow diagrams, and design input and output records. The projects listed at the end of this chapter ask you to modify the cases and implement system improvements. They describe specific tasks to be carried out on each case problem.

These cases offer more guidance than the projects provided at the end of each chapter. You should find them helpful to bridge the gap between the chapter projects and the more detailed problem descriptions given in the Analyst at Work cases. These cases are designed to integrate your learning. Situations experienced on the job do not always fall into neatly labeled categories, and it will be valuable for you to assess the nature of a problem and how it should be solved.

For each case, a brief summary describes the business firm and places the system in the context in which it functions. Pictures and design diagrams illustrate important aspects and graphically trace the flow of information throughout the system. A system evaluation discusses the limitations as well as the benefits of the system. The cases are drawn from actual business situations and illustrate practical, real-world information systems.

MICROCOMPUTER WORD PROCESSING SYSTEM: TOP FLIGHT INSURANCE AGENCY

Description of Firm

Top Flight is an insurance agency that sells a line of life, health, and accident policies. It represents about 30 different insurance carriers and has 25 agents who work out of a local office, selling policies via the mail, telephone, and personal contacts.

Top Flight processes a high volume of correspondence, including proposals, price quotations, claims forms, letters, and memos. Each agent prepares between 50 to 100 pieces of correspondence per week. Dozens of sales brochures and price quotations are mailed to prospective clients. Documents must be neatly typed and reflect the professional character of the firm. The speed with which they are prepared is essential when processing claims or changes in policy status.

Description of System

Top Flight has installed a group of stand-alone microcomputers to provide word processing for each of its sales agents. Each microcomputer is equipped with a display monitor, a letter-quality printer, and a word processing software package. A microcomputer is located near the desk of each sales agent.

When an agent wishes to prepare a letter or other piece of correspondence, he or she loads a word processing program from floppy disk storage. Various standard letters and form reports are stored on the disk. The agent enters the relevant information and prints the letter. Copies of important letters are saved on a floppy disk.

System Evaluation

This system has several advantages for Top Flight. The microcomputer's ability to store text eliminates the need for retyping, produces error-free drafts, and improves neatness of the finished documents. It also permits accessing a large number of standard letters.

Another advantage is that the turnaround time for preparation of correspondence has been reduced from several days to a few minutes. The system's ability to print out one or more drafts of a document without retyping is an important advantage. It allows revisions, corrections, and additions to be made easily in a document.

MULTIUSER WORD PROCESSING SYSTEM: INDUSTRIAL EQUIPMENT SUPPLY COMPANY

Description of Firm

Industrial Equipment Supply Company is a leading equipment dealer marketing industrial equipment and machinery. A staff of 50 salespeople serves a large geographic area. The sales personnel spend most of their time in the territory to which they are assigned, calling upon accounts. Periodically, they visit the home office for sales meetings.

When salespeople make calls, customers often ask them to mail price

FIGURE 18.1

**Multiuser Word
Processing System**

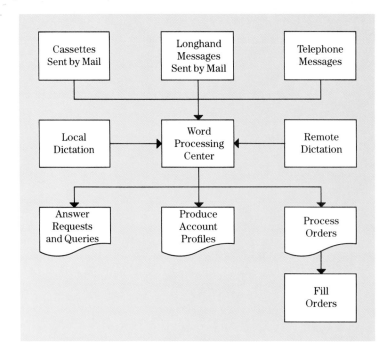

FIGURE 18.1

**Multiuser Word
Processing System**

quotations or specification sheets, or to answer questions or requests. Since representatives are in the field for several weeks at a time, they must depend upon the word processing center in the home office to handle these requests.

The sales staff also relies on the center to route orders and in some instances to follow up on complaints or delivery schedules. Salespeople also use the system to forward vital trade information picked up in the field to the home office sales manager for use in planning future sales strategies.

Description of System

Industrial Equipment's home office provides good service to its customers and efficient, reliable support to its sales staff in the field. A multiuser word processing and message-handling system meets these needs (see Fig. 18.1).

The heart of the system is the word processing center located in the home office. The center is designed specifically for preparing letters, memos, and reports and processing orders and complaints. It is equipped with both remote and local dictation equipment, as well as word processing machines.

The center also has a supply of catalogs, bulletins, and folders on Industrial Equipment's products. This material helps employees handle orders, complaints, and requests for prices promptly and accurately. Data is input to the system in four ways.

1. Salespeople in the field telephone the word processing center and are

connected to remote dictation machines. They dictate messages or letters over the telephone, which are automatically recorded on cassettes.

Periodically, operators in the center remove the cassettes and place them on transcribing machines. The contents are keyboarded and stored in the word processing machine. The letters, reports, orders, or complaints are then appropriately processed.

2. Salespeople carry portable dictation equipment in their briefcases or automobiles. This allows them to record messages, orders, or requests on cassettes in the field. At the end of each day the salespeople mail the cassettes to the center for processing. There the contents are transcribed and the documents processed.

3. Some salespeople mail or hand carry letters, memos, or reports in longhand to the word processing center. Operators at the center transcribe the text and prepare the finished documents.

4. Occasionally, the sales staff visits the home office for meetings or to catch up on paperwork. In these instances, cassette dictation equipment available in the home office is used. Messages and memos are recorded on cassettes and processed by the center just as though they had been mailed from the field.

System Evaluation

This system has several advantages for Industrial Equipment. It enables the company to centralize its stenographic and word processing services, making them more efficient. Letters and memos are prepared in a consistent form and style, orders are processed promptly, and complaints and requests for literature are handled expeditiously.

Another advantage is that the salespeople have the full resources of the center at their disposal, even when they are traveling in the field. The system also has benefits for management. Information regarding orders, customers, or new accounts is quickly sent back to the home office for analysis and referral. This input allows management to make more efficient and responsive decisions about marketing strategy.

PRODUCTION CONTROL SYSTEM: NUTS AND BOLTS MANUFACTURING COMPANY

Description of Firm

Nuts and Bolts specializes in the manufacture and assembly of small appliances and household hard goods. Most goods are manufactured to order and carry private brand labels or nameplates.

In a typical production cycle, a customer orders goods from Nuts and Bolts to be assembled with a private brand name. Nuts and Bolts assigns a job number to the order and begins processing. First, the necessary raw materials are ordered and placed in inventory as they arrive; some are pulled directly from the storage warehouse. When all the materials are available, the job is ready for the assembly line. Fabrication usually requires a period of several weeks. Finally, the finished goods are shipped and billed.

Nuts and Bolts requires a system that facilitates efficient and accurate order processing, inventory control, and production control. Not only must the proper quantity and quality of raw materials be obtained for each order, but they must be available at the right time to meet assembly schedules. Therefore, the company must know what materials are in stock and which are on order at all times. They must know which goods have been assembled, which are ready for shipping, and which have been billed.

Description of System

This system handles the order processing, production control, inventory, and billing and invoicing activities for a medium-size manufacturing firm. The system monitors the status of orders from the purchase of the raw materials through production and assembly to the billing process. It is typical of the systems used by manufacturing, fabricating, and assembly companies.

The system is designed around a computer and several terminals. These terminals, located in key departments around the plant, are connected online to the central computer. The terminals in the order department, the production supervisor's office, and shipping and receiving departments allow operators to enter information regarding the movement and status of material and orders into a database. The records in the database are organized by the job number assigned when the order first came in.

Figure 18.2 illustrates the flow of data through the system. The cycle starts when an order for a job is received. The order department writes it up and assigns a job number. A computer file for this account is opened under the job number.

A production schedule for the job is developed with the aid of programs stored on the computer. Another schedule is drawn up so that the raw materials needed to produce the finished goods will be available at the right time. Orders for materials that must be purchased are sent out.

Data indicating the materials that are taken from the company's own inventory of stock is noted on a terminal in the storage department. A computer program updates the inventory file to maintain an accurate, current picture of the quantity still in stock. As the raw materials arrive or are picked from stock, this information is entered from the terminals in the receiving department and incorporated into the file for that job.

At the appropriate points in the schedule, assembly of the goods begins. At various stages, data indicating the job's current status is entered from the production line to update the account file. After the finished goods have been

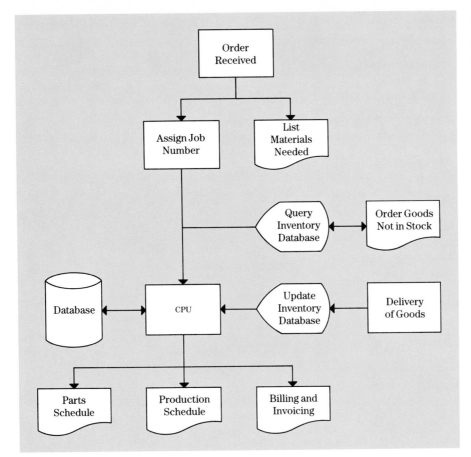

FIGURE 18.2

Production Control System

assembled, their shipping dates are recorded from a terminal in the shipping department. Finally, the accounting department uses a computer program to prepare the billing documents from the data recorded under the job number. At any time while the order is being processed in the manufacturing plant, its status can be determined by querying the database.

System Evaluation

The scheduling programs ensure that raw materials will be available when they are needed. This facilitates maintaining a more efficient assembly line and avoids delays or interruptions.

Accurate inventory control methods reduce unexpected problems caused by items being in short supply. Machines and workstations can be operated at their optimum level of production efficiency, reducing operating costs. This system results in faster delivery of goods and increases the level of output. Computer facilities expedite the billing and invoicing procedures of finished goods.

Being able to ascertain the status of any item in the inventory or any job under production enables the company to monitor schedules and performances constantly, and to respond promptly to changes in the environment.

Finally, the system produces a group of useful management reports concerning overall plant operations. These reports give important historical data and cost accounting information. The charge-back system allows accountants to determine overhead and operating costs with precision. Ultimately, these advantages lead to improved management decision-making practices.

RETAIL ACCOUNTING SYSTEM: SHIRT AND SKIRT COMPANY

Description of Firm

Shirt and Skirt Company is a small clothing retailer specializing in men's and women's high fashion clothing. The company has about 20 employees. The greatest percentage of sales are cash transactions; the remainder are charge account sales. Appropriate records must be kept on both types of sales for tax, audit, inventory, billing, and other purposes.

Most of Shirt and Skirt's success is due to the selection of the high-style clothing they stock. Buyers rely on up-to-date information regarding sales and current inventory status in order to identify the lines, colors, and styles enjoying the greatest sales appeal. They select new stock based upon this data.

Shirt and Skirt also carries its own accounts. Each month statements must be sent to charge customers. Past due accounts receive letters or notices from the credit manager requesting payment.

Description of System

Shirt and Skirt has installed a small computer system equipped with OCR scanning equipment and software that serves the accounting department. This retail accounting system performs the inventory, ledger, sales, credits, and collections activities for the company (see Fig. 18.3). Each article of clothing has a tag with a bar code identifying the manufacturer, type of garment, and price. When a sale is made, the clerk prints the customer's name, address, and other information on a specially designed optical scanning form and places the form in a cash register equipped with a bar code reader. The clerk scans the ticket attached to the garment, which enters additional data into the register. The register then prints out a sales slip with price and other data shown.

The system is programmed to print out daily inventory reports and sales by classification code. Periodically, the program generates turnover, accounts receivables, and age analysis reports. The credit manager uses the credit, col-

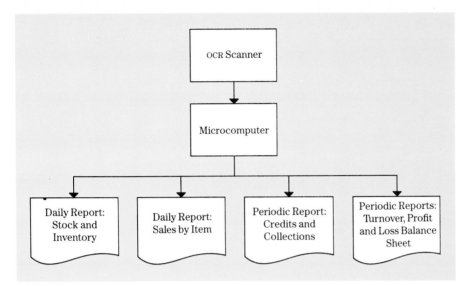

FIGURE 18.3

Retail Accounting System

lections, and age analysis reports to facilitate collection of accounts. Merchandise buyers carefully study the inventory reports. At less frequent intervals, the computer prepares profit and loss statements and balance sheets for accounting, tax, audit, and management purposes.

System Evaluation

The computerized cash registers and optical character scanning equipment enable Shirt and Skirt to give customers rapid retail service while at the same time providing the company with an excellent accounting system. A complete set of reports that facilitates inventory control, cash flow, credit reports, and other tasks is generated periodically. The system eliminates much manual data entry, thus greatly speeding up the processing of register transactions.

LOCAL AREA NETWORK (LAN): PIONEER DEVELOPMENT COMPANY

Description of Firm

Pioneer is a research and development company employing dozens of engineers and scientists. A large portion of the firm's work involves experimental designs of new equipment and hardware. In signing new projects, Pioneer prepares a detailed written proposal for its customers. Engineers and scientists

FIGURE 18.4

Local Area Network (LAN)

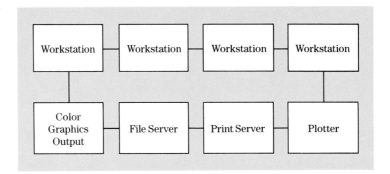

contribute technical information to the report. As a proposal moves through the preparation process many drafts are prepared.

The engineers and scientists who work on these reports are located in several buildings, all on the Pioneer plant site. After the proposal has been approved, Pioneer personnel develop numerous developmental reports. Upon completion, detailed final reports are prepared. At delivery of the final prototypes, Pioneer provides its customers with detailed and comprehensive documentation, including test reports, installation manuals, and operator guides.

Description of System

Pioneer has installed a local area network (LAN) (see Fig. 18.4) to assist personnel in the preparation of reports and documents. The LAN connects dozens of workstations, each consisting of a microcomputer with keyboard and display monitor. Also wired to the system are print servers, which provide high-speed printer output. A file server, using a high-speed mass storage device, provides additional storage.

The system also includes various plotters, color graphics display devices, and data communications equipment. All the devices on the system are wired together with coaxial cable and located on the plant site. There are relatively short distances between buildings.

System Evaluation

The LAN installed at Pioneer serves many functions. It facilitates the preparation of reports by enabling many individuals to make contributions from their local workstations. Interoffice memos are easily transmitted from workstation to workstation via the electronic mail system. Color graphics terminals, plotters, and high-speed printers are also available on the network. A major benefit of the LAN is its flexibility. Devices can be added, relocated, or removed from the system by tapping into the coaxial cable. This avoids costly system rewiring.

REAL-TIME INVENTORY AND ORDER-PROCESSING SYSTEM: WHOLESALE PAPER DISTRIBUTORS

Description of Firm

Wholesale Paper Distributors (WPD) is a large paper supplier with branch sales offices and warehouses located in major cities in several states. The company stocks a variety of paper styles in different widths and colors. WPD often accepts order for goods in one office but may ship them from the stock available in another branch, creating a sizable and involved warehousing and inventory job.

WPD's sales staff calls upon printers, publishers, advertising agencies, and others. These salespeople must know the exact quantity of goods available in stock, especially when a large amount of paper is involved in the order. Insufficient supply of an item in stock could delay the shipment of goods to the customer, resulting in the loss of good will and possibly future sales.

Sales are also made at the branch offices to customers who pick up goods at the will-call counters. These transactions must be entered into the inventory file immediately.

Description of System

A computer system with disk storage capability has been installed in WPD's main office. The master inventory is stored on the disk system. Remote terminals are connected to the computer by dial-up telephone lines or by leased lines (see Fig. 18.5). These terminals are located at sales desks and order, warehouse, shipping, and receiving departments of all the branches.

Because of the real-time capabilities of the system, transactions are recorded as they occur. As new stock is added or items are sold, information is immediately entered into the inventory file. The status of this file can be queried from each terminal. This allows salespeople in the field to call the order desk and immediately learn the quantity in stock, price, or other information about any item.

To facilitate transactions at the will-call counters, WPD has installed a group of point-of-sale terminals at each order desk and in the stockroom. Data from these transactions are entered into the database as they occur.

FIGURE 18.5

Real-Time Inventory and Order-Processing System

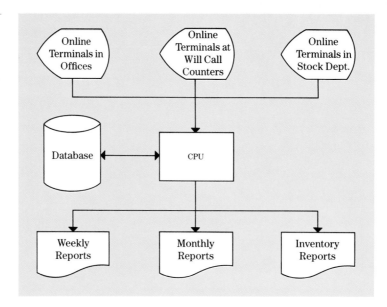

At weekly and monthly intervals, the system is programmed to prepare management and inventory reports. One report lists each item in stock and indicates its turnover ratio. Another report flags each item in short supply. Additional reports list sales by salesperson, type of goods, branch, department, and vendor.

System Evaluation

The system works very well for WPD. The instant accessibility of accurate stock information has improved the company's performance in a competitive marketplace and increased its ability to win large sales orders. Errors in maintaining inventory records have been reduced, resulting in fewer instances of goods out of stock and encouraging customer good will and dependency.

Service at the will-call counters is prompt and efficient. The point-of-sale terminals have speeded up the processing of these sales. Reports prepared by the system encourage better management practices. Reports that flag items in short supply give valuable information to buyers, who must determine the popular items and the vendor lines that move the fastest.

An accurate picture of sales performance is generated by the report showing the activity of each salesperson, branch, and product line. Information on discontinued merchandise and outdated colors and sizes can be easily gathered and disseminated.

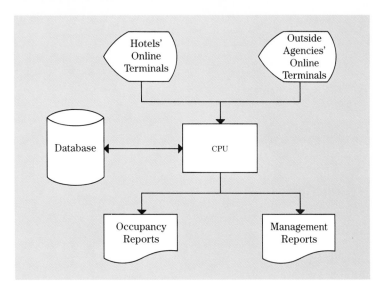

FIGURE 18.6

Reservation System

RESERVATION SYSTEM: CARRIAGE INN HOTELS

Description of Firm

The Carriage Inn Hotel chain operates 30 hotels and motels located in several major cities in different states. Each facility has different types of accommodations, including singles, doubles, rooms for families, and suites. Rates vary depending upon the season, size of room, number of beds, and the location of the hotel or motel. Some facilities grant discounts to selected commercial firms who are regular and frequent clients. Names of these accounts are kept in a database.

Reservations for all accommodations can be made directly from any of the 30 members of the Carriage Inn chain. They can also be made via telephone from outside agencies.

Description of System

Figure 18.6 illustrates the reservation system used by the Carriage Inn chain. A central computer is located in the administrative office at the company's headquarters. The database of accommodations available at all units in the chain is stored on a magnetic disk storage device connected online to the computer. AT&T 800 Service has been installed to allow outside ticket agencies and travel agents to place reservations without toll charges.

The operator determines the type of accommodation needed, location of facility, and dates. The computer accesses the database and displays all accommodations available for a specific facility on the date requested. If it is not possible to fill the request, the computer displays alternate selections—different dates or other combinations of beds and rooms.

After the customer has made a selection, the data is keyed into the terminal and a hold is placed on that particular accommodation. Written confirmation is handed or mailed to the customer, showing the date, price, and other pertinent data.

The computer periodically prints out several reports on the activity of the various hotels and motels in the chain. These reports indicate such things as average length of stay, percentage of time each type of accommodation is utilized, number of reservations canceled, and number lost due to unavailability of facilities.

System Evaluation

The Carriage Inn chain gains several advantages from using a real-time computerized reservation system instead of telephone operators or mail facilities alone. The efficiency of the system results in maximum occupancy of each hotel in the chain. The accommodations available in a given facility may change rapidly, depending upon such factors as weather and travel conditions. Losses from unused accommodations are less when information about cancellations or other such data is immediately available to ticketing agencies. Since printed confirmations indicating the number of days of stay, type of room, cost, and other details are mailed to customers, errors and no-shows are minimized.

SIMULATION AND MODELING SYSTEM: TROPICAL FRUIT DISTRIBUTORS

Description of Firm

Tropical Fruit Distributors (TFD) maintains a fleet of oceangoing vessels that ship bananas and other tropical fruits from several major ports worldwide. The fleet contains 12 ships varying in tonnage and cargo-carrying capacity. The cargoes are shipped to various ports in the United States where TFD operates dockside unloading facilities. After they are unloaded, the goods are sent via rail or truck to markets in major inland cities.

The challenge is to find the most profitable schedule for shipping the produce to market. This is a complex situation with many factors to be considered, including the needs and schedules of the customers buying the fruit and

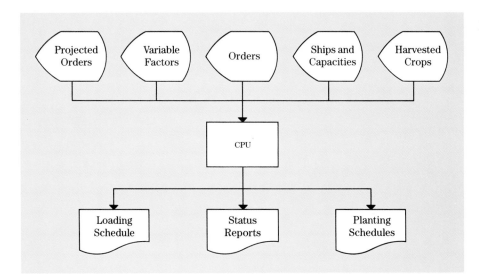

FIGURE 18.7

Simulation and Modeling System

the threat of spoilage. These factors create a complicated, intricate scheduling problem.

In the past, a traffic manager was assigned to this task. But with the myriad of elements to be considered, such as bad weather, human error, and various unexpected problems, this job became too complicated to be handled efficiently by one person. Computerization was obviously required.

Another of TFD's problems is to determine the best combination of crops to be grown and the optimum times to plant them to meet projected customer needs at harvest. These planting decisions must be made many months before the orders come in and, of course, well before the harvest. Factors such as weather or variations in productivity must be considered. Harvesting times and degree of product ripeness must be coordinated, since fruit picked too soon will not ripen properly and fruit picked too late will spoil in transit. Errors in judging any of these factors will cost TFD money.

Description of System

Figure 18.7 illustrates the system developed by TFD. A computer located at company headquarters is programmed to generate schedules and run computer simulations and models. A planning program develops the itinerary schedules, and a linear programming technique is used to determine the best combination of fruits for the cargoes of the various ships.

A modeling program of the entire shipping and cargo operation gives TFD the capability of simulating many of the effects of varying conditions. It allows the company to experiment with loading arrangements, routes, and schedules. The modeling program is also used to develop several planting schedules that consider all possible changes in conditions and factors.

The system is designed to produce several reports. One indicates the status of all orders in the house. Another lists the cargo and destination of each vessel in the fleet. Other reports and tables show departure times and ports of embarkation and arrival. The planting schedule is carefully defined in detail by another report. Status rosters are prepared for each dock to indicate when shipments are due, how the cargo should be processed, and what surface transportation should be employed to take the fruit to its final destination.

System Evaluation

This computerized system gives TFD several advantages over manual scheduling methods. Goods are shipped faster and arrive in better condition at the customer's facilities. Fruit does not remain on the docks waiting for ships to arrive, risking spoilage due to scheduling errors or poor planning.

Increased efficiency in loading cargoes has led to lower operating costs and larger profit margins. The status reports for the docks and other workstations facilitate planning work schedules for personnel and equipment.

Finally, the schedules generated for planting crops have increased TFD's ability to make sound decisions regarding future harvests and projected demand. They allow the company to study alternative planting schedules and crop mixes.

MICROFILM INDEX AND DISPLAY SYSTEM: THE NATIONAL JOURNAL

Description of Firm

National Journal is a daily newspaper employing dozens of editors, copywriters, reporters, and news analysts. The reporters' duties include checking the accuracy of news items and researching background information on current stories. They frequently review dozens of clippings, articles, or old newspaper pages when pursuing a news story.

National Journal has been published for over 50 years and maintains an extensive morgue (a morgue is a file of newspaper articles, pictures, and clippings on important people, events, and happenings). The file contains a permanent copy of every edition of the newspaper, providing a source of important research data. The morgue is frequently queried to check names, dates, and other historical information.

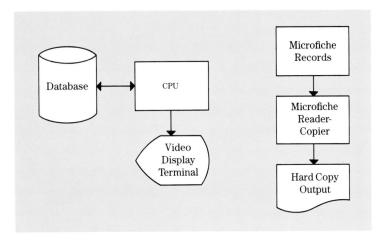

FIGURE 18.8

**Microfilm Index
and Display
System**

Description of System

Figure 18.8 illustrates the major aspects of the filing and retrieval system. There are two essential elements: the microfilm files and the computer-based indexing system.

Every day National Journal librarians duplicate pages from the current edition onto microfiche records, each record containing up to 80 pages. Clippings and pictures are copied onto microfilm. To view the microfilm or microfiche records, the operator places the record in a reader. The reader enlarges the images back to their original size for easy viewing.

Indexing is important in this system. An index record is prepared for each item as it is microfilmed. This record is stored in a computerized database. Each index record contains key words called descriptors that describe the items. Index records containing related or allied key words are also included in the file to cross-reference items.

To look up an item, a reporter accesses the database from a terminal and enters a primary descriptor and related key words. All the related items in the file are displayed on the screen, together with the microfilm reference number. The reporter prints out this information to assist in locating the appropriate microfilm records. For example, to obtain information on South American rubber plantations, the reporter lists the descriptor "rubber," followed by the modifiers "plantation" and "South America." The computer searches the files and displays the reference numbers of all related documents in the file. The reporter selects the appropriate records.

If a permanent copy of the record is needed, the microfilm reader can make one. The reader enlarges the image to original size and outputs a permanent copy of the original clipping or article.

System Evaluation

This system enables employees to search important records quickly, easily, and thoroughly. The comprehensive index system of related key terms facilitates expanding searches into allied areas.

Since microfilm records can be copied, the risk of loss and damage to paper originals is avoided. A backup copy of all records is kept in an archival storage file in case a microfilm or microfiche record is lost or destroyed.

The system provides an economical method of storing large volumes of visual and graphic data. Considerably less space and filing equipment are required than would be needed to store copies of the newspapers and documents in their original form.

DECISION SUPPORT SYSTEM (DSS): FAIRVIEW MUNICIPAL GOVERNMENT

Description of Organization

Fairview is a medium-size city with about 600,000 people and has its own police, fire, and health departments. The municipal government issues business licenses, collects taxes, and supports an animal shelter, road maintenance department, and court system.

Each business day a considerable number of transactions occur between the city agencies and departments and the citizens of Fairview. Licenses are issued, court cases processed, fines collected, stolen property reports filed, and so forth.

These activities generate data that must be processed. Some is needed immediately for handling requests, making decisions, answering questions, and so on. Some is used to guide expenditures and allocation of city resources. Other information is used for tax purposes, and some is of a historical nature.

Description of System

Fairview's decision support system (DSS) holds the city's vital data (see Fig. 18.9). The database is a collection of master files composed of the records from the various operating departments in the city. The files are updated from facts generated as transactions occur in the various departments. Video display terminals (VDTs) are located in various city offices, such as the police, fire, business license, and court facilities. City personnel access the database from these terminals to retrieve information and, in some instances, enter new data.

Two types of services are available on this system. One is the online query

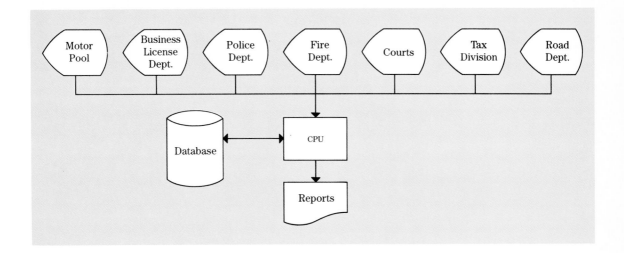

service available via the video terminals in the various departments. The second is hard copy printouts of reports and documents.

A large number of reports are generated by the system for the various city agencies. The value of these reports is directly related to the quality of the data used in their preparation. Reports based on accurate and current data help the agencies respond efficiently and intelligently to the demands placed on the city government.

Reports on the court caseload are generated to expedite scheduling of courtrooms and personnel and to anticipate trends and future needs. Studies of changes in the tax base are used when calculating the next year's tax rate. A schedule listing the dates for servicing the motor vehicles in the city-owned fleet is prepared for the motor pool. This helps to coordinate maintenance and improve efficiency.

The speed and ease of data retrieval is also an important factor. This is particularly true for the activities of the police and fire departments.

FIGURE 18.9

Decision Support System (DSS)

System Evaluation

This is an efficient DSS. Since all major city services are integrated into the system, the municipality functions as a coordinated, interrelated unit. Each department has access to all the data gathered by the other agencies as well as its own. This improves the quality and efficiency of government and reduces operating costs.

The reports generated by the system represent an accurate, up-to-date picture of the activities of the various departments. This provides a sound, reliable base for the governing agencies and improves their decision-making practices. The accessibility of the data in the database enables the governing agencies to serve the public faster and more efficiently.

Projects

Perform the following tasks for each of the cases presented in this chapter.

1. The systems described call for a variety of pieces of documentation. Prepare the required documentation for each system.

2. Modify the data flow diagram to change, alter, or improve the system. Document the changes.

3. Suppose the changes proposed above were to be implemented. What steps would you take to see that they are implemented in an orderly manner?

4. Assume the transaction volume handled in each system were to double. What changes or modifications in procedure, policies, methods, personnel, and equipment would be necessary?

5. Assume the transaction volume handled in each system were to be reduced by half. What changes or modifications in procedures, policies, methods, personnel, and equipment would be necessary?

HOW TO PREPARE FLOWCHARTS

Flowcharts have been used to document systems for many years. Recently, however, other techniques, including data flow diagrams, structure charts and HIPO charts, have gained popularity because they lend themselves to structured programming. These techniques and others were described in Chapter 4. Nevertheless, flowcharting remains a valuable tool in the systems analyst's repertoire.

One of the reasons why flowcharting continues to be used is that a standard set of symbols has been approved by the American National Standards Institute (ANSI) in their X3.5-1970 standard. In addition, an international standard has been adopted by the International Standards Institute (ISO). This appendix describes flowcharting principles and techniques.

SYMBOL DESCRIPTION AND USAGE

Flowcharts are drawn using a standard set of symbols, shown in Fig. A.1. ANSI separates the symbols into several categories. The two major groups are basic and specialized symbols. Acceptable flowcharts may be drawn using only the basic symbols. Specialized symbols are more specific and give more information about an operation; therefore, they are preferable to basic symbols. Both the shape of the symbol and the text within it convey descriptive information about the step being represented.

Some of the symbols, such as the extract and punched card, are peculiar to unit record systems. Their usage is becoming obsolete. They are included here because they frequently appear on standard flowchart templates.

General Input/Output Symbol

A parallelogram is the symbol that represents input or output media or operations. This is a generalized form that may be used for a variety of input and output media such as line printers, optical character scanners, and keyboards. It also indicates all types of input or output processes, such as reading in a payroll from time cards, reading sales slips, and printing out invoices or reports.

Online Storage

The online storage symbol refers to input/output operations performed on electronic media that are connected to a computer and are capable of storing the data. The symbol indicates that a file is recorded on an online storage device, that new data is to be written on the device, or that data already recorded is being accessed. This symbol may represent magnetic tape or disk units. An example is preparing the monthly billing from files and programs recorded on an online storage device.

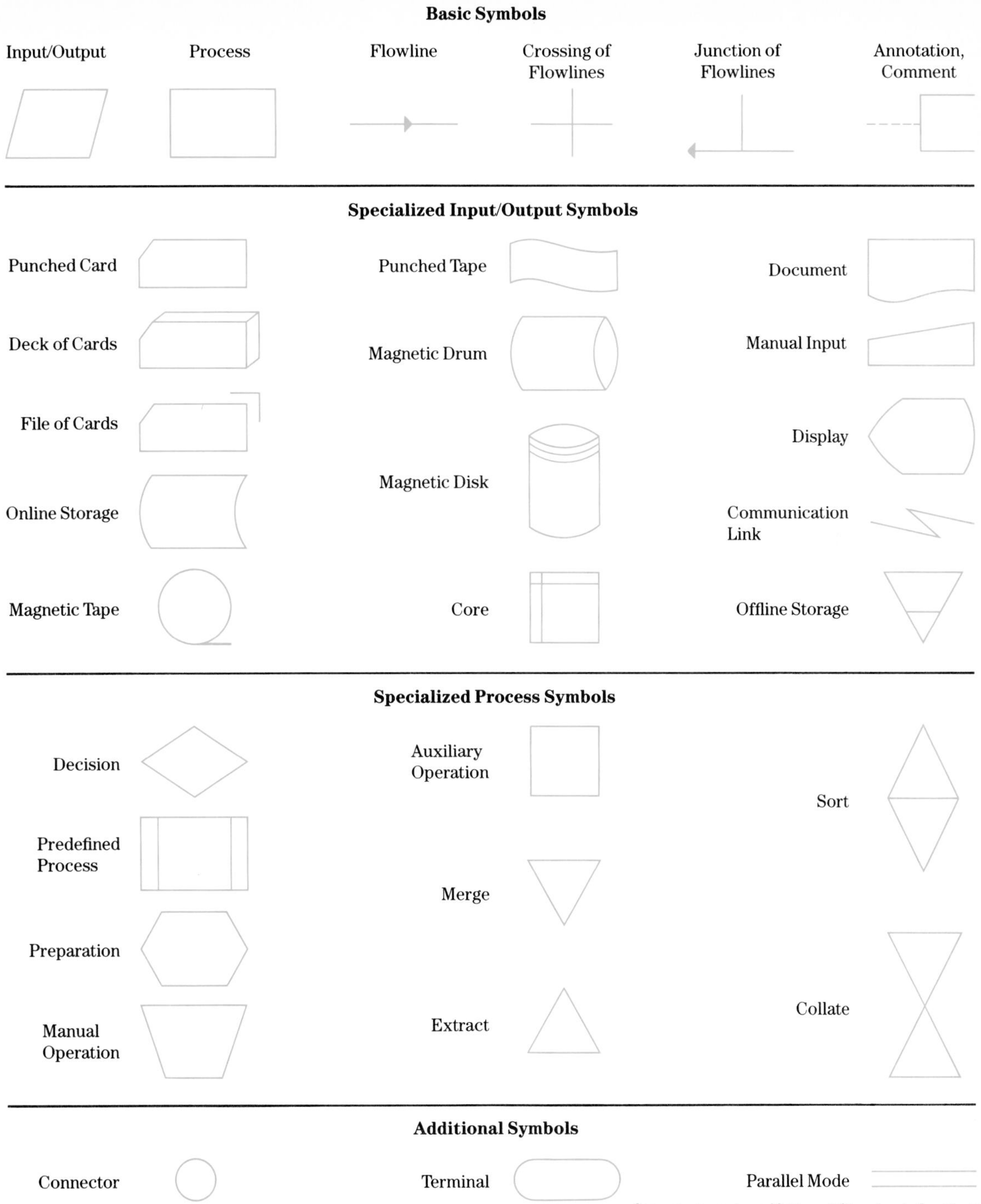

Basic Symbols

Input/Output	Process	Flowline	Crossing of Flowlines	Junction of Flowlines	Annotation, Comment

Specialized Input/Output Symbols

Punched Card		Punched Tape		Document	
Deck of Cards		Magnetic Drum		Manual Input	
File of Cards				Display	
Online Storage		Magnetic Disk		Communication Link	
Magnetic Tape		Core		Offline Storage	

Specialized Process Symbols

Decision		Auxiliary Operation		Sort	
Predefined Process		Merge			
Preparation				Collate	
Manual Operation		Extract			

Additional Symbols

Connector	Terminal	Parallel Mode

Source: American National Standards Institute

FIGURE A.1

Standard Flowchart Symbols

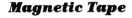

Magnetic Tape

A symbol shaped like a reel of tape specifies an input or output operation performed on magnetic tape. Examples include a parts inventory list stored on magnetic tape and a file of students' names on magnetic tape used to generate a report.

Primary Storage

This symbol, labeled "core" in Fig. A.1, specifies that data is being input or output from a primary memory device. Examples include a list of parts and their wholesale costs stored in the primary memory system of a computer, or a quality control program stored in a microcomputer.

Magnetic Drum

A cylinder-shaped symbol specifies input or output operations being performed on a magnetic drum storage device. An example would be a computer program that prepares a payroll stored on a magnetic drum unit.

Magnetic Disk

A symbol resembling a group of disks specifies input or output operations on magnetic disk storage devices. Examples include files such as alphabetic lists of employees' names or professional periodicals recorded on a magnetic medium such as a floppy disk.

Offline Storage

This symbol refers to input/output operations performed on data storage media not connected to a computer. It indicates that a file is stored on that media, that new data is being recorded, or that stored data is being accessed.

Punched Card

A symbol shaped like a punched card is used to show that data is stored or being input or output on punched cards.

Document

A symbol shaped like a torn piece of paper shows that data is to be recorded or stored on a hard copy document, or that the output will be a written, printed, or typed hard copy document. Preparation or storage of reports, signatures, forms, invoices, and statements are shown using this symbol.

Punched Tape

A symbol shaped like a piece of paper tape specifies data stored on or being punched into paper tape. This symbol indicates that the data is being accessed by a paper tape reader, that a file is available on paper tape, or that the output of a process will be on paper tape.

Manual Input

This symbol represents a manual input operation. It is used to show those steps in a system in which data is entered for processing using pencil and paper or a keyboard.

Display

This symbol is used whenever an input or output operation in a system involves a video display device. For example, this symbol could be used in a reservation system to show that airline flight departures and arrivals are displayed on a video device.

Communications Link

A symbol shaped like a lightning bolt signifies that elements in a flowchart are connected via some form of communications link. Microwave, telephone lines, and private leased lines over which data can be transmitted are shown with this symbol. Examples include branch offices of a firm connected by telephone lines, data being processed on a remote computer, or credit check queries placed by telephone.

Process Symbol

A rectangular box is the generalized process symbol. It indicates any process operation, such as sorting, merging files, manipulating data, performing calculations, testing data, or executing a computer program. Examples include calculations necessary to prepare a profit and loss statement, or computing payroll deductions.

Manual Process

This symbol indicates that a process is being performed manually, without the use of machine or computer. Examples would be filing records, calculating loan information with pen and paper, or taking inventory.

Auxiliary Operation

A square specifies that an operation will be carried out on equipment not connected to a computer. It is used to indicate operations such as listing records recorded on magnetic tape or a line printer.

Merge

The inverted triangle shows that two or more files are to be combined into one. This symbol can indicate a manual or computer operation. Examples include merging a detail file showing payments with the records in the master file showing account balances, or merging a list of new employees into the payroll file.

Extract

A triangle indicates data or records being pulled from a file manually or electronically. Examples include selecting the delinquent accounts in a file, removing names of terminated employees from a personnel file, or marking any items in a list of expenses that are not within the expected cost range.

Sort

This specialized symbol indicates that a sorting operation is being performed on files or records. The process can be executed manually or by computer. Examples include ordering a file alphabetically, numerically, or by account or stock number; separating local and out-of-town shipments; or sorting a group of sales by department.

Collate

This symbol shows that two or more files are to be combined into one file that may or may not be in the same order as any of the original files. A common example of collating is when a file of payments is merged with the master account file and the records of customers who have not paid are listed.

Flowline Symbol

The direction of flow or movement between elements of a system is shown with the flowline symbol, a line that connects both points in the flowchart. An arrowhead at one end of the line indicates the direction of flow. If no arrowhead is shown, it is assumed that flow moves from left to right, or from the top of the page to the bottom. Arrowheads are also used to show where flowlines join and to indicate their new direction. Lines that cross each other and continue in separate directions are assumed to be unrelated.

Connector Symbol

The connector symbol, a small circle with a letter or number inside, shows flow or movement between elements in a system. One symbol is used at the terminal point of a sequence and a second symbol with a matching label points to the beginning of the next sequence where flow resumes. Arrowheads indicate the direction of flow.

This symbol is often more convenient to use in flowcharts than flowlines. It eliminates lines that cross or form confusing junctions. It is useful for directing flow to sequences on other pages in a multipage flowchart. It improves the appearance and clarity of flowcharts.

Annotation Symbol

Notes or comments can be added to a flowchart with the annotation symbol. This symbol, an open-ended box, encloses additional explanations or descriptive text related to a given step. A broken line points to the step in the flowchart that it describes.

The other symbols that appear in Fig. A.1 are used primarily on program flowcharts.

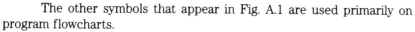

HOW TO DRAW FLOWCHARTS

The rules and symbols used in the preparation of a flowchart are standardized and easy to understand. They represent an almost universal language for communications between systems analysts.

The care and detail used when preparing a given flowchart varies according to the chart's immediate purpose. For preliminary planning and experimentation, the symbols are drawn freehand and show only the major elements in a sequence or system. Later the chart may be expanded, refined, improved, and drawn permanently using a template, ruler, pen, and ink.

Physical Considerations

Flowcharts should be drawn on 8½ × 11 inch paper (or other standard page size if required). If the charts are to be kept permanently, a good grade of 20-pound bond paper should be used.

Leave adequate margins (a minimum of 1 inch on all sides of the page, 1½ inches if binding is a consideration). Leave sufficient space between symbols. Label the flowchart at the top with the name of the system or subsystem to which it relates and other important details, such as the date and revision number. If several pages are required for a single flowchart, number them consecutively.

Use a template to make sure that the shape of each symbol adheres to recognized standards. Figure A.2 shows a plastic template that contains the ANSI standard symbols.

Content Considerations

There are a few techniques and conventions that should be followed when drawing flowcharts.

1. Wherever possible, draw the direction of flow from left to right and from the top of the page to the bottom. Use arrowheads to indicate the direction of flow.

2. A symbol may vary in size, but its shape must adhere to the proportions stated in the ANSI standard and its orientation on the page must be unchanged.

3. Always show a data flow path in the simplest way and avoid crossing flowlines whenever possible. Use the connector symbol to prevent crossing lines.

4. Many analysts prefer to have flowlines enter a box from the top only. If more than one line is involved, they are joined before entering so that only one line actually goes to the box. Several flowlines may leave a box,

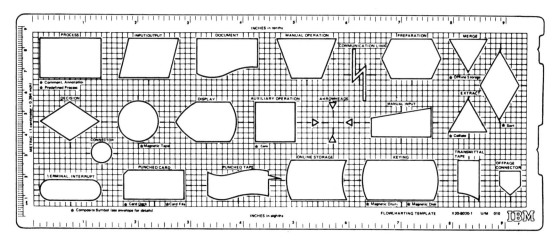

Courtesy of International Business Machines Corporation

either from separate points in the box or from one line which then separates into several branches.

5. Include descriptive text within each symbol to describe the operation represented by the box. Use short, concise terms and avoid ambiguity. For example, "Print Pick List" is better than "Print Report" and "Compute Net Commission" gives more information than "Commission."

6. Use the annotation or comment symbol liberally throughout a flowchart. Annotative text should contain important information about data, data paths, processes, reports, media, and workstations that cannot be conveniently included within a symbol.

Several levels of flowcharts are often used to describe a single system. A block diagram flowchart may show only the major elements. These are called macroflowcharts. Detailed charts may include more elements or break out blocks into smaller components. These are called detail or microflowcharts. The level of detail shown on a flowchart should be consistent. All equivalent elements in a system should be represented with the same degree of emphasis and specification.

FIGURE A.2

Flowchart Template

EXAMPLES OF SYSTEM FLOWCHARTS

We present two simplified system flowcharts to illustrate how system flowcharting symbols are used. One is for a typical payroll processing system that produces reports and paychecks. The other is for a financial system for a savings and loan association. In this system, teller terminals located in several branches of the bank are connected to a central computer via ordinary telephone lines.

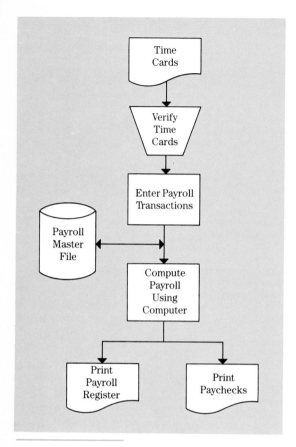

FIGURE A.3

Payroll-Processing System

Time Card		
Lois Montgomery		
Name		
15 – 4380		
Employee No.		
Quality Control		
Dept.		

Day	In	Out
Monday	9:10	5:15
Tuesday	8:55	5:10
Wednesday	7:30	5:00
Thursday	9:05	5:05
Friday	8:40	4:30
Saturday		
Sunday		
Overtime		

FIGURE A.4

Time Card Source data originates on the time card

Payroll-Processing System

Figure A.3 is a system flowchart of a payroll-processing system for a company with several hundred employees. There are two sources of data for the system: time cards and the master payroll file sorted on magnetic disks. The system produces a payroll ledger and prints paychecks.

Source data originates with the time cards, shown in Fig. A.4. The time cards are stamped each day on a time clock and record the number of regular and overtime hours worked by each employee. At the end of each week the cards are verified by the department supervisor and sent to the computer for processing. The data recorded on each time card is keyboarded by an operator.

The master payroll file, stored on disk, contains permanent data on each employee, such as the date of employment, pay rate, overtime rate, accumulated

FIGURE A.5

Savings and Loan Financial System

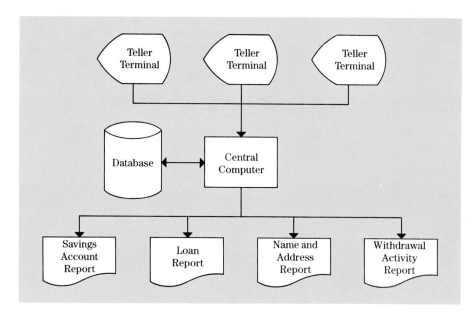

withholding tax contributions, number of exemptions, credit union deductions, and retirement contribution rate. As entries are made, the master payroll file is updated. Once each week the file is processed by a computer program to produce payroll checks. This file is later used for the preparation of quarterly and yearly tax reports and forms.

The computer also prepares a payroll register. This is a hard copy printout listing each employee by name, number, number of hours worked, and other pertinent information such as deductions and net earnings. This report is kept in the manager's office.

Savings and Loan Financial System

Figure A.5 is an example of a system used by savings and loan associations to process teller transactions. Data on transactions is entered on remote computer terminals located at each branch and relayed to a central computer via ordinary telephone lines. The information is transmitted directly to the computer at the time of the transaction while the customer remains at the window.

Data on deposits, withdrawals, name changes, deletions, and other file maintenance procedures, as well as data regarding loan payments or new loans, are transmitted and processed. The computer maintains a database showing all accounts, current balances, and related data. Immediate results are returned to each terminal.

The system is called online because each terminal is connected directly to the computer and is served immediately. At the end of the day a program is run to prepare various reports based on the transactions that occurred during the day. These include savings account reports, loan reports, name and address reports, and withdrawal activity reports.

Data recorded in the database is used to generate monthly and quarterly special reports for the government, annual earning reports, and personnel reports.

G L O S S A R Y

Abstract　A short, written description of a program's function, logic, and general routines.

Access time　The amount of time required to locate a given record in storage.

Accuracy　The measure of the freedom from errors achieved by a system.

Action entry　The part of the decision table that describes the actions to be followed for each set of conditions.

Action stub　The part of the decision table that lists all possible actions that may be taken.

Address　The numerical reference to a location where data is stored.

Algorithm　The logical steps or sequences of operations that are followed to arrive at a solution to a problem. The strategy for solving a given problem.

All-at-once changeover　A method of abandoning an old system and implementing a new one on a specific date.

Alphabetic data　Alphabetic letters.

Alphanumeric data　A combination of alphabetic letters and numbers.

Analysis phase　The second step in the SDLC during which the analyst analyzes and documents an in-place system.

Applications package　A program that performs many end-user tasks and does not require users to have knowledge of a specific programming language.

Assembler language　Programming instructions written in mnemonic abbreviations known as operation codes.

Audit　A review of a record, file, or database to uncover information.

Audit trail　A track that enables information or data flow through a system to be traced.

Backup system　A second system put in place during a transition to insure against the failure of a primary system.

Batch processing　A system that processes groups (batches) of input data some time after the original transactions take place; also called offline data entry.

Batch total　The sum of all values in a given field.

Benchmark test A test used to evaluate hardware and software performance.

Beta testing The testing of a computer program by end users before its final release.

Bit The smallest unit of data that can be stored or manipulated on a computer.

Boundary The perimeter or line of demarcation between a system and the environment distinguishing between the elements that make up the system and the outside world with which it interacts.

Business system A collection of policies, procedures, methods, people, machines, and other elements that interact and enable the organization to reach its goals.

Byte A group of eight bits that form a character.

Carbon interleaved form Forms bound at one edge, separated by carbon paper.

Cause and effect A relationship in which the cause will always generate the same effect.

Cell An intersection of a row and a column on a spreadsheet.

Centralized system A system in which processing is done at a central point.

Changeover timetable A schedule of dates that establishes checkpoints during systems implementation.

Check digit code A digit appended to the end of a number to detect errors or transpositions.

Closed system A system in which the result or output can be predicted with certainty.

Cluster sample A technique that samples according to groups, such as geographic area, race, or age.

Code The conversion of logical steps into instructions that the computer can understand.

Committee organization A structure in which a position or responsibility is assigned to a group of individuals rather than to a single person.

Communication The transmission of a message through a medium, such as the spoken or written word, from a sender to a receiver.

Compiler A program to convert English or mathematic instructions into machine language.

Computer-aided software engineering (CASE) The application of the computer to the software development process.

Computer output microfilm (COM) An output medium in which images are reduced in size on rolls of film.

Condition entry The part of the decision table that lists all possible combinations of conditions that may occur.

Condition stub The part of the decision table that lists all possible conditions that could arise in making a decision.

Constraints   Limits or controls set upon a problem. The outer limits or rules by which a problem may be solved.

Consultant   An individual or organization that provides specialized system services for a fee.

Consumer documentation   Documents prepared for the consumer of an organization's services or goods.

Context diagram   A data flow diagram that illustrates an entire system as one generalized element.

Continuous form   A form that is attached to the form before and after it, separated by rows of perforations.

Cost analysis   The assessment of the cost for processing a given unit of work.

Cost/benefit analysis   An assessment of the costs and benefits that result from the implementation of a new system.

Critical path   The key path that defines which steps must be completed on time in order to meet a schedule.

Critical path method (CPM)   A scheduling technique that shows the key events that must be completed in order for a project to be finished on time.

Cursor   A marker on a screen showing where the next character can be entered.

Cut form   A loose form to be inserted manually into a printer or other output device.

Data   A representation of facts, concepts, or instructions in a formalized manner suitable for communication, interpretation, or processing by humans or by automatic means. Facts, figures, names, lists, and tables that are of value to a business enterprise.

Database   A comprehensive collection of libraries of data. For example, one line of an invoice may form an item; a complete invoice may form a record; a complete set of such records may form a file; the collection of inventory control files may form a library; and the libraries used by an organization are known as its database.

Database administrator   The individual responsible for coordinating software, records, file design, and data management activities.

Data cycle   The sequence of input, processing, and output.

Data dictionary   A repository of descriptions of the form, style, and content of data, and of the methods that will be used to process and report it.

Data element   The smallest unit of data that can be processed or become part of a record.

Data entity   A term that describes the properties and relationships of an item of data.

Data flow   A specific pathway for moving data.

Data flow diagram   A figure that illustrates the flow of data within a system and operations performed on the data.

Data map   The code generated by Excelerator software.

Data model entity   A construct that defines what records and elements will be treated as a unit.

Data processing   The restructuring of data to improve its utility to the business enterprise. To change the order, form, or method of storage of data by such operations as sorting, collating, merging, or sequencing.

Data record   A collection of elements or sequences of records that are treated as a unit.

Data store   A point in a system where data is permanently or temporarily stored.

Debugging   Finding and removing errors from a program.

Decentralized system   *See* Distributed data processing system.

Decision support system (DSS)   A system of managing data based upon the needs of the end user or decision maker.

Decision table   A chart that shows the actions to be taken in light of various conditions.

Decision tree   A diagram that illustrates the branches or logic in a program or solution to a problem.

Decompose   *See* Explode.

Deliverable   *See* Work product.

Design diagram   A graphic or visual representation of a structure.

Design phase   The third step in the systems analysis process, in which new or revised systems are generated.

Design walkthrough   A procedure in which a programmer manually checks each block of program code for accuracy and completeness.

Detail file   A file that contains records related to specific transactions or activities.

Detail record   A record containing data on a specific transaction or activity.

Development phase   The fourth step in the SDLC, in which a system is actually assembled and constructed.

Direct observation   A means of gathering data by watching a system in operation and keeping records.

Distributed database   A system in which databases are physically distributed in several different locations.

Distributed data processing system   A system in which data is distributed throughout a network and may be available to all users on the system.

Documentation   Written manuals, diagrams, narratives, layouts, or drawings that describe how a system functions.

Dumb terminal   A keyboard terminal without a microprocessor.

Entity   An element that describes relationships or properties attributed to a unit of data.

Environment   The people, facilities, rules, policies, and regulations that surround a system.

Error rate   A measure of the accuracy rate in a transmission.

Expansion costs   Costs incurred when a system is modified, revised, or altered.

Explode   To explain an operation in increasingly more detailed levels.

External communications   Communications that take place between an organization or system and those beyond its boundaries.

External entity   A symbol represented by a square box on a data flow diagram that specifies either the source or the destination of data.

Facilities inventory   A compilation of the physical assets and facilities used in a system.

Fan-folded form   *See* Continuous form.

Feasibility study   An initial system study undertaken to determine whether additional study or resources are needed to solve a problem.

Field   A group of related bytes or characters.

File   A collection of records that can be manipulated by people or machines.

File processing   A system that manipulates records based upon files.

Final report   A study that states conclusions, expected benefits, and outcomes.

Fixed costs   *See* Overhead.

Fixed-length record   A record that consumes the same amount of space in a storage device regardless of how much data is stored on it.

Floppy disk   A flexible magnetic storage medium used on desktop computers.

Flowchart   A graphic representation of the steps in the solution of a problem, in which symbols are used to show data flow, hardware, and the system plan.

Flowline   A vector that connects external entities, process, or data store elements on a flowchart.

Formal organization   The official plan that clearly shows the chain of command and the lines of authority and responsibility of personnel within an organization.

Formatted input   An input mode that provides blanks where data is to be entered.

Forms control   Procedures that provide an orderly movement of forms throughout a system.

Forms manuals   Collections of all the business forms used in a system.

Fourth-generation language   A high-level programming language that does not require strict adherence to syntax and structure rules.

Gantt chart   A scheduling tool that diagrams starting and ending dates of tasks.

Gradual changeover   Introducing a new system and phasing out the old system in gradual steps.

Graph entity   A term that describes where a diagram is stored and the entities within the diagram.

Hand holding   Technical assistance and support provided by a vendor after the installation of equipment.

Hard copy   A permanent document, such as a piece of paper or printed form.

Hard copy output   Documents, forms, or reports typed or printed on paper.

Hard disk   A rigid magnetic storage medium that can hold millions of characters of data.

Hardware   The physical equipment used in a system; generally, computers, terminals, typewriters, desks, and telephones.

Hawthorne effect   The phenomenon that employees who know they are the subject of a study behave differently from those who do not.

Help screen   A display on a computer terminal to assist the operator in using software.

Hierarchy plus input-process-output (HIPO)   A structured diagram that defines procedures and operations in a hierarchical manner.

Horizontal communications   The transfer of data and information among individuals at the same level on the organization chart.

If-then logic   A logical process in which alternatives are assessed and compared.

Impact printer   A device that strikes a letter against a ribbon, transferring ink to the paper.

Implementation phase   The last step in the SDLC, in which a change is made to a new or revised system.

Implementation schedule   A timetable to guide the transition from an old system to a new one.

Indexed file access   Storing records in sequential blocks, and within each block in random order.

Information   Meaningful data. Facts, figures, names, and so on that have been organized or processed to increase their value to the business enterprise. The product that results from processing or manipulating raw data.

Information security   Keeping records safe, confidential, and under system control.

Information system   A collection of procedures, programs, equipment, and methods that process data and make it available to management for decision making.

Input   The capturing or entering of data into a system.

Input-process-output (IPO)   A chart that describes a sequence of processing activities.

Inputs   Those items that enter the boundaries of the system from the environment and are manipulated by the system.

Internal communications   Communications that originate and terminate within the same organization.

Investigative study   A detailed study, part of a feasibility study, that outlines specific solutions.

Job description   A document that outlines the specific duties and responsibilities of an employee.

Junior analyst   A position that requires less skills and knowledge than that of a senior analyst.

Labor costs   The amount of money paid to employees to perform given operations.

Laser beam scanner   A device that sweeps a beam of coherent light to read data for input.

Laser beam storage   An optical storage medium that stores data on plastic or metal disks.

Laser printer   An output device using a technology akin to an electrostatic office copier.

Last digit code   A trailing character placed after a field to indicate the class to which it belongs.

Lead time   The time between ordering a piece of equipment and its actual delivery.

Learning curve   A graph illustrating the relationship between continued practice at a given task and the resulting gains in proficiency, speed, and accuracy.

Lessee   One who acquires equipment on a lease.

Lessor   One who provides equipment on a lease.

Letter-quality output   Printouts that are composed of fully formed letters.

Library   A collection of related files.

Line organization   A classical structure resembling a pyramid, where relationships are shown by lines drawn on a chart.

Line and staff organization   A form of business structure in which line positions refer to the formal chain of command and staff positions refer to departments that provide advisory services to the firm.

Linked-list schema   A file organization that uses pointers to direct the computer to the next record.

Logical design   The plan or structure of a system before it is physically implemented.

Logical record   A collection of related items that may or may not be stored on the same physical record.

Machine language   Programming instructions written in strings of ones and zeros.

Machine readable   Data stored in a form that can be read by computers or machines.

Magnetic ink character recognition (MICR)   A device that senses the magnetic properties of an image and converts them to pulses for entry.

Magnetic storage media   Devices for storing data that has been converted from source documents into electrical pulses.

Magnetic tape   Data may be stored on a reel of magnetic tape and accessed with a read/write head.

Mainframe   A large computer serving many I/O devices with large secondary storage capacity.

Maintenance costs   The costs for the physical plant, office equipment, communications equipment, and the like.

Management information system (MIS)   A user-oriented system for manipulating data and generating reports.

Manual data entry   Input done in longhand or on a typewriter.

Mark sense reader   A device that senses penciled-in areas and converts them to electrical pulses for entry.

Master file   A file that contains records of a permanent nature.

Master record   A record containing data of a permanent nature.

Menu   A group of options from which a selection is to be made.

Microfiche   A form of output in which images are generated on 4 × 6 inch film records.

Microfilm   *See* Computer output microfilm.

Mnemonic code   A coding system that uses shortened or contracted code symbols.

Module   A small component or element of a larger system.

Morale   The amount of satisfaction and acceptance that employees feel toward their jobs.

Nassi-Shneiderman chart   A structured chart that clearly shows a program's logic.

NCR form   A form that eliminates the need for carbons by using specially treated paper.

Nonimpact printer   A printer that produces an image without striking a letter form against paper.

Numeric data   Numbers or digits.

Objective   A goal toward which effort is directed. An aim or end of action. Objectives are the designated results or outcomes of a system.

Offline data entry   *See* Batch processing.

Ongoing committee   A group of individuals with continuing responsibility for a problem-solving task.

Online data entry   *See* Transaction-oriented processing.

Open system   A system in which the output or results cannot be determined precisely, but can only be guessed at; also called probabilistic system.

Optical character reader   A device that scans printed, handwritten, or typed characters for input.

Optical scanning device   A device that reads filled-in areas or characters by their optical characteristics.

Optimization   The process of reentering the problem-solving loop to improve results.

Order-processing manuals   Documentation defining how orders are to be written and processed.

Organization chart   A visual, graphic device that shows the lines of authority and chain of command in an organization.

Organization manuals   Documentation describing lines of authority in a firm and responsibilities of personnel.

Output   The delivery of the results of processing.

Overhead   System costs that do not change with the volume of output produced.

Padded form   Forms bound together at one edge with a rubber-based adhesive.

Paper substance   *See* Paper weight.

Paper weight   A measure of the thickness of paper stock.

Parallel system operation   Operating both old and new systems concurrently for a period of time.

Parameter   A variable that is given a constant value for a specified procedure or process. The limits or boundaries that define a given problem.

Parent record   A record that possesses subordinate records.

Performance criteria   Characteristics that are assessed to ensure that system goals have been reached.

Physical design   A plan or structure of a system after its logical design has been converted to functional elements.

Physical record   A tangible record, such as an optical scanning form.

Pin feed form   *See* Continuous form.

Pipe   *See* Flowline.

Planning phase   The part of the SDLC during which analysts recognize, diagnose, and define the problem.

Plotter   A device that can draw charts, graphs, lines, or curves.

Pointer   An indicator that directs the computer to the next record in a logical sequence.

Policy   A specific course or method of action, selected from among alternatives and in light of given conditions, to guide and determine present and future decisions. A set of rules upon which present and future decisions are made.

Policy manuals   Documents that state the goals of the system.

Population   All the cases under study.

Preliminary phase   The first or planning step in systems analysis.

Preliminary study   An early study conducted as part of a feasibility study to assess needs.

Presentation graph   A visual chart that shows the flow of data through a system in a nontechnical manner.

Problem definition   A statement of a problem given in precise terms to facilitate its solution.

Problem recognition   A phase in the planning process in which the analyst is made aware of a problem.

Problem solving   A logical approach developed for finding sound solutions for problems.

Procedural language   A high-level language such as COBOL or PL/I.

Procedure   The course of action taken or the steps that must be followed to solve a problem.

Procedure manuals   Documents that detail the steps of routines or actions.

Process entity   A term that describes processes, destinations, and sources of data.

Processing   The restructuring or manipulation of data to increase its usefulness to an organization.

Process symbol   A rectangular symbol representing the transformation or processing of data within a system.

Productivity   A measure of system performance that states the relationship or ratio between input and output.

Program   An ongoing endeavor to generate a series of products or to reach a series of goals.

Program flowchart   A diagram that illustrates the flow of data throughout a computer program.

Project   A planned undertaking of scheduled activities to reach a goal.

Project director   An individual entrusted with the responsibility of conducting a systems study or guiding a project through to its completion.

Project management   The coordination of a project to ensure that it is completed on time and within assigned constraints.

Project manager   *See* Project director.

Project team   *See* Task force.

Prompt   A query on a terminal display to assist in entering data.

Proposal   A document by a vendor specifying an organization's needs and how the vendor will fulfill them.

Prototype   A mockup or developmental model of a system for test purposes.

Prototype installation   A pilot installation designed to test system hardware or software.

Pseudocode   *See* Structured English.

Purchase order   A document that directs a vendor to supply software or hardware.

Qualitative expression   A variable stated in general or subjective terms.

Quantitative expression   A variable expressed in numeric terms rather than general qualities or characteristics.

Query language   A database language similar to English that requires little programming knowledge.

Questionnaire   A means of gathering information by having respondents answer written questions on specific topics.

Quota sample   A sample structured so that a specific number from given groups is selected.

Random access storage   Magnetic storage media that can retrieve data without searching every record in sequence.

Random clock observation   Observations made throughout the day, based upon a random table of times.

Random order   Records in a file that are placed one after the other without regard to succession.

Random sampling   A technique in which all members of a population have an equal chance of being selected for the sample.

Real-time processing   *See* Transaction-oriented processing.

Record   A fundamental unit of an information system; it contains a group of fields.

Record lock   The capability of preventing more than one user from accessing a database simultaneously.

Relational database   A file organization in which relationships are defined by tables.

Request for proposal (RFP)   A document sent to vendors stating an intent to purchase.

Request for services   A form that provides space to describe a problem and outline services needed from the systems department.

Response time   The time that elapses before a system responds to a demand placed upon it.

Rule   A vertical column of a decision table that specifies the actions to be taken for each set of conditions.

Sample   A subset or selection of units that is representative of a population.

Scheduling   Programming activities to see that they occur at the proper time in a sequence of events.

Schema   The model or plan around which fields, records, and files are organized.

Scientific method   A procedure for solving problems that systematically deals with causes and effects and evaluates results.

Scratch file   A temporary file used during a processing operation.

Screen and report entity   A term that describes the details related to a screen or report and its entities.

Senior analyst   An analyst with many years of practical experience and extensive postgraduate training.

Sequence code   A coding system in which a group of items is assigned numbers in sequence.

Sequential access storage   A medium such as magnetic tape that must be searched in sequence until a desired record is located.

Sequential order   Records that are filed successively according to a particular arrangement, such as alphabetically or chronologically.

Significant digit code   Each element in the code represents a different characteristic of the data item.

Sink   A point outside a system that receives data.

Smart terminal   A keyboard terminal with an integrated microprocessor.

Soft copy output   A nonpermanent, temporary document displayed on a terminal screen.

Software   The computer programs, procedures, and associated documentation concerned with the operation of a data processing system. Includes manuals, diagrams, flowcharts, and language translators used in data processing.

Software development life cycle   The sequence of steps followed in writing a computer program.

Software documentation   Manuals, instructions, and tutorials for a software package.

Software package   A ready-to-use program designed to perform such things as database management or spreadsheet analysis.

Source   A point outside a system that generates data.

Source document   A record made at the time an original transaction takes place.

Spreadsheet   An electronic ledger sheet containing rows and columns.

Statistical analysis   The use of the computer and mathematics to describe system characteristics.

Stratified sample   A sample selected from a population according to predefined groups.

Structure chart   *See* Visual table of contents.

Structured design tools   Tools that emphasize the visual or graphic nature of a problem.

Structured English   A means of indicating language commands in an English-like form; pseudocode.

Structured interview   An interview in which prepared questions are asked in a specific sequence.

Structured systems analysis   A method for describing systems using figures and flowlines rather than written narratives.

Subsystem   One of the parts or components of a system, which performs a specified task that is consonant with the goals of the larger system of which it is a part.

System   A regularly interacting or interdependent group of elements forming a unified whole; a collection of related parts treated as a unit where its components interact.

Systematic sample   A sample selected from a population according to an organized pattern.

System flowchart   A diagram that illustrates the movement of data throughout an organization.

System model   A representation of an in-place or proposed system that describes the data flow throughout the structure.

Systems analysis   The scientific study of the systems process, including investigation of inputs and outputs, in order to find better, more economical, and more efficient means of processing.

Systems analyst   An individual charged with the responsibility of assessing business data flow problems, planning, modifying, evaluating, and implementing systems.

Systems department   The organizational unit charged with the responsibilities of systems design, implementation, planning, and evaluation.

Systems design   The reduction of a plan or concept to a set of specifications that describe a new or modified system.

Systems development   *See* Development phase.

Systems development life cycle (SDLC)   A five-step approach to solving business problems.

Systems evaluation   The systematic assessment of system performance to determine whether system goals have been reached.

Systems implementation   The planned and orderly process of converting from an existing system to a new one.

Systems manuals   Documentation tracing the flow of information or goods throughout a system.

Systems optimization   The redesign and refinement of system components to improve their performance.

Task force   A group of individuals charged with a one-time responsibility of solving a systems problem or managing a project.

Task list A short list of key steps that will be followed in carrying out a task.

Terminal screen layout form A ruled sheet of paper used for planning and designing terminal screen layouts.

Throughput A measure of the volume of traffic or jobs handled by a system, measured in transmission rate of information bits (TRIB).

Time and motion study Observations made with stopwatches and cameras to document a task.

Top-down structure A logical design that creates a hierarchy of detail.

Traffic survey A technique used to analyze the communications links of a system.

Training costs Costs of training personnel to operate a new system.

Training manuals Documentation describing the programs that prepare personnel to operate the system.

Transaction file *See* Detail file.

Transaction-oriented processing A system that processes data at the time transactions occur, in real time; also called online data entry.

Transaction record *See* Detail record.

Transmission rate of information bits (TRIB) *See* Throughput.

Tree schema A file organization resembling an inverted tree with a trunk and branches.

Turnaround time The period during which a system carries out a demand placed upon it.

Unstructured interview An interview with no fixed sequence of questions.

User-friendly system A system that addresses human, physical, and psychological aspects in its design.

Variable costs Those costs that change with the volume of output.

Variable-length record A record that consumes only the amount of space needed to store a piece of data on a medium.

Vendor A provider of resources.

Verification A check for accuracy of data transferred from one document to another by comparison.

Vertical communications The transfer of information between individuals on different levels of the organization chart.

Video display terminal (VDT) A soft copy output device equipped with a cathode ray tube (CRT).

Visual table of contents (VTOC) A diagram that shows levels of detail increasing from top to bottom.

Voice recognition device A device that interprets human voice or speech.

Voice synthesizer A soft copy output device that generates spoken words, tones, or audible sounds.

Warnier-Orr diagram A structure chart that shows general modules on the left and detailed modules on the right.

Warranty A document stating the terms and conditions for handling defective goods.

What-if analysis A spreadsheet technique that allows assumptions to be changed and values to be recalculated.

Winchester disk storage A magnetic storage medium that holds millions of characters on a hard disk.

Work product A finite, measurable amount of work; also called a deliverable.

I N D E X